No Longer Invisible

Afro-Latin Americans today

Minority Rights Group is an international non-governmental organization whose aims are to ensure justice for minority (and non-dominant majority) groups suffering discrimination by:

1. Researching and publishing the facts as widely as possible to raise public knowledge and awareness of minority issues worldwide.

2. Advocating on all aspects of human rights of minorities to aid the prevention of dangerous and destructive conflicts.

3. Educating through its schools programme on issues relating to prejudice, discrimination and group conflicts.

If you would like to know more about the work of Minority Rights Group, please contact Alan Phillips (Director), MRG, 379 Brixton Road, London SW9 7DE, United Kingdom.

m

Minority Rights Publications is a series of books from Minority Rights Group. Through the series, we aim to make available to a wide audience reliable data on, and objective analyses of, specific minority issues. The series draws on the expertise and authority built up by Minority Rights Group over two decades of publishing.

Other titles in the book series are:

Armenia and Karabagh: The Struggle for Unity
Edited by Christopher J. Walker (1991)

The Kurds: A Nation Denied
by David McDowall (1992)

Refugees: Asylum in Europe?
by Danièle Joly *et al* (1992)

The Balkans: Minorities and States in Conflict, 2nd edition
by Hugh Poulton (1993)

Polar Peoples: Self-Determination and Development
by Beach, Creery, Korsmo, Nuttall, Vakhtin (1994)

The Palestinians: The Road to Nationhood
by David McDowall (1994)

Cutting the Rose – Female Genital Mutilation: The Practice and its Prevention
by Efua Dorkenoo (1994)

NO LONGER INVISIBLE

AFRO-LATIN AMERICANS TODAY

Edited by
Minority Rights Group

Minority Rights Publications

First published in the United Kingdom in 1995 by
Minority Rights Publications
379 Brixton Road
London SW9 7DE

British Library Cataloguing in Publication Data
A CIP catalogue record of this book is available from the British Library.

ISBN 1 873194 80 3 hardback
ISBN 1 873194 85 4 paperback

Library of Congress Cataloguing in Publication Data
CIP Data available from the Library of Congress

Cover design by Brixton Graphics
Typeset by Brixton Graphics in Stone Serif
Printed on chlorine-free paper in the UK by Redwood Books

Cover photo of Cuban cooperative worker by
Barry Lewis/Network

CONTENTS

Preface and Acknowledgements

'Race' and ethnicity are a social construct rather than a biological fact, particularly in the case of Latin America, where people of African, European and indigenous ancestry have intermixed through the generations to an enormous degree. Who should be considered, or consider themselves, Afro-Latin American is a question of more than academic interest. Such identifications allow the experience and situation of different ethnic groups to be compared; they provide indicators of economic, social and political well-being; and they thereby suggest constructive new ways of meeting different community needs within states.

In the case of Afro-Latin Americans there is a notable lack of reliable contemporary research and evidence. Today, most Latin American states do not collect ethnic data; others, while officially recognizing Afro-Latin ethnicity, tend to include in this category only people of 'pure' African ancestry. Various countries in the region have claimed that their black populations are insignificantly small, in defiance of contradictory evidence. By such means, identities can be misrepresented, and the historical legacy of oppression and discrimination can be denied.

Ideologies of *blanqueamiento* (whitening) and *mestizaje* (race mixture) offer perhaps the clearest explanation for this. Latin American nations have long associated the loss or 'dilution' of African physical and cultural characteristics with the idea of 'progress'; hence Latin Americans have tended, both individually and collectively, to deny what is African in themselves and their culture. In numerous cases, too, countries in the region adopted policies specifically designed to achieve a physical and cultural whitening of the population.

Among Afro-Latin organizations and others concerned with

enhancing democracy, human rights and social justice, however, there is much concern to overcome this 'invisibility' by identifying, strengthening and celebrating what is African in the Latin American heritage. MRG would argue that this is essential for the fulfilment of the terms of the UN Declaration on the Rights of Minorities (see Appendix, pp. 371-2). As part of this process, a more realistic assessment of Afro-Latin Americans' socio-economic, cultural and political experience is sorely needed. To this purpose, the Organization of Africans in the Americas, based in Washington, DC, estimates that inhabitants of the region who have some degree of African ancestry number between 130 million and 170 million, constituting approximately one-third of Latin America's 450 million people (see map, pp. xii-xiii).

No Longer Invisible: Afro-Latin Americans Today is published as the result of a collaborative effort involving the work of the contributing writers and of numerous others. MRG sees the role of the book as part of the effort to gain recognition for the experience and situation of Afro-Latin American communities, to identify both their needs and the resources that they can offer to the wider society. The subject is not an entirely new one for MRG, which published a report some years ago on *The Position of Blacks in Brazilian and Cuban Society* (1971, 1979), one of whose authors has contributed to the present volume, and has continued in its work to draw attention to minority rights issues in Latin America. Although an understanding of the Afro-Latin American experience must be rooted in the age of slavery and its aftermath, contributors have also turned their attention to more recent and contemporary events and to a consideration of future prospects. Past neglect of Afro-Latin Americans – perhaps one of the least studied of all the world's larger minorities – has made the fulfilment of the project both more urgent and more difficult.

The region has been broadly defined for the purpose of this volume as the Spanish- and Portuguese-speaking countries of Central and South America and the Caribbean. French-speaking Haiti, for example, is not covered as such, although its close relationship with the Dominican Republic has resulted in some consideration of the Haitian experience. Inevitably, perhaps, gaps remain. It has not been possible to include an account of the small Afro-Latin communities of coastal Guatemala and El Salvador; the approximately 156,000 known Paraguayans of African descent; the former British, Dutch and French colonies of Guyana, Suriname and French Guiana, home to perhaps half a million African-descended people; or the expatriate Afro-Latin Americans of the United States. In a future edition it may be possible for MRG to make good such omissions. Argentina and, to a lesser extent, Chile undoubtedly had identifiable Afro-Latin populations at one time, but there is little evidence of their contemporary survival.

MRG owes a debt of gratitude to the many scholars, minority rights campaigners and others who gave generously of their time and expertise during the preparation of the book. Above all, they are the writers whose work appears here, but also those who took an active interest in the project and helped it to fruition: Jaime Arocha, Andy Atkins, Eduardo Bermúdez, Osvaldo Cárdenas, Darién J. Davis, Jualynne Dodson, Anani Dzidzienyo, Debbie Ewens, Michael Franklin, Jane Freeland, Nina S. de Friedemann, José Luciano, Alejandrina da Luz, Gayle McGarrity, Jameelah S. Muhammad, Patricia Odber de Baubeta, Jenny Pearce, Pedro Pérez Sarduy, Franklin Perry, Angelina Pollak-Eltz, Diego Quiroga, Humberto Rodriguez Pastor, Sunny Salibian, Kelvin A. Santiago-Valles, Kathleen Sawyers Royal, Rachel Sieder, José de Souza Martins, Alison Spedding, Pat Stocker, Jean Stubbs, María Matilde Suárez, Arlene Torres, Silvio Torres-Saillant, Gwendolyn Twillie, Rosângela Maria Vieira, Peter Wade and Norman E. Whitten Jr. MRG also wishes to thank those, some of whom contributed to the book as authors, who helped by reading and advising on the content: Sue Branford, Darién J. Davis, James Ferguson, Brenda Lipson, Patricia Odber de Baubeta, Jenny Pearce, Pedro Pérez Sarduy, Jean Stubbs, Peter Wade and Kate Whittle. Thanks are also due to all those who kindly supplied photographs; to Alan Biggins and colleagues at the Institute of Latin American Studies Library, London; to Anna Keene for her translation work; to Raja Jarrah, who originally suggested the idea for the book; and to Miles Litvinoff, who coordinated the project on behalf of MRG.

With the publishing of this book, MRG has followed, as

always, a rigorous process of independent review of the text by specialist readers. It is nevertheless virtually impossible to produce a study of this length and detail without some errors inadvertently slipping in, no matter how diligently those involved do their work. The problem is compounded when the subject is surrounded by considerable dispute and controversy. MRG will attempt to rectify in future editions any significant errors to which its attention is drawn. It is intended, above all, that *No Longer Invisible* should be a timely and useful contribution to a wider understanding of the African presence in Latin America and to a future for the region characterized by increasing social and economic justice.

Alan Phillips
Director

PHOTOGRAPHS

Afro-Latin American populations: minimum and maximum estimates, early to mid-1990s, with percentages of total country populations, allowing for differences in classification and self-perception; high upper estimates usually include all or most people with some degree of African ethnicity.

Based on Oviedo, R.M., 'Are we or aren't we?', *NACLA Report on the Americas: The Black Americas 1492-1992*, vol. 25, no. 4, 1992, p. 19, copyright 1992 by the North American Congress on Latin America, 475 Riverside Drive, #454, New York, NY 10115; supplemented by individual country sources.

NICARAGUA
Managua

Caribbean Sea

BARBADOS

TRINIDAD AND
TOBAGO

COSTA
RICA San José
Panamá

PANAMA

Caracas

Bogotá

VENEZUELA
min. 1.9 million (9%)
max. 14 million (70%)

Georgetown

Paramaribo

Cayenne

**GUYANA, SURINAME &
FRENCH GUIANA**
min. 405,000 (33%)
max. 530,000 (44%)

COLOMBIA
min. 4.9 million (14%)
max. 15 million (43%)

Quito

ECUADOR
min. 573,000 (5%)
max. 1.1 million (10%)

PERU
min. 1.4 million (6%)
max. 2.2 million (10%)

Lima

BRAZIL
min. 53 million (33%)
max. 120 million (75%)

Brasilia

La Paz

BOLIVIA
min.
max. } 158,000 (2%)

Asunción

PARAGUAY
min.
max. } 156,000 (3.5%)

S O U T H

P A C I F I C

Santiago

Buenos
Aires

Montevideo

URUGUAY
min.
max. } 38,000 (1%)

CHILE
no figure available

ARGENTINA
no figure available

A T L A N T I C

O C E A N

O C E A N

Scale 1:59,700,000
0 250 500 750 1000 1250 1500 kilometres

Cape Horn

xiii

1

INTRODUCTION

Pedro Pérez Sarduy and Jean Stubbs

The millions of Africans, of different ethnic groupings, shipped halfway across the world to labour the sugar, coffee, tobacco and rice plantations and the mines of the New World brought with them their religions, their languages, their dance, their music and their instruments. European colonial might did its utmost to strip them of their freedom, their dignity and their culture, but culture was perhaps the easiest of the three for peoples of African descent to continue to subvert.

From the US South and the Mexico altiplano in the north, to the Peruvian coastal lowlands and the Argentine pampas down south, the rhythms of Africa continued to beat. The *samba* and Candomblé of Brazil; the *son* and Santería of Cuba; the street carnivals of Salvador de Bahia, Río de Janeiro and a host of other towns and cities; the *merengue* of the Dominican Republic and Venezuela; modern-day *salsa;* the very ingredients of the languages spoken and the foods eaten; family, community and other organizational forms: in all lie manifestations of the strivings of Afro-Latin Americans to create a viable reality in which life could then, and can now, be lived with dignity.

Colonial and post-colonial society partitioned off people, classifying and categorizing skin pigmentation with a bewildering array of legal codes and linguistic terms (170 such terms in Brazil alone). In this context, bettering or whitening the race denoted upward social mobility, while blackening was equated with backwardness, poverty and underdevelopment. The exceptions to

1

racial hostility and oppression are pitifully thin at the national level, and testify to the stigma of a perverse colonial legacy.

The chapters in this book therefore document a history of oppression, struggle and achievement, seeking to help meet a need for further knowledge and action. Implied in the title is that Afro-Latin Americans have not been visible, and must now be made so. In the history of Latin America, however, there have been times and places where Afro-Latin Americans have constituted a majority, and the race issue has been uppermost, hence visible. But the prevailing currents of the region's history, dominated by an excluding sense of 'Europeanness', have repeatedly undermined and denied awareness of the African heritage, forcing Afro-Latin Americans to rediscover their ancestry and culture and renew the struggle for rights.

For this reason, if none other, the present volume is timely. We approach the twenty-first century with an urgent need to keep open the race debate and to redress what many have interpreted to be a resurgence of racism in Latin America, as elsewhere in the world. The country studies contained here – written by academics and activists, both women and men, many themselves from the countries in question and of African descent – go towards articulating an authentic Afro-Latin American voice in that debate.

The chapters also highlight a central challenge: the need to bridge the gap between the wealth of study and comparative knowledge on race in Latin America, often (though not exclusively) the work of white scholars, and the more localized knowledge-base, vision and self-perception of Afro-Latin Americans themselves. Three key areas of conceptual debate concern the variants of Afro-Latin American race relations, Africa and the Atlantic world, and black self-liberation. By outlining in this Introduction issues raised in each area, we hope to establish a framework for contextualizing the country studies that follow. If we draw most on Cuba and the Caribbean by way of example, it is because we know these best.

Variants in race relations

A key variant occurs between the relatively fluid race relations of, say, Brazil and Cuba and the more bipolar situation in the United States and the non-Hispanic Caribbean. This has been explained in terms of colonial cultures and stages of development. One side of the argument is that the reason for the difference is not economic but cultural. Iberians, it is claimed, instituted a more benign form of slavery than North-West Europeans, because of the strong Moorish influences on, and the nature of feudalism and Catholicism in, the Iberian peninsula. The counter-argument is that there are powerful underlying economic explanations for racism tied to the growth of the plantation economy in the Americas. Thus, it makes little sense to compare nineteenth-century Cuba and Puerto Rico; although both were Spanish colonies, Puerto Rico was an imperial backwater, with no significant development of the plantation or slavery, whereas Cuba was a booming slave plantation economy.

Both the 'imperial cultures' and the 'economic materialism' approaches tend to focus on power structures and 'officialist' thinking, whereas a third argument highlights the extent to which people have been active agents in shaping their own history, building and abolishing slavery, erecting and transgressing the intricacies of colour and class codes. A distinction has been made between public and private, between the rules of behaviour regulating contact between racial groups and actual intimate personal relations. According to this view, Iberian differed from non-Iberian America far more in the public than in the private.

No part of the world, it has been claimed, ever witnessed such a gigantic mixing of races as what took place in Latin America and the Caribbean. It has been found useful, however, to think of the region in terms of a threefold division between *Afro-Latin America* – the slave-plantation-based Caribbean and north-east Brazil; *Euro-Latin America* – Argentina, Uruguay, southern Chile and south Brazil, which received great waves of European immigrants over the last 100 years; and *mestizo America* – with scattered enclaves of indigenous populations in Mexico, Guatemala, the Andes and the Amazon Basin.

The extent of race mixing in Latin America might have engendered hopes of a new 'cosmic race', but it also meant that there has been no generally agreed racial classification, and racial distinctions are necessarily vague. What is considered black in one context might be white in another. This depends, to a large extent, on the tensions between prevailing definitions of race – as phenotype, or physical characteristics, and as genotype, or heredity – and on how far there has been cultural as well as biological mixing.

Throughout Latin America, after plantation slavery, a general hardening of race prejudice occurred, incorporating nineteenth-century European pseudo-scientific eugenicist notions. These sat uneasily with Latin American intellectual thinking, which romanticized indigenism and Africanism, and celebrated *mestizaje* (race mixture) as the new symbiosis. As a result, notions of *mestizaje* were also permeated with a 'whitening' superiority. Hence, the contradiction between the myth of racial democracy and the prevalence of discrimination and prejudice against indigenous peoples, blacks and mulattos.

Africa and the Atlantic world

Essential to a contemporary understanding of the Afro-Latin American reality is the legacy of almost 400 years of plantation slavery and what is today recognized to have been the largest forced migration in modern history. Between 10 and 50 million Africans were shipped to the Americas, with by far the largest numbers going to Brazil, Cuba, the Caribbean and the United States. Several countries in the region not usually thought of as associated with the slave traffic also had a substantial African presence, such as Mexico, which received an estimated half-million black captives.

Two aspects of this process have been much debated. The first is the commodity-driven nature of New World slavery, in contrast to Old World slave-based civilizations. The second is the deculturation of Africans in the trauma of the Middle Passage and what followed. Deculturation was seen as an inherent consequence of every form of colonial or neo-colonial exploitation. It was usual for the dominant class to protect and even stimulate isolated cultural values of the dominated class, but only in so far as those values helped reinforce the desired social structure. The dominated class was forced to seek refuge in its culture as a means of identity preservation and survival.

The vast and tortured movement of African peoples across the Atlantic was a major turning point in world history, facilitating the beginnings of the modern world capitalist economy and the emergence of empires spanning oceans. In the field of Atlantic studies, a key unresolved question is the extent to which both Eurocentric and Afrocentric approaches converge in depicting Africa and Africans as passive victims. How active a partner were Africa's political and economic elites in trade involvement with Europe? How far did African slaves accommodate to or resist slavery in the Americas? How strong was African culture in the re-creation of Afro-Latin American societies?

To understand the Africa of Latin America therefore requires more than a retracing of African footsteps. We must grasp how African, along with European, indigenous and Asian social groups created new and complex societies that differed from their component parts. After independence and the abolition of slavery, a racist simplism gained currency in Latin America, whereby the chaotic situation was explained in terms of, among other things, blacks being the obstacle to development. Blaming the victim – perhaps the most damning outcome of the denial of the African past – made subsequent re-evaluations of the African contribution to the development of Latin American society imperative. This has proved no mean task when racial values were constantly being socially reworked and codified, re-created and reproduced.

The legal end of slavery, which came last to Cuba (1886) and Brazil (1888), did not end its legacy, and in the struggle over land and labour the process of emancipation proved as varied, long and bloody as abolition. Its impact wrought major changes in the nineteenth-century Latin American and world economy, including the collapse of older production centres. It ushered in waves of indentured Asian and immigrant European labour, and massive out-migrations of Afro-Latin Americans from poor and marginal lands to cities and overseas.

From slavery to the present, the predominant – though far from universal – experience for Afro-Latin Americans has been of oppression and inferiorization. There have, however, been times when they have demonstrated great individual and collective achievement, awareness and organization in challenging their oppression, eliciting official concern and recognition, gaining in political power and establishing themselves as an accepted part of the culture and national self-identity.

Black self-liberation

An important lesson of history is that political leadership matters. Race and ethnicity hold strategic, not inherent or absolute, value. Ethnic and racial identity take on different meanings in different contexts, depending on who uses them and for what purposes. They are relative, situational categories. Competition and conflict between racial and ethnic groups may occur but need not necessarily do so, and may or may not be institutionalized in the political system at a societal level. Political systems may generate heightened racial or ethnic sentiments, but they can also channel negotiations and cross-cutting alliances, allowing scope for individual and collective action.

In the context of Latin America, we can distinguish between three forms of political systems: those where one dominant segment of the population claimed that its racial or ethnic identity was the only legitimate one in the nation; those where new power elites sought legitimacy by promoting a synthetic national culture, tending to discourage racial or ethnic thinking that might separate citizens from the nation; and those where groups shared more equally in the political life of the nation in proportion to their population, and where citizenship encompassed different yet compatible ethnic identities together constituting the nation.

The first was more likely to occur when a relatively large settler group from the colonizing power attained independence without a social revolution – the US model but one that, to a lesser degree, might be applied to Puerto Rico, the Dominican Republic, Mexico and South American Andean countries. The second has been perhaps the most common, certainly in Brazil,

Cuba, Colombia and Venezuela, with their evidently significant numbers of African-descent peoples. Central and South American countries, with their smaller Afro-Caribbean and Afro-Latin American enclave peoples, would fall somewhere between the two. The third case, harbouring what might be the closest approximation to racial democracy in the region, is arguably only attributable in part to Belize.

Any meaningful notion of racial democracy must encompass black self-liberation. Studies of Afro-Latin America continue to reflect the racist denigration of blacks as primitive, backward, anti-intellectual beings. Anti-slavery continues to be seen more as a transatlantic than a regional phenomenon, with its own philosophical and ideological underpinnings, involving localized resistance and awareness. Yet black-led anti-slavery represented a critical element at the core of transatlantic abolitionism and might be seen as the first international political movement of modern times.

In the context of the modern-day 'black Atlantic', African-descended identities and cultures jostle between asserting an absolutist sense of difference and recognizing an awareness of the double consciousness of trying to face (at least) two ways at once, between closure and openness in what have been called 'cultures of mediation'.

The gender parameters of cultures of mediation, as well as the Afro-Latin American presence, are still to be explored in full. The slaves brought over from Africa were predominantly male, and hence skewed the population. As the model transformed into one that was slave-reproducing rather than slave-importing, this was also a highly gendered process. Later Afro-Caribbean migrant workers on the Panama Canal and on Costa Rican and Cuban plantations were also mainly male. Conversely, the more recent Puerto Rican out-migration was significantly Afro-female-led into the New York garment industry.

Moreover, family and kinship patterns, and accompanying value systems, linked with pronatalist or antinatalist state policies, have all been crucial in shaping the emergent societies. A modern-day example of this was Puerto Rico's Operation Bootstrap, which was accompanied by a drastic sterilization programme that targeted poor and black women.

Prevailing ideas on gender differ markedly in Latin America and the Caribbean, especially where the family and sexuality are concerned, and largely along race lines. The polarized stereotypes are of the white Ibero-American patriarch (with repressed, controlled female) and the black Afro-Caribbean matriarch (with marginal, emasculated male). Though only briefly touched on in the present volume, these are areas that continue to command attention.

Afro-Latin America: the country studies

By far the most common thread in the chapters that follow is the country-by-country tale of the marginalization and inferioriza-tion of Afro-Latin Americans in a region where racial groups have intermixed to an astonishing degree. This has clear socio-economic dimensions, with black people generally among the poorest and least empowered inhabitants of this region of strik-ing inequalities and multiple unmet human needs. It also has a more subtle and elusive manifestation in prevailing attitudes and beliefs, with Latin America having historically tended to sup-press the sense of possessing an African heritage.

One of the principal agents of this suppression, the myth of 'racial democracy', is attacked in the chapters on Brazil and Cuba, though largely accepted for Venezuela. However, in virtu-ally every chapter the persistent denial of race and the silences surrounding the Afro-Latin American presence arouse a sense of anger and a determination to work for a fuller and more truthful recognition of past and present realities.

Rosângela Maria Vieira, writing on Brazil, and Gail McGarrity and Osvaldo Cárdenas, on Cuba, seek to unpick the pervasive myth of racial harmony. Vieira is impassioned in her cry for acceptance of Brazil's African ancestry, and angry over the stereo-typing and denigration of Afro-Brazilians beneath the veneer of racial accord, as expressed in Brazilian national thinking. She shows the degree to which Africans had a part in creating the very language that Brazilians speak – a phenomenon that has parallels in other countries of the region – as well as in other forms of cultural creation and production. Despite the existence of an energetic and well-organized black cultural, social and political movement, whose origins reach back to the early twentieth century, Vieira reveals the severity of the obstacles still confronting Afro-Brazilians in their search for justice. Death-squad killings of predominantly black street children are just one such manifestation of this; and her overriding concern is that the continuing race denial in Brazil will be a persistent source of future injustice and conflict unless honestly faced.

In their account of Colombia, Nina de Friedemann and Jaime Arocha highlight the widespread problem that arises when a national culture seeks to edit out black people's history. They make an illuminating parallel between black and indigenous land claims, investigating the close ties that bind Afro-Colombians to particular regions of the country; and their detailed account of Afro-Colombians as rainforest farmers may be a revelation for some readers. In addition to providing abundant detail about pre-twentieth-century Afro-Colombian history, de Friedemann and Arocha deal at length with black political movements of the 1990s, the outcomes of whose endeavours are still in the balance.

Gail McGarrity and Osvaldo Cárdenas argue that awareness of race as an issue of major historical and contemporary significance has been suppressed and denied in Cuba. They see this as the result of the working of several forces, including an ideology inherited from the nineteenth-century Spanish colonial plantocracy, and the limitations of twentieth-century socialist/communist politics, which carried over into the post-revolutionary period. For them, prevailing 'officialist' thinking permeates popular conceptions, an interpretation that contrasts strikingly with Silvio Torres-Saillant's understanding of the relation between official ideology and popular sentiment in the Dominican Republic.

Even so, at the height of nineteenth-century slavery in Cuba, with blacks outnumbering whites, contrary elements were forcefully present: maroonage (the escaping of slaves to the rural hinterlands); black leadership and involvement in rebellions and in the struggle for abolition and independence; a solid free black and coloured bourgeoisie; and Spanish colonial concessions to black institutions, beliefs and awareness. Cuba's early-twentieth-century independent coloured party and the 1912 race war were precursors to 1920s *negrismo* (Negritude) and 1940s black nationalism. The post-1959 period witnessed significant socio-economic advances for the Afro-Cuban population and a resurgence of Afro-Cuban study. None the less, as McGarrity and Cárdenas graphically demonstrate, in a multiplicity of ways Afro-Cubans continue to be disadvantaged. This needs to be monitored with the increasing racism of the crisis 1990s, as overseas (white) investment is encouraged, and the threat of a far whiter Miami Cuban return looms large.

The studies of Brazil, Cuba and the Dominican Republic – which, along with Colombia, are today among the most visibly racially mixed nations in the Americas – prove particularly fruitful when read together. Of the three, slavery was least prevalent in the Dominican Republic, and yet the race question has been problematized by its shared island history with Haiti. Dominican *antihaitianismo* emerged as a demonization of the black 'other' and the most blatant denial of race, reaching its height under the twentieth-century Trujillo and Balaguer administrations, with the term *negro* being reserved for Haitians, and *afro-dominicano* euphemistically becoming *indio* (denoting a more acceptable indigenous, as opposed to African, past). In his chapter Silvio Torres-Saillant focuses on aspects of black and mulatto Dominican history which belie the 'officialist' ideology; he argues that Dominicans never really bought into that way of thinking, but rather subverted it.

Kelvin Santiago-Valles focuses our attention on key issues facing Puerto Rico today: the way the island's black working class has been excluded from the socio-economic mainstream; and how young black people have been 'criminalized' – or crime 'racialized' – with accompanying manifestations of discrimination and prejudice. As Santiago-Valles clearly shows, these injustices result to a large extent from the success with which 'official' guardians of Puerto Rican culture and thought have denied and suppressed the African element in the island's demographic and historical make-up, celebrating instead the 'triumph' of the Hispanic. Courageously, a number of thinkers and activists have striven to affirm a more complex reality.

In an absorbing piece on Mexico, Jameelah Muhammad establishes that as many as perhaps half a million Africans were brought into the country, and that the African presence remained significant, with black Mexicans prominent throughout Mexico's independence struggles. Yet, as so much encountered throughout the region, Mexico's and Mexicans' denial of what is African in themselves remains widespread and deepseated – despite the survival of towns that are virtual Afro-Mexican enclaves, as Muhammad ably documents.

Mexico witnessed an Afro-Caribbean migration to Veracruz and Quintana Roo, especially from the eighteenth century onwards, and this is of particular interest in connection with the experience of Afro-Caribbean migrant enclaves in Atlantic coastal regions of the Central American nations. Of the five countries of Central America discussed in the book, Nicaragua constitutes a somewhat special case. Atlantic coast Afro-Nicaraguans historically emerged as an English-speaking buffer group between US companies, Pacific coast Hispanics and the indigenous Miskitu and Suma peoples, as well as the Garífuna (Black Caribs). Jane Freeland's skilful investigation touches on nerve centres of contradiction for this Afro-Creole people, particularly after the 1979 Sandinista revolution. She considers problems associated with the subsequent 'autonomy process', and issues surrounding the national ascendancy of Hispanic Nicaraguans, as well as Miskitu and Suma involvement in the *contra* war. Freeland concludes with a strong assertion of the validity of the autonomy principle for regional minorities.

Panama and Costa Rica illustrate a familiar pattern of male enclave Afro-Caribbean migrant labour. Darién Davis, on Panama, provides a succinct and contemporary account of the dual character of the Afro-Panamanian community, which consists of both *nativos,* or Afro-Panamanians who predate the Caribbean migration, and *antillanos,* who came from the West Indies over a long period but in greatest numbers after the 1870s to work on the Panama Canal. Davis helps clarify our understanding both of Afro-Panamanian social movements and of the additional problems caused by the 1989–90 US invasion.

Writing about Costa Rica, Kathleen Sawyers Royal and Franklin Perry provide a parallel study of West Indian – especially Jamaican – migrant labour in coastal Limón Province. Here work opportunities for the migrants arose from railway construction and the associated cultivation of bananas for United Fruit. Sawyers Royal and Perry describe the strong influence of Garveyism in this relegated enclave area; and, like all the contributors to this volume, they give testimony to the hardships that Afro-Latin Americans have endured and to the resilience and ingenuity with which they have adapted to their circumstances.

Debbie Ewens, on Belize, draws attention to two factors that have made the experience of Afro-Belizeans unusual: first, that black Belizeans were traditionally the most numerous racial group in the territory; and second, the close ties that have bound Belize to the English-speaking world. Despite Afro-Belizeans' forming the majority grouping until the relatively recent influx of Central American migrants, Ewens shows that black people have experienced discrimination and stereotyping, while lighter-skinned *mestizos* have enjoyed greater upward mobility. She concludes that 'multiracial tensions', rather than 'multiracial harmony', are the essence of the Belizean case.

On Honduras, Rachel Seider discusses the experience and situation of the Garífuna (Black Carib) people. While Honduras has perhaps the most significant Garífuna population in Central America, the group also has a sizeable presence in Belize and Nicaragua; this suggests a need for comparative work on all three communities. Like others in this collection, Seider's study provides fascinating insight into the processes and effects of syncretism, whereby in this case Garífuna culture combines African, indigenous and European elements, most notably in religious practices. Land rights are also a major issue here.

Eduardo Bermúdez and María Matilde Suárez chart the heterogeneous origins of the Afro-Venezuelan population and the process of ethnic integration, family formation and whitening, with a wealth of historical detail. Their evident interest in Afro-Venezuelan religious forms and beliefs has resulted in an absorbing investigation. Paradoxically, however, ultimately for them class, and not race, is the prime issue; and in this sense their integrationist approach stands out from the viewpoint of most of the other contributors.

In their discussion of Peru, José Luciano and Humberto

Rodriguez Pastor impart a sharp sense of a demographically small but nevertheless significant community, whose experience in key historical periods has many similarities with that of Afro-Hispanics of Colombia and Venezuela. Unusually, however, Afro-Peruvians have been a mainly urban community. The authors include a valuable account of the rebirth of black cultural and social movements in recent decades.

Norman Whitten and Diego Quiroga, in their erudite and accessible account of Afro-Ecuador, look in detail at six areas of the country, both urban and rural, which have sizeable concentrations of people of African ancestry. Like several of the contributions here, their chapter analyses the various meanings and connotations of such racial terminology as *negro* and *moreno*. Whitten and Quiroga also provide important insights into black cultural forms and social movements; and they call for a renewed interest in community studies, as well as for greater interest in the Afro-Hispanic reality and for enhanced opportunities for Afro-Latin Americans themselves.

Alison Spedding charts a fascinating process of a dwindling Afro-Bolivian population through race mixture and assimilation, especially with indigenous Aymara peasant communities. She considers relations between the two groups, and with *mestizos* and 'whites', including a discussion of the stereotyping of black Bolivians. Spedding provides illuminating insight into both traditional Afro-Bolivian culture and the revived social movement, although like other writers she is uncertain about the future prospects of the latter.

In her study of Uruguay, Alejandrina da Luz addresses the historical ambiguities of the position of people of African descent in a country that followed the end of slavery with a declaration of egalitarianism but where a strong undercurrent of racism persisted and developed into twentieth-century neo-Nazism. She tells a story of self-hating internalized racism, salvaged in part by an influx of Brazilians. This country study is one among several to show how awareness and validating of 'Africanness' have both grown and diminished over time, with Afro-Uruguayan activism reaching a peak during the 1940s from which, da Luz argues, it has since declined.

Following the country studies, Anani Dzidzienyo in his Conclusions considers how problems raised in the foregoing discussion might be addressed in the future. He rightly identifies that issues of racial inclusion and exclusion are the essence of the Afro-Latin American predicament, and he demonstrates the complexity surrounding them. Emphasizing the need to transcend the uniqueness of each country's experience, he suggests that the contributions in this collection could serve as a foundation for future programmes and projects that help raise the profile of Afro-Latin America and help us reach a new validation of 'the multiple meanings of Africa'. Ultimately, Dzidzienyo argues, the liberation of Afro-Latin Americans requires a political dimension.

Darién Davis's thoughtful Postscript, describing the Seminar on Xenophobia and Racism held in Montevideo, Uruguay, in December 1994, shows some of the forms that future political action might take.

A culture of survival?

If we had not met him in 1995, we would not have known that 35-year-old Elio Charlot, an Afro-Cuban sugar worker, had been sent to Britain, accompanied by his 59-year-old father, for a delicate genito-urinary tract operation in Middlesex Hospital, on the outskirts of London, paid for by the Cuban government. Born with the Cuban Revolution, Elio speaks of not having experienced his father's misfortunes of having been poor and black in pre-revolutionary Cuba. The operation was only possible, his father Roberto said, 'thanks to the revolution'. 'We had no alternative,' added Elio; 'although we know it costs a lot, the government said we had to come here. I was even willing to wait so the government could save that money. And there are thousands like me every year.'

Elsewhere in Latin America and the Caribbean, it would be hard to find a sugar worker like Elio being paid for out of state funds to have such a delicate and expensive operation done at home, much less abroad. As we write, however, it is not clear how much of the social justice attained in Cuba for the poor and black, especially in the fields of health and education, can be preserved.

14

Moreover, it can be argued that the Cuban social revolution was less successful in the broader ramifications of race politics than might have been hoped. Writing in the 1940s, Cuban ethnologist Fernando Ortiz, who pioneered the term 'Afro-Cuban', articulated a plea for an end to racial essentialism and denigration, outlining five phases in race relations encompassed in his theory of transculturation: hostility, compromise, adaptation, vindication and integration. He saw integration as a 'rite of social communion', the phase of the tomorrow that was dawning, a third identity and culture, where racial factors would lose their ill-intent. Fifty years later, it is a phase proving highly elusive.

Can there be a just racial order fashioned out of the injustices, chaos and eclecticism that have shaped Latin America and the Caribbean? We would like to think so, and to argue that lessons may be wrought from the region's cultural fusion, whereby the African is a major component part in what might be termed a culture of survival.

Throughout the Americas, as with oppressed peoples elsewhere in the world, a distorted vision of Afro-Latin Americans has been historically refashioned, negating their powers of individual and collective self-determination and expression. And yet, where politics and economics pushed the races apart, people have demonstrated a determined and expressive coming together, as expressed in the written, visual, performing and festival arts. The continent might do well to borrow a leaf from the cultural book in moving forward to celebrate racial pluralism rather than to fear, denigrate and manipulate race difference.

Select bibliography

Afro-Hispanic Review.
Benítez-Rojo, A., *The Repeating Island: The Caribbean and the Postmodern Perspective*, trans. J.E. Maraniss, Durham, NC, and London, Duke University Press, 1992.
Bailey, B., Brereton, B. and Mohammed, P. (eds), *Engendering Caribbean History*, London, James Currey, and Kingston, Jamaica, Ian Randle, 1995.
Beckles, H., Caribbean anti-slavery: the self-liberation ethos of enslaved blacks', *Journal of Caribbean History*, vol. 22, nos 1-2, 1988.
Bolland, O.N., *Colonialism and Resistance in Belize: Essays in Historical Sociology*, Benque Viejo del Carmen, Belize, Cubola Productions, 1988.

Bourgois, P.I., *Ethnicity at Work: Divided Labor on a Central American Banana Plantation*, Baltimore, MD, Johns Hopkins University Press, 1989.

Coniff, M. and Davis, T.J., *Africans in the Americas*, London, Macmillan, 1994.

Crayhan, M.E. and Knight, F.W. (eds), *Africa and the Caribbean: The Legacies of a Link*, Baltimore, MD, Johns Hopkins University Press, 1979.

Curtin, P.D., *The Atlantic Slave Trade: A Census*, Madison, WI, University of Wisconsin Press, 1969.

Davis, D.J. (ed.), *Slavery and Beyond: The African Impact on Latin America and the Caribbean*, Wilmington, DE, Scholarly Resources/Jaguar Books, 1995.

Farris-Thompson, R., *Flash of the Spirit: African and Afro-American Art and Philosophy*, New York, Vintage Books, 1983.

Freyre, G., *The Masters and the Slaves*, New York, Knopf, 1946.

Gilroy, P., *The Black Atlantic: Modernity and Double Consciousness*, London, Verso, 1993.

Graham, R. (ed.), *The Idea of Race in Latin America, 1870-1940*, Austin, TX, University of Texas Press, 1990.

Harris, M., *Patterns of Race in the Americas*, New York, Walker, 1964.

Hoetink, H., *The Two Variants in Caribbean Race Relations: A Contribution to the Sociology of Segmented Societies*, trans. E.M. Hooykaas, New York and London, Oxford University Press, 1967.

Klein, H.S., *African Slavery in Latin America and the Caribbean*, New York, Oxford University Press, 1986.

Lewis, G., *Main Currents in Caribbean Thought*, Kingston, Jamaica, and Port of Spain, Trinidad and Tobago, Heinemann, 1983.

Maingot, A.P., 'Race, color, and class in the Caribbean', in A. Stepan (ed.), *Americas: New Interpretative Essays*, New York, Oxford University Press, 1992.

Mintz, S.W. and Price, R., *An Anthropological Approach to the Afro-American Past: A Caribbean Perspective*, Philadelphia, PA, Institute for the Study of Human Issues, 1976.

Momsen, J.H. (ed.), *Women and Change in the Caribbean*, London, James Currey, Kingston, Jamaica, Ian Randle, and Bloomington, IN, Indiana University Press, 1993.

Moreno Fraginals, M. (ed.), *Africa in Latin America*, New York: Holmes & Meier, 1984.

Morner, M., *Race Mixture in the History of Latin America*, Boston, MA, Little, Brown, 1967.

Morner, M. (ed.), *Race and Class in Latin America*, New York, Columbia University Press, 1970.

North American Congress on Latin America, *Report on the Americas: The Black Americas 1492-1992*, New York, NACLA, vol. 25, no. 4, 1992.

Ortiz, F., 'For a Cuban integration of whites and blacks', in P. Pérez Sarduy and J. Stubbs (eds), *AfroCuba: An Anthology of Cuban Writing on Race, Politics and Culture*, London, Latin America Bureau, and Melbourne, Ocean Press, 1993.

Thornton, J., *Africa and Africans in the Making of the Atlantic World, 1400-1680*, Cambridge, Cambridge University Press, 1992.

Sage Race Relations Abstracts.
Serbin, A., 'Relations between the English-speaking Caribbean and Latin America', *Caribbean Affairs,* vol. 2, no. 4, 1989.
Tannenbaum, F., *Slave and Citizen,* New York, Knopf, 1947.
Williams, E., *Capitalism and Slavery,* Chapel Hill, NC, University of North Carolina Press, 1944.

2

BRAZIL

Rosângela Maria Vieira

The history and culture of Afro-Brazilians are not cultivated in schools. Our children do not become aware of Blacks' participation in the history of Brazil. Such teachings, when they occur, are conveyed in total misrepresentation, generating in the minds of our children a distorted view of reality.[1]

Racism has long been an issue of importance in Brazil. Yet many Brazilians take pride in denying its existence and portraying Brazil as the world's true melting pot, a model of racial equality, harmony and opportunities for all. It is considered 'impolite', as well as mistaken, to raise problematic issues of ethnicity.[2] Many Brazilians of African ancestry, however, are aware of the degree to which their cultural, religious, socio-economic and political identities have been suppressed. There is thus a serious discrepancy between the usual portrayal of racial matters in the country and the reality as experienced in the lives of millions of Afro-Brazilian people.[3]

The African contribution to Brazilian life has been one of the most significant factors in its formation and development, but there is little official acknowledgement of its importance. Instead, black Brazilians tend to be conceived and presented as undignified stereotypes; and they have been led to believe that *embranquecimento* (whitening) offers by and large the only route to improvement and mobility.

According to estimates made by the Brazilian black movement and various scholars, people of partly or wholly African ancestry account for between 68 per cent and 75 per cent of the national population,[4] or well over 100 million individuals. Even the official census, which arrives at a lower figure, largely because people choose their ethnic classification for census purposes, indicates that they represent almost half of the population (46 per cent). These differences are of more than academic interest, because black affairs are arguably a *majority* concern in Brazil, rather than the minority interest that the government classifies them as. Whatever the precise numerical reality, however, Afro-Brazilians as a group clearly lack economic power, political influence and effective representation. They are generally the poorest of the poor in their own country. Infant mortality rates for black children are higher than among the white population, and many black children who survive infancy live in fear of sudden violent death at the hands of death squads. The vast majority of Afro-Brazilians are inadequately housed, most notably those who inhabit the city *favelas* (slums). Black people are overrepresented in the country's violent prisons but underrepresented in the media, except as 'stars' of entertainment and sport, or as comic figures. Their educational and employment opportunities are strictly limited, with vast numbers forced to depend on low-paid and informal-sector work for survival. While many white Brazilians also endure hardship and poverty in this polarized and stratified society, Afro-Brazilians tend to fare worst of all. It has perhaps rightly been argued that a concealed form of apartheid operates in Brazil.

The weight of such evidence has nevertheless had little impact on the prevailing view that Brazil is a 'racial democracy' whose social problems stem mainly or entirely from differences of 'class' and of personal qualities – initiative, enterprise, ability – that result in unequal outcomes. Where it is admitted that a mild form of racism may exist, this tends to be spoken of as 'prejudice' rather than outright discrimination.[5]

About Brazil

Brazil is the largest country in Latin America and the fifth largest in the world. Its landscape is dominated by two prominent features: the Amazon River, with its surrounding lowland basin, and the Central Highlands plateau to the south of the great river. Brazil has one of the most extensive river systems in the world. Its climate is varied, ranging from the temperate conditions in the south to the steamy humidity of the tropical jungle. The country is extremely rich in such natural resources as iron ore, manganese, bauxite and nickel, as well as having large reserves of uranium, potassium, phosphate, tungsten, cassiterite, lead, graphite, chrome, gold, zirconium and the rare mineral thorium. It is also the world's leading producer of semi-precious gems.

The northern region was once of major importance for rubber collection and contains the world's largest remaining tropical forest. The north-east has major oil reserves, although it remains Brazil's poorest region. The south-east is Brazil's richest region, with its industrial sector, offshore minerals and advanced agricultural production of coffee, grains, fresh and processed food, milk and meat. Southern Brazil has one of the largest hydroelectric dams in the world at Itaipú. West-central Brazil, where Brasília, the new capital, was founded in 1960, is relatively undeveloped. The current national population is estimated at about 156 million.

No single ethnic group dominates in Brazil. The nation is a racial mixture of African, indigenous, European, Asian and Middle Eastern (especially Lebanese) elements. The country's religious groups include those of African origin – Candomblé, Umbanda – the Catholic and Protestant churches, Spiritists, Mormons, Jews, Muslims and Buddhists. Many cults are also widely practised.

Brazil is the only Portuguese-speaking country in South America. The Portuguese occupation began in AD 1500 and ended on 7 September 1822, with independence. Salvador da Bahia, founded in 1540, was the first national capital. The capital was transferred to Rio de Janeiro in the later eighteenth century, and on 21 April 1960 to Brasília.

Official histories indicate that Brazilian expansion began after the mid-1500s with the work of *bandeirantes,* who explored the interior of the country. In reality, the *bandeirantes,* were men of violence, hired by the colonial rulers to cut their way through the forest and march across the inland plateau to hunt down, capture or kill indigenous and African slaves who had escaped from the plantations and taken refuge in the interior. The economy was based mainly on sugar cultivation during early colonial times. After the decline of sugar consumption in the late seventeenth century, the Portuguese discovered and exploited reserves of gold and diamonds, mainly for export. Then, during the eighteenth and nineteenth centuries, coffee replaced precious minerals and became one of Brazil's most important sources of wealth, remaining so today.

Nationalistic sentiments developed with great intensity during this period, and Brazilians saw the need to expel their Portuguese, French and Dutch exploiters. Inspired by the ideals of the American Revolution and the French Encyclopedists, Joaquim José da Silva Xavier 'Tiradentes', a young cavalry officer and intellectual from Minas Gerais State, in 1792 led the first independence movement, known as the Inconfidência Mineira. His heroic efforts were discovered by the Portuguese, who condemned Tiradentes to die by hanging in a public square as an example to all.

During the years 1808-21, when the Portuguese court was transferred to Brazil, the country went from colony to a united kingdom with Portugal. King Dom João VI returned to Portugal in 1821 but left his son, Dom Pedro I, as ruler of Brazil. In 1822 Pedro I proclaimed Brazilian independence and declared the country his empire; he inherited it officially after the death of his father in 1826. His son, Dom Pedro II, became the second Emperor (1831-89) while still a minor. Slavery was abolished during this period, in 1888, by Dom Pedro II's daughter, Princess Isabel, who was acting as regent because of her father's absence from the country. The First Republic was inaugurated on 15 November 1889, with Brazil's first military coup d'état, and the Emperor and his family were ousted from Brazil. There followed a long period of civilian rule, with the franchise limited to landowners and property owners. In 1930, after leading a movement which overthrew the government of the First Republic, Getúlio Vargas became President. This dictator lost the presidency in elections in 1945 to General Eurico Gaspar Dutra, who ruled until 1951. Vargas was then re-elected President; but in 1954, amid an intense political crisis, he committed suicide.

In 1964 the military overthrew the civilian government, beginning a period of military rule which lasted until 1985. This was a time of terror, when freedoms were revoked, censorship was imposed, and several hundred Brazilians were kidnapped, tortured or killed for their left-wing views or opposition to the military. Others fled into exile. Five military generals became President of Brazil in turn during these years, the last of whom, General João Batista Figueiredo, initiated the *processo de abertura,* the political opening which led to the end of this painful chapter of Brazilian history. In January 1985 Tancredo de Almeida Neves was chosen as the country's first civilian President in twenty-one years. On the eve of his inauguration, however, Neves fell ill and was taken to hospital, where he died. José Sarney, the vice-president, was sworn in as President instead, and a new constitution was proclaimed on 15 October 1988. Today Sarney continues to be active in the political arena.

In 1989, in the first direct election held since 1960, Brazilians were heavily influenced by the country's media and other powerful economic and political sectors in electing Fernando Collor de Mello to the presidency, whose main campaign promise had been to rid the country of corruption and incompetent leaders. Following accusations made by his own brother, Collor de Mello and several of his top advisers were investigated for the theft of many millions of dollars. He resigned in December 1992, after being tried by the Senate, but was then largely exonerated in 1994. Itamar Franco, the vice-president, became President until replaced by Fernando Henrique Cardoso in January 1995, following the elections of October 1994.

Colonial slavery

After the Portuguese Dom Pedro Alvares Cabral 'discovered' Brazil in 1500, an estimated 3,650,000 African slaves were brought to Brazilian soil as a source of labour to exploit the territory. Indigenous Brazilians had proved 'unreliable' in the Portuguese quest to build the new nation. The above figure is many times greater than, for instance, the approximately 427,000 Africans sent to what would become the United States.[6] The Portuguese colonial rulers were the largest importers of black people to the Americas, having also been the first modern Europeans to enslave Africans, beginning in 1441.[7] Indeed, although Africans had enslaved each other prior to the arrival of Europeans on their continent, their slavery as we know it today was the invention of the Portuguese, who monopolized the slave traffic throughout the sixteenth century. With the colonial conquest, the Portuguese promoted both the ethnic and cultural dismembering of Africa,[8] the cradle of human civilization and knowledge, and the genocide of indigenous Brazilians. Today, the native Brazilian population has been reduced to a mere 2 per cent of the national total, and their numbers continue to decline. The Portuguese were also among the first Europeans to take advantage of political instability, wars and general unrest in Africa, an involvement that lasted from the fifteenth century until the mid-1970s.

Among the Africans brought to Brazil were Afantis, Axantis, Jejes, Peuls and Muslim Hausas, called Malês in Salvador da Bahia, as well as Nagos and Yoruba peoples. At first they came mainly from Guinea and the Congo. One West African port alone sent Portugal a thousand slaves a year during the second half of the sixteenth century. During the eighteenth century new waves of the trade brought slaves from Sudan and the Bight of Benin. After about 1830 – by which time Britain, the USA, France and Spain had abolished the slave trade – an illicit trade began to develop. Slaves came to Brazil in the nineteenth century from many different places, with Mozambique and Angola by far the largest sources of supply. East Africa supplied 75 per cent of the slaves imported to Brazil at this time, compared with only 3 per cent for the period 1790-1811.[9] Overall, Brazil imported 38 per cent of the approximate 9,500,000 Africans forcibly brought to the Americas.

Throughout Brazil, especially in the northern provinces, perhaps 40 per cent of African slaves worked in agriculture, cultivating sugar-cane, tobacco, spices, cotton, coconut, corn, tomatoes, potatoes and other crops. Smaller numbers worked in the owners' mansions, occupied with house chores, child care and the general upkeep of the house, grounds and domestic stock. After the decline of sugar, and throughout the eighteenth and nineteenth centuries, blacks were shifted to work in southern Brazil, where large numbers worked in the gold-mines of Minas Gerais and in the coffee plantations of the São Paulo region.

The Cape Verde Islands, where sugar plantations developed after 1460, became a centre for the trade in slaves from the African coast between Senegal and present-day Sierra Leone. The importance of Cape Verde did not begin to decline until the middle of the sixteenth century, when English and French traffickers first set up operations in Gambia.[10] Among the companies which controlled and profited most from the enslavement and selling of Africans was the Royal African Company of England, which extended its influence along the coast of Guinea, present-day Ghana and Dahomey. By the eighteenth century 70 per cent of the slaves destined for the Antilles and North America were carried by British slavers, and 101 slave ships were registered at the port of Liverpool.[11] Yet Britain was the nation which exercised the most pressure on the United States, Brazil and other countries in the Americas to stop the traffic and abolish slavery.

By the dawn of the nineteenth century Britain had already acquired great wealth from the traffic of slaves, and saw the need to direct its investments and interests elsewhere, notably into the textile industry. Under the Methuen Treaty of 1703 Britain supplied textile products to Portugal, which paid for them with gold extracted from Brazilian mines using the forced labour of Afro-Brazilian slaves. Thus Brazilian gold ended up in London and helped finance the Industrial Revolution. Not wishing to benefit directly from slavery any longer, Britain policed the Atlantic seas to rid the world of slave traffic. Brazil officially abolished its traffic on 28 September 1850, going on to abolish the institution of slavery itself on 13 May 1888, the last nation in the western hemisphere to free its black population.

The experience and legacy of slavery

Africans who came to Brazil in fetters preserved their cultural heritage and religions despite the lack of a common language among them. The Portuguese deliberately mixed together slaves from different African nations and regions, breaking up familial and linguistic links, as they distributed them among the various *capitanias* (states of the colony); this was done to make communication among the Africans more difficult and to prevent collective defiance or mutiny. The strategy was largely unsuccessful, however; the slaves, bonded in grief, developed what Yeda Pessoa de Castro has called a *dialeto das senzalas* (dialect of the slave quarters)[12] – a form of linguistic expression combining Yoruba, Bantu and Kwa elements, among others. In addition, when using the language of their masters, the slaves would change the pronunciation of certain words, both to confuse the Portuguese and to facilitate communication among themselves.

In such ways the process of 'creolization' took place. Brazilian Portuguese was richly influenced by the speech of such African peoples as the Afantis, Axantis, Jejes, Peuls, Hausas, Nagos, Yorubas and those from Benin, Angola and Mozambique. The language became 'softer' and more melodious, losing the monotony and nasality of European Portuguese, as a result of the way the slaves and their descendants altered and simplified it, reducing inflexions and sometimes doing away with verbs and other linguistic elements altogether in order to make their communication harder for whites to comprehend. Through this process the word *filho* (son) became *fio*; *fazer* (to do) was pronounced and then written as *faze*. A new Afro-Brazilian vocabulary developed whereby words such as *molambo* (rags), *moleque* (adolescent), *mucama* (nurse), *mandinga* (witch doctor) and *caçula* (youngest child) were incorporated into mainstream Brazilian Portuguese.[13] When giving orders or otherwise communicating with the slaves, the Portuguese would at times use their own language or in other instances borrow the slaves' terminology for faster and more effective communication, hastening the creolization process.

Today in modern *quilombos* (black communities), such as Quilombo da Rãs, forms of linguistic expression persist that are essentially African. In other contemporary black communities such as Cafundó, São Paulo State, as Michael Mitchell observes, one encounters an Afro-Brazilian community 'clinging to the past through its African language'.[14] Mitchell's work on Cafundó has been much influenced by that of a group of anthropologists from the Universidade Estadual de Campinas – Carlos Vogt, Peter Fry and Maurício Gnere – whose studies are probably the first serious descriptions of this surviving African community.[15] As Vogt, Fry, Gnere and Mitchell explain, the language spoken at Cafundó represents an oral tradition which was transformed into a *caipira* (a rural Brazilian Portuguese dialect), and is probably of Bantu origin. In some cases, complete sentences are formed by fusing Portuguese grammatical structures with Bantu stems.[16]

As in most colonized societies, and wherever African slaves were found, miscegenation took place – chiefly, particularly at first, in such abusive or violent forms as rape and even father–daughter incest. During the first decades of Portuguese occupation, African and indigenous women were the only ones available to Portuguese men; white Portuguese women would not come to the colony until many years later. The great numbers of interracial children generated from these liaisons formed a class denominated as *mulato*. The Portuguese words *mulato* and *mulata* are by implication highly offensive to black people, signifying that the person concerned is the offspring of the crossing of a mule with a horse. The implication was that the child born from the union of a female African-Brazilian slave (the mule) with a white Portuguese man (the horse) would benefit from the genetic transformation thus conferred. By the time of the 1980 census, Brazilians had coined 136 terms of racial categorization by which to define themselves. Such a range was needed because lighter-skinned black people tended to object to being classified in the same group as people of a darker complexion.

The Portuguese believed that the 'black race' would 'improve' in essence and appearance and eventually disappear. Such sentiments are still expressed throughout Latin America. Even today in Brazil mulattos are often said to be a 'breed apart', and their ethnic classification is rarely black; indeed, many dark-skinned mulatto Brazilians refer to themselves as 'white',. However, white Brazilians generally do not allow mulattos full 'promotion' into their ethnic category nor acceptance as 'white' until the fourth or fifth generation (with Pelé, the former soccer star and now Minister for Sport, being the most notable exception). This way of thinking is at the core of Brazilian racism, for it denies the black presence and Afro-

Brazilian identity, and emphasizes the mulatto's 'whiteness' as perhaps the key factor in the achievement of better opportunities in a white-dominated world. In addition, historic exploitation of *mulata* women in Brazil dates from colonial times, attributing to them exaggerated libidinous characteristics and desirability as a sexual partner – the subject of many popular songs.

Despite all such negative connotations, however, sexual and familial relationships in Brazil, as elsewhere in the region, may cross ethnic boundaries and still be based upon mutual affection and respect. The celebrated mixing of races during Carnival represents a genuine desire among many Brazilians to unite black with white. Clearly, then, Brazilians have contradictory responses to such matters.

Whitening of the race became an official priority in Brazil in 1850, when the slave traffic was declared illegal, and after the abolition of slavery in 1888. By the first decades of the nineteenth century the government had begun actively to encourage white European immigration, hoping to transform the ethnic composition of the nation and to provide labourers for the coffee plantations. White Europeans took an active role in this process by intermixing with Afro-Brazilians. And it is true that Brazilian mulattos have long experienced more social mobility than Brazilians who are more easily identified as blacks. In colonial times many members of the mulatto class achieved relatively comfortable living conditions; some, such as the nineteenth-century novelist José Maria Machado de Assis, enjoyed great prominence in society.

Africans in colonial Brazil sought to preserve their culture through religious practices and exclusive confraternities (brotherhoods and sisterhoods). In the late seventeenth century, for example, the Confraternização Nosso Senhor da Baixa dos Sapateiros in Bahia admitted only Angolan slaves, and the Confraternização Nosso Senhor da Redenção comprised only Gegé slaves. A few other such groups were composed of mulattos alone. After the eighteenth century the confraternities, which sought to promote black unity, became more integrated and racially diverse. African religions, based on the worship of ancestors – a practice partially disrupted by the enslavement and consequent destruc-

28

tion of African families – were regarded as pagan by the Portuguese and hence repressed. One way the slaves found to overcome this obstacle and to preserve their heritage was to incorporate Catholic rituals and saints into their African worship. In the blending of Catholicism with Candomblé, brought to Brazil by Yoruba slaves from Nigeria and Benin, for example, Oxalá, a male god of procreation and harvest, is identified with Cristo (Jesus); and Iemanjá, goddess of the sea, is associated with Nossa Senhora da Conceição (Our Lady of Conception). The Portuguese permitted such adaptations but would not acknowledge the association of their Christian faith and doctrine with African forms of worship, which they despised. African religions survive in Brazil today and give testimony to the strength of Brazil's African heritage and to the powerful sense of solidarity among Africans brought to the country. They felt the need to forge a new culture that would be their original response to the difficulties of the new environment in which they were forced to live.[17]

Life expectancy for slaves was short, especially for those who worked on the plantations. The Portuguese, seeking to maximize returns on their investment, imposed long hours of work on their captives, often in the harshest of weather conditions, and neglected the Africans' nutritional and clothing needs. Corporal punishment was commonplace, and a great many diseases went without treatment in circumstances which led to the early death of countless slaves. Many died of neglect or exhaustion once they became sick; others committed suicide in large numbers. Those Africans who survived into old age tended to die in miserable abandonment, especially after 1885, when the Sexagenarian Law was passed, which conveniently liberated older and unproductive slaves, thus freeing the slave owners from any responsibility for their upkeep. Many thousands of slaves over the age of 60 were freed as a direct result of this law.

The Portuguese slave regime was therefore generally a brutal one. Even so, the myth that it was somehow 'benevolent' has persisted into contemporary times and helped mask the true nature of Brazilian race relations. Commentators have judged the Portuguese more 'humane' in their treatment of slaves than, say, the Anglo-Saxons in North America, in part because as

Catholics they are said to have recognized that their captives might have immortal souls worthy of salvation. The classic expression of this myth of 'good masters' and 'docile slaves' is in the work of the Brazilian sociologist Gilberto Freyre. In theory, admittedly, Brazilian slaves had such legal rights as the right to buy their freedom or to make a formal complaint of ill-treatment; but in reality these rights could rarely be exercised.[18]

Early resistance and struggle

Even in colonial times, black Brazilians continually organized and protested against their enslavement. Some had the opportunity to work to acquire their freedom, as did Chico Rei, an African king sent to Minas Gerais. Chico Rei worked to free his son and all the members of his tribe who had been sold to Portuguese mercenaries. Other African-Brazilians resisted on the plantations by refusing to work efficiently during the sixteen-hour work-day required by their masters. A further form of resistance was to escape and join other former slaves in the *quilombos* – remote and self-sufficient resistance communities founded and governed by black people. Several *quilombos* became virtual independent nations. Escaped slaves set up *quilombos* in the Ilha de Marajó, in Mato Grosso, Bahia, Sergipe, Alagoas, Pernambuco, Paraíba, Minas Gerais, Rio de Janeiro, São Paulo, Santa Catarina and Porto Alegre. These communities had to be well organized to maintain their freedom and, while they existed, represented the enduring hope for a free society.[19] Some *quilombos*, like Palmares, survived for over a century, although most were eventually wiped out by the Luso-Brazilian state.

Palmares was situated in the Serra da Barriga of northern Brazil. This community resisted two attacks by the Dutch, who occupied north-east Brazil for twenty-four years during the first half of the seventeenth century, and several other incursions by Portuguese forces between 1625 and 1694, when it was finally destroyed by the mercenary Domingo Jorge Velho. Zumbi, Palmares's African king and last leader, survived all attacks against his nation but was captured and killed on 20 November 1695 while trying to regroup and rebuild the *quilombo*. Betrayed by one of his own, who had revealed the location of his hideout after being tortured by the Portuguese, Zumbi was decapitated, and his head was displayed in public. He is still remembered by Brazilians of African ancestry as a hero who fought for freedom.[20] The history of such *quilombos* illustrates the extent and effectiveness of black resistance in Brazil, and it is notable that women often had important roles in these communities, including, in some cases, acting as leaders.[21]

Other black revolts and resistance movements sprang up from colonial to post-abolitionist times. The Sastre Rebellion of 1798 in Bahia, for instance, occurred after gold had been discovered, following the decline of sugar production. The rebels intended their movement to lead to the establishment of a free and democratic republican government, accessible to all peoples; but their rising was defeated in its early stages, and the leaders were all hanged. Many slave rebellions took place between 1807 and 1835. Decolonization and the establishment of a nation state created two kinds of tension in Bahia: tension within the slave class, and within the class of free Brazilians, where there was conflict between the interests of the elite and those of the remainder of the non-slave population. In 1807 in Bahia the rebellion of Muslim Hausa slaves, who were known as Malês, called for the extermination of white people by poisoning them in their homes and at public water fountains, and sought to seize any slave ships found in Bahian harbours in order to return to Africa, the motherland. As with the Sastre revolt, the Portuguese got wind of the plot orchestrated by the Malês and sentenced all leaders and participants to death. Similar rebellions by Muslim slaves broke out in 1810, 1813 and 1816. One major uprising occurred in 1814, during the period leading up to independence, when Napoleon's armies had begun their invasion of Portugal and the Portuguese monarch, Dom João VI, had fled to Rio de Janeiro, where he would stay until 1821. This was the rebellion of severely deprived and malnourished slaves from Itapoã, in the state of Bahia de Todos os Santos. This era was one of the worst periods for the treatment of African slaves in Brazil; hunger, neglect and torture of slaves prevailed as never before. In desperation, the slaves of Itapoã took to the streets to demand better treatment, but were all killed by Luso-Brazilian forces.

The period immediately after the proclamation of independence on 7 September 1822 also witnessed the Jehad (1835) and Black Nagôs (1826-35) revolts. Like the Malês rising of 1807, these rebellions had religious characteristics, the goal being both to kill whites and to expel the Christian religion from Brazil in the name of Allah.[22] The Sabinada revolt soon followed, in 1837, and hundreds of black women, children and older slaves were slaughtered with such intensity by Luso-Brazilian forces that rebellious movements ceased for a considerable time afterwards in Bahia. Outside of Bahia, however, several insurrections took place during the years of Dom Pedro I's and Dom Pedro II's empire: the rebellion of the slaves from the Fazenda Freguesia of 1838, led by the *quilombo* chief Manoel Congo; the Manuel Balaio revolt of 1839; and the Vassouras rebellion of 1847. The lack of long-term objectives, planning and specific strategies allowed all such risings to be swiftly crushed by the authorities; and, as on previous occasions, all the rebel leaders were executed. In the late nineteenth century the Canudo and Beata revolts similarly ended in the mass killing of participants.

Slavery ended in Brazil in 1888, but in the years just before abolition slaves were in constant rebellion. They were also escaping the plantations, fleeing to the *quilombos,* in great numbers. The Brazilian army no longer hunted them down as effectively as before. There was general political instability and a war with Paraguay. The driving force of the economy had moved from the sugar-growing slave plantations of the north-east to the coffee plantations of the south-east which used free labour. Brazil's white elite was now subject to international political and economic pressures to abolish slavery and move towards a free society. Despite such pressures, particularly on the part of Britain, the Brazilian state was slow to act. It passed a series of self-serving laws, such as the Law of the Free Womb (1871) and the Sexagenarian Law (1885), which did little except favour the interests of white slave owners and sustain the criminality of the slave system.

The years following abolition were extremely hard for Afro-Brazilians. To survive, they had to find alternatives to plantation life; but newly freed blacks had no opportunity to prepare for the emerging industrial economy. The white population, ignoring the major role that black people had played in building the nation and creating its wealth, was instead preoccupied with the fear that Brazil would become a 'black nation'. Their response to this situation, after the declaration of the first republic in 1889, was to open their country to hundreds of thousands of white European immigrants. White newcomers were given preference over black Brazilians in jobs, housing and education wherever they lived, but especially in the emerging south-east. Afro-Brazilians, many of whose skills equalled those of the white immigrants, were pushed into low-paying occupations and unemployment.[23]

Afro-Brazilian cultural forms have long been an important element in the struggle of black Brazilians to survive their oppression, most notably in the north-east state of Bahia, where a clear majority of the population is Afro-Brazilian. The enrichment of Portuguese with African vocabulary helped the first generations of Afro-Brazilians portray their experience and preserve their sense of reality. Indeed, storytelling was a significant activity through which the African inheritance was retained and reproduced. The legendary Bahian woman Sinhá Inocência, for example, used the Nago language of the Yoruba for some of her tales.[24]

Similarly, the African-descended religion Candomblé preserved the beliefs and practices of the Yoruba people, although it remained a hidden practice, banned by the Portuguese, for many years and reappeared in public only in the nineteenth century, linked in various ways to Catholicism. Involving many deities that control the forces of nature and human fortunes, Candomblé still is central to the lives of many Afro-Brazilians, for whom its festivals are days of major significance. Another aspect of the Yoruba inheritance that has persisted until today is the exercise form known as Capoeira, combining elements of dance and martial arts.

Brazil's best-known cultural export, Carnival, has developed as a further product of the Afro-Brazilian survival instinct, especially in the most 'Africanized' form that it takes in Bahia. Here the widespread involvement of the population in Afro-Brazilian percussion groups, the wearing of African costumes and the singing of traditional African and black Brazilian songs continue a centuries-old process of ethnic affirmation and celebration.[25]

Contemporary organizations

After the end of slavery, resistance to racism was evident among the many Afro-Brazilians who participated in black popular organizations.[26] Such forms of activism were linked to the fight against poverty, which remained severe among black people. In particular, the years between the two world wars, during which the Brazilian New State was established under the dictatorship of Getúlio Vargas, witnessed the emergence of several notable Afro-Brazilian organizations,[26] whose goals were to achieve better life opportunities and social justice for all Afro-Brazilians. Numerical estimates vary, but today many hundreds of black consciousness and civil rights organizations are actively at work in Brazil.

The rise of these organizations has been made possible in part by the strong promotion of black awareness on the part of journals which emerged in the first decades of the twentieth century. At first, such journals mainly promoted social events; but in time, the sense of social awareness grew, and more and more social and political campaigns were mounted through their pages. These publications have been instrumental in examining the experience of Afro-Brazilians, enabling them to see the common bonds that exist between them. Underscoring the need to take into account the pluralistic experience of black Brazilians, this community-based press has had a major role as a catalyst for organizing, for the claiming of rights and for fighting racism.

Notable among the many black people's newspapers published from the beginning of this century until now are *O Manelic* (founded in 1915), *A Rua* and *O Xauter* (1916), *O Alfinete* and *O Bandeirante* (1918), *A Liberdade* (1919), *A Sentinela* (1920), *O Kosmos* (1922), *O Getulino* (1923) and *O Clarim d'Alvorada* (an important newspaper, founded by the journalists Jayme Aguiar and José Correia Leite). Other important journals were *Elite* (founded in 1924), *Auriverde, O Patrocinio* and *Progresso* (1928), *Chibata* (1932), *A Evolução* and *A Voz da Raça* (1933), *O Clarim, O Estímulo, A Raça* and *Tribuna Negra* (1935), *A Alvorada* (1936), *Senzala* (1946), *Mundo Novo* (1950), *O Novo Horizonte* (1954), *Notícias de Ébano* (1957), *O Mutirão* (1958), *Hífen* and *Niger* (1960), *Nosso Jornal* (1961) and *Correio d'Ébano* (1963).[27]

A new wave of journals established since the 1970s includes *Gazeta Afro-Latina de Porto Alegre*, *Revista do Movimento Negro Unificado* (MNU), *Jornal Negô* (MNU, Bahia), *Jornal Nacional do MNU*, *Eparrei* (published by Entidade Casa da Mulher Negra), *Jornal do Conselho da Comunidade Negra*, *Sinbá*, *Jornegro*, *Jornal da Maioria Falante*, *Cecune*, *Jornal do Centro Ecumênico de Cultura Negra*, *Cadernos Negros* (published by the literary group Quilombhoje), *Jornal do Centro de Estudos Afro-Asiáticos* and *Revista do Instituto das Mulheres Negras* (published by Geledés).

Afro-Brazilian ideals and aesthetics were strongly expressed through the work of many black organizations founded during the first decades of the twentieth century. Among the most prominent of these was the Centro Cívico Palmares (Palmares Civic Centre), established in 1927, which was initially conceived as an educational organization but soon became a focus for the Afro-Brazilian fight against poverty, racial discrimination and social inequalities. A few years later, in 1931, the Frente Negra Brasileira (FNB) was founded in São Paulo; its aims also included community education among black and mulatto Brazilians, as well as the promotion of more active Afro-Brazilian participation in the socio-economic and political life of the country. Women – who gained the vote in 1932 – had a notable role in the FNB through a women's section that campaigned against sexual discrimination and exploitation; by the mid-decade a significant group of assertive working-class women, known as *frentenegrinas*, had emerged through the organization.[28] The FNB had developed into a political party by 1936, but it was outlawed for a period by the dictator Getúlio Vargas, and subsequently became a cultural rather than a political organization.

During the 1940s there occurred a black renaissance in arts and letters, especially as a result of the work of the Afro-Brazilian intellectual Abdias do Nascimento, who in 1944 founded the Teatro Experimental do Negro (TEN). This group sought to promote black pride through the arts, to defend black consciousness and to speak against whitening. TEN's main activities included the promotion of Afro-Brazilian dramatic art as a means of portraying black people's reality and the need for social change, as well as the creation of a space for black people in Brazilian arts and literature. As Darién J. Davis points out in an invaluable account of the activism of twentieth-century Afro-Brazilian women, TEN embraced gender issues, just as the FNB had done: it published articles featuring exemplary Afro-Brazilian women and its journal *Quilombo* regularly featured a column entitled 'Fala Mulher' (Woman Speaks) by the writer Maria Nascimento. In later years women involved in TEN set up various women's organizations and ran literacy and educational programmes.[29]

In 1950 the Primeiro Congresso do Negro Brasileiro was founded as a forum for the promotion of Afro-Brazilian awareness and the struggle for rights.

More recently, among the leading black people's organizations set up since the 1970s and still active, are the following. The Movimento Negro Unificado (MNU) of São Paulo, which dates from 1978, was established to emphasize the need for change in Brazilian government policies towards black people, to strive for black communal rights and to fight the historical injustices which have been inflicted by the Brazilian state on the black population. With representatives throughout Brazil, the MNU is one of the most active organizations addressing issues faced by Afro-Brazilians today.

Women have long been active in the MNU, to the extent that conflicts of interest have surfaced between men and women in the movement, with women frequently more concerned with educational goals rather than the more overtly political interests of the men. MNU women in Bahia, for example, have run educational campaigns inspired by the radical approaches of the pioneering Brazilian social educator Paulo Freire.[30] In the political sphere, the MNU has forged links with the Workers' Party and the Democratic Workers' Party, encouraging Afro-Brazilians to stand as election candidates. As a result, Benedita da Silva, a working-class Afro-Brazilian from Rio de Janeiro, became first a city councillor, then the first black Brazilian member of Congress in 1987 and, in 1992, the first Afro-Brazilian woman to run for the office of mayor of the city – a contest that she only narrowly lost. In 1994 she was elected Brazil's first black woman senator.

Geledés Instituto da Mulher Negra (Black Women's Institute) is a non-governmental organization established in São Paulo in

1988, the centenary year of the abolition of slavery in Brazil, when many Brazilians of African ancestry began to re-examine their history. The main goals of Geledés are to combat gender oppression and racism, and its major programmes are in the fields of civil rights and women's health. One such programme, the SOS-Racismo project, offers free legal assistance for black people who are victims of discrimination. This work has led to a re-examination of Brazil's anti-discriminatory legislation, which has yet to become truly effective. The health programme developed by Geledés among Afro-Brazilian women seeks to stimulate and help them recover their self-esteem and dignity. Geledés health workshops teach contraceptive methods and preventive measures against sexually transmitted diseases. Many of the symposiums promoted by the organization address issues of women's health, abortion, family planning, violence and forced sterilization. Geledés also runs a rappers' project to promote self-esteem and political consciousness among Afro-Brazilian youth through music. Project participants write, produce and record their own music, and their lyrics express the need to build a united black front against racism worldwide, as well as to further the liberation of black Brazilians. The project also publishes a magazine, *Pode Crê* (You Can Believe It!). Black rappers in Brazil are under constant surveillance by the police, and some have been arrested for 'inciting violence' with their candid and assertive lyrics.

Another collective organization, the Centro de Articulação de Populações Marginalizadas (CEAP – Centre for the Mobilization of Marginalized Populations), in Rio de Janeiro, was set up to work with and help street children and to combat the sexual abuse of young Brazilian girls of African ancestry – many of whom become prostitutes as young as 8 years of age – as well as the forced sterilization of black women. CEAP is one of the leading Brazilian organizations campaigning against the killing of children and adolescents by off-duty police and death squad members; it is supported by UNICEF and other international agencies concerned with the killing of minors in Brazil.

In the cultural arena, groups such as Olodum (led by João Jorge Rodriguez), Illiaé and Quilombhoje (a collective of Afro-Brazilian writers) are energetic promoters of Afro-Brazilian music, arts and literature, both nationally and internationally. Their music and writings are much admired. Members of these groups also speak out against racism and work for the advancement of Afro-Brazilians through education and political mobilization.

For all its achievements, however, the Afro-Brazilian movement has far to go before it can mobilize the majority of black Brazilians. The anthropologist John Burdick reports being told by one activist: 'Ninety percent of all *negros* in Brazil don't acknowledge their blackness; they want to forget their slave past. That's what we're up against.' In general, as Burdick found, activists still tend to be better-educated, middle-class people, whereas working-class black Brazilians are more likely to identify primarily with class struggles and only secondarily with issues of race.[32]

Afro-Brazilian life chances today

In terms of the law, all Brazilians enjoy equality. The weak Afonso Arinos Law of 1951 and the follow-up legislation of recent years have made racial and colour discrimination a criminal offence. However, a marked difference remains between the existence of such legal provisions and the reality, because racial discrimination is very difficult to prove in the courts.

The majority of Afro-Brazilians remain – along with many of their impoverished white and indigenous compatriots – virtual second-class citizens. At birth a black Brazilian has a 30 per cent greater chance of dying before the age of 5 than has a white Brazilian. Among those who survive into adulthood, black Brazilians die, on average, at the age of 50, whereas white Brazilians enjoy a life expectancy of 63 years.[33] Almost half of the black and mulatto population subsists on income levels at or below the national minimum wage, whereas the same applies to less than a quarter of Brazilian whites.[34]

As for employment and earnings, a 1980 study produced by the Instituto Brasileiro de Geografia e Estatística (IBGE – Brazilian Institute of Geography and Statistics) indicates that in São Paulo and Recife, on average, the income of a black doctor is 22 per cent lower than that of a white person of the same occupation, and that of a black secretary 40 per cent lower than a white secretary's; a black engineer earns 19 per cent less than a white one, black teachers 18 per cent less than white teachers, black truck drivers 19 per cent less than whites and black brick-layers 11 per cent less than whites. At the offices of the National Employment System (SINE) in São Paulo, several thousands of jobs are reportedly coded to indicate the ethnic preference of employers, in particular to show jobs for which the employer does not want black applicants. One public official has been quoted as stating that more than 60 per cent of registered companies restrict entry to jobs on racial grounds. IBGE sociologist Tereza Cristina Araújo has stated that in Brazil there are two separate labour markets, one for blacks and one for whites. Black people make up 60 per cent of the 10 million poorest Brazilian families.[35]

There are, of course, dark-complexioned Brazilians who have achieved prominence and success in a limited number of fields. The leading example is Minister for Sport Edson Arantes do Nascimento, better known as Pelé, the great soccer player. As Anani Dzidzienyo puts it, Pelé, as

> the 'King of Football', was an invaluable ally of the Brazilian authorities, constantly used to demonstrate the validity of their 'racial democracy' propaganda. He himself claimed that there is no racism in Brazil ... Pelé happens to be the best known of these tokenist 'honorable exceptions', but he is by no means the only one.

Dzidzienyo goes on to comment that Afro-Brazilian entertainers and sports stars frequently perform to exclusively white audiences, thus achieving little in terms of challenging the master–servant emphasis of the relationship.[36]

Educational outcomes are similarly disquieting. Twenty-five per cent of white Brazilians are illiterate, which is bad enough, but for black and mulatto Brazilians the literacy rate rises to approximately 40 per cent.[37] Less than 2 per cent of Afro-Brazilians attend college, and fewer than 1 per cent graduate.[38] Only a handful of Afro-Brazilian women reach senior positions in the university system. Perhaps the most notable exception was Lélia Gonzales, an academic who had also been active in the collective struggle until her untimely death in 1994. In the mid-1970s at the Federal University of Rio de Janeiro Gonzales set up the country's first university-level course on African culture.[39]

Large numbers of Brazilians of all ethnic groups live in poor social conditions. Sixty-nine per cent of the national population – more than 100 million people – have inadequate domestic sanitation, and 33 per cent – over 50 million people – lack access to safe drinking water.[40] Four hundred thousand Brazilians die each year of curable diseases due to insanitary conditions and inadequate health facilities, and inevitably a high proportion of these casualties of 'underdevelopment' are blacks and mulattos. Black Brazilians comprise probably the majority of residents of the nation's *favelas*, or modern 'slave quarters'. It is also estimated that between 78 per cent and 88 per cent of Brazilian prison inmates are of African descent.[42]

In the cultural sphere, the mixture and sharing of African and European cultural elements by white and black Brazilians is not of course something to be condemned. However, the commercialization and frequent misrepresentation of Afro-Brazilian folklore, religion, art, music and heritage are forms of exploitation that do not benefit black Brazilian communities. Historical and educational books often give a distorted portrayal of black legends, folk tales and folklore, and of the relationship between white and black Brazilians. African religions have been widely embraced by white people, both as adepts of African cults and through such business enterprises as the production of African religious symbols and images in books and visual art forms to sell in specialized stores. Moreover, despite the richness of Afro-Brazilian religious culture, self-denial runs deep. The recently appointed leader of the National Conference of Bishops, the conservative Bahian churchman Dom Lucas Moreira, is known for his fierce condemnation of Candomblé and all Afro-Brazilian religious forms as the Devil's work. Dom Lucas is himself a black Brazilian.[43] This also illustrates that not all Afro-Brazilians endorse or feel culturally obliged to practise African religions.

African-Brazilian music, such as the *samba*, has become a national form of expression through which white as well as black people communicate their sense of life; but Afro-Brazilian *sambistas* are often obliged to sign contracts with white-owned recording companies and thus see their music and careers managed by people outside their own community. White elites also control, and reap most of the profits from, tourism, whose major source of income is derived from the Carnival, which is largely of Afro-Brazilian provenance. Black Brazilians participating in the samba schools competitions receive prizes that have little or no monetary value compared to the profits made by the people who promote such events, which depend almost entirely on Afro-Brazilian creativity and physical endurance.

Brazil is faced with a serious problem of street children, many of them homeless, orphans or runaways. According to figures released by UNICEF and CEAP, there are 50 million street children in Latin America, half the world's total. Of these, more than 7 million are Brazilians, the vast majority of whom are of African ancestry. In scavenging a living on the streets, these hungry children become involved in a range of undesirable activities, including petty crime, small-scale drug-running and, in a great many cases, glue sniffing. Some go home to sleep at night and spend only the daytime on the streets, but virtually all of them live in fear of the brutal death squads – often composed of off-duty or retired policemen – who mete out a terrible form of 'social cleansing'. The killers are frequently hired by local storeowners and other business people to rid a neighbourhood of juvenile petty crime. They sometimes refer to themselves as 'the judges', and they may torture their victims before killing them.[44]

The problem appears to be escalating. Estimates made by the National Movement of Street Children and the Brazilian Institute for Social and Economic Analysis indicate that 1,937 such children and adolescents were killed during the period 1984-9; and according to Brazil's Attorney-General, 5,644 children between the ages of 5 and 17 were victims of violent death between 1988 and 1991. State government statistics record that 424 children under the age of 18 were victims of homicide in Rio de Janeiro in 1992, while the International Child Resource Institute asserts that 298 children were killed in Rio de Janeiro State in the first six months of 1993, most of whom had no previous police records. The perpetrators of such murders have been known to justify their crimes by saying that if they kill a black street child today they will not have to bother about killing a full-grown black criminal in the future.

Official responses to these killings are frequently inadequate. In June 1994 the governor of Amazonas State, Gilberto Mestrinho, is said to have prohibited the reporting of the murder of five adolescents in Manaus in the media. When seven boys were killed in Alagoas between late January and early February of the same year the state government insisted that their death was the result of gang wars, although the official prosecutor publicly declared that the children were victims of a death squad. In at least one case, in Acari in July 1990, the key witness, who accused police officers of being involved in the abduction and killing of ten teenagers, was also subsequently murdered. In Espírito Santo investigations into death squad activities have proven to be extremely dangerous, leading the state authorities to request assistance from the federal police in their efforts to stop the killing of children.

One of the cruellest examples of the phenomenon was the Candelária massacre. On 23 July 1993 five men opened fire on a group of eight sleeping children in front of the Candelária Catholic church in downtown Rio de Janeiro. Rio state troopers were subsequently charged for the crime, but in 1994 reports from Brazilian news outlets indicated that the two main investigators of the murders had also been killed. Hermogenes da Silva e Almeida Filho, a 40-year-old investigator and Afro-Brazilian poet, and Reinalgo Guedes Miranda, 37, were found murdered in a car; both had multiple gunshot wounds.[45]

Conclusions and future prospects

Despite a degree of democratization over the past decade, and some loosening of its traditionally rigid structure, Brazilian society is likely to remain sharply divided for many years to come. Meanwhile Afro-Brazilian activists, and those who share their aspirations, envision a process whereby the inequalities of life chances in their country, which affect indigenous and white as well as black Brazilians, may be reduced, to the benefit of all. For this to happen, state and federal governments must come to understand that a polarized society is a violent one, and that the healing of Brazil's historic inter-ethnic wounds requires a new openness about racial issues, whose reality must be faced.

Nothing less than full formal public recognition of the African contribution to the nation will be enough – not as a single statement but as a long-term process of national rediscovery. This will involve a more inclusive assessment of the African presence in the population and of the African legacy that has so enriched Brazilian culture. The programme might also adopt policies advocated by the Washington-based Organization of Africans in the Americas: for example, the establishment of a ministerial department to collect and analyse Afro-Brazilian demographic data; public educational and media campaigns aimed at rooting out the ideology of whitening and racial prejudice; and promotion of a sense of pride in the African (as well as the indigenous) heritage. Work of this kind at the federal and state levels would create a climate in which the grass-roots efforts of Afro-Brazilian community organizations could flourish.

The international community has a part to play. International loans and investments for social and economic development could be channelled specifically to those programmes and projects most likely to enhance the opportunities of Brazil's dispossessed millions directly, rather than through 'trickle-down' economics. This is a far more ambitious – but also more worthwhile – aim than to continue pouring short-term money into the most lucrative ventures. In this regard protection of Brazil's street children is clearly a matter of urgency.

In the long term, Brazil's legacy of racism can be overcome. But change will be slow unless Afro-Brazilians themselves take a major role and become the protagonists of their own liberation; without their full participation the process will be incomplete and ineffective. One first step would be to trace and follow the basic strategies employed in the civil rights and liberation struggles of the United States and South Africa, adapting them to the Brazilian reality. Black Brazilians must become totally committed and proud of who they are; they must confront the identity issues which have historically divided them and weakened the Afro-Brazilian movement and struggle. They should reject the use of pejorative terms such as *mulato/a*, *moreno/a* and *pardo/a* and redefine themselves as black Brazilians, Negroes (acceptable in the Brazilian context), Afro-Brazilians or Brazilians of African ancestry. Strength and victory will come in solidarity, not in separatism; black Brazilians must start to celebrate what unites them, rather than the differences that were imposed on them by historical circumstance. They will need to confront both the institution of racism and the cycle of black self-hatred. As Afro-Brazilians work to construct a new self-image, and to rekindle pride in their ethnicity, they will surely garner external support in their bid to overcome historical injustices.

Notes

1 Galdino, A.M., *Brasil negro*, São Paulo, Pannartz, 1991, p. 18.
2 On the 'etiquette' of Brazilian race relations, see Dzidzienyo, A., 'The position of blacks in Brazilian society', in A. Dzidzienyo and L. Casal, *The Position of Blacks in Brazilian and Cuban Society*, London, Minority Rights Group, 1971, 1979, p. 3.
3 E.g. Whitaker, C., 'Blacks in Brazil: the myth and the reality', *Ebony*, no. 46, 1991, pp. 58-62. Throughout this chapter I will refer to Brazilians of African ancestry as blacks, Afro-Brazilians or African-Brazilians, without consideration to whether or not they have been exposed to whitening, which the majority have.
4 Oliveira, E., 'Manifesto à nação brasileira e à comunidade negra de São Paulo', *Cadernos Cândido Mendes, Estudos Afro-Asiáticos*, Rio de Janeiro, Aug.-Sept. 1983, pp. 24-5.
5 Dzidzienyo, op. cit., pp. 4, 6.
6 Hellwig, D.J. (ed.), *African-American Reflections on Brazil's Racial Paradise*, Philadelphia, PA, Temple University Press, 1992, p. 3.
7 Rodrigues da Silva, M., *O negro no Brasil*, São Paulo, Editora FTD, 1987, p. 8.
8 Moura, C., *Dialética racial do Brasil negro*, São Paulo, Editora Anita, 1994, p.125.
9 Mattoso, K.M.Q. de, *To Be a Slave in Brazil*, trans. A. Goldhammer, New Brunswick NJ, Rutgers University Press, 1986, p. 13.
10 Ibid., p. 10.
11 Ibid., pp. 12-36.
12 Castro, Y.P. de, *Os falares africanos na interação do Brasil colônia*, Salvador, Universidade Federal da Bahia, 1980, p. 15.
13 Mattoso, op. cit., p. 98.
14 Mitchell, M., 'Cafundó: counterpoint on a Brazilian African survival', *Centennial Review*, vol. 28, no. 3, 1984, p. 186.

15 E.g. Vogt, C., Fry, P. and Gnere, M., 'Las lenguas secretas de Cafundó', *Punto de Vista*, vol. 3, no. 9, 1980, pp. 26-32; and 'Mafambura e Caxapura: na encruzilhada da identidade', paper presented at the fourth meeting of the National Association of Social Science Research, Rio de Janeiro, 28-30 October 1980.

16 Mitchell, op. cit.

17 Mattoso, op. cit., p. 92.

18 Dzidzienyo, op. cit., p. 5; Freyre, G., *The Masters and the Slaves: A Study in the Development of Brazilian Civilization*, New York, Knopf, 1946.

19 Rodrigues da Silva, op. cit., p. 22.

20 Carneiro, E., *Guerra de los Palmares*, Panaco, Mexico, Fondo de Cultura Económica, 1946, pp. 9-12

21 Davis, D.J., 'Afro-Brazilian women, civil rights and political participation', in D.J. Davis (ed.), *Slavery and Beyond: The African Impact on Latin America and the Caribbean*, Wilmington, DA, Scholarly Resources/ Jaguar Books, 1995, p. 255.

22 Carneiro, op. cit., p. 13.

23 Lopes, H.T. et al., *Negro e cultura no Brasil*, Rio de Janeiro, Unibrade, 1987, p. 23.

24 Davis, op. cit., p. 255.

25 Dunn, C., 'Afro-Bahian carnival: a stage for protest', *Afro-Hispanic Review*, vol. II, nos 1-3, 1992, pp. 11-20.

26 See Carneiro, op. cit., p. 14.

27 Moura, C., *Sociología do negro brasieiro*, São Paulo, Atica, 1988, pp. 205-17.

28 Davis, op. cit., pp. 255-6.

29 Ibid., pp. 256-9.

30 Ibid., pp. 261-2.

31 Burdick, J., 'Brazil's black consciousness movement', *Report on the Americas: The Black Americas 1492-1992*, North American Congress on Latin America, vol.25, no. 4, 1992, p. 25; Davis, op. cit., p. 262.

32 Burdick, op. cit., p. 25.

33 Alencastro, L.F., 'Being black in Brazil', *World Press Review*, no. 2, 1988, p. 56.

34 Francisco, D., 'Comunicação', *Cadernos Cândido Mendes, Estudos Afro-Asiáticos*, Aug.-Sept. 1983, p. 28.

35 Alencastro, op. cit., p. 57.

36 Dzidzienyo, op. cit., p. 7.

37 Roland, E., 'A realidade da mulher negra', in M. Baptista (ed.), *Povo negro*, São Paulo, Edições Loyola, 1988, p. 16; Francisco, op. cit., p. 28.

38 Roland, op. cit., p. 16.

39 Davis, op. cit., pp. 259-60.

40 *O Estado de São Paulo*, 7 July 1994.

41 Hering, T., 'Emancipaçao racial no Brasil: uma continuidade histórica', *Journal of Afro-Latin American Studies and Literatures*, vol. II, no. 1, 1994, Washington, DC, p. 29.

42 Oliveira, op. cit., p. 24.

43 Reported in the *Guardian* (London and Manchester), 26 May 1995.
44 Information on killings of street children from the International
    Child Resource Institute.
45 United Press International, C&T Radiobras: Internet <bras-eua-
    l@indiana.edu>, 14 June 1994.

Select bibliography

Andrews, G.R., *Blacks and Whites in São Paulo, Brazil, 1888-1988*, Madi-
son, WI, University of Wisconsin Press, 1991.
Covin, D., 'Afrocentricity in o Movimento Negro Unificado', *Journal of
Black Studies*, no. 21, 1990, pp. 126-44.
Davis, D.J., 'Afro-Brazilian women, civil rights and political participa-
tion', in D.J. Davis (ed.), *Slavery and Beyond: The African Impact on Latin
America and the Caribbean*, Wilmington, DA, Scholarly
Resources/Jaguar Books, 1995, pp. 253-63.
Dzidzienyo, A. and Casal, L., *The Position of Blacks in Brazilian and Cuban
Society*, London, Minority Rights Group, 1971, 1979.
Hasenbalg, C., *Discriminacão e desigualdades raciais no Brasil*, Rio de
Janeiro, 1979.
Hellwig, D.J. (ed.), *African-American Reflections on Brazil's Racial Paradise*,
Philadelphia, PA, Temple University Press, 1992.
Lemelle, S., *Pan-Africanism for Beginners*, New York, Writers & Readers,
1992.
McAdam, D., *Political Process and the Development of Black Insurgency,
1930-1970*, Chicago, IL, University of Chicago Press, 1982.
McCartney, J.T., *Black Power Ideologies*, Philadelphia, PA, Temple Universi-
ty Press, 1992.
Macedo, S.D., *Crônica do negro no Brasil*, São Paulo, Distribuidora Record,
1974.
Mattoso, K.M.Q. de, *To Be a Slave in Brazil*, trans. A. Goldhammer, New
Brunswick, NJ, Rutgers University Press, 1986.
Mintz, S.W. and Price, R., *The Birth of African-American Culture*, Boston,
MA, Beacon Press, 1976.
Mitchell, M., 'Cafundó: counterpoint on a Brazilian African survival',
Centennial Review, vol. 28, no. 3, 1984, pp. 185-203.
Querino, M.A., *Raça africana e os seus costumes*, Salvador de Bahia,
Livraria Progresso Editora, 1955.
Scisinio, A.E., *Escravidão e a saga de Manoel Congo*, Rio de Janeiro, Achi-
ame, 1988.
Silva, M.J., *Racismo à brasileira*, Brasilia, Thesaurus, 1987.
Vainfas, R., *Ideologia e escravidão*, Petrópolis, Vozes, 1986.
Wilson, W.J., *The Declining Significance of Race*, Chicago, IL, University of
Chicago Press, 1978.

3

COLOMBIA

Nina S. de Friedemann and Jaime Arocha

Most schools in Colombia today still teach their students to behave in ways which may have been expected during the Spanish colonial period but which are now the basis of human rights violations. Colombian education has generally excluded from the country's past the history of the people enslaved from the ports of Africa and that of their descendants; Afro-Colombians have also been edited out of the national vision of present-day reality. Yet few Colombians recognize that to make Afro-American cultural, economic, political, religious and artistic contributions invisible is a pernicious form of ethnic discrimination.

In the face of this persistence of racist thinking and conduct, the Afro-Colombian experience represents a multifaceted historical saga of political resistance, continuing up to the present day, in which a close relationship has been forged between the search for freedom, on the one hand, and cultural creation, production and transformation, on the other. This complex and long-term process of struggle, intimately linked to the geographical locations where it has taken place, has resulted in the gradual making visible of Afro-Colombians.

African origins

Many of the roots of contemporary forms of Afro-Colombian cultural innovation and resistance to oppression lie in West and Central Africa. They constitute an ethno-historical bridge that

47

joins the continents of Africa and South America as part of a process of historical reconstruction. How did the original historical dislocation occur?

From the beginning of the sixteenth century black Africans began arriving in the territory that 300 years later would be known as Colombia. Cartagena de Indias, on the Atlantic seaboard, was the main port for the introduction and distribution of African captives. However, many traders smuggled enslaved people through other Atlantic ports. Some of the slaves were quickly taken along the Magdalena, Cauca, San Jorge, Patia, Atrato and San Juan rivers to the Pacific coastal region, under a system of forced labour placing.

Throughout the seventeenth and eighteenth centuries the Spanish colony was entirely dependent on African slave labour. Mining, agriculture, cattle raising, commerce, pearl fishing, domestic work and craft production were all performed by slaves. Mining was the activity that employed most Africans and sustained the economy of the New Kingdom of Granada.

Among the conquistadors who came to the New World in the earlier colonial period were also descendants of an African pre-Columbian diaspora in the Iberian peninsula.[1] Many owed their ancestry to African soldiers who had arrived with the Islamic conquerors of the peninsula in AD 711, others to Africans who had settled there after 1445 as a result of Henry the Navigator's maritime expeditions. During colonial times these Ibericized Africans, who observed Portuguese and Spanish customs and spoke Iberian languages, were known as *negros ladinos*.

Many such Africans first appear embarking in Seville for the New World as they registered in the lists of the *Catálogo de pasajeros a Indias* between 1509 and 1559. Fray Pedro Simón mentions that in 1538 more than 100 black men and women were part of one expedition from Cartagena to Uraba. How many black people came from the Iberian pre-Columbian diaspora to the New World as free individuals and how many of them as slaves? What were the relations between these two groups, and between them and the Spaniards? These questions come to mind reading testimonies such as that of the scribe Andres de Valderrabano, who in 1513 noted the presence of a black man named Nuflo de Olano accompanying Vasco Nuñez de Balboa in the heights of Quarequa to see and 'discover' the Pacific Ocean.[2]

Documentation on *asientos* – licences for transportation from Africa to the American ports and accounts of sale – has permitted a preliminary general mapping of the regions from which the captives were taken. Subsequent studies of Afro-Colombian languages, religious forms, music and oral traditions have confirmed the arrival in Cartagena of people from particular African groups at certain periods of time: between 1533 and 1580 the Yolofos; from 1580 to 1640 people from Angola and the Congo; from 1640 to 1703 Arara people from the region of Benin, and Mina from the coast of Pimienta; Arara and Carabali people from Benin from 1703 to 1740; and Carabali (Benin) with others from Angola, Congo and Mozambique from 1740 to 1811.[3]

The African origins of the inhabitants of the Colombian archipelago of San Andres y Providencia are linked with English colonial history in the Caribbean. Cultural and linguistic research, such as that into the creole language spoken in the archipelago as well as in Jamaica, the Caiman Islands and other Caribbean territories, has shown the influence there of the Fanti-Ashanti peoples of West Africa.

With the beginning of the slave traffic, the Spanish Crown issued laws governing relationships between masters and slaves, which were gathered by 1789 into a single document known as the *Black Code*.[4] This code specified working hours as from sunrise to dusk, as well as detailing the punishments allowed to slave owners. Owners would not be prosecuted if they slashed or cut the ears and noses of those who struggled for freedom or who sought to ease the conditions of their slavery. However, punishable offences by the masters included castration or any form of mutilation that could endanger the reproduction of the labour force.

The denial of history

In Colombia the history and demography of the early African diaspora have so far been denied the full attention they merit as major constituents in the building of the nation. Nevertheless, several works analyse early colonial society, describing the numbers and prices of slaves, their African provenance and their role in the economy.

Data drawn from studies of the slave trade by European and American historians do not dwell, however, on the social and cultural roles of Africans in the construction of new societies in Colombia. And few of these works have integrated data and thought offered by African historians on the subject of the slave trade and the processes of change taking place among Africans at the time. There is no mention, for example, of the war of resistance against the slave trade waged in Guinea by the Bijagos, or in the Congo by the Jagas, between 1568 and 1587.[5] At that time squadrons of men and women, operating from camps called *kilombos*, invaded and devastated parts of the Congo in an attempt to destroy the political and military structures of those African kingdoms that were allied to the Portuguese in the slave trade.

Controversy has surrounded Colombian debates about the extent and conditions of the traffic. In 1979 Germán Colmenares referred to a total of 9 million African slaves coming to the Americas, whereas in 1966 Jaime Jaramillo Uribe had mentioned only 2 million. These numbers are conservative when compared with Herbert Klein's 10 to 15 million.[6] Official Colombian historiography makes no mention of the number of captives dead in slave raids or wars in Africa during the trade or during the transatlantic voyage, which some historians estimate as at least 10 million.[7]

Philip D. Curtin[8] finds a total of 200,000 African slaves arriving in the area which today corresponds to Colombia, Panama and Ecuador. Based on these numbers and his own research, Germán Colmenares concluded that a total of 120,000 Africans entered Colombia as slaves.

Yet new questions have arisen with data such as those from Nicolás del Castillo, who in 1981 calculated that 169,371 African slaves entered the port of Cartagena de Indias alone between 1580 and 1640. These numbers do not take into account the Dutch contraband through Curaçao and the English through Jamaica.

For many historians the main focus of interest in the period of slavery has been trade and its economic significance, regardless of the permanent uprooting of Africans and the transformation of their cultural life. A significant number of historical works have even been animated by an ahistorical ideology involving a belief that, following captivity, the Africans and Afro-Americans were people stripped of their culture and history.

The Spanish rulers of the New Kingdom of Granada shared this ignorant, ahistorical view of their subject peoples from Africa. Africans who had not acquired any cultural experience with Iberians in Africa, Spain or Portugal were considered *bozales* (wild men) when they disembarked in America. They became *ladinos* when they acquired some Spanish behaviour and language, *cimarrones* (rough or wild men) when they revolted against their slavery, and *libres* (freemen) when they bought their freedom. But above all, early Afro-Colombians were described as *negros*. During the colonial and early republican periods, then, Africans were considered not as human beings but as 'merchandise'.

In 1851, when slavery was abolished, and as the republic and the new century settled in, the word *moreno* (dark brown) was adopted as a polite term of reference. *Negro* related to African and 'savage', remaining an offensive reference by non-black people, and was understood as such by Afro-Colombians until recently.

Regions of Afro-Colombian settlement

Several parts of Colombia have traditionally been, and remain, characteristically Afro-Colombian, their development and history closely involving the descendants of African slaves. These regions include the archipelago of San Andres, Providencia and Santa Catalina, where descendants of Akan and Ewe-Fon slaves brought from Jamaica once had a subsistence economy based on agriculture and fishing, after having emerged from slavery on small plantations run by English Puritans during the early 1700s. Today these people, who speak an English-based creole, are fighting the tourist industry for their cultural survival.

Another such characteristic area is the Palenque de San Basilio, on the Caribbean flatlands near the former slave port of

Cartagena. Here, during the early 1600s Bijago Africans stirred other captives to revolt against slavery, fleeing to inaccessible places where they built fortified villages, known as *palenques*. Today their descendants still speak a creole with Ki-Kongo and Ki-Mbundu elements, until recently defined as 'savage' or, at best, 'bad Spanish' by the dominant regional society. The *palenqueros* are agriculturalists and cattle raisers, many now working on high-technology livestock ranches. They have shared this area with indigenous and white people for 500 years.

The Tumaco inlet on the Pacific Ocean is another region of major Afro-Colombian settlement. Here, women who probably have Fanti-Ashanti origins specialize in gathering the shells that lie deep in the mangrove swamps, while black peasants in places such as Chajal go to sea during the low tide and use a variety of techniques to capture sharks, crabs, shrimp or squid. They return to their cultivated plots during high tide and grow cacao, fruits, plantains, sugar-cane and rice.[9]

The river valleys and forests of the Pacific coast, also known as the bio-geographical region of Chocó, are an endangered paradise of tropical rainforest bounded by Panama, Ecuador and the western Andes. This region of mega-biodiversity has survived intact at least in part because of the ingenious way that Afro-Colombian people, comprising 84 per cent of the regional population, and indigenous people, 4 per cent, have managed their economic activities in harmony with seasonal cycles.

A significant number of Afro-Chocoans descend from Ewe-Fon, Yoruba, Fanti-Ashanti, Akan, Ibo, Ibibo and Efik Africans brought to the area as slave-miners during the Second Gold Mining Cycle (between 1680 and 1810).[10] After 1750 many bought their freedom and established themselves as independent miners and farmers, centring their communal life on strong kinship networks.

In later years members of these black rural communities migrated to ports such as Buenaventura and large cities like Popayán, Cali and Medellin. Many Afro-Chocoan women went to urban areas to work as domestic servants, the men as construction workers; both also entered the informal sector as street vendors. On Sundays and holidays, urban Afro-Chocoans of both sexes cluster around bars and discotheques which play *salsa, vallenato* and other Afro-American music. Afro-Colombians of such origins gradually became involved in professional and political activities, both regionally and nationally.[11]

Survival of cultural heritage

As in Panama, Venezuela, Ecuador and Peru, in Colombia the African cultural heritage is implicit rather than explicit. There are neither the Abacuá secret societies of Cuba, nor the Candoblé of Bahia, Brazil. Several factors explain why a system like the Haitian voodoo did not take root in this part of South America. First, the massive importation of slaves ended after the mid-1700s. From that time on, the labour demands of the mining districts were met by American-born slaves.[12] So African cultural traditions in Colombia lacked sources of renewal and reinforcement which other countries had.

Second, in Colombia there were no large plantations geared for export with barracks housing several hundred slaves. Most of the captives were distributed in small groups in different regions. Many went to the gold-mines, which rarely held more than five dozen slaves, along the rivers of the Chocó region. Something similar happened on the cattle ranches and in what were known as *haciendas de trapiche*, the small sugar plantations and mills which supplied local and regional markets with raw sugar and *aguardiente* (liquor) but were not geared for export.

Third, Spanish Inquisitors in New Granada were more attentive to African religious manifestations than to those of the indigenous people. Between 1618 and 1637, 80 per cent of those tried by the Inquisitorial tribunal were slaves who had struggled for their freedom by practising magic spells and religious ceremonies believed by the Spaniards to be African.[13] Military and religious repression was so strong that much of the Bijago, Bran, Zape, Biáfara, Lucumi and Bantu culture that was preserved became clandestine. People of African descent did not reject their ethnic identity but they did refrain from displaying it. This form of secrecy had been practised in Africa by Ki-Kongo-speakers when facing people of different cultural affiliation.[14]

The fact that the African cultural heritage is often not explicit in Colombia does not mean that it is meaningless. On the contrary, its persistence in a context so unfavourable to its survival indicates a resilience and an unusual degree of vitality. Its continuation was also the result of processes of cultural creation, innovation and reinvention that took place within the space contested between Spanish punishment and annihilation of diversity and Afro-Colombian resistance. The latter forms of political action – from armed maroonage to legal purchases of freedom – have left deep imprints on the processes of cultural expression.

Maroonage and the culture of resistance

Despite the forces ranged against them during the colonial period and later, Afro-Colombians did on occasion exercise their ethnicity with success. A major instance was the establishment of fortified villages by maroon (escaped) slaves. This form of rebellion was so prevalent during the late 1600s and early 1700s that it could not be controlled by the Spanish military apparatus. Hence arose the political negotiations which resulted in the liberation of what some authors have called the first free people of America; a royal injunction of 1691 granted freedom to the inhabitants of mountain *palenques* at Sierra de la María, near Cartagena.

During the mid-1500s the first imported Spanish cattle arrived in Cartagena from Santo Domingo. Fifty years later, using African slave labourers, cattle ranches had extended throughout the lowlands of the Caribbean coast.[15] The 1600s in the province of Cartagena are known as the century of terror. The *palenques* faced the Spanish soldiers and their hunting dogs, while across the province maroons terrorized and kidnapped the Spanish, burned their haciendas and stole their cattle.

Today the historical record allows us to draw comparative maps of the way the maroon insurgency grew over three centuries. For the sixteenth century, there are only a few dots in the Caribbean lowlands. However, such was the magnitude of the phenomenon over the next 200 years that *palenques* were set up in most of the main river valleys, and one was even located almost on the outskirts of Bogotá, at Guayabal de Siquima.[16]

In the early 1800s the wars of liberation against Spain helped to render meaningless the insurgency of the *palenques*. But in 1851, when slavery was abolished, Afro-Colombians without land or tools left mining camps and haciendas and, mindful of the unfulfilled promises of freedom made by Libertador Simón Bolívar, developed new forms of resistance.

During the late 1800s, as the republican regime was consolidated, members of the dominant elite manipulated land titles and bribed officials in order to monopolize significant acreage of the Caribbean flatlands. They left the Palenque de San Basilio without pastureland and the *palenqueros* as cattle-raisers with few cattle. Today, however, the cultural identification of these Afro-Colombians with cattle-raising remains vigorous, encompassing their social and economic organization.

Geographical isolation and continued cultural resistance have allowed the Palenque de San Basilio proudly to retain its maroon legacy. The village is organized into opposing halves, each divided by age groups known as *cuagros*, in which boys and girls have life membership. Their ritual battles and war games indicate a socialization system within which training for combat was a priority. Further evidence of the same system is the creole tongue spoken in San Basilio; historical documents show how, during the late 1600s and early 1700s, this language served the *palenqueros* as a code used for espionage and insurgency.

Today the same creole language is used by emigrants from the area to places in the Gulf of Maracaibo and even Caracas to propagate news about the Venezuelan police's attempt to deport illegal aliens. Other cultural memories dating further back – to origins in the Congo and Angola – are found in local people's vision of the cosmos, oral traditions, funeral rituals, dance, music and musical instruments.[17]

The vitality of the *cuagro* can also be clearly appreciated at the mourning ritual known as *lumbalu*. Women and men, old and young, perform particular roles in the funeral space that symbolizes a cosmological view. Drums played by the men symbolically penetrate the firmament in order to ease the way for the women's voices to reach heaven.[18]

Contemporary ethnographers and linguists have studied the

sacred chants sung by senior female members of high-status *cua-gros*. They have also analysed the games played by youngsters affiliated to children's *cuagros*. The way both phenomena have been decodified has allowed for comparative studies which clearly indicate the Central African Bantu ancestry of both the *palen-quero* creole language and religion.[19]

During the mid-seventeenth century, in the Cauca gold-mining district of the north, enslaved people of African descent used strategies of symbolic violence in the struggle for freedom. A study of two women – one a Bran and the other a Zape – tried for witchcraft by the Inquisitorial tribunal of Cartagena speaks of the way recently disembarked African slaves tried to reconstruct their ancestral rituals and ceremonies.[20] They formed what the Inquisitor termed *juntas* – stratified secret religious groups, whose membership depended upon agreements to denounce publicly the Roman Catholic faith into which they had been baptized, as well as to use their traditional spiritual knowledge to terrorize the slave owners. Those who were condemned by the Spanish appear to have attempted to keep their beliefs secret by copying the Europeans' way of discrediting non-Christian religious phenomena with such terms as 'Satanic cult' and 'demons'.[21] The success of this strategy perhaps explains the persistence of this form of political resistance.

Today the imprint of maroonage based on the use of symbolic violence can be clearly seen in regions such as the hot dry valley of the Patia River. Here the heirs of the rebels call themselves *empautados*, because of the pacts they make with devils thought capable of helping them win machete duels or achieve success in cattle raids against the area's large ranch owners.[22]

In the flatlands of the northern zone of the Department of Cauca expressions of African-influenced 'witchcraft' provide a sharp contrast to the heavy industrialization process that has occurred over the past twenty years. Afro-Colombian proletarians who work as cane-cutters for the monopolistic industrial sugar plantations make deals with the Devil, aspiring to achieve success either in their jobs or in attempts to sabotage their employers' business.[23]

Autonomy, independence and the Antioqueños

Personal surnames like Carabali and Biáfara survive in the flatlands of the south-western region of Colombia to bear witness to
the African origins of the slaves brought to work in the colonial
haciendas de trapiche. Their frequent uprisings gave birth to a
clandestine enclave to which they escaped to ease the hardships
of forced labour, and where they grew their own food. Named
the Indiviso de San Fernando, this area acted as the core of subsequent rebellions which during the late 1800s led to the partial
dismembering of the large landholdings between the towns of
Puerto Tejada and Villarica.[24]

The former slaves began to exert autonomous control over
these areas, establishing *fincurrias* – small plots where they plant-
ed coffee intermixed with cacao and plantains, under the shade
of *yarumo* trees. As happens with other multi-crop systems, production was constant throughout the year, because periods of
low coffee production were compensated by high plantain yield,
while fertilizers were supplied by the decomposition of leaves
falling from the branches of the shade trees.

But the success of this low-energy system was brought to an
end through illusions about the 'soya miracle' created by the
'green revolution' of the 1970s.[25] Afro-Caucan peasants began to
replace their *fincurrias* with soybean *sembraderos* (sown fields),
which failed due to lack of the pesticides and fertilizers needed
for monocropping. At the same time, large landowners tried to
expand their soya fields and began to press the small cultivators
for their lands. Black peasant resistance was crushed with military repression and with aerial spraying of chemical defoliants;
the latter damaged the small plantations, forcing their owners to
abandon them and seek work in the industrialized sugar plantations.

Afro-Colombian peasants of the region had combined caring
for their *fincurrias* and working in the *ingenios* (sugar factories).
By 1976 the tie between traditional and modern economic systems had become so fixed that it was hard to imagine how one
could survive without the other. The small landholdings saved
the sugar industry from the need to invest in housing and other

facilities for workers, such as had to be constructed by the sugar mills that flourished during the 1960s further north; they also freed the industry from potential conflicts with full-time unionized labour. In turn, faced by declining yields, peasants began to subsidize their landholdings through their jobs in the industrialized sugar plantations and mills.

Expressions of resistance among miners during the early 1700s in the lower Cauca Valley had included deliberate destruction of tools to slow the work.[26] This so jeopardized the profitability of gold-mining that many owners opted to free their slaves. After gaining their freedom, some former slaves began to earn their livelihood by driving mules between Santafé de Antioquia – the mining capital of the region – and supply points to the east. They also established *fondas*, or vending and resting posts, which later became well-furnished stores along the mule trails.

These Afro-Colombians' search for independence, as well as their stubborn struggle for the success of their small businesses, can be counted among the modelling forces in what has been portrayed as the entrepreneurial, industrious, honest, disciplined, well-ordered, ambitious, expansionist and highly dominant Antioqueño culture. However, the orthodox version of this history hides the contribution of people of African ancestry. Instead it has exaltated the legacies of other immigrants, such as Basques and former Jews, in order to mythologize the qualities of Antioqueños. The North American historian James Parsons, for example, labelled them the 'Yankees of South America'.[27]

Mining and farming communities

From the early days of the colony, Spanish legislation specified those instances in which the African slaves could purchase their freedom.[28] This stimulated the enslaved to find ways to free themselves within a legitimate framework. Many began to make long-term plans and to undertake extra work on Sundays and holidays, either in the enterprises of their owners or elsewhere. After 1750 self-manumissions became a new locus of Afro-Colombian resistance in the struggle for liberty. Between then and 1810 gold-mining began to reach its greatest profitability, while the much needed forced labourers progressively stopped coming from Africa and began to be supplied locally.[29] This change – whose explanation may have human rights implications, to be elucidated by future historical research – occurred as, perhaps unconsciously, owners implemented what was, in effect, a policy of human breeding, as indicated by the growing frequency of accusations made by slave women against their owners of rape and concubinage. The increase in the number of American-born slaves (*criollos*) coincided with higher profits in mining for both owners and slaves, which the latter began to apply to free themselves and their close relatives.

In the Pacific coastal region it is feasible that many of these freed people (*libres* or *libertos*) moved away from the main mining districts, such as that of Barbacoas, on the Telembi River, and settled along the banks of more isolated rivers, like the Güel-mambi, a tributary of the Telembi. There they built a mining economy, supplemented by subsistence agriculture.[30] Others, like those who emigrated from the Citara mining district to the Baudo Valley, established agricultural communities rather than mining ones. The adoption of such diverse livelihoods demonstrates the individual and collective creativity of Afro-Colombians.

Traditional Afro-Colombian mining villages have between twenty and seventy houses strung out along the riverbank.[31] Miners paddle their dug-out canoes, the only available vehicle of transportation, through the rivers, streams and swamps that permeate the soggy jungle. Rain drips continually from the palm-thatched roofs of their houses, which are raised on wooden pillars two metres or more above ground. In the space below, pigs, chickens and canoes are kept.

Some households have a hand-press for processing sugar; others have an earthen oven for baking bread. The rocky debris left from the mining process is used to pave the areas around the house. At least once a month there is a *velorio*, a celebration with singing and drumming to bid farewell to the soul of a dead person, or to honour Catholic saints whose attributes, in their Afro-American interpretations, evoke memories of African deities. The *velorio* is the occasion to renew genealogical knowledge of *troncos*, ancestors and rights. The *tronco* is a kinship group whose members trace their descent to a founder-ancestor with a quasi-mythological profile. Members claim affiliation through their father's or their mother's line. The functions of the *tronco* involve the regulation of individual, family and collective domains in the mining community. These elements include the village, the extended family subsistence garden, the little mining cut for the nuclear family, the communal mining cut and the collectively shared forest where miners hunt for the animal protein their people need, and cut wood for tools and domestic use. Given the high degree of mobility of miners, members of *troncos* must know how to elicit their genealogical links, or they may loose their territorial rights during long absences from the mine.

These miners' settlements have lasted for at least 200 years, as indicated by the time depth of their genealogies, whose frequent recapitulation is fundamental to the functioning of their social organization. Their house beams also provide evidence of longevity of settlement; they are made of very hard and lasting wood, and the beams are passed from one generation to the next.

Other sources of proof of the exercise of ancestral domain over their territories are essential to the mining communities so that they can disprove an allegation routinely made by Colombian government officials that they are squatters on vacant state-owned lands. For many years those functionaries have denied traditional Afro-Pacific territorial claims and have 'legally' transferred surface exploitation rights from the miners to other parties, or have extended subsoil concessions to industrial mining enterprises.

Many Afro-Colombians settled the upper Baudo River Valley after buying freedom from slavery. This is the north-western strip of tropical rainforest that lies just below the Darién Gulf, west of the Baudo mountain ridge, and reaches to the Pacific. The Afro-Baudoseños have developed a diversified agricultural system which synchronizes plot alternation and productive activities with seasonal and climatic changes, preserving their lands as an oasis of tropical mega-biodiversity.[32]

Afro-Baudoseño forest-farming communities grow rice, corn,

plantains and fruit trees on one of the riverbanks, while keeping free-roaming pigs on the other. After harvesting, and when the *colinos* (plots of plantain) are left only with broken corn canes, fallen plantain stems or dry rice straws, the farmers switch to the other side of the river to clear new plots, while moving their pigs across in the opposite direction to where the animals will have plenty of agricultural leftovers to eat.

Afro-Baudoseños are not alone in their operation of this sophisticated farming system, because they delegate animal husbandry and other agricultural tasks to the indigenous Embera people. Traditional ties of *compadrazgo* (ritually sanctioned Roman Catholic co-parenthood) are the basis of a complex form of coexistence which integrates the two peoples. The resulting inter-ethnic dialogue may be tense at times, but it has permitted the carving out of territories shared by both groups.

Until the inauguration of President Ernesto Samper's government on 7 August 1994, along with parts of the Atrato and San Juan river valleys also in the Chocó region, the Baudo Valley was a refuge of peace, where people settled territorial and political disputes without violence. Nowadays, as in other valleys of the region, the Afro-Baudoseños face unpredictable guerrillas of uncertain affiliation. The outcome of this situation cannot be predicted. By the end of 1994, confronted by previously unknown forms of violence, the Afro-Baudoseños began to seek refuge in non-violent areas where they could call on membership of extended and corporate families.

The Afro-Baudoseño forest farmers are, not surprisingly, excellent botanists. When collecting leaves and stems to prepare their medicines, their healers softly touch and identify plants, also identifying their curative attributes. Herbs are very important to the community, not only in terms of their medicinal powers but because personal baptism includes rituals involving the forging of spiritual ties with plants and animals. The umbilical sac is buried together with the growing seed of a tree, such as a coconut palm. As the person grows, they refer to that tree as their 'navel'. When the baby loses his or her umbilical cord, powders prepared with parts of a particular animal – perhaps a wild pig – are spread on the baby's navel to impregnate him or her with the qualities of that animal. This explains why Afro-Baudoseños behave so respectfully when visiting their cultivation plots. It is usual for a person to stop at the foot of a tall tree, to take off their hat and to say a prayer.

Like other inhabitants of the Pacific coast, Afro-Baudoseños practise a form of religion whose iconography and ritual bear resemblances to the African cult of Shango. For a long time social scientists referred to these peoples' ties with the environment as 'animism'. Many of those who studied customs in West and Central Africa comparable with those of the Baudo classified the latter as inferior or retarded forms of African religious behaviour. Yet today the future of the delicate tropical rainforest ecosystems has been shown to depend on the survival of people who treat their immediate surroundings as part of their own souls and not as places to mercilessly exploit natural resources. Thus, the Afro-Colombian political movement struggles not only for its ancestral territories but also for a better future for humanity.

Women and children

Although chronicles and historical studies of Africans in New Granada, and later in Colombia, mention women and children, the role of these people is hardly considered. Even today, despite growing interest in gender issues, the significance of Afro-Colombian women has been widely ignored by historians, largely on account of their African ancestry.[33]

During colonial times black women's exploitation as slaves was centred on their fertility, which was valued as the reproductive source of slave labour. High prices were commanded by healthy young women. A black woman brought as a cook to a mining camp became the mother of children fathered by several of the slave workers, a fact that embarrassed neither owners nor the Catholic Church.[34]

This was not widespread throughout the colony, however. Historical and literary works record slave families on the haciendas comprising one or two grandparents, parents and children. Thus, diverse historical and cultural factors have contributed to the existing type of Afro-Colombian family and to the roles that women have had. But discussion of the Afro-Colombian family and gender issues is still pervaded by stereotyped concepts of familial instability and disintegration, and a high degree of illegitimacy, centring on the woman. Looked at in this way, and myopically assuming that the nuclear family is the only valid model, the problem has been explained in terms of the effects of conjugal couplings outside the Catholic Church.[35]

The reality is somewhat different. In contemporary traditional Afro-Colombian gold-mining communities on the Pacific coast, nuclear families form part of extended families in which men and women have equal rights and duties. The socialization of children as mine workers begins at an early age; and when men leave temporarily in search of waged work elsewhere, women take over their mining and agricultural tasks in order to preserve the family's rights. This is an expression of female self-reliance rather than of male peripherality, showing the strong contribution of Afro-Colombian women to the perpetuation of their mining system.

A different situation applied in the case of maroon communities during colonial times. There, women and children formed the social core, while men were occupied in resisting the Spanish soldiers – although there were cases in Colombia, as in Africa,[36] of women also taking up arms against slavery. At that time, male peripherality was a fact. But the importance of consanguinity in the family remained, as shown in accounts of maroon children being caught at the doors of the prisons in Cartagena by the Spanish authorities. These children were sent by their mothers to find out about their imprisoned fathers; on being questioned in court they refused to give any information.

Nowadays the type of family in Palenque de San Basilio may still represent the legacy of the old maroon warfare system, but it also suggests memories of the African polygamous family. Women exercise authority and independence in household and economic spheres, while special sacred roles of mystical power in the realm of rites of death and life are ascribed to female lineages in the social organization of the village.[37]

Since colonial times Afro-Colombian women have adapted the

laws and customs of the dominant Hispanic majority for their own ends, helping to sustain their own communities. In the eighteenth century, for example, the Spaniards' African concubines were legally allowed to sell wine, and they used their earnings to buy their freedom. Later, in the nineteenth century, slave women in Cartagena were adorned during carnival time with the jewels of their masters for a Catholic parade which was the occasion for the display of wealth and social power. After taking part in these promenades, slaves were allowed to go to their *cabildos* and enjoy their own celebrations, whose drumming, singing and dancing would bring Afro-Colombians together.[38]

In contemporary semi-rural and urban areas where migration has taken place, Afro-Colombian women – alone or with their children and members of their family – are taking up varied alternatives in their organization, trying to reproduce or modify traditional social structures in new circumstances. And in the political sphere, popular votes have recently gone for the first time to an Afro-Colombian woman standing for Congress. Zulia Mena campaigned in 1994 as part of Afro-Colombians' struggle for legal recognition of their culture.

Mestizaje and *blanqueamiento*

Throughout the nineteenth century the close association of *mestizaje* (racial mixture) and 'equality' gave the notion of 'liberty' a peculiar meaning in Colombia. When the indigenous peoples were made 'equals', for example, they lost their protected status and with it the communal reserves that the Spanish Crown had recognized in order to prevent their total annihilation. For Afro-Colombians, national independence meant only that children conceived after the conclusive break with Spain in 1819 would be free.[39]

It is widely believed that conditions worsened when slavery was abolished in 1851. Slavery laws were replaced by those which outlawed vagrancy. Disoriented slaves who had gained their freedom left the haciendas and mines, but only to be forced back in because they were 'vagrants'.[40] For many years the abolition of slavery did not mean that free Afro-Colombian people

were integrated into the national education system. Until recently Afro-Colombian men were not allowed to become naval officers, and only a few of them ascended into the hierarchy of the
Catholic Church. The essence of Colombia's 1886 constitution
was an 'either/or' proposition in which 'people' equalled
mestizos, and 'not people' equalled indigenous people. The constitution glorified as the goal of progress the conversion of
Colombians into a single 'race', speaking one language and
believing in a single God. Using such binary acrobatics, the elite
sought to negate the existence of those descendants of African
slaves who, because of geographic isolation or political resistance, did not have children with white or indigenous partners –
just as they denied the identities of other Colombians of Afro-
American culture. The former constitute approximately 10 per
cent of the population, the latter 30 per cent – hardly insignificant compared with the 2 per cent who are indigenous.

In 1890 Law 89 ratified colonial titles to communal lands and
conferred autonomous self-government on the indigenous peoples – but only on a transitional basis, while the 'savages' were
integrated into national society or became *mestizos*. The large
haciendas were not economically viable without the indigenous
labour concentrated in the reserves.

In 1922 the ideology of whitening (*blanqueamiento*) as a necessary condition for national progress was used to legitimize Law
114, which authorized the immigration of whites. The law for-
bade the immigration of people who could be 'inconvenient' for
the nation and for the development of the Colombian 'race'.

In 1928 the politician Laureano Gómez, who would later be
President, defined the status of Afro-Colombians in reasoning
that supported the immigration of whites to 'upgrade' the mixed
population: 'The black is a plague. In the countries where he has
disappeared, as in Argentina, Chile and Paraguay, it has been
possible to establish an economic and political organization on a
strong and stable basis.'[41]

Twenty-five years later, changing social and economic condi-
tions in the country called for a different political approach.
Population growth and the rural–urban migration of Afro-
Colombians, indigenous people and other peasants created a

new sense of the country as comprising a diversity of peoples. *Mestizo*, a term previously understood as describing the mixture of white and indigenous peoples, started being applied to Afro-Colombians in order to disguise socio-ethnic differences and discrimination against indigenous and black Colombians. Statements such as 'Here no one is white' and 'We all are *mestizos*' began to be employed in political demagogy. Thus, in a nation governed by a class minority, *mestizaje* as a concept emerged as a strategy to counteract ethnic and ethno-social claims.

The diversity of non-indigenous Colombians was made invisible by diffusion and consolidation of the idea that Colombia was a nation of *mestizos* and that *mestizaje* represented a democratic force. This notion was based on the belief that equality of rights is not compatible with the conservation of identity. In other words, to accede to such rights one must neither perceive nor declare oneself to be different or belong to a different people. In 1964 the government census disclosed a national population of 25 million people among whom 30 per cent were referred to as blacks and mulattos. The census data shed light on the racism implicit in ideologies of *mestizaje* and *blanqueamiento*, which went back to colonial times when Colombian society was modelled on a caste system. Afro-Colombians and indigenous people were at the bottom of the social pyramid, with white people at the top. Upward movement was slow, involving several generations and intense genetic and cultural whitening. The process was both socially and linguistically delimited: *mulato*, *mestizo*, *zambo* and *cuarterón* were some of the terms that qualified both the *mestizaje* and the whitening towards the apex of the pyramid.

Years later, during the 1980s, official claims about a 'racial democracy in the making' through *mestizaje* were echoed by the intellectual left and the guerrilla movements, which used similar reasons to exclude Afro-Colombian participation as such, refusing to recognize ethnic rights. Thus, claims of Afro-Colombians interested in their unique social and ethnic identity were rejected and subsumed under the *mestizaje* category.

In 1992 an issue of *Report on the Americas*, using several independent and international sources, indicated that Afro-Colombians now constituted between 14 and 21 per cent of the national population of nearly 35 million.[42] The official census of 1993 – shortly after the approval of Law 70, which recognized the ethnic rights of Afro-Colombians – acknowledged the existence of this sizeable minority and asked for the first time ever: 'To which ethnic group do you belong?' Results of the census have still not been disclosed.

Violent discrimination

From the birth of the colonial racial caste system, criminal permissiveness regarding the abuse of the human rights of Africans gave rise to an implicit typology of almost legitimate forms of violence. Colombia's republican system of social classes was constructed upon the colonial system, and consequently the national society has retained the perception of certain types of violent behaviour as relatively acceptable.

A current example that emerged during the mid-1980s is the so-called 'social cleansing' murder of prostitutes, homosexuals, drug users and street children. Lately it has been reported that most of the adolescent victims are black,[43] which is predictable given the persistence of the intersection between class and race. However, precise data bearing on the racial overtones of these crimes are unavailable.

Political and constitutional struggles

During the late 1980s the Afro-Colombian political movement began to gain momentum in its struggle against those versions of Colombia's development which systematically conceal the centuries-old Afro-Colombian heritage. Amid growing concern among Afro-Colombians to rediscover their African origins, the term *negro*, signifying African descent, began to be reclaimed, alongside increasing reference to the community's experience as 'Afro-American' and 'Afro-Colombian'.

A major turning point occurred in 1990, when the new Constituent Assembly began work to replace the 1886 constitution, following an earlier plebiscite. This assembly was unique; for the first time in Colombia's history an elected national public body included representatives of indigenous, religious and political minorities. The assembly began trying to imagine an inclusive nation by making permanent the indigenous peoples' rights recognized by Law 89 of 1890. In turn, the Afro-Colombian movement attempted to extend those rights to members of its own community who had traditionally exerted communal ancestral domain.[44]

Colombia's indigenous peoples and some leftist politicians elected to the assembly set themselves the task of boosting the sovereignty of the indigenous communal land reserves, as well as the political autonomy of the councils governing those territories. Excluded from this new ethnic space, organizations representing Afro-Colombian communities began to gather signatures for petitions requesting the introduction of an article granting them collective titles to riverbanks and jungles of the Pacific coastal region and other areas over which they had exerted ancestral territorial domain. To accomplish this, ethnic and political leaders travelled to the areas of most concentrated Afro-Colombian settlement.

Besides the unusual strength of the geo-social integration of these Afro-Colombian communities, the strong kinship networks that tie the people of the Pacific coast to neighbourhoods in Medellin and other cities inspired several communal leaders to propose in the Constituent Assembly to define the Afro-Chocoan territory as composed of rural areas *plus* Afro-Colombian urban sites. Their proposal was rejected on grounds of the problematic implications of a form of collective landownership that could include sections of major cities.

Since the early 1980s the Asociación Campesina Integral del Atrato had been struggling in favour of legal recognition of Afro-Chocoan ancestral communal territorial domain.[45] Its members were able to demonstrate that, according to agreements between the Colombian government and the International Labour Organization, ratified by Congress, Afro-Colombian peasants of the Atrato River Valley had the right to claim an ethnic territory.[46] However, their arguments were rejected by members of the Colombian Institute for Agrarian Reform, who were charged with studying the claims. These officials insisted that in Colombia there were no ethnic minorities apart from the indigenous peoples.[47]

In October 1990 President César Gaviria's government set up commissions to prepare materials for the constitutional convention. The Subcommission on Equality and Ethnic Rights produced a compromise proposal, approved by the indigenous and Afro-Colombian organizations which took part, as well as by their advisers and lawyers and by those who participated as concerned academics. The proposal broadened the concept of ethnic territory to make room for river valley communities of the Pacific coast.[48] Although this document resulted from a process of complex negotiation, it was disregarded by some members of the Constituent Assembly, who denied that the majority of Afro-Colombians had any ethnicity at all.[49]

In May 1991 these objections were discussed and denounced at a huge meeting of Afro-Colombian leaders and campaigners held in Cali, where it was decided to continue the struggle against the exclusion of black people. The movement organized urban and rural committees and held discussions on ethnic identity as a source of rights. In the Department of Chocó, public demonstrators peacefully seized the city halls of Quibdo and Pie de Pato.[50]

Reacting to these pressures, those who opposed Afro-Colombian rights assumed a more radical position, which was fought for by an ad hoc committee appointed by the National Organization of Colombian Indigenous Peoples. Two members of this committee, the sociologist Orlando Fals, and Francisco Rojas of the indigenous Embera, were chosen to write and submit for voting what would later be known as Transitory Article 55. Several of the group's leaders identified with Fals's and Rojas's efforts; but others considered that, by insisting on classifying the lands occupied by Afro-Pacific people as 'vacant', Transitory Article 55 had not broken away from the tradition of injustice that had been contested since the beginning of the reform process.

In July 1991 the old constitution was replaced by one which changed the nature of the Colombian nation from bi-ethnic and monocultural to pluri-ethnic and multicultural. For Afro-Colombian organizations, the time had come to prepare the law implementing the rights which the 1991 constitution barely delineated. The following year, the government set up the Special Commission for Black Communities which was required for the implementation of Transitory Article 55.[51] Its members included delegates from government agencies, members of Congress, academics, and Afro-Colombian leaders from the advisory committees which had been formed in the Pacific departments of Chocó, Valle, Cauca and Nariño.

Afro-Colombian members of the special commission had to contend with the government's inefficiency in failing to allocate sufficient funds for them to travel from their riverbank and forest communities to Bogotá, where the monthly commission sessions took place, or for them to implement a public education and information programme.

New threats: land and resource rights

The failure of the Afro-Colombian educational campaign – which was to include a programme to raise public awareness of traditional Afro-Colombian environmental wisdom – for lack of the promised funds was catastrophic. The constituent process portrayed the indigenous peoples as the only non-predator Colombians. Afro-Colombians were thus excluded from negotiations involving the exchange of ecological knowledge for territorial autonomy, and from participation in the debate about, and funding of, sustainable development.

Meanwhile, in an attempt to maximize the alleged benefits of the new international opening of trade frontiers, the Colombian government began to offer to the economies of the Pacific Rim the Chocó region's rich resources of gold, platinum, timber, fish and shellfish, and to advance incentives to Colombian investors to expand high-technology monoculture plantations there.

By late 1992 it had become imperative to spread the message that 'progress' could not be what the industrial enterprises of Colombia were promoting.[52] Maderas del Darién, the largest firm in the national logging industry, lobbied the government to allow it to extract timber from 23,640 hectares of virgin forest, rich in endangered species, in the lower Atrato River Valley. The request had been opposed by the Special Commission for Black

Communities while it considered the future granting of collective title on Afro-Chocoan territories. The commission also objected because, according to information presented by the Organización Campesina del Bajo Atrato, the timber company's environmental impact studies had excluded any consideration of the peasant communities.

In spite of these arguments, the government granted permission for the forest to be exploited. Officials explained that Afro-Colombian timber company workers had demanded that the government obey the constitution in reference to their right to work and survive. The special commission continued its opposition on the grounds of the constitutional mandate which requires the state to plan the management and use of natural resources in order to promote their conservation, renewal or replacement, and to guarantee sustainable development.

Class consciousness overcame ethnic identity. Black forestry workers attacked the special commission for defending collective ownership, allegedly an 'inferior' form of property. They also claimed to hold the commission responsible for advocating a type of apartheid that could spread to the Chocó.[53] This outcome bears witness to the workings of an educational system that denies and negates Afro-Colombian people's ancestry and achievements.

Despite this setback, the new ethnic legislation, Law 70, was passed in August 1993. It is the only law which Afro-Colombian peasants, miners and fisherfolk can use to retain and protect their ancestral territories. If their political organizations are successful, their achievement will consist in the defence of their lands against foreign and national monopolistic intrusion, as well as in the nation's recognition of the way enslaved Africans and their descendants have helped create the national culture.

Towards the future

The breathing space of two years offered by the constituent process to the indigenous peoples has allowed groups like the Regional Organization of the Embera and Waunan of the Pacific coast to exert further pressures on the government to have their communal reservations expanded. Considering only the situation of the Dapartment of Chocó, by 1993 1 million of its 4 million usable hectares had passed to the jurisdiction of seventy-eight indigenous communal land reservations. Unfortunately, at times this successful growth has taken place at the expense of those Afro-Colombian ancestral territories whose legitimacy depended upon approval of Law 70. This tendency may accelerate the fragmentation of *compadrazgo* and other traditional means of peaceful inter-ethnic coexistence.[54]

To counteract this trend, members of the Peasant Association of the San Juan River have promoted the unification of the struggles of both indigenous peoples and Afro-Colombians. In that valley a new and paradigmatic form of bi-ethnic communal territorial domain has been consolidating during the past four or five years of political upheaval.

Within this context, the achievements of Law 70 acquire particular relevance. One important feature comprises the recognition of Afro-Colombian ancestral territorial rights, including rights to use plant and animal resources and to mine for gold and platinum. Another involves the possibility of defending Afro-Colombian cultural and historical identities by means of special education programmes, and a third concerns the influence and control that Afro-Colombian communities have gained over the planning and implementation of socio-economic development.[55]

These advantageous developments have quickly led to political participation. Rudecindo Castro, president of the Peasant Association of Baudo, and Zulia Mena, president of the Organization of Popular Barrios – both former members of the Special Commission for Black Communities – stood as candidates in the 1994 congressional elections. Zulia Mena obtained 40,000 votes, a much larger share than that obtained by the candidates of the traditional leftist parties.

Thus, by struggling in the legal and political arenas, Afro-Colombians are becoming visible.

Notes

1 Whitten, N.E. and Torres, A., 'A pre-Columbian diaspora', *Report on the Americas: The Black Americas 1492-1992*, North American Congress on Latin America (NACLA), vol. 25, no. 4, 1986, p. 20.
2 Friedemann, N.S. de, *La saga del negro: presencia africana en Colombia*, Bogotá, Pontificia Universidad Javeriana, 1993.
3 Ibid, p. 51.
4 Friedemann, N.S. de and Arocha, J., *De sol a sol: génesis, transformación y presencia de los negros en Colombia*, Bogotá, Planeta Editorial Colombiana, 1986, pp. 15, 16.
5 Lara, O., *Resistencia y esclavitud: de Africa a la América negra, la trata negrera del siglo XV al XIX*, Paris, Serbal/UNESCO, 1981.
6 Friedemann and Arocha, op. cit., pp. 15-47.
7 Friedemann, op. cit., pp. 41-54.
8 Curtin, P.D., *The Atlantic Slave Trade*, Madison,WI, University of Wisconsin Press, 1969, p. 46.
9 Friedemann and Arocha, op. cit., pp. 347-55, 364-76.
10 Maya, A., 'Afrocolombianos: se lleva la misma sangre', *Colombia País de Regiones*, no. 30, Medellin, El Colombiano-Centro de Investigación y Educación Popular (CINEP), 1993.
11 Wade, P., *Blackness and Race Mixture: The Dynamics of Racial Identity in Colombia*, Baltimore, MD, Johns Hopkins University Press, 1993, pp. 3-28.
12 Sharp, W., *Slavery on the Spanish Frontier: The Colombian Chocó 1680-1810*, Oklahoma City, OA, Oklahoma University Press, 1976.
13 Maya, A., 'Las brujas de Zaragoza', *América Negra*, no. 4, Bogotá, Pontificia Universidad Javeriana, 1992, pp. 85-98.
14 Schwegler, A., 'Hacia una arqueología afrocolombiana: restos de tradiciones religiosas bantues en una comunidad negro-colombiana', *América Negra*, no. 4, Bogotá, Pontificia Universidad Javeriana, 1992, pp. 35-84.
15 Friedemann, N.S. de and Cross, R., *MaNgombe: guerreros y ganaderos en Palenque*, Bogotá, Carlos Valencia Editores, 1979.
16 Friedemann, op. cit., pp. 70-1.
17 Friedemann, N.S. de, 'Lumbalu: ritos de la muerte en Palenque de San Basilio', *América Negra*, no. 1, Bogotá, Pontificia Universidad Javeriana, 1991, pp. 43-64; Schwegler, A., 'Africa en América: los juegos de velorio y otros cantos funerarios afrohispanos remanentes en la costa atlantica de Colombia', in J.R. Dow and T. Stolz (eds), *Akten des Essener Kolloquium Uber Sprachminoritatenspachen*, vols 15-17, Essen, Universität von Essen, 1990.
18 Friedemann, N.S. de, 'Vida y muerte en el Caribe afrocolombiano: cielo, tierra, cantos y tambores', *América Negra*, no. 8, Bogotá, Pontificia Universidad Javeriana, 1994.
19 Friedemann, N.S. de and Patiño, C., *Lengua y sociedad en el Palenque de San Basilio*, Bogotá, Instituto Caro y Cuervo, 1983; Schwegler, op. cit.
20 Maya, op. cit., 'Las brujas de Zaragoza'.
21 Ibid., pp. 94-8.

22 Ussa, C., 'De los empauta'os a 1930', unpublished thesis, Popayán, Universidad del Cauca, 1989.
23 Taussig, M., *The Devil and Commodity Fetishism in South America*, Chapel Hill, NC, University of Carolina Press, 1980; Friedemann, G., 'The Devil among blacks of the Pacific littoral and the Cauca Valley in Colombia: cultural constructions', *América Negra*, no. 8, Bogotá, Pontificia Universidad Javeriana,1994.
24 Friedemann and Arocha., op. cit., pp. 198-217.
25 Ibid., pp. 198-230.
26 Ibid., pp. 241-57.
27 Parsons, J., *'Antioqueño' Colonization in Western Colombia*, Berkeley, CA, University of California Press, 1968.
28 Maya, op. cit., 'Afrocolombianos: se lleva la misma sangre'.
29 Ibid.
30 Friedemann, N.S. de, *'Troncos* among black miners in Colombia', in T. Greaves and W. Culver (eds), *Miners and Mining in the Americas*, Manchester, Manchester University Press, 1985, pp. 204-25.
31 On Afro-Colombian mining communities, see ibid.
32 On these Afro-Colombian agriculturalists, see Arocha, J., 'El sentipensamiento de los pueblos negros en la construcción de Colombia', in C. Uribe (ed.), *Simposio: la construcción de las Américas. Memorias del VI Congreso nacional de antropologia*, Bogotá, Universidad de los Andes, 1993, pp 159-72; and 'Sentipensamiento, cacharreo y convivencia en el Baudo, Departamento del Chocó', *Señales Abiertas*, no. 4, 1993, pp. 98-111.
33 See Friedemann, N.S. de and Espinozea, M., 'La mujer negra en la historia de Colombia', in *La mujer en la historia de Colombia*, in press.
34 Romero, M.D., 'Sociedades negras: esclavos y libres en la costa pacífica colombiana', *América Negra*, no. 2, Bogotá, Pontificia Universidad Javeriana, 1991, pp. 137-56.
35 Gutierrez de Pineda, V., *La familia en Colombia*, Serie Socioecónomica no. 7, Bogotá, Centro de Investigaciones Sociales Cis, 1962; and *Familia y cultura en Colombia*, Bogotá, Departamento de Sociología de la Universidad Nacional and Ediciones Tercer Mundo, 1968.
36 Friedemann and Cross., op. cit.; Friedemann, op. cit., *La saga*.
37 Friedemann, op. cit., 'Vida y muerte'.
38 Posada, G., *Memorias histórico-políticas*, Bogotá, Imprenta Nacional, 1929.
39 Tirado, A., *Introducción a la historia económica de Colombia*, Bogotá, La Carreta, p. 64.
40 Friedemann, op. cit., *La saga*.
41 Friedemann, N.S. de., 'Estudios de negros en la antropología colombiana', in J. Arocha and N.S. de Friedemann (eds), *Un siglo de investigación social-antropología en Colombia*, Bogotá, Etno, 1984, pp. 507-72.
42 *Report on the Americas: The Black Americas 1492-1992*, NACLA, vol. 25, no. 4, 1992, p. 19.
43 '"Social cleansing" in Colombia and Brazil: genocide of the poor', *Human Rights Working Paper*, vol. 1, no. 17, Bogatá, Instituto Latinamericano de Servicios Legales Alternativos, 1993.

44 Arocha, J., 'Hacia una nación para los excluídos', *Magazin Dominical de El Espectador*, no. 329, Bogotá, 1989.
45 Arocha, J., 'Cultura afrocolombiana, entorno y derechos territoriales', *La Política Social en los 90*, Bogotá, Facultad de Ciencias Humanas, Universidad Nacional de Colombia, 1994, p. 94.
46 Vasquez, M., *Las caras lindas de mi gente negra: legislación histórica para las comunidades negras de Colombia*, Bogotá, Instituto Colombiano de Antropología, PNR, PNUD, 1994, pp. 38-46.
47 'Conceptos sobre identidad cultural en las comunidades negras', *América Negra*, no. 6, Bogotá, Pontificia Universidad Javeriana, 1993, pp. 173-96.
48 Arocha, J., 'Afro-Colombia denied', *Report on the Americas: The Black Americas 1492-1992*, NACLA, vol. 25, no. 4, 1992, p. 30.
49 Ibid., p. 31.
50 Arocha, op. cit., 'Cultura afrocolombiana', pp. 96, 97.
51 Ibid., pp. 98, 99.
52 Ibid., pp. 101-2.
53 Ibid., pp. 99-100.
54 Losonczy, A.M., 'Almas, tierras y convivencia', in *Contribución africana a la cultura de las Américas*, Bogotá, Biopacífico, Instituto Colombiano de Antropología, 1993, pp. 189-91.
55 Vasquez, op. cit., pp. 53-61.

Select bibliography

Arocha, J., 'Afro-Colombia denied', *Report on the Americas: The Black Americas 1492-1992*, North American Congress on Latin America (NACLA), vol. 25, no. 4, 1992.
Arocha, J. and Friedemann, N.S. de (eds), *Un siglo de investigación social-antropológico en Colombia*, Bogotá, Etno, 1984.
Friedemann, N.S. de, *La saga del negro: presencia africana en Colombia*, Bogotá, Pontificia Universidad Javeriana, 1993.
Friedemann, N.S. de, '*Troncos* among black miners in Colombia', in T. Greaves and W. Culver (eds), *Miners and Mining in the Americas*, Manchester, Manchester University Press, 1985, pp. 204-25.
Friedemann, N.S. de and Arocha, J., *De sol a sol: génesis, transformación y presencia de los negros en Colombia*, Bogotá, Planeta Editorial Colombiana, 1986.
Lara, O., *Resistencia y esclavitud: de Africa a la América negra – la trata negrera del siglo XV al XIX*, Paris, Serbal/UNESCO, 1981.
Sharp, W., *Slavery on the Spanish Frontier: The Colombian Chocó 1680-1810*, Oklahoma City, OA, Oklahoma University Press, 1976.
Taussig, M., *The Devil and Commodity Fetishism in South America*, Chapel Hill, NC, University of Carolina Press, 1980.
Ulloa, A. (ed.), *Contribución africana a la cultura de las Américas*, Bogotá, Biopacífico, Instituto Colombiano de Antropología, 1993.
Wade, P., *Blackness and Race Mixture: The Dynamics of Racial Identity in Colombia*, Baltimore, MD, Johns Hopkins University Press, 1993.

West, R., *The Pacific Lowlands of Colombia*, Baton Rouge, LA, Louisiana University Press, 1957.

Whitten, N.E., *Black Frontiersmen: A South American Case*, New York, Wiley, 1974.

Whitten, N.E. and Torres, A., 'A pre-Columbian diaspora', *Report on the Americas: The Black Americas 1492-1992*, NACLA, vol. 25, no. 4,, 1986, p. 20.

4

CUBA

Gayle McGarrity and Osvaldo Cárdenas

Given the historical precedents and contemporary power structure, it is not difficult to fathom why the problem of race continues to have a central role in today's Caribbean. This is particularly true in the case of Cuba, despite the fact that establishment literature and official discourse have maintained the contrary for more than two hundred years, through the course of radically different socio-economic systems.

Rise of the nation

In the nineteenth century Cuba was the largest sugar plantation economy in the Caribbean, an economy based on African slave labour. Cuba was also the last Caribbean country to abolish slavery, doing so in 1886. The only other countries in which slavery was as important and persisted so long were Brazil and the United States, and in both countries racism and race segregation continue to be distinctive features of contemporary life.

The struggle for the abolition of slavery and the fear of a slave rebellion and a repetition of the events in Haiti occupied a dominant position in nineteenth-century Cuban political thought:

> *Cuban thinkers, prior to the War of 1868, were all pro-slavery. None ... adopted a progressive stance as regards the institution and some maintained an explicitly racial position on the evolution of Cuban society ... [they] also were convinced that the hope of civilization in Cuba lay in white supremacy and the elimination of the black population.*[1]

While the Luso-Hispanic colonies of mainland America gained

their independence during the first quarter of the nineteenth century, Cuba remained faithful to the Spanish Crown. This adherence to colonial status can be traced to the economic boom resulting from the relatively late expansion of the sugar industry, stimulated by the destruction of sugar production in Haiti and the ensuing unfettered access to the North American market. 'As Cuban society was based on slave production and the slaves were of a different race to the dominant class, the ideologues of the latter ... justified this shameless exploitation of man by man on the grounds of racial inferiority.'[2]

A sharp division characterized nineteenth-century Cuba – between the great masses of slaves, artisans, peasants, small tobacco-growers, professionals, and the poorer population in general, on the one hand, and the colonial regime, Spanish merchants and Creole landowners, on the other.[3] The other major division occurred between Creole landowners, on the one hand, and the Crown and Spanish merchants, on the other, over taxes, onerous tariffs and the economic, social, religious and politico-administrative discrimination to which the former were subjected. Within this context the Cuban nation emerged, after barely two centuries of colonialism, experiencing rapid fusion and re-creation in an intense process of transculturation and syncretism.

Contemporary Cuban historical writing, including the post-revolutionary brand, frequently begins with the premise that the Creole is the embryo from which the Cuban nation emerges. Some writers even refer to the integration of black people and mulattos into a Cuban nation created by Creoles. The term 'Afro-Cuban', introduced into Cuban socio-historical literature by Fernando Ortíz[4] in the 1930s, has often been inappropriately used, as Nicolás Guillén[5] reminded us. Little that is Cuban can be divorced from its largely African roots. In 1869 the largest ethnic group in Cuba comprised the Africans and their descendants.

The birth of the nation, the brutal oppression to which Cubans were subjected and the economic interests of both Cuban landowners and Spanish merchants in preserving slavery interacted to give rise to the three ideological and political currents that dominated Cuban thought throughout the nineteenth century:

reformism, independentism and the movement for the annexation of Cuba to the United States. Many nineteenth-century Cuban political figures inclined towards more than one of these currents during the course of their careers. Of the three modes of thought, only independentism was consistent with the development of a Cuban nation. Nevertheless, all of them influenced the way the nation arose and contributed to its final shape.

It has been falsely assumed that Cuba's Guerra de los Diez Años (Ten Years' War) erased racial differences, and that the emergent nation was a product solely of independentist thoughts, both anti-slavery and anti-racist. Some historians and politicians, have even affirmed that a problem as serious, complex and deeply entrenched in the Cuban psyche as racism simply vanished during the armed struggle of 1868-78, and that racism was reintroduced only subsequently, during and after the North American military occupation at the end of the century. Such views are a travesty of the historical reality.

Reformism, annexationism, independentism

Reformist thought and the social movement that accompanied it embodied the interests of the Cuban landowning class, who suffered disadvantages vis-à-vis the metropolis and Spanish merchants and aimed to modify the colonial relationship to their benefit. They sought an agreement with Spain which would allow them to control the internal affairs of the colony, while modifying the commercial and financial monopoly enjoyed by Spanish merchants. The reformists hoped to obtain these goals without upsetting the social order in so violent a manner that slavery, on which their power depended, might be eliminated.

During the early development of the sugar plantation economy the reformists were staunch and often outspoken defenders of slavery. But after 1840, particularly after the Conspiración de la Escalera (1844), the slave trade was attacked by the most brilliant minds of the *sacarocracia*.[6] Their position was influenced by fear of the enormous number of black people, both free and slave, already on the island; by increasing difficulties in obtaining slaves; by the rising market price of slaves; and by constant rumours of conspiracies and actual rebellions that aroused fears of a repeat of the Haitian Revolution.

The reformists formulated different proposals to eliminate black people from the Cuban social setting. The most cynical was the policy of dividing black people from mulattos and according privileges to the latter, while assimilating them, within limits, as allies. Many of these policies and practices are still reflected in the state of race relations in twentieth-century Cuba. Subject to oppression and ignorance for centuries, many Cuban black people came to identify their depressed socio-economic status with the colour of their skin. As the colonial regime left open the possibility of *blanqueamiento* (whitening), the alienation of both black people and mulattos led to a tendency for the collective and individual efforts of this enormous oppressed sector of society to be characterized by the desire of black people to transform themselves into mulattos, and of mulattos, in turn, to evolve into white people. This pattern of behaviour is reflected in the attitudes of large numbers of black and mulatto Cubans today, although clearly not all black people aspire to be white.

The break-up of the Junta de Información in 1867, when the absolutist Spanish regime rejected the essentially reformist demands of the representatives of Cuba, closed off the option of self-government for the time being. Many discouraged reformists moved into the independentist camp and participated in the movement which led to the Guerra de los Diez Años in 1868. Reformism exerted a conservative influence over the revolutionary movement throughout the struggle for independence, contributing to its repeated failure in 1868-78 and 1895-8. In the inter-war period most of the reformists were grouped around the Liberal Autonomist Party, which represented the interests of the landowners and urban middle classes and was overtly racist. The most radical sector of the Liberal Autonomist Party joined the War of Independence in 1895, while the majority opposed the struggle and supported US intervention in 1898.

This faction expressed the interests, as well as the fears, of a sector of the landowning and slave-owning class, and of Spanish merchants, who saw their interests threatened by the Spanish Crown's weakness in the face of pressures, mainly from the

British government, to end the slave trade and abolish slavery. Confronted with this prospect, this powerful lobby proposed the incorporation of Cuba into the United States as a means of preserving the institution of slavery. In spite of their opposing interests on some issues, Cuban landowners and Spanish merchants were of like mind when it came to the slave question.

The annexationist movement was at its height between 1850 and 1865. The armed confrontations that took place in Cuba during the two decades prior to 1865 were annexationist in character. Following the defeat of the southern states in the US Civil War (1861-5) and the subsequent abolition of slavery in the USA, the pro-slavery annexationists suffered a severe blow, and many joined the struggle for independence in 1868.

Not all those who adhered to and promoted annexationist positions in the nineteenth century were reactionaries. Nor were all those who opposed annexation progressive. The best-known Cuban anti-annexationist of the period, José A. Saco, was also a champion of the pro-slavery landowning class; and the foremost leaders of the insurrectionist movement in 1868, and many prominent revolutionary leaders in the 1895 War of Independence, were, at some stage, annexationist. The annexationist ideology has surfaced at intervals throughout contemporary Cuban history, propelled by the USA's proximity and by the traditional US perception of the Caribbean as its 'backyard'.

The independence movement began on 10 October 1868, on the eastern part of the island, and came to be known as the Guerra de los Diez Años (1868-78). This movement was not, as has sometimes been incorrectly stated, headed by representatives of the landowning class who declared the abolition of slavery and were committed from the outset to Cuba's total independence. Such assumptions, held by many Cubans today, are untrue, because sugar production was concentrated on the western side of the island, an area never touched by the Guerra de los Diez Años.[7]

In fact, the revolution started and developed mainly in regions where sugar and slavery were not significant. The leaders of the early revolutionary movement were predominantly small and medium-size landowners and professionals. The rank and file of the insurrectionist forces were peasants, former slaves, labourers, artisans, tobacco-growers and other members of the intermediate and lower social strata.

The conservative attitude taken by the majority of the leaders of the movement at the beginning of the revolution was due to the predominance of reformist and annexationist tendencies, as well as to their hope of obtaining the support of big landowners from western Cuba, and from liberals in Spain and in the US government. The 1868 revolution 'began being pro-slavery, later applying stringent regulations to the working conditions of the freed men and finally, after 1871, became radically pro-abolition'.[8]

The focus of the revolution thus gradually shifted towards the popular classes, and this trend was consistent with changes in the composition of the Independence Army, more than 70 per cent of whose ranks were, it has been estimated, filled by black people and mulattos.[9] This is especially significant in view of the fact that black and mulatto Cubans constituted only about 43 per cent of the population, according to the 1869 census.

The leadership of the war passed into the hands of radicals and populist white leaders like the Dominicans Modesto Diaz and Máximo Gómez and the Cuban Calixto García. The mulatto Vicente García was another important leader of the period. The role and influence of black and mulatto leaders such as Antonio and José Maceo, Guillermón Moncada, Flor Crombet and Quintín Bandera grew day by day. Fear of the 'black threat' rose within the ranks of the conservative wing of the revolution. One of the main reasons for the failure of the war was white people's trepidation at the prospect of the ascendancy of black and mulatto military chiefs.

The war came to an end with the Pacto del Zanjón.[10] The process was presided over by the conservative wing of the revolutionary movement, people who did not call for the total abolition of slavery. The rebellious position of General Antonio Maceo at the Mangos de Baraqua meeting resurrected the revolutionary banner of abolition: 'The man who protested the selling out of the revolution also decried the abandonment of the exploited classes ... [A] peasant and not a landowner ... lifted high the banners of abolition ... The leadership of the revolution had shifted.'[11]

In 1886 slavery was abolished and former slaves became the bulk of the working class. Black and mulatto Cubans continued to suffer from discrimination and segregation. The black population had diminished, in relative terms, as a consequence of the gradual demise of the slave trade and the impact of the war on the revolutionary army and on the black and mulatto population in general. It also declined as a result of the policy of *blanqueamiento* pursued by the colonial authorities. Between 1893 and 1895, 224,000 Spanish immigrants entered the island, although only 82,000 remained.[12] According to the 1887 census, black people and mulattos represented only around 32 per cent of the population. North American capital made considerable inroads during this period, displacing the Cuban landowning class and coming to dominate the economy. Meanwhile, recently freed slaves, confronted with intense racial discrimination and segregation, were driven to renew the struggle for civil rights and equality.

The great Cuban thinker and revolutionary José Martí (not himself of African descent), who spent much of his life in exile for his political ideas, was to carry the concept of Cuban independence to full maturity. Martí, arguably the greatest Cuban intellectual of all times, was the creator of the idea of a democratic and sovereign republic, composed of all Cubans and governed in their best interests. His radical, anti-racist and egalitarian views, his vision of Latin American unity (reminiscent of Simón Bolívar's thought), his lucid grasp of the danger to Cuba and to the rest of Latin America of North American imperialist expansion, crystallized in the drafting in 1892 of the constitution of the Partido Revolucionario Cubano (PRC) in the United States.

The PRC delegate in Cuba was Juan Gualberto Gómez, a black man, son of slaves, who was to become one of the foremost political and intellectual leaders of the War of Independence, as well as of the first few years of the republic. To begin the Guerra Necesaria, Martí needed the collaboration of the great heroes of the Guerra de los Diez Años, especially the distinguished, popular and much admired General Antonio Maceo.

Martí was himself virtually unknown in Cuba at this time. Imprisoned as a young man, he had made his escape to Spain, where he graduated in law, philosophy and letters. Martí then travelled to France, Mexico and Guatemala, returning to Cuba after the Pacto del Zanjón in 1878. His pro-independence activities brought him into conflict again with the authorities, and he had to go abroad once more in 1879, settling in New York. In 1895 Martí returned to Cuba again, soon to die in battle.[13]

In Havana, Juan Gualberto Gómez used as an organizational base for the PRC the *sociedades de color* (societies of coloured people, both black and mulatto). Martí raised funds and organized logistical support for the independence movement among members of the Cuban expatriate community in the USA. When the War of Independence started in 1895, Máximo Gómez assumed the position of military chief, while Antonio Maceo became *lugarteniente general* of the Liberation Army. This time, not only the rank-and-file troops but also the majority of officers were blacks and mulattos, and in social terms workers, peasants, manual labourers, students, professionals and artisans. The three main leaders of the movement – Maceo, Martí and Gómez – were radically pro-independence and nationalist, and firmly opposed to US intervention in Cuban affairs.

Martí and Maceo were killed before they could witness the achievement of independence. The latter lost his life in a minor skirmish after leading his forces more than 1,000 kilometres from the east to the west of the island – one of the most extraordinary military achievements of the nineteenth century and the most important in Cuban history.

Although the independence movement was now relatively mature and possessed a clearer ideological position and a seasoned leadership, it was still hampered by the presence of reformists and annexationists within its ranks. These sentiments found succour and nurturance among wealthy Cuban immigrants in the USA. The premature death of Martí and Maceo, combined with the US government's designs on Cuba, favoured these tendencies.

Black and mulatto Cuban veterans of the independence struggle later commented on how General Maceo, due to the colour of his skin, had to decline the military leadership of the movement – although the majority of the fighters were black and mulatto people, and Maceo both had the military skills and was the most popular Cuban of his time. Many revolutionary fighters insisted that Maceo's death in an isolated skirmish was proof of a plot within the revolutionary ranks to assassinate him and prevent him from assuming his rightful position as independent Cuba's first President:

> *The rebel leaders, who were working towards the achievement of total and unconditional independence for Cuba, sought support from blacks and mulattos; but the majority of the white landowners, who looked to the United States government for support, were, in fact, opposed to the idea of independence. In this arena of conflict, the United States appears as the veritable saviour of white Cubans, and by extension, as the enemy of Afro-Cubans.*[14]

Race relations in the puppet republic

The first group of US troops set foot in Cuba in 1898, an event that represented a serious step backwards in the process of realizing the dreams for which so many Cubans had fought and died. US military intervention proved to be disastrous for the revolutionaries and for the Cuban people. The US government never extended recognition to the Cuban patriots. Despite the decisive role played by the Liberation Army in the defeat of the Spanish troops, especially of those stationed in Santiago de Cuba, in the last battle of the war, Cuban freedom fighters were not even allowed to enter the city limits. The insurgents were also excluded from the negotiation process that led to the Paris Treaty, which effectively transferred sovereignty over Cuba from Spanish to US hands.

The occupation forces found support from wealthy Spaniards and Cubans, as well as from North American business interests, which had come to dominate the Cuban economy. The dissolution of the Liberation Army left its former members poor and marginalized, cut off from the national political process. The USA converted a now unarmed and defenceless Cuba into a protectorate, imposing the Platt Amendment on the Cuban constitution of 1901. The best summary of its implications was given by Leonard Wood, head of the US occupationary government:

> *The Platt Amendment has left very little, if any, independence in Cuba, and the only reasonable course now is to seek annexation. This process will, of course, take time, during which it is desirable that Cuba will have its own government ... They will not be able to sign certain treaties without our consent, nor will they be able to obtain loans above certain limits ... [A]ll of which should prove ... that Cuba is clearly in the palm of our hands ... The control that we have over Cuba, a control that will soon be transformed into possession, will enable us to eventually exercise total control over the world sugar market.*[15]

The racism which had been endemic to colonial society found fertile ground during the occupation and in the nascent republic. The 1901 constitution was inspired by its US counterpart. Although it proclaimed equality of all human beings, this remained a purely theoretical assertion for the descendants of African slaves. The policy of *blanqueamiento* continued: 'Between 1902 and 1919, over 400,000 Spanish immigrants entered Cuba, making the Spanish-born population, by 1930, increase to 16 per cent of the total and making Cuba the most Spanish of Latin American countries.'[16]

The immigration of black people was prohibited by law. Yet the expansion of the sugar industry and the pressures of North American capital in need of cheap labour and a mechanism to keep wages low compelled the government to import thousands of black temporary workers from other Caribbean islands, while unemployment remained high among Cuban-born workers. Racial tensions increased.[17]

Many Cuban landowners and Cuban exiles in the USA had acquired US citizenship. Among this group was Tomás Estrada Palma, the first President of Cuba, whose pro-annexation ideas and racism were well known. Affluent Spanish merchants, now owners of large stretches of Cuban land, were granted preferential treatment by officers of the occupation forces. Proudly and adamantly white, 'uncontaminated' as they saw it by African blood, they made an alliance with carefully selected members of the Liberation Army who shared their racial status and racist ideas. Together, first under the US military occupation and later with US support, they established and reinforced an exclusionary and racist social order.

Cuban history was rewritten. The anti-imperialist and nationalistic thought of José Martí and Antonio Maceo was relegated to the obscure corners of Cuban intellectual life. Martí became the 'Apóstol' (Apostle), an intellectual who turned the struggle for independence into a religion and who felt deep sympathy for the impoverished masses – masses portrayed as mysteriously devoid of colour. In Cuba when colour is not mentioned, it is implicitly white. Maceo's role was reduced to his military contribution and stripped of his political brilliance. No more the outstanding Cuban warrior, he became merely one of the more prominent generals, and not black any more, but mulatto.

The Guerra de los Diez Años was presented as the work of the Cuban landowning class, who gave freedom to their slaves in a purely altruistic fashion and were committed to independence from the start. Tomás Estrada Palma, comfortably exiled in the USA during the War of Independence, and other conservatives were promoted as the great champions of Cuban independence; outstanding black and mulatto generals of the war were marginalized.

In this new version of history there was no reference to the race issue or to the ethnicity of the majority of the revolutionary forces, who therefore become, by implication, white. The reformists, annexationists and racists of the past were transformed into anti-slavery thinkers. Mulattos were transformed into *mestizos*.[18] Black people and mulattos came officially to be viewed as a minority, although there was no evidence that African descendants constituted a minority of the Cuban population – just as there is no such evidence today.

Danzón – once the dance of the black people, which white racists excluded from their ninteenth-century social gatherings – now gained respectability as the national (and therefore white) dance form. African religions and secret societies (Abakuá and *ñañigos*), which played a crucial role in the formation of Cuba's nationhood during and after the independence struggle, and continued profoundly to influence the lives of millions of Cubans, were transformed into 'witchcraft' and the ignorant expression of superstition by backward black people. They were repressed, while Catholicism, which was never popular in Cuba, and whose predominantly Spanish hierarchy supported colonialism and slavery, received privileged status.

The racist and pro-slavery novel *Cecilia Valdés*, by the pro-annexation writer Cirilo Villaverde, was touted as being anti-slavery and anti-racist. The hispanophile, racist and colonialist daily newspaper *Diario de la Marina* became the great organ of the Cuban republic. Racism penetrated every pore of the civil society, converting black people and mulattos into second-class citizens. There were white nationalists, such as the radical intellectual and politician Manuel Sangüily and the widely admired philosopher Enrique José Varona, who had joined the struggle for independence and now took a stand against US domination. But although such people condemned the worst expressions of racism, they tended to behave paternalistically.

Frustrated in their struggle for independence and for a better society, excluded from many areas of employment and national life, black and mulatto Cubans were now divided into three main tendencies. Some followed the revolutionary black leader Juan Gualberto Gómez, who dreamed of creating a predominantly black political party combining the struggle for a sovereign and democratic republic with those for racial equality and social justice. A second group supported the mulatto intellectual and orator Martín Morúa Delgado, one of the leaders of the Liberal Party. In spite of political differences and personal rivalry, Gómez and Morúa were in favour of a gradual uplifting of the black and mulatto population and were willing to work within the established order.[19] The third group was the Independientes de Color movement, led by Evaristo Estenoz and Pedro Ivonet. More radical and impatient than the other two groups, they were ready to resort to military means to achieve equality and justice for black Cubans. Many veterans of the independence wars belonged to this group.

In the face of official indifference and neglect, Estenoz launched the Partido de los Independientes de Color in 1908, in an attempt to bring together black people and mulattos with the aim of creating the kind of republic which the revolutionaries of 1895 had struggled for. The party was falsely accused of racism and of seeking to create a black republic, although, in fact, its political platform was the most progressive of the first two decades of republican history, and the only one to address the question of the achievement of a genuine racial democracy.

In 1910 the Partido Liberal, which traditionally attracted a majority of the black vote through a mixture of demagogy and patronage, introduced an amendment to the Electoral Law. This prohibited the participation in the elections of parties organized along class or racial lines. The amendment was introduced by a mulatto member of the Senate in an attempt to hide its racist motivation. From 1910 to 1912 the Independientes de Color exhausted all legal mechanisms to oppose this amendment, which barred their partipation in national elections; then they resorted to arms.

The Cuban oligarchy reacted in panic, and the US government expressed concern. President José Miguel Gómez used all the force of the newly created army rapidly and violently to suppress the poorly organized and underequipped rising. According to official records, more than 3,000 blacks and mulattos were killed, while black people were terrorized throughout the island. Estenoz died fighting. US troops based at Guantanamo intervened to support the repression.

A conspiratorial silence afterwards enshrouded the dramatic events of 1912. Most white nationalists had supported the government's action; black and mulatto leaders condoned the massacre, kept silent or condemned it only weakly. Recently, progressive historians, while condemning the massacre and the racist ideology and practices that provoked the uprising, have stopped short of approving the attempt of the Independientes de Color to bring together black and mulatto Cubans to combat racism, depicting it rather as a mistaken tactic.

The frustrated revolution

A combination of international events and movements shook Cuban society in the 1920s: the Mexican Revolution; the University Reform Movement, which began in Argentina in 1918 and swept the continent; and the socialist October Revolution in

Russia. In Cuba itself, administrative and political corruption reached hitherto unprecedented heights, and economic crises shook the nation following the brief economic boom during the First World War. The expansionist cycle of the sugar industry came to an end, after strengthening its dominion over the Cuban economy. The urban centres had expanded, and, along with them, the urban working class, the petty bourgeoisie, the intellectual sector and the middle and professional classes.

All these developments coincided with the emergence of a new generation who carried with them the interests, values and aspirations of the new evolving social classes and sectors. Frustration, engendered by corrupt governments as well as by foreign domination, fuelled increasing confrontation with the established order, expressed most dramatically in the Protesta de los Trece, the Movimiento de Veteranos y Patriotas, the Liga Antimperialista and the Universidade Popular José Martí. Two young charismatic leaders distinguished themselves: Julio Antonio Mella and Rubén Martínez Villena. Although both died young, they were pivotal figures in the Partido Comunista de Cuba, established in 1925, which would play a decisive role in the organization of workers, displacing reformist and anarchist influence on the trade union movement in the 1930s.

The Partido Comunista resurrected the demands of the Partido de los Independientes de Color, assuming the role of defender of the rights of a working class that was overwhelmingly composed of blacks and mulattos, along with black immigrant workers from the Caribbean. This attracted many black and mulatto Cubans and gave prominence to the issue of race.[20] These early communists even proposed the creation of a black republic in Oriente Province. The creation of soviets was central to their agenda, and a major attempt in this direction was coordinated by the black leader León Alvarez. The influence of the regional movement led by Marcus Garvey was also significant among West Indian sugar workers in Camaguey and Oriente provinces.

The Partido Comunista and the workers' movement of which it was the vanguard played a decisive role in the revolution which overthrew the tyrant Geraldo Machado in 1933. The Platt Amendment was annulled. However, in the long run, the 1933 revolution was thwarted by North American pressures, betrayal by army chief Colonel Fulgencio Batista and contradictions within the revolutionary ranks.[21]

The racial question was a constantly underlying factor. Although the 1933 revolution failed, the trade union movement emerged strengthened. The three main union leaders of this period were black members of the Partido Comunista: Lázaro Peña, Jesús Menéndez and Aracelio Iglesia. They were incorruptible men, loved and admired by Cuban workers, and provided excellent leadership until the end of the 1940s. About 80 per cent of Cuban union members were people of colour.[22]

Changes in the strategy of the Communist International under Stalin's influence in the 1930s led to grave errors. In a simplistic and reductionist manner, all social conflicts were to be left to the mechanistic resolution of an ethnically homogenized class struggle. This had serious repercussions for the development of the struggle against racial oppression throughout the world. The understanding within the heart of the communist movement that racism, like capitalism, is an international system was retarded, leading to dramatic mistakes in the political approach to multiracial class societies on the part of communists everywhere.

In Cuba the Partido Comunista moderated its traditional militant posture towards racial conflict in keeping with directives from the regional office of the Communist International in New York. Members of the US Communist Party were unable to grasp the complexities of the racial issue in Cuba just as they could not comprehend the nature of racism in their own country.

Nevertheless, the Partido Comunista was the only national political organization of the day to assume a committed and positive posture towards racial conflict. Cuba's communists criticized the racial discrimination to which black people were subjected, although there was a tendency to consign the final resolution of the problem to the victory of the working class, thus obscuring the complexities of racism as an ideology and delaying the possibility of advance in the anti-racist struggle. Even so, the party was the only political grouping in which black Cubans were present to a significant degree, both at the base and within the leadership, although other social organizations also struggled for racial equality.

The 1930s were a decade of far-reaching and profound change worldwide. In Cuba a new generation of young intellectuals and artists initiated a cultural renaissance as a result of the convergence of Cuban nationalism, anti-imperialist reactions to US interference and prevailing artistic and intellectual currents.

This was the exciting era of the Afrocentric poetry of Nicolás Guillén and Zacarias Tallet; the proletariat poetry of Regino Pedroso; the anthropological and ethnological research of Fernando Ortíz, emphasizing the contribution of Africans and their descendants to the formation of the Cuban nation and culture; and the contribution of historians Ramiro Guerra and Emilio Roig to a clarification of Cuba's past. Alejo Carpentier's 'magic realism' opened up to Cuban readers the world of the Caribbean and the role of Africa within it. The *cubanismo* of Lezama Lima's literature; the journalism of Pablo de la Torriente Brau; the essays of Juan Marinello, Raúl Roa and Jorge Manach; the Cuban rhythms and melodies in the music of Amadeo Roldán, Alejandro García Caturla and Ernesto Lecuona; the popular *sones* of Miguel Metamoro and Sindo Garay; the painting of Abela, Victor Manuel, Amelia Pelaez, Wilfredo Lam and Portocarrero; and the coquetish beauty of the diva Rita Montaner: all were part of the search for the national and the universal in Cuban culture, reflecting Cuban national identity and social psychology and revealing the African foundations of the country's culture in a unique synthesis.

Unfortunately for the Cuban people, this explosive and tumultuous cultural rebirth was brought to an abrupt halt. Fulgencio Batista, a young mulatto of humble origin, assumed the reigns of power, rising from sergeant to colonel amid a revolt of non-commissioned officers that was an integral part of the 1933 revolution. Batista would later deny both his class and his ethnic origin, proving to be a subservient puppet of the Cuban upper classes and a staunch defender of US interests. He restructured the army along lines of patronage and personal allegiance, and his power over the military made him the arbiter of Cuban destiny until his defeat in 1959.

After the collapse of the 1933 revolution, the Batista–Mendieta administration took a moderate position towards the workers' movement. Faced with increasing attacks from the conservative opposition, Batista tried to seek support among the workers. This led him to ingratiate himself with the Partido Comunista. In 1937 he allowed the communists, socialists and other leftists to organize themselves into the Partido Unión Revolucionaria; and in 1938 the Partido Comunista was legalized and soon after changed its name to the Partido Socialista Popular (PSP). This political opening allowed for considerable labour organizing and permitted the party to exercise much influence over the workers' movement. In 1939 a centralized trade union organization was launched, the Confederación de Trabajadores de Cuba, under the leadership of the black communist Lázaro Pena.

The shortcomings of the PSP as regards the racial issue can be traced to its inheritance of the dogmatic and reductionist stand of the Communist International. By subsuming the anti-racist fight within the general struggle for socialism, the communists and socialists unconsciously deprived the black struggle against racism of its most brilliant, courageous and prestigious black leaders. Although some Marxist intellectuals developed an alternative view of Cuban history, they still failed to challenge such aspects as the presumption that the Cuban landowning class had led the 1868 revolution, ignorance of the political implications of *blanqueamiento*, the minimizing of the contribution of African culture and African religions to the formation of the Cuban nation, and the lack of official recognition of the true racial composition of the population.

In 1940 a constitutional convention was held in Havana. There were six communists among the delegates, and they had a decisive role in the approval of a very advanced labour code and many other progressive measures, including some on the racial issue, rendering the Cuban constitution one of the most progressive in Latin America. The PSP alliance with the Batista regime and his accommodationist stance on the proletariat movement were in keeping with US policy during the Second World War.

In 1944 Ramón Grau San Martín, leader of the Partido Revolucionario Auténtico, became President of Cuba. His party would remain in power until 1952. As the USA reversed its previous tolerant policy towards communism, following the end of the war, the weak and corrupt Cuban government followed suit. Grau's anti-communist offensive was unleashed in 1946. Attacks against union headquarters, and the detention and assassination of union and other leaders, culminated in the murder of Jesús Menéndez, the popular black organizer of the sugar workers and a PSP senator.

Carlos Prío replaced Grau in 1948. Under his government, the PSP was banned; communists and others were persecuted, jailed, tortured and assassinated; trade union offices were seized; the left-wing media were supressed. Black people continued to be discriminated against, systematically excluded from higher positions in employment, public service and politics. There were no black people in managerial or clerical jobs, nor in banks, the telephone company, mines or electrical companies. They predominated in manual and unskilled employment, such as in the sugar fields and the construction industry. Few black people owned land or other property.[23]

There were schools from which black people were excluded, especially private Catholic schools; areas in the cities where they could not rent homes or enter hotels, restaurants or barber shops; beaches and sections of parks from which they were banned; and so on. There was, nevertheless, a growing black and mulatto middle class; and the process of *blanqueamiento* intensified, making many mulattos into whites and blacks into mulattos.

In 1952 Batista, now an army general, overthrew the Prío government and installed his unprecedentedly corrupt and bloody dictatorship. Prostitution and gambling assumed massive proportions, while poverty and unemployment increased, particularly among black Cubans. The government and armed forces placed themselves unabashedly at the service of the local ruling elite and of foreign capital. With a mulatto who claimed to be 'Indian' the reins of power, discrimination against the black population persisted.

The struggle against Batista was waged by people from many sectors of Cuban society, some, but not all, organized politically. The Movimiento Revolucionario 26 de Julio was the most important grouping, led by the young attorney Fidel Castro Ruz. Other groups were the Directorio Estudiantil Universitario, led by José

Antonio Echeverría, president of the Federación Estudiantil Universitaria, and the PSP, under the leadership of the mulatto Blas Roca Calderio. Of the three organizations, only the PSP was explicitly committed to the eradication of racial discrimination. The 26 de Julio and Directorio Revolucionario movements, by contrast, were multi-class and multiracial, with anti-racist positions implicit in their more general demands for social justice.

Rejection of the Batista regime in a country afflicted by racism often took a racist tone, even within the ranks of the revolutionary movement. It was commonly heard in revolutionary circles that Batista enjoyed the support of the majority of the black population, which was untrue, although he sometimes used his racial origin demagogically. It was also falsely rumoured that the Ejército Rebelde did not welcome black people.

Race relations in socialist Cuba

The triumph of the Cuban Revolution on 1 January 1959 represented the culmination of the struggle for liberty and justice waged by Cubans for almost a century. For the first time revolutionary forces had achieved victory and found themselves positioned to be architects of their own destiny.

Class privileges were severely curtailed. Opportunities never before available to the poor and disenfranchised proliferated. A social order was established that was infinitely more just than any that had hitherto existed in Cuba. The revolution was blessed with the support of the vast majority of the population, and especially of the black population.

The gigantic task that the inexperienced young revolutionaries faced, and the almost insurmountable obstacles, such as persistent US hostility, seemed to justify and pardon mistakes, excesses and even flagrant injustices. Many black revolutionaries rationalized to themselves that, as the goal of the revolutionary process was so laudable, they would overlook persistent racism, trusting that its elimination would soon receive top priority. They also believed that many racist attitudes would fade away, a conviction that has proved naïve.

In its early years the revolution eliminated the structural bases of institutional racism, attacking the moral and ethical foundations of the ideology and eliminating its more vulgar and offensive social manifestations. In this process, the position of Fidel Castro was exemplary. For the first time the black population gained access to most workplaces and to education, as well as to recreational institutions. The popular economic, social and political measures implemented benefited mainly people of humble origin and thus most blacks and mulattos.

Cubans regained pride and dignity. Their revolution mirrored the international liberation process that swept Africa and Asia at the time. Close relations were established with Third World peoples and governments. However, progress towards elimination of the more subtle and damaging forms of racism at home moved at a snail's pace. The leadership generally lacked understanding of the racial issue. As the revolution took a socialist orientation, the influence of the PSP grew. The communist stand on racism became the official position of the revolution: the socialist commitment and strictly fair nature of the new regime would eventually assure the gradual and spontaneous resolution of the racial question.

It was true that profound transformations in the social and economic structure of the country needed to occur before racism could be successfully uprooted. Threats and attacks emanating from the USA, combined with Cuba's hemispheric isolation, led the revolutionary leadership to prioritize the maintenance of the monolithic unity of the population. It was incorrectly asserted that little space remained for debate, criticism or a diversity of ideas. With national unity considered paramount, it was officially determined that any reference to race relations represented a threat that could divide the population along racial lines. The leadership sincerely believed, and was able to persuade the majority of black Cubans, that there were other problems more urgent and pressing to be solved.

But not everybody accepted the official stance. A small but significant group of young intellectuals and professionals, mainly black, tried to articulate their proposals on the racial issue in the late 1960s. Although most of them supported the revolution, they were 'penetrated' by the state security police and dealt with as members of a counter-revolutionary group. This aborted effort and the harsh measures taken against some of its protagonists became an unforgettable lesson for anyone distressed by the persistence of racism in Cuba.

The racial issue was always viewed in a simplistic manner, as a passing phenomenon, because the majority of Cuban leaders considered themselves, and are considered by others, to be white – although many of them are, in reality, light-skinned mulattos. Perception in this case is more important than fact. These leaders were born and raised in a profoundly racist environment in which white supremacy was taken for granted.

Revealing a misunderstanding of the dynamics of Latin American and Caribbean race relations, resulting from an adherence to US racial categorization, some Afro-American writers have declared that Fidel Castro cannot help but be a champion of black people's rights in Cuba, as he himself is of African descent.[24] Yet, although Castro, like a great many Cubans, may have some African ancestry on his mother's side, his upper-class origin and white appearance define him as unquestionably white in the Cuban context.

Educational policy and official culture are still strongly Eurocentric. African traditions are relegated to the category of folklore, and centuries-old African religious systems are dismissed as cults and sects – despite representing the form of religious belief and expression of perhaps most Cubans, including the elite.[25]

The role of Cuba in African affairs, especially in Angola and Ethiopia, raised Cuban prestige on the continent and among black people in the diaspora but did not produce significant changes in race relations in Cuba. Even black Cubans tend to look paternalistically upon their sisters and brothers from Africa. In the mass media, especially television, the racial imbalance is more marked than in the USA, for example.

In recent years the proportion of black people in high positions has diminished from the levels of the 1960s and 1970s. People who are socially white dominate the political leadership, the state apparatus, mass organizations, the army and the Ministry of the Interior, although there are some black leaders. Black people are underrepresented in the diplomatic corps. Cuba now has many white ambassadors in predominantly black countries, as well as in the rest of the world. Black people are also relatively rare in the rapidly developing tourist sector, in the newly established joint-venture enterprises and in other prominent, prestigious and relatively well-paid occupations.

Massaging of demographic statistics, minimizing the African component of the population, continues. Although more than a million Cubans, mostly white, left the country in the post-revolutionary period, according to official statistics the proportion of whites to non-whites remains constant. The official tendency to regard blacks and their culture as 'minority' persists.

At the Third Congress of the Communist Party in 1986, for the first time after almost two decades, Fidel Castro addressed the evident persistence of racism and the underrepresentation of black Cubans in leading social positions. However, no significant change took place, and the situation has worsened. His and Raúl Castro's speeches on the subject were never carried by the Cuban media, nor ever published.

Thus, in Cuba people who are socially defined as white exercise a disproportionate hegemonic influence on national life, contributing to the perpetuation of racial stereotypes, prejudices and the persistence of racism. Although this pattern is common throughout Latin America, no other nation in the region has undergone a comparable socialist revolution that raised expectations that racism would be confronted and uprooted.

Race relations during the 'special period'

Due primarily to the collapse of state socialism in Eastern Europe and the former Soviet Union, the socio-economic situation of Cuba deteriorated rapidly after 1989-90. Gross domestic product has declined sharply, while imports of petroleum, agrochemicals, animal feed and spare machine parts have 'dwindled to a trickle'.[26] The abrupt curtailing of economic ties with the former USSR and Eastern Europe, the impact of the US blockade and the highly bureaucratic and inefficient strategies left over from earlier decades have led to Cuba's present economic crisis.

This crisis, known euphemistically as the 'special period in peacetime', is the most acute of the post-revolutionary period.

All aspects of daily life – food, clothing, transport, communica-tions, housing, energy supplies and the provision of utilities, medicines, spare parts and raw materials, military supplies and employment – are affected. Cuba's outstanding achievements in health, education, culture and sports are also under threat. With socialism in decline worldwide, and with a change of guard in the Cuban revolutionary leadership seemingly imminent, the country appears increasingly vulnerable.

The leadership is trying to develop a strategy to overcome the crisis, involving the development of tourism, a gradual and selec-tive opening to foreign investment and the introduction of mar-ket reforms. The persistence of racial prejudice has assumed new dimensions. As the majority of tourists visiting Cuba are Euro-pean, and Cubans do not have access to most tourist establish-ments, the security guards at the entrance of these places decide who has and who does not have access. Their assessment is based, more often than not, on external appearance: clothing, behaviour, hairstyle, age and, above all, skin colour. Many tourists from the Caribbean have suffered from this form of racism. The explanation most frequently given is: 'The problem is that you look Cuban.'

Growth of the tourist sector has led to increasing business for private taxis, guest houses and restaurants, sectors in which white Cubans – who have the necessary vehicles and houses in upper-class neighbourhoods – predominate. Meanwhile the acute shortage of everyday essential goods has led the govern-ment to reinforce the strict rationing established more than three decades ago. Products supplied under the ration system at a subsidized low cost for Cubans on low incomes, who are pre-dominantly black and mulatto, are insufficient. On the other hand, the government has opened foreign-currency stores which sell all the commodities that can be found abroad. Cubans who worked abroad or in foreign embassies in Havana were among the first to be paid in foreign currency; more recently many more Cubans have gained access to foreign currency, although the distributon is still racially skewed.

These circumstances have led to a realignment and to the emergence of new classes and sectors, with complex racial and gender implications. Black Cubans are dramatically underrepresented in the activities that provide legal access to foreign currency, and a new class is emerging, composed of the following: mainly young and white (*de buena apariencia*; 'good-looking'), and mostly male, Cubans working for foreign enterprises in Cuba, who drive foreign cars (while Cuban doctors and engineers ride bicycles) and eat and drink in foriegn-currency restaurants and bars; young and generally white service employees in hotels and restaurants, who receive tips in foreign currency; mostly white Cubans of all ages, educational levels and class origins, and of both sexes, who receive foreign currency as family remittances from other countries, mainly the USA; government officials, mostly white and male, who receive some foreign currency via their work; entertainers, performers, artists, artisans, athletes and members of the nation's sports teams, who are paid in foreign currency for work done outside Cuba. The number of black and mulatto Cubans in this last group is relatively high, and the age and sex range is also broad.

Simultaneously, the illegal underground economy has grown to unprecedented size and complexity. Huge quantities of all types of products are bought and sold every day through such channels. In Havana a broad spectrum of the population steals, buys or consumes products from this source. Black Cubans, being predominant in such manual jobs as longshoreman, truck driving, and warehouse, construction and hospital work, handle or transport most products and resources; as a result, the number of black people among the *macetas* and *ninjas*[27] of the underground economy is relatively high.

The combination of a rapidly growing tourist sector and worsening economic difficulties and shortages has resulted in a resurgence of prostitution. Highly qualified professionals, university students and married women and men may be involved (sometimes with a partner's or a family's consent), and the stereotyping of black and mulatto women as sexual objects has intensified. White female prostitutes are subject to less police harassment and social ostracism than their brown and black counterparts.

With regard to housing conditions, black Cubans disproportionately inhabit the most neglected urban districts. Mainly but not exclusively in Havana, the housing crisis has become severe, due both to the shortage of new homes and to the level of deterioration of existing buildings. The mayor of Havana recently stated that 49 per cent of the houses in the capital are in need of urgent repair. In neighbourhoods like the largely black 10 de Octubre, the most crowded in Havana, more than 70 per cent of houses need urgent repair. In such overpopulated areas criminal and antisocial behaviour, including gambling and drug trafficking, is rife and increasing, although still perhaps not of the same magnitude as in several other Latin American capitals.

Cuba has a very large prison population, about 100,000 inmates, and it is estimated that more than 70 per cent of prisoners may be black. This can be explained by the socio-economic conditions of the Afro-Cuban population, but it also results from the level of police repression, especially that experienced by black youths, despite the fact that many police officers are themselves black.

The economic difficulties particularly affect women, especially working women, in a country in which more than 40 per cent of the labour force is female. The revolutionary leaders argued that the employment of women was their path to liberation, but the attitude of men towards sharing domestic responsibilities has not changed as rapidly. Cuba also has one of the highest rates of divorce in Latin America and the Caribbean; divorced women usually assume responsibility for children, while men restrict themselves to mandatory financial contributions and sporadic parental visits.

Before the special period an official report based on a survey of working women in Havana stated that these women spent an average of five hours daily travelling around the city. With the deterioration of transport and infrastructure, this situation has almost certainly worsened. The circumstances of Cuban working women have, in fact, become almost unbearable at times, resulting in a high rate of psychological and psychiatric disorders, as well as suicide.

The Revolution facilitated and encouraged black women to study. Many of them became professionals, intellectuals, artists or public officials. However, racist standards continue to permeate popular culture and personal relationships. Although there are, of course, numerous cases of long-lasting and affectionate interpersonal relationships of all possible inter-ethnic combinations, black women often suffer rejection by both lighter- and dark-skinned men. The higher social status frequently attached to white and light mulatto women leads many black and mulatto men to continue the historical pattern consistent with *blanqueamiento* of selecting whiter women as mates. Among mixed-race couples who have spent time together in both Cuba and the USA, many report more harassment from white people in Cuba than in the USA.

The racial composition of those fleeing Cuba has changed in recent years. In the 1960s the majority of people going into exile were white; among those leaving the island during and since the 1980s, including the 'boat people' of the 1990s, the proportion of black and mulatto Cubans has increased substantially.

Double standards and confused attitudes

After years during which the expression of both foreign and local black culture was repressed, dreadlocked Rastafarians can now be seen on the island. Religions of African origin that were viewed as manifestations of superstition, backwardness and irrationality have been elevated to the status of reflections of Cuba's 'exotic' Caribbean culture. The reason may lie in official recognition that tourists have to be provided with 'local culture' to consume. Foreigners can be initiated into Santería by paying in US dollars, and even Cubans often have to pay in *divisas* (foreign currency) as this becomes the unofficial national currency.

However, the same police and state security officers who in the past harassed black Cubans with Afro hairstyles, and who broke up Afrocentric cultural and social meetings in the 1970s, often trim dreadlocked Rastafarians, as well as other Afro-style youths, and make life hard for those who organize reggae events, *toques de santos* and other African-rooted cultural activities.

Double standards persist and seem to be deeply rooted in today's Cuba. Whereas reference to a person as *blanco, blanquito* or *rubio* rarely has a pejorative connotation, labelling someone *prieto* (dark) or *negro* is more likely to be combined with a disapproving tone of voice and facial expressions associated with negativity. More 'acceptable' means of referring to people of decidedly African appearance involve euphemistically altering their racial status to mulatto, *moreno* (coloured) or *trigueño* (wheat- or olive-skinned).

A consequence of the exodus of whiter and wealthier Cubans is that light-skinned mulatto islanders have been socially promoted to the status of *blanco*. This allows the official racial breakdown of the population to remain more or less constant. Behaviour continues largely to determine racial categorization. The jazz musician Arturo Sandoval was socially *un blanco* when he lived in Cuba; once he left and joined the exile community, white officials commonly referred to him as a *mulato mal agradecido* (ungrateful mulatto). Social status is also a determinant, as is hair type. A mixed-race foreign woman was described as *trigueña, india* and in some cases *blanca* when she first lived in Cuba in the early 1980s; in time, as she associated more with black Cubans, changed her hairstyle from straight to curly and came to be socially viewed as more Cuban, she was increasingly perceived as *mulata santiaguera* (a mulatto from Santiago Province) and advised by sympathetic white people to revert to the straighter hairstyle.

In Cuba there has been relatively little development of a progressive consciousness of racism and of anti-racist strategies, perhaps partly because of the island's relative isolation from the international Black Power and black consciousness movements that swept North America, the English-speaking Caribbean, much of Southern Africa and Western Europe in the 1960s and 1970s. Although Cuban political leaders were in touch with and supported the struggle in the USA, they did not understand the movement's relevance to Cuba. With only limited possibilities for a debate on the racial issue, and linguistic and cultural differences, in Cuba the movement touched only a small group of black intellectuals, professionals and some government officials.

Lack of understanding of the Afro-American movement on the part of the Cuban establishment was a source of conflict with many of the black activists who lived in Cuba during the period, and it helped stifle the development of a theoretical context in which contemporary Cuban racism could be analysed and interpreted.

A light-skinned *mulata* woman in Havana recently complained that she and her black husband were often subjected to racial harassment in public places. However, in the same conversation, she lamented that most black people seemed to no longer 'know their place'; they had got 'too big for their boots now' through access to US dollars, she complained. Despite clearly feeling uncomfortable about what she said, the woman lacked an analytical framework through which to interpret her contrasting perceptions.

Recent white and light-skinned Cuban migrants to Jamaica have displayed similar internal conflicts. While admitting that they were initiates in Afro-Cuban religions, and that they had black relatives in Cuba, they spoke of feeling socially uncomfortable in Jamaica. It was not the language barrier, the different cultural context or problems of drugs and crime. The more assertive posture of black Jamaicans, as contrasted with their Cuban counterparts, disturbed them.

Conclusions and future prospects

The revolution did not create racism in Cuba. Modern-day racism was born with colonialism and slavery, and nurtured by the white Cuban oligarchy and North American imperialism. However, the revolution has the duty and the power to remove the scourge of this historical injustice. By failing to confront, denounce and expose racism, Cuba's rulers, in effect, facilitate its continuation. Yet racism will not disappear as a result of patronizing acts of goodwill on the part of the political leadership alone; its demise also requires the conscious action of black and mulatto Cubans themselves. Our work is a modest attempt to contribute to this process.

Notes

1 Cepero Bonilla, R., *Azúcar y abolición*, Havana, Editorial de Ciencias Sociales, 1971, p. 23.
2 Ibid., p. 125.
3 The Creoles were those Spaniards born on the island. The largest landowners and slave owners in nineteenth-century Cuba were Creole.
4 Ortíz was the leading modern Cuban anthropologist and ethnographer, and his writings are essential to an understanding of the paramount influence of Africa on Cuban culture.
5 Guillén, Cuba's greatest modern poet, shows in his work the centrality of the African roots of Cuban culture.
6 The term *sacarocracia*, coined by M. Moreno Fraginals, refers to the nineteenth-century Cuban sugar plantation oligarchy.
7 See e.g. Moreno Fraginals, M., *El ingenio*, vol. I, Havana, Edición Comisión Nacional de la UNESCO, 1964, p. 67.
8 Cepero Bonilla, op. cit., p. 177.
9 Aguirre, S., 'El cincuentenario de un gran crimen', in *Historia de Cuba 1868-1921: materiales de estudio*, Havana, Editorial Pueblo y Educación, 1986, p. 361.
10 El Pacto del Zanjón was the agreement signed in 1878 between the Cuban Independence Army and the Spanish Army to end the Ten Years' War.
11 Cepero Bonilla, op. cit., p. 259.
12 Hennessy, A., 'Cuba', in M. Falcoff and F.B. Pike (eds), *The Spanish Civil War 1936-39: American Hemispheric Perspectives*, Lincoln, NE, and London, University of Nebraska Press, 1982, p. 105.
13 See Ruíz, R.E., *Cuba: génesis de una revolución*, Barcelona and Madrid, Editorial Noguer, 1977, p. 39.
14 Ibid., p. 61.
15 Quoted in Le Riverend, J., *La república*, Havana, Editorial de Ciencias Sociales, 1975, p. 218.
16 Hennessy, op. cit., p. 105.
17 See Ruíz, op. cit., p. 61.
18 A *mestizo* was the son of a white person and a member of the indigenous population.
19 See Serviat, P., 'The black problem in Cuba and its definitive solution', in P. Pérez Sarduy and J. Stubbs (eds), *AfroCuba: An Anthology of Cuban Writing on Race, Politics and Culture*, London, Latin America Bureau, 1993, pp. 77-8.
20 See Ruíz, op. cit., p. 172.
21 Batista was made colonel and army chief under the revolutionary government of 1933. Betraying the revolution, and with US support, he controlled the government from 1935 to 1940, ruling as President in 1940-4. In 1952 he overthrew Prío's government and seized and kept the presidency until defeated by the Revolution of 1959.
22 Ronaina, T.F., *El negro en Cuba 1902-1958*, Havana, Editorial de Ciencias Sociales, 1961, p. 92.

23 See e.g. Roca Calderio, B., *Los fundamentos del socialismo en Cuba,* Havana, Ediciones Populares, 1961, p. 92.
24 Brock, L. and Cunningham, O., 'Race and the Cuban revolution: a critique of Carlos Moore's *Castro, the Blacks and Africa', Cuban Studies Review*, vol. 21, 1991.
25 McGarrity, G., 'Race, culture and social change in contemporary Cuba', in S. Halebsky and J. Kirk (eds), *Cuba in Transition*, New York, Westview Press, 1992, p. 199.
26 Deere, C.D., Pérez, N. and González, E., 'The view from below: Cuban agriculture, "the special period in peacetime"', *Journal of Peasant Studies*, vol. 21, no. 2, 1994, p. 195.
27 *Maceta* refers to a person who accumulates a large amount of money, usually illegally; a *ninja* is somebody who steals from a government enterprise with the complicity of managers or workers.

Select bibliography

Alquelles, L., 'Stratification in the Miami Cuban enclave', *Contemporary Marxism*, 1982.

Booth, D., 'Cuba, color and the revolution', *Science and Society*, vol. XI, no. 2, 1976, pp. 129-72.

Carbonnel, W., *Como surgió la cultura nacional*, Havana, Biblioteca Nacional, 1961.

Cepero Bonilla, R., *Azúcar y abolición*, Havana, Editorial de Ciencas Sociales, 1971.

Deere, C.D., Pérez, N. and González, E., 'The view from below: Cuban agriculture, "the special period in peacetime"', *Journal of Peasant Studies*, vol. 21, no. 2, 1994.

Dzidzienyo, A. and Casal, L., *The Position of Blacks in Brazilian and Cuban Society*, London, Minority Rights Group, 1971, 1979.

Fermoselle y López, R., *Política y color en Cuba: la guerrita de 1912*, Montevideo, Ediciones Géminis, 1974.

Fernández Robaina, T., *El negro en Cuba 1902-1958*, Havana, Editorial de Ciencias Sociales, 1990.

Fernández Robaina, T., *Hablen paleros y santeros*, Havana, Editorial de Ciencias Sociales, 1994.

Fox, G.E., 'Race and class in contemporary Cuba', in I.L. Horowitz (ed.), *Cuban Communism*, New Brunswick, NJ, Transaction Books, 1977.

López Segrera, F., *Cuba: capitalismo dependiente y subdesarollo (1510-1959)*, Havana, Editorial de Ciencias Sociales, 1981.

McGarrity, G., 'Race, culture and social change in contemporary Cuba', in S. Halebsky and J. Kirk (eds), *Cuba in Transition*, New York, Westview Press, 1992.

Martínez-Alier, V., *Marriage, Class and Color in Nineteenth-Century Cuba*, New York, Cambridge University Press, 1974.

Moore, C., *Castro, the Blacks and Africa*, Los Angeles, Center for Afro-American Studies, University of California, 1989.

Moreno Fraginals, M. (ed.), *Africa in Latin America*, New York, UNESCO, 1977.

Murphy, J.M., *Santería: An African Religion in America*, Boston, MA, Beacon Press, 1988.

Ortíz, F., *Cuban Counterpoint: Tobacco and Sugar*, New York, Knopf, 1947.

Pérez Sarduy, P. and Stubbs, J. (eds), *AfroCuba: An Anthology of Cuban Writing on Race, Politics and Culture*, London, Latin America Bureau, and Stanmore, Australia, Ocean Press, 1993.

Ruíz, R.E., *Cuba: génesis de una revolución*, Barcelona and Madrid, Editorial Noguer, 1977.

Saco, J.A., *Contra la anexión*, vol. I, Havana, 1938.

Stubbs, J., *Cuba: The Test of Time*, London, Latin America Bureau, 1989.

Wagner, E., 'The Cuba identity in the Americas: some parallel values in the exile and revolutionary societies', *Caribbean Review*, Fall 1981.

5

THE DOMINICAN REPUBLIC

Silvio Torres-Saillant

Dominicans occupy the eastern two-thirds of Hispaniola, the second largest Caribbean island, located between Cuba and Puerto Rico. The territory was conquered and colonized by Spain from 1492 onwards, and from the first decades of the seventeenth century Spain had to vie with France for its control. By the second half of the seventeenth century the lands of western Hispaniola were occupied by French settlements. The Peace of Ryswick signed in 1697 between the two colonial powers was tantamount to a formal partition of the island into two distinct colonial spaces, Spanish Santo Domingo in the east and French Saint Domingue in the west. In time, two distinct national communities would evolve from the local populations that lived in the two contiguous territories: the Dominican Republic and the Republic of Haiti. A successful slave insurrection against the French in Saint Domingue resulted in the founding in 1804 of the Republic of Haiti, the first black republic in the Americas. In Santo Domingo the fervour for independence manifested itself against the French in 1808 and against the Spanish in 1821. But only in 1844, after twenty-two years of living under direct Haitian rule, did the Creole elites show enough political maturity to create a separate country with its own national sovereignty.

The fact that Dominican independence, the formal emergence of Dominicans as a people, occurred as a separation from the black republic of Haiti has complicated the racial identity of Afro-Dominicans, inducing in the population a reticence

109

towards their own blackness. In terms of their physical presence in the country, people of African descent abound in the Dominican Republic. A demographic assessment taking account of racial distinctions would show blacks and mulattos as making up as much as 90 per cent of the country's nearly 8 million inhabitants. Yet Afro-Dominicans have failed to assert their ethnicity in advancing a collective civil and human rights agenda. At the same time, the country's African-descended majority has always stood out in its fight for equality, as one can gather from the many black and mulatto Dominicans who have become revered household names. Negrophobia and negrophilia, in other words, have historically coexisted in Dominican society. This chapter seeks to show that paradoxical reality and discuss the strenuous conditions it has created for the Afro-Dominican population.

Early historical background

Dominican society is the cradle of blackness in the Americas. Santo Domingo served as the port of entry to the first African slaves who arrived in Spain's newly conquered territories following the transatlantic voyage of Christopher Columbus in 1492. Nine years into the conquest of what thenceforward became known as the New World, King Ferdinand and Queen Isabella appointed Fray Nicolás de Ovando as the new Governor of Santo Domingo, authorizing him to bring 'black slaves' to their colony.[1] Ovando's fleet arrived in Hispaniola in July 1502, marking the start of the black experience in the western hemisphere.

The number of black people in Hispaniola grew dramatically as the Spanish settlers' need for slave labour increased with the rapid decimation of the aboriginal Taino population. A census of the colony taken in 1508 showed that a mere 60,000 Tainos remained from the original 400,000 found by the Spaniards in 1492.[2] The high mortality rate of the native workforce and the need for able bodies in the gold-mines caused the Crown to overrule an earlier decree that had permitted the importation only of those black slaves who, born to a Spanish master, had received a Christian upbringing. Colonists in 1511 could secure their labourers through the slave traffic directly from Africa.[3] By

1519 the Taino population had shrunk to 3,000.[4] The gold-mines had exhausted their deposits. Whites had begun to emigrate massively, a trend that would become accentuated with the mineral riches subsequently discovered in the mainland colonies of Mexico (1522) and Peru (1531). And sugar-cane cultivation had become part of the colonial reality, brought by Columbus to Hispaniola during his second voyage in 1493. Industrial sugar-cane processing went through successive periods of trial and error until in 1516 an entrepreneur named Gonzalo de Vellosa turned it into a lucrative enterprise.

The success of Vellosa's experiment led to the rise of the sugar industry as the pre-eminent economic institution of the island. By 1522 plantations had spread throughout the colony with the participation of the most notable members of the ruling class.[5] Since the plantation drew its labour force almost exclusively from African slaves, the black presence in the colony grew enormously, while the emigration of whites continued unabated. The development of the plantation economy in sixteenth-century Santo Domingo may provide the clue to the historical origins of anti-black racism in the modern world. In an insightfully lucid chapter, Pedro Mir has convincingly argued that the triumph of Vellosa's industrial technology marks a turning point in the colonial transaction. It worsened the plight of the black population by begetting a conceptual association between slavery and race: 'From then on slavery acquires new traits and shows the characteristics of a modern institution. It becomes a coloured institution.'[6] A subsequent study of the colonial origins of racial prejudice supports Mir's argument in claiming that, prior to the rise of the sugar industry in Santo Domingo, 'a racial prejudice against the black slave did not exist in the Americas with any meaningful centrality as an argument of the ideology of slavery'.[7] In equating sugar with blackness, Vellosa's success inaugurated the racialization of slavery.

Naturally, the importing of African slaves to Santo Domingo gained momentum, with the result that from the second decade of the colonization of the island the black population invariably outnumbered the white, often by a very wide margin. In 1552 alone the colonists of Santo Domingo made 3,000 requests for licences to import Africans, and many of them smuggled in slaves unknown to the Spanish authorities.[8] The population differential between 1,157 white settlers and 9,648 blacks assessed by a census in 1606 would widen in the decades that followed.[9] The numerical disparity would become greater as the plantation lost the vitality of its beginnings, and the Spanish settlers continued emigrating.

With the downfall of the plantation economy in Santo Domingo, the colony went through a long period of impoverishment. Slavery lost its economic base, and many slave labourers gained their freedom. Blacks did not have the option of leaving, so they stayed and multiplied: 'Either slave or free, [they] continued to grow in number, and ... spread throughout the colony.'[10] Following the depopulation of western Hispaniola in 1605-6 by Governor Antonio de Osorio, the inhabitants of the colony became concentrated in the east, and the vacant territories of the island would eventually become the French colony of Saint Domingue, where blacks would also outnumber whites. In the Spanish colony of Santo Domingo the African presence in the ethnic composition of the population may be gathered from a report by Archbishop Alvarez de Abreu, who in 1739 spoke of 12,259 inhabitants, with a majority of free blacks.[11]

Black interaction: Hispaniola east and west

Dominican blacks and mulattos owe their predominance to successive waves of importation of slaves to the island of Hispaniola and to their biological multiplication through intra- and interracial reproduction. Colonial masters took care to import an adequate number of women among their slaves so as to ensure the reproduction of their coerced labourers. There was also considerable mating between white men and the black women they owned. In addition, various events in the island's history contributed to increasing the black presence. The rise of the French colony of Saint Domingue on western Hispaniola, whose prosperous plantation economy made intensive use of African slaves, led to further integration of blacks into the population of Santo Domingo, since slaves often crossed the border to the eastern side to escape the brutality of their condition. Runaway slaves from the west came to eastern Hispaniola in 1678 and founded San Lorenzo de los Minas, a neighbourhood that still thrives today in the midst of the Dominican capital.[12]

During the period known as the Haitian Revolution, when a black insurrection overturned the French colonial system on the island, many Saint Domingue slaves sought their freedom by fighting as soldiers of the Spanish monarch. Among the many who crossed to the Spanish-speaking colony, Pablo Ali became most prominent, achieving great military distinction in Santo Domingo and appearing by 1820 as colonel of the prestigious Batallón de Morenos. When in November 1821 a Creole elite, headed by José Núñez de Cáceres, proclaimed their juridical separation from Spain – the short-lived enterprise that historians call 'the ephemeral independence' – Ali served as their chief military commander. This illustrates the importance of the ex-slave in the armed forces of Santo Domingo at the time.[13]

The black population of Santo Domingo received another numerical boost in January 1801 when the former Saint Domingue slave Toussaint Louverture led his troops across the border to take possession of the Spanish territory for republican France. By unifying the island under French rule, Toussaint gave physical form to the terms of the 1795 Treaty of Basel, whereby Spain had ceded to France the control of its Hispaniola colony. While in Santo Domingo, Toussaint abolished slavery, eliminated racial privileges and restructured the colonial economy, producing a period of momentary prosperity. Toussaint's efficiency, leadership and sense of equity as 'general and governor' earned him the 'love and respect' of the people of Santo Domingo, and 'the blessing of Dominicans', as the authors Antonio Del Monte y Tejada and Alejandro Llenas affirmed in the nineteenth century.[14] Toussaint's government, however, did not last. With the fall of the republic and the rise of Napoleon in France, an interest developed in regaining colonial control over Saint Domingue. In January 1802, 21,000 French soldiers led by Napoleon's brother-in-law General Leclerc invaded the island. Toussaint's army had to abandon the eastern lands to strengthen its defences in the west, which allowed the French army to occupy Spanish-speaking Santo Domingo and immediately restore slavery. Though we may not know how many of Toussaint's black troops, if any, remained in eastern Hispaniola when the insurgents returned to Saint Domingue, they did leave behind a constructive example of social justice which would have repercussions in local movements against racial oppression.

Santo Domingo remained under French rule until the War of Reconquest, which ended in 1809. A faction of the landowning Creole oligarchy that had grown dissatisfied with some of the French government's economic measures rose up with support from the Spanish governor of Puerto Rico. Led by Juan Sánchez Ramírez, the Creoles expelled the French and turned the sovereignty of the land over to Spain. That their political choice did not meet with widespread approval is suggested by the conspiracies that ensued, one of which involved people of African descent. In August 1812, following the death of Sánchez Ramírez, blacks and mulattos, slave and free, rose against Santo Domingo's governing structure, which was headed by Núñez de Cáceres. They planned to overthrow the ruling class and to bring the land under Haitian jurisdiction.[15] But the authorities discovered the plot, crushed the insurrection and killed the leaders. To set an example for the rest of the population, they publicly dragged the bodies of the conspirators through the streets and fried their remains in coal-tar.[16]

But a faction that favoured the unification of Santo Domingo with Haiti continued to exist among the predominantly black and mulatto population. The leaders of a 'pro-Haitian party', as Moya Pons calls it, actually declared in 1821 their independence from Spanish rule in the cities of Dajabón and Montecristi and sought, through communication with the Cap Haitien authorities, 'to place themselves under the protection of Haitian laws', requesting 'munition and weapons to defend themselves'.[17] Fifteen days later, the news of that event triggered the proclamation of independence by Núñez de Cáceres and led his group to seek a federative association of Santo Domingo with Simón Bolívar's nascent Gran Colombia.[18] Haitian President Jean Pierre Boyer, in turn, claimed that unification alone would safeguard the sovereignty of the whole island from European powers. Thus in February 1822, only several weeks after the installation of Núñez de Cáceres's government, Boyer and 12,000 Haitian soldiers took over Santo Domingo.

The unification of Santo Domingo with Haiti, which lasted twenty-two years, marked another watershed for the black and mulatto population of the land. Despite the claim by an inveterate anti-Haitian and conservative elite that Dominicans never mingled with Haitians, unification brought about an intensified rapport between the two populations. As soon as Boyer took power, he abolished slavery, which the Creole government of Núñez de Cáceres had failed to do.[19] This measure, while hurting the interests of the Creole ruling class, must have earned him the sympathy of the African-descended majority. The occupation, at any rate, intensified the daily interaction of Haitians and Dominicans, adding to the vibrant commercial and cultural contact that had for long taken place along the border areas.

African-Americans, West Indians and Haitians

During the Haitian period in Santo Domingo, another event further augmented the black population. Between 1824 and 1825 over 6,000 free African-Americans from the United States came to settle in lands of their own in Hispaniola upon the invitation of President Boyer. A good many of them settled in Samaná and Puerto Plata, where they became 'perfectly adapted'.[20] A study of those who settled in Puerto Plata, roughly 2,000 according to the author, indicates that African-Americans easily accommodated themselves to the way of life of the Creole population in both the rural and the urban sectors of that city, where they also contributed significantly to the quality of life.[21]

During the republican period, which began with independence in 1844, two other black contingents became part of the Dominican population, both connected with the growth of the modern sugar industry that started in the 1870s.[22] The first resulted from the decision of the Dominican government, pressured by the demands of expanding foreign capital, to authorize the importation of labour from the 'Africanized' area of the

British West Indies. Efforts to coerce native Dominican workers into accepting the menial salaries and the miserable living conditions of the sugar mills had proved unsuccessful. In 1884, for instance, Dominican labourers in the sugar mills went on strike, 'refusing to work for the wages offered', arguing that with existing salaries they could not even satisfy 'basic necessities'.[23]

Despite occasional expressions of disapproval by the negrophobic elite, the needs of capital prevailed, and black West Indian labour grew numerically. From a first 500 Anglophone Caribbean labourers registered in 1884, we find by 1918 as many as 7,000 in San Pedro de Macorís alone.[24] Immigrants from the Leeward Islands made up approximately 20 per cent of the population of Montecristi by 1914 and roughly 10 per cent of the inhabitants of Puerto Plata by 1917.[25] West Indian workers continued to be brought in until the early 1940s. Their descendants now form part of Dominican society, even if their strong cultural traditions and social norms still make them recognizable as a distinct ethnic subgroup, which other Dominicans refer to as the *cocolo* community.[26]

The US occupation of the Dominican Republic in 1916 brought about the other important addition to the black population. The North Americans preferred Haiti, which they had invaded the year before, as the primary source of labour for the sugar plantations. Thus, the first major contingent of Haitian workers arrived in 1916. In keeping with the labour demands of the sugar industry, by 1920 a national census recorded 28,258 Haitian residents in the country, a figure which would rise to 52,657 by 1935.[27] In 1980 official sources gave the figure of 113,150 Haitian workers active in the country's agricultural production. Scholars agree, however, that due to an existing trend of clandestine or illegal traffic of Haitian *braceros* (sugar-cane cutters), as well as to the informal migration patterns of individual workers, the official sources cannot guarantee an accurate count of their presence in the Dominican Republic.[28]

Today, 'The job of cutting the sugar cane is performed almost exclusively by the Haitian *braceros*',[29] which means, in essence, that one of the primary sources of the Dominican Republic's national wealth rests on the shoulders of Haitian workers. Nor do they toil in particularly enviable conditions. Once recruited into the *bateyes* (sugar plantations), by means of an arrangement involving the Dominican and Haitian governments as well as private capitalists and their watchdogs, the workers endure a process of dehumanization for wages that are so low as to make it difficult even to recover the energy they spend in the fields. Formal regulations deprive them of freedom of movement, and some voices have denounced their oppressive situation as 'a tale of modern slavery'.[30] Maurice Lemoine's discussion of the ignominy endured by Haitian workers in the *bateyes* concludes that 'They are officially kept in servitude, precisely the servitude of slavery.'[31]

Irrespective of whether the penury endured by the Haitian *braceros* in the Dominican sugar industry accurately fits the technical definition of slavery, enough data exist to confirm their unspeakable plight. In 1983 Moya Pons led a team of researchers, under contract to the State Sugar Board, to study the state-owned and -operated plantations, producing a voluminous report that details diverse aspects of the *batey* experience. Among its multiple findings, the study showed the physical conditions of the barracks where the workers live: 64.9 per cent of the housing units surveyed (4,099) lacked electricity and any other form of illumination; 70.6 per cent (4,464) had no running water; and of 5,515 housing units examined, 87.3 per cent made no provision for the workers to urinate or defecate.[32] It is therefore unsurprising that native Dominican workers should not regard sugar cutting as a viable area of employment. Contrary to the insinuations of the preachers of anti-Haitian hatred, most Dominicans do not blame Haitian immigrants for displacing them from the workforce. Rather, they seem to recognize Haitians as the ones who bear the brunt of a most dehumanizing industry. In the words of a Dominican worker interviewed by the research team cited above, Haitian immigrants 'take the jobs that nobody wants'.[33] Equally, an earlier study had suggested that Haitians maintained a generally favourable view of the Dominican people.[34]

Legacy of resistance

Dominican history bears witness to the courage, perseverance, creativity and commitment to social justice that characterized people of African descent from the dawn of the colonial transaction. In their quest for equality and freedom they often had to confront the repressive measures of an entrenched colonial elite. In 1784 the Spanish colonial authorities in the metropolis, wishing to have their counterpart of the French *Code Noir*, compiled the *Código Negro Carolino* to regulate the 'economic, political, and moral government of blacks', based on the recommendations of a select number of landholders, colonial functionaries and clerical authorities from Santo Domingo.[35] The *Código*, whose laws never got to the point of formal implementation, shows the depravity of a mind-set that can conceive other humans as cattle or mere fuel for industry. But its nervous pages of endless precautions and prohibitions speak eloquently of the fear that the slave and free black population aroused among the minority colonial elite. In an introductory paragraph, the *Código* ascribes to 'slaves and free blacks' the primary responsibility for reducing Santo Domingo to 'poverty and the most deplorable situation' through their 'shameful idleness, independence, and pride, as well as the continuous thefts and disturbances they commit in the woods and farms'.[36] Thus, the text argues, they must be governed strictly. A decree in the *Código* makes it unlawful, on severe physical punishment, for anyone to dispense 'arsenic, corrosive sublimate, or realgar' as well as 'medicines' of any kind to blacks 'of any class or condition' without a clearance from the proper authorities.

The fear and resulting loathing of blacks contained in the pages of the *Código* attest to the oppressed community's age-old struggle to dismantle the unjust ruling structure of the colonial system. The above quotes would seem to indicate that the oppressed masses sought to subvert the established order both by passive forms of dissent, as the reference to their 'shameful idleness' would insinuate, and by wiley stratagems such as plotting to poison their colonial masters, as the prohibitions in the *Código* would suggest. Lurking behind the fears also was a long history of open rebellion which had started in December 1522, with the first black slave insurrection registered in the hemisphere. It happened near the river La Isabela in the city of Santo Domingo during the administration of Diego Colón, the Admiral's brother. Dominican historiography did not record the names of the leaders of that movement. The leadership of many other uprisings against the colonial regime also remains anonymous; among those whose named commanders have come down to us, the list of heads includes: Diego de Guzmán (1545) in Baoruco, Juan Vaquero (1546) in Santo Domingo, Sebastián Lemba (1548) in Higüey, Diego de Ocampo (1555) in La Vega and the mid-sixteenth-century rebel leader Juan Criollo, whose revolt in Higüey 'persisted for more than fifteen years'.[37]

Clearly slaves in Santo Domingo always imagined the possibility of leading a life outside the oppressive colonial structure and sought to do something about it. Individual and small bands of slaves ran away from the jurisdiction of their masters as soon as they set foot on the island. A letter by Governor Ovando in 1503, only one year after he had brought the very first contingent of blacks to the island, already whines about runaways.[38] Subsequently, we witness the emergence and proliferation of maroon settlements, called by historians *manieles* or *palenques*. These were tantamount to alternative societies of runaway slaves, which existed outside the boundaries of the colonial system in various parts of the island. Santo Domingo maroons settled most frequently in Ocoa, Neiba, Baoruco, Cotui, Buenaventura, Samaná, Higüey, Azua and San Juan de la Maguana. A recent archaeological exploration adds the province of Altagracia as a setting, since there in the early eighteenth century the maroons of the formerly unknown José Leta *maniel* may have operated.[39] The best-known maroon society in Santo Domingo, whose population was crushed by the troops of a Captain Villalobos in 1666, had its camp in the *maniel* of San José de Ocoa. And the one historically closest to us existed in Neiba, a section of present Barahona, a *maniel* whose maroon leaders in 1783 negotiated an agreement with the Spanish authorities and consented to become integrated into the larger colonial society.[40]

Blackness and nineteenth-century politics

Consistent with their large presence, Dominicans of African descent have exhibited active and decisive political participation in their country. From a survey of selected historical moments one could get a sense of their outstanding role and the high regard they have enjoyed in the eyes of their people. One could begin with the mulatto Francisco del Rosario Sánchez (1817-61), one of the founding fathers of the nation. Dominicans honour him for championing the birth of the republic in 1844. The black general José Joaquín Puello (1808-47) also played a decisive role in bringing the dream of Dominican independence to fruition. Other blacks and mulattos, who rebelled in Monte Grande, in the vicinity of Santo Domingo, in defiance of the original separatist movement, ensured the nation's formally espousing democratic ideals. In February 1844, when the Santo Domingo elites declared independence from Haiti, a fearful uncertainty emerged in the black and mulatto population as to the effect of the impending political change on their well-being, particularly in light of the pro-Spanish leanings of some important supporters of the separation. Indeed, a projected national anthem written by the poet Félix María Del Monte (1819-99) emboldened the patriots with the exhortation 'Rise up in arms, o Spaniards!'[41]

An association of the nascent republic with imperial Spain, which still enslaved blacks in the nearby colonies of Cuba and Puerto Rico, would have imperilled the freedom of many Dominicans. As a result, within hours of the independence proclamation, an uprising of Afro-Dominicans in Monte Grande challenged the new government. The rebellion forced the leaders of the incipient nation to reaffirm the abolition of slavery 'for ever in the Dominican Republic' and to integrate the black Santiago Basora, leader of the Monte Grande uprising, in the country's governing structure.[42] Among various gestures to allay the concerns of blacks and mulattos, the fledgling Dominican government went on to publish on 17 July 1844 a law that, apart from stressing the finality of abolition, outlawed slave traffic of any kind as a capital crime and decreed that slaves from any provenance would instantly gain their freedom upon 'setting a foot on the territory of the Dominican Republic'.[43]

Less than twenty years after independence, an unpatriotic elite negotiated the annexation of the Dominican Republic to imperial Spain. An armed rebellion to recover lost sovereignty promptly ensued, and the black General Gregorio Luperón outshined all other patriots as the supreme guardian of national liberation. The participation of people of African descent in that chapter of Dominican history, which is known as the War of Restoration, became significant both in the high command and in the rank and file. Spain had sent its white troops to secure its newly regained Dominican colony, and the colour of the invaders contrasted sharply with that of the Creoles, giving the war racial overtones. With the 'massive integration' of the peasant population, 'which consisted mainly of blacks and mulattos', the armed struggle 'soon became a racial war' against a white supremacist power that preserved slavery.[44] The military clash became 'a truly popular war, as it directed all the energies of the nation toward achieving independence and restoring sovereignty'.[45] General José de la Gándara, the military commander of the invading Spanish forces, has left his impression of how the racial attitudes of his soldiers, who were 'used to viewing the black race and people of mixed ancestry as inferior people', deepened the opposition of Dominicans to the annexation and brought its downfall.[46]

Dominicans commemorate the War of Restoration, fought against white Spaniards, with as much patriotic fervour as they do the War of Independence, fought against black Haitians. And the black General Luperón, who helped to restore the nation's sovereignty, inspires as much respect and admiration as the white Creole Juan Pablo Duarte, the ideological founder of the republic. Another salient figure of the Restoration War, the black Ulises Heureaux, whose heroic exploits against the imperial Spanish army gained him national prestige, came to dominate the country politically for over fifteen years. After achieving distinction in various high government positions following the war effort, he ran for President of the country and was elected for the first time in 1882. He became head of state through electoral

channels twice more, and he then extended his power by dicta-
torial imposition until 1899, when he met a violent death at the
hands of opposition leaders.

Blackness and twentieth-century social movements

Many of the country's most memorable instances of patriotic
resistance and struggle against tyranny in the present century
feature the leadership and courageous actions of Afro-Dominicans. Among the nationalists who resisted the occupation of the
country by US troops in 1916, Ramón Natera, a black man,
launched such an effective campaign of guerrilla warfare that the
US forces thought it best to negotiate an armistice with him.[47]
Another black named Gregorio Urbano Gilbert (1898-1970)
became so incensed by the passive acceptance he witnessed in
the 'nationalist' youth of San Pedro de Macorís as the army of
occupation disembarked that he got himself a 32-calibre revolver
and went to the seaport by himself to fight the invaders. The
skirmish left one US officer dead, and Gilbert fled to the mountains to join the forces of a guerrilla leader named Vicente Evan-
gelista. Caught by the marines and sentenced to death, he
somehow obtained his release in 1922, after which he left the
country and went on to join the insurgent movement led by
Augusto César Sandino in Nicaragua.

During the ruthless dictatorship of the mulatto Rafael
Leónidas Trujillo, a trainee of the US army, few attempts at
open opposition achieved as much distinction as the one led
by Mauricio Báez, a black labour organizer from the eastern
part of the country. From an outstanding involvement in a
workers' strike that took place in La Romana in 1942, his visibility grew nationally. He played a leadership role in coordinating a 1946 strike against many eastern sugar plantations.
President of the Federación Provincial de Trabajadores de San
Pedro de Macorís, he suffered persecution by the dictator's
police, having to seek asylum in the Mexican Embassy. Neither
exile nor the terrorism of the regime dissuaded Báez from his
activism, which, unlike the anti-Trujillo campaign of a middle-
class intelligentsia that attained recognition in exile, did have

an impressive grass-roots following. In 1950, while in Cuba, assassins probably hired by the regime put an end to his life. But many of the rights that Dominican workers enjoy today are owed to the struggle of people like Báez and the mostly African-descended workers who joined him. Paradoxically, since the Dominican Republic is a country with a predominantly black and mulatto population, one must say that Trujillo's soldiers, whose job was to combat the workers, were also an overwhelmingly African-descended army.

A different sort of dissidence, also involving sectors of the black and mulatto population, dates back to the beginning of the century: the rise in San Juan de la Maguana of Liborio Mateo, a black man who presided over a modern maroon community that for more than a decade enjoyed political, economic, religious and military autonomy from the rest of the country. Efforts of the Dominican government, both peaceful and violent, prompted by the Catholic Church, to bring Liborio's people under the political and moral jurisdiction of the state, proved unsuccessful. Their detachment from official Dominican society and adoption of an alternative social order was, as one scholar has put it, a 'reaction to oppressive social structures and a ruling system that kept the lower classes in a state of abject poverty'.[48] Only with the military might of the invading US forces did the insurgent community come to an end, after years of persecution and violent confrontations, in June 1922 after a long battle that left a heavy toll of casualties on both sides.

The emergence in more recent times of a movement that 'aimed to revive the cult of Liborio Mateo' in Palma Sola, a part of San Juan de la Maguana, suggests that the legacy of those early twentieth-century maroons lives on.[49] There too a community developed, predominantly Afro-Dominican, which challenged the ideology of the state in economic, political and religious matters. Thousands of peasants, under the direction of leaders known as 'Los Mellizos' (the Twins), threatened the 'Christian values' of Dominican society, as the official daily *El Caribe* charged on 8 December 1962. Subsequently, the conservative newspaper denounced the deleterious effect of the Palma Sola community on 'commercial activity' in the country's south-east and sounded the alarm that the congregation might have 'political leanings' which Los Mellizos could manipulate to favour distinct political parties.[50] Urged by the social sectors that spoke through the pages of *El Caribe*, the government ordered the armed forces to march against the Palma Sola peasants on 28 December 1962. The soldiers there perpetrated, as an author has put it, 'one of the most horrendous massacres the country has seen'.[51] Once again, Afro-Dominican soldiers violently repressed their dark-skinned compatriots.

The slaughter of the Palma Sola community took place during the provisional government that ruled the Dominican Republic following the death of Trujillo and the escape of Joaquín Balaguer, the former dictator's 'front-man' President. Arguably, many of the progressive measures that Juan Bosch tried to implement when he became President of the country in 1963 may have come from his awareness of the people's desperate yearning for fairer political options as made evident in the civil disobedience of the Palma Sola peasants. In any event, Bosch did not last as President, being overthrown by the military only seven months after his swearing-in ceremony. Years of social upheaval ensued: protest movements of various kinds, an unsuccessful guerrilla campaign, a civil war in 1965 and another US military invasion to support the conservative sectors. In 1966, supported by the national oligarchy and the United States, Balaguer, a member of the old Trujillo guard, became President of the Republic, remaining uninterruptedly so until 1978. After a hiatus of eight years Balaguer returned to the presidency in 1986 and was still the head of state in 1995.

Like his political mentor Trujillo, Balaguer had to confront the opposition of remarkable Afro-Dominicans such as Maximiliano Gómez (1943-71), the young leader of the left-wing party Movimiento Popular Dominicano. Joining the underground movement in 1962, Gómez soon established his leadership as a foremost ideologue and strategist. Holding the highest rank in his organization, he upheld the view that the revolutionary movement in the country needed to emancipate itself from subservience to the European classics of socialist thought and pay closer attention to the discrete historical experience and socio-cultural peculiarity of the Dominican people. Incarcerated by Balaguer's police in 1970, Gómez subsequently went into exile as a result of an exchange of prisoners orchestrated by an anti-Balaguer 'commando' that held a US officer hostage. He died mysteriously in Brussels the following year.[52]

Another important contribution to the cause of social justice during the Balaguer regime came from Florinda Muñoz Soriano, an older black woman who is known in Dominican popular song and folklore as Mamá Tingó. In 1974, at the age of 60, she championed the cause of peasants in Hato Viejo, Yamasá. They fought against the efforts of a powerful landholder to drive them out of the lands where they had worked and lived for half a century. Under her leadership, the peasants resisted intimidation, coercion and violence, prevailing upon the municipal authorities to intervene as mediator in the litigation. On 1 November 1974, on the way from court, one of the landowner's foremen shot her dead. The social indignation caused by the brutal murder of Mamá Tingó led the Balaguer government, if not to side with peasants against the landowning class, at least to declare the disputed lands state property with the declared purpose of employing them in the implementation of land reforms.

Contributions to culture

People of African descent have excelled in the realm of cultural activity in Dominican society. The country's history registers the achievements of many black and mulatto thinkers and artists. The Dominican feminist movement, for instance, owes a great deal to three black women: Petronila Gómez, Altagracia Domínguez and Evangelina Rodríguez, who in the 1920s promoted a revolutionary creed of social, economic and political equity between males and females.[53] Rodríguez (1879-1947) distinguished herself by being the first Dominican woman physician, in defiance of the male-centred academic establishment. Two black male physicians, Francisco Eugenio Moscoso Puello and Heriberto Pieter Bennet, left a remarkable legacy as practitioners and scholars of medical science during the first half of the present century.

In the field of literature, Dominican artistic writing began to exhibit a distinct voice with the compositions of the mulatto Meso Mónica in the eighteenth century. Another mulatto, the Jesuit priest Antonio Sánchez Valverde (1734-90), wrote the seminal *La idea del valor de la Isla Española* (1785), the most important work of erudition to appear in eighteenth-century Santo Domingo. In the latter half of the nineteenth century the mulatto poet Gastón Fernando Deligne (1861-1913) achieved great literary prestige. Scholars normally group him with Salomé Ureña (1850-97) and José Joaquín Pérez (1845-1900) among the founders of modern Dominican poetry, and the scholar Pedro Henríquez Ureña (1884-1946) lavished more passionate praise on him than on any other Dominican literary figure.[54]

Black and mulatto Dominicans have been no less visible in twentieth-century literature. The black author Ramón Marrero Aristy (1913-59), wrote the novel *Over*, the most frequently read and highly regarded Dominican work of fiction from the first half of the century. Aída Cartagena Portalatín (1918-94), a mulatto woman poet, is the most revered twentieth-century Dominican female writer. Cartagena Portalatín, unlike many of the writers of her generation, openly asserted 'her own racially mixed background'.[55] In evoking the legacy of the sixteenth-century slaves Teodora and Micaela Ginés, who as young women managed to travel from Santo Domingo across to the neighbouring island of Cuba and there contributed their talent to the development of popular music, Cartagena Portalatín calls them 'Dominican black women', presenting the exploration of their lives as a way to 'look for our roots'.[56]

The African presence in Dominican culture transcends, of course, the creative contributions of individuals. Most elements of African cultural survival in Dominican society belong to a popular heritage whose traces even appear in the language Dominicans speak. The 'ethnolinguistic modalities' that characterize the people's handling of Spanish, showing peculiarities in the 'lexical structure' as well as in the 'phonetics, morphosyntax, and intonation' suggest retentions from the languages of African slaves in colonial times.[57] The original culture of the slaves has probably found its way also into the oral tradition of the

Dominican people. Some scholarly research suggests the existence of 'a type of tale of African origins ... among us which forms part of the oral literary heritage of Dominicans'.[58] Much can be said also to highlight the contribution of blacks to Dominican cuisine, both in the form of cultural transmissions brought by the slaves from Africa and as creole innovations traceable to the 'plantation regime'.[59] But, without a doubt, African cultural forms manifest themselves most evidently in Dominican society in the realm of spiritual expression.

Carlos Esteban Deive has convincingly indicated the existence of a Dominican *vodoun* or voodoo with an indigenous pantheon and other characteristics of its own that distinguish it from Haitian *vodoun*.[60] As the author argues, people of diverse class extractions normally have recourse to the services and rituals of this folk religion, which has as much currency in urban areas as in the rural ones.[61] Probably contributing to the spread and persistence of this and other African-descended forms of worship is the syncretic nature of Dominican culture, which allows for their unproblematic coexistence with religious expressions of European origin. In fact, the majority of *vodoun* practitioners consider themselves 'officially Catholic', having received their baptism and remaining active in the worship of that faith.[62]

Further research has not only supported the existence of *vodoun* as 'part of Dominican folk religious expression' but has also identified its utility as a crucial resource for popular medicine.[63] The anthropologist Martha Ellen Davis has highlighted certain kinds of folk spiritual expressions with 'strong African influences' that provide aid to the Dominican people in many of the social functions of their daily lives.[64] Following the insight of such scholars as Deive and Davis, recently a team combining mental health and social science specialists has stressed the importance of *vodoun* and other folk spiritual manifestations to an understanding of the Dominican people from the 'perspective of psychiatry and psychology'.[65]

A religious expression with strong links to the African past but emerging on Dominican soil in connection with the modern sugar industry is the Gaga cult. Reflecting a profound religious sense, the Afro-Dominican Gaga cult, born of the interaction of

Haitian and Dominican popular traditions in the vicinity of sugar plantations, constitutes the coming together of two spiritual sources which are themselves different expressions of African and European transculturation.[66] In her pioneering monograph on this folk spiritual form, the anthropologist June Rosenberg argued that 'the celebration of the Gaga is part of the cultural richness of the Dominican people'.[67]

The state-funded guardians of the official culture, intent on stressing the predominance of the Hispanic heritage among Dominicans, have vigorously rejected any trace of 'pagan' forms of worship in Dominican society. Unable to deny that Dominicans do engage in African-descended spirituality, they have proceeded to ascribe that predilection to an unwelcome foreign influence, a logic that often has justified the persecution of folk religious practices as a threat to morality, Christian values and national integrity. Thus, the nineteenth-century poet Félix María Del Monte construed *vodoun* as a savage, cannibalistic ritual, and a 1862 police ordinance proscribed a series of dances and festivities that involved expressions of African origin.[68] During the Trujillo dictatorship, the period when the Dominican state became most emphatically committed to promoting Eurocentric and white-supremacist views of Dominicanness, the official daily *El Listín Diario* of 16 August 1939 reported the arrest of two men for commemorating the War of Restoration by engaging in *vodoun* practices along with other men and women who had managed to escape. They had surrendered themselves frantically, the newspaper said, to a 'ritual that the police has so tenaciously persecuted'.[69]

The Trujillo regime found it necessary to pass Executive Law 391 on 20 September 1943 prohibiting participation in *vodoun* ceremonies. The decree imposed a penalty of up to one year in prison plus a fine of 500 pesos for anyone found guilty of the crime by either direct commission or indirect collusion.[70] That the government's campaign to eradicate African spiritual expressions in Dominican society would not relent is clear from an article published in the newspaper *La Nación* on 5 October 1945 by the light-skinned mulatto Emilio Rodríguez Demorizi, an apologist for the Trujillo regime. There the author denounced 'cucaya dance, cannibalism, vodoun, witchcraft, and other evil arts and customs' as Haitian rituals that had occasionally tarnished 'the simple habits of Dominicans', although he reassured his readers that the 'dark roots' of those influences left no perceptible vestiges in the people.[71] But, of course, in such affirmations Rodríguez Demorizi was merely indulging in wishful thinking. For even he, a consummate negrophobe, would know that, if his claim were true, the regime's police persecution, the legislative actions and his own article, which he militantly entitled 'Against Vodoun', would all have been unnecessary.

Afro-Dominicans and race

Despite the aberrant negrophobia of the ruling class from colonial times to the present, nobody can seriously dispute the omnipresence of blacks in all aspects of Dominican life. In addition to the areas of endeavour surveyed above, one could speak of the success and celebrity enjoyed by Afro-Dominicans in the fields of sports and popular music. Blacks have by no means lacked representation in the public sphere nor in the regard of the Dominican people. The overwhelming popular victory during the 1994 elections of black presidential candidate José Francisco Peña Gómez of the Partido Revolucionario Dominicano, against the two white elders Juan Bosch, of the Partido de la Liberación Dominicana, and incumbent Joaquín Balaguer, of the Partido Reformista Social Cristiano, speaks eloquently. The manoeuvres of Balaguer's government did not permit the people's choice to materialize, and the octogenarian politician stayed in power. Nevertheless, the opposition's documentation of the fraud[72] and the indignation of the international community caused the ruling party to agree to reduce its administration by two years and convene new elections for 1996, thereby admitting to the illegality of Balaguer's 're-election'.

That Peña Gómez did not become President of the Republic matters less for the present discussion than the fact that the majority of the Dominican population went to the polls and cast their ballot in favour of a black man who, in addition, reputedly comes from Haitian parents. In voting for him massively, the

Dominican people disregarded an elaborate, insistent and virulent campaign orchestrated by the government and the conservative elite that aimed to cast doubt on the Dominicanness of the candidate on account of his race and presumed Haitian ancestry. The campaign, which employed the resources of the state and all the available media on a daily basis, insidiously sought to render it unpatriotic for voters to elect the black Peña Gómez. But the majority of Dominicans showed through their action that they have a mind of their own.

Afro-Dominicans today live in a country which in the 1990s has suffered shortages of gasoline, electricity, running water, flour, sugar, milk and other basic foodstuffs. As Moya Pons has pointed out, 'without transportation, police protection, schools or hospitals, the Dominican people lived through the most depressing crisis in modern history'.[73] The country still lacks social security, adequate schools and health services. An ailing and malnourished population still lives in the grips of an entrenched conservative and authoritarian political regime headed by 87-year-old Joaquín Balaguer, the former Trujillo henchman. In addition to the publicly documented fraudulent scheme whereby the President achieved 're-election' in 1994, corruption and embezzlement of public funds have been uncovered in various government departments including the Ministry of Education and the Customs Division. The unconditional support of the Catholic Church leadership and the obsequiousness of the press, both of which have received abundant economic favours from the government, are largely responsible for Balaguer's survival and perpetuity as head of state.

The situation of Afro-Dominicans, then, corresponds to the precarious condition of the majority of the people in this country whose population is arguably nine-tenths black and mulatto. This makes it difficult to associate the pitiful lot of most Dominican people primarily with their colour or ethnicity. Indeed, among the most violent henchmen of the conservative regime are distinctly black individuals like Major General Enrique Pérez y Pérez, one of Balaguer's staunchest allies. Similarly, among the fiercest proponents of Eurocentric and Hispanicist definitions of Dominican culture are phenotypically black scholars like the young essayist Manuel Núñez and the present Assistant Secretary of Education Jorge Tena Reyes. As a result, no voices of group rights have come to articulate the cause of Afro-Dominicans. There has been no sustained effort to explain the oppression of the Dominican masses in ethnic or racial terms, given the fact that the oppressors often share the ethnicity of their victims.

While one can discern the development of a racial discourse and the existence of racial attitudes, one cannot so easily fathom the dynamics of Dominican race relations. One can hardly speak meaningfully about the socio-economic and political situation of blacks as a differentiated ethnic group in the country. To measure the living conditions of Dominican blacks and mulattos would mean no more than to assess the social status of the masses of the people, which would lead to an analysis of class inequalities and the social injustices bred by dependent capitalism. This is not to say that there are no racial tensions or instances of racism in Dominican society. But there is a coexistence between the population's self-awareness as a people of African descent and the negrophobia contained in the Creole elite's prevalent definitions of Dominicanness. Dominican blacks and mulattos seem to tolerate passively the rigid Eurocentrism of the official cultural discourse. For instance, Balaguer has publicly proclaimed the mental and moral superiority of whites and dreadfully warned about the country's 'Africanization' without ever needing to recant his racist statements. Dominicans do possess the ability to discern the phenotypical characteristics that distinguish one racial group from another, and they do recognize the traces of Africa in their ethnicity despite the insistent efforts of the conservative intellectual elite to define them as part of a Western, Caucasian community. Yet Afro-Dominicans do not see blackness as the central component of their identity. They tend to privilege their nationality instead, which implies participation in a culture, a language community, and the sharing of a lived experience.

Consistent with the racially mixed ancestry of the population, the ethnic vocabulary of Dominicans is rich in words describing gradations of skin colour. A scholar looking at the city of Santiago de los Caballeros alone arrived at an elaborate classification of twenty-one terms used by the people there to denote racial traits.[74] Generally devoid of the language of racial polarity current in the United States, Dominicans have little familiarity with a discourse of black affirmation. Nothing in their history indicates to the masses of the Dominican people that their precarious material conditions or the overall indignities they suffer constitute a strictly racial form of oppression. As a result, they have not developed a discourse of racial self-defence among their strategies of social resistance. This, no doubt, bewilders observers coming from societies like the United States where race tends to outweigh many other elements of human identity. But the specific history Dominicans have lived simply did not beget the rigid racial codes found in North America. Thus, they have no difficulty recognizing a valid identity in their racial fusion, and, for the most part, would not experience the troubling perplexity of the speaker in Langston Hughes's short poem 'Cross', who struggles with the dilemma of having a white father and a black mother: 'My old man died in a fine big house / My ma died in a shack / I wonder where I'm gonna die, / Being neither white nor black.'[75]

Also, because of the overwhelming racial fusion of the Dominican population, one cannot easily speak of blacks versus whites or identify cases in which people align themselves politically along racial lines. For that reason Afro-Dominicans have lacked the incentive to construct a discourse of racial self-assertion and have remained indifferently unmoved by the negrophobia of the elite. Thus, the racist ideas of the ruling class have triggered no retaliation. Balaguer can find it expedient to advocate the implementation of measures to halt 'the Africanization of the Dominican people' so that, in due time, the population may 'gradually improve its anthropological traits', ascribe the country's moral decay to 'the contact with blacks' and assert the 'imperceptible' influence of Africa on Dominican culture, without provoking the immediate enmity of the black and mulatto majority of the population.[76]

In the recent past, the openness of the Dominican concept of race lent itself to the manipulation of the Trujillo regime, whose scribes exploited its flexibility for their ends. They effected the historical identification of the Dominican population with the indigenous Taino inhabitants of Hispaniola, who endured oppression and total extermination at the hands of Spanish conquerors at the outset of the colonial experience. Ethnically the Taino represented a category typified by non-whiteness as well as non-blackness, which could easily accommodate the racial in-betweenness of the Dominican mulatto. Thus, the regime gave currency to the term *indio* (Indian) to denominate the complexion of people of mixed ancestry. The term assumed official status in so far as the national identification card (*cédula*) gave it as a racial category designation during the three decades of the dictatorship. While, in the minds of most Dominicans who use it, the term merely describes a colour gradation somewhere between the polar extremes of whiteness and blackness, much in the same way that the term 'mulatto' does, the cultural commissars of the Trujillo regime preferred it primarily because the term was devoid of any semantic allusion to the African heritage and would thus accord with their negrophobic definition of Dominicanness.

Conclusions

Dominicans survived the alienating negrophobia induced by their malignant education under Trujillo. Despite a long history of state-funded conspiracy against their mental health, Afro-Dominicans exhibit a reasonable degree of self-esteem. They have not succumbed to state-sponsored inducements against Haitian immigrants in the country and have stayed clear of collective racial misconduct. Their successful escape from psychological atrophy may have to do in large part with the resilience of their open concept of race. We cannot overlook the social utility of such a concept. For, due to their history of pervasive racial mixture, one can chance upon two Dominican children with strikingly different phenotypical characteristics legitimately belonging in the same nuclear family unit. A flexible concept of race, permitting people with disparate features to share a common identity space, removes the psycho-social turmoil provoked in other societies by the sight of two people, one visibly white and the other visibly black, who identify themselves as biological siblings. The open concept of race saves Dominicans from a good deal of embarrassment and pain. However, the mental liberation of Dominicans in racial matters will come only when, political power having been wrenched from Trujillo's henchmen, the intelligentsia can succeed in instituting an official definition of national ethnic identity that accurately reflects the true colours, shades and ethnic origins of Afro-Dominicans.

Notes

1. Saco, J.A., *Historia de la esclavitud*, Madrid, Ediciones Jucar, 1974, p. 164.
2. Moya Pons, F., *Manual de historia dominicana*, Santo Domingo, Caribbean Publishers, 9th edn, 1992, p. 26.
3. Saco, op. cit., pp. 166-7.
4. Moya Pons, op. cit., p. 293.
5. Saco, op. cit., p. 175; Moya Pons, op. cit., pp. 32-3.
6. Mir, P., *Tres leyendas de colores*, Santo Domingo, Taller, 3rd edn, 1984, p. 219.
7. Tolentino Dipp, H., *Raza e historia en Santo Domingo: los orígenes del prejuicio racial en América*, Santo Domingo, Fundación Cultural Dominicana, 2nd edn, 1992, p. 189.
8. Larrazabal Blanco, C., *Los negros y la esclavitud en Santo Domingo*, Santo Domingo, Julio D. Postigo e Hijos Editores, 1967, pp. 37-8.
9. 'Esclavitud', *Enciclopedia Dominicana*, 3rd edn, 1988, vol. 3, p. 77.
10. Larrazabal Blanco, op. cit., p. 182.
11. Ibid., p. 183.
12. Lizardo, F., *Cultura africana en Santo Domingo*, Santo Domingo, Sociedad Industrial Dominicana, 1979, p. 55.
13. Deive, C.E., *La esclavitud del negro en Santo Domingo (1492-1844)*, 2 vols, Santo Domingo, Museo del Hombre Dominicano, 1980, pp. 426-7.
14. Ibid., pp. 220-1.
15. Ibid., p. 122.
16. Franco, F.J., *Santo Domingo: cultura, política e ideología*, Santo Domingo, Editora Nacional, 1979, pp. 36-7.
17. Moya Pons, F., *The Dominican Republic: A National History*, New York, Hispaniola Books, 1994, p. 122.
18. Ibid., p. 122.
19. Deive, op. cit., p. 228.
20. Ibid., p. 612.
21. Ortiz Puig, J.A., *Emigración de libertos norteamericanos a Puerto Plata en la primera mitad del siglo XIX: la iglesia metodista Wesleyana*, Santo Domingo, Editora Alfa y Omega, 1978, pp. 7, 153.
22. Castillo, J. del, 'The formation of the sugar industry: from competi-

tion to monopoly, from national semiproletariat to foreign proletariat', in M. Moreno Fraginals, F. Moya Pons and S.L. Engerman (eds), *Between Slavery and Free Labor: The Spanish-Speaking Caribbean in the Nineteenth Century*, Baltimore, MD, and London, Johns Hopkins University Press, 1985, p. 217.

23 Bryan, P.E., 'The question of labour in the sugar industry of the Dominican Republic in the nineteenth and twentieth centuries', ibid., pp. 236-8.

24 Mota Acosta, J.C., *Los cocolos en Santo Domingo*, Santo Domingo, Editorial La Gaviota, 1977, p. 12.

25 Bryan, op. cit., pp. 239-40.

26 Mota Acosta, op. cit., pp. 140-1

27 Hernández, F.M., 'La emigración haitiana en la República Dominicana', *Eme Eme: Estudios Dominicanos*, no. 1, 1973, pp. 34-5.

28 Ibid., p. 53; Báez Evertsz, F., *Braceros haitianos en la República Dominicana*, Santo Domingo, Instituto Dominicano de Investigaciones Sociales, 1986, p. 194.

29 Báez Evertsz, op. cit., p. 193.

30 Plant, R., *Sugar and Modern Slavery: A Tale of Two Countries*, London and Atlantic Highlands, NJ, Zed Books, 1987, p. 159.

31 Lemoine, M., *Sucre amer: esclaves aujourd'hui dans les Caraïbes*, Paris, Nouvelle Societé des Editions, 1981, p. 280.

32 Moya Pons, F. (ed.), *El batey: estudio socioeconómico de los bateyes del Consejo Estatal del Azúcar*, Santo Domingo, Fondo para el Avance de las Ciencias Sociales, 1986, pp. 521, 515, 509.

33 Ibid., p. 223.

34 Hernández, op. cit., p. 53.

35 Malagón Barceló, J. (ed.), *Código Negro Carolino (1784)* , Santo Domingo, Ediciones Taller, 1974, p. 81.

36 Ibid., p. 162.

37 Arrom, J.J. and García Arévalo, M.A., *Cimarrón*, Serie Monográfica no. 18, Santo Domingo, Fundación García-Arévalo, 1986, p. 46.

38 Deive, C.E., *Los guerrileros negros: esclavos fugitivos y cimarrones en Santo Domingo* , Santo Domingo, Fundación Cultural Dominicana, 1989, p. 20.

39 Arrom and García Arévalo, op. cit., pp. 41-3, 53.

40 Deive, C.E., *Los cimarrones del maniel de Neiba: historia y etnografía*, Santo Domingo, Banco Central de la República Dominicana, 1985, p. 99.

41 Franco, F.J., *Los negros, los mulatos y la nación dominicana* , Santo Domingo, Editora Nacional, 7th edn, 1984, pp. 161-2.

42 Ibid., pp. 161-2.

43 'Esclavitud', op. cit., p. 81.

44 Franco, F.J., *Historia del pueblo dominicano*, Santo Domingo, Instituto del Libro, 1992, vol. 1, p. 277.

45 Moya Pons, op. cit., *The Dominican Republic*, p. 213.

46 Gándara, J. de la, *Anexión y guerra de Santo Domingo*, Santo Domingo, Editora Santo Domingo, 1975, pp. 237-8.

47 Ferreras, R.A., *Negros*, Serie Media Isla, Santo Domingo, Editorial del Nordeste, 1983, vol. 4, p. 174.

48 'Liborio-liborismo', *Enciclopedia Dominicana*, 3rd edn, 1986, vol. 4, p. 127.
49 Ferreras, op. cit., p. 332.
50 Ibid., pp. 318-20.
51 Ibid., p. 328.
52 'Gómez Horacio, Maximiliano', *Enciclopedia Dominicana*, 3rd edn, 1988, vol. 3, p. 226.
53 Zaglul, A., *Despreciada en la vida y olvidada en la muerte: biografía de Evangelina Rodríguez*, Santo Domingo, Taller, 1980, p. 86.
54 Henríquez Ureña, P., *La utopía de América* , ed. A. Rama and R. Gutiérrez Girardot, Caracas, Biblioteca Ayacucho, 1978, pp. 315-25.
55 Cocco de Filippis, D. (ed.), *From Desolation to Compromise: Bilingual Anthology of the Poetry of Aída Cartagena Portalatín*, trans. E.J. Robinett, Santo Domingo, Taller, 1988, pp. 15-16.
56 Cartagena Portalatín, A., *Culturas africanas: rebeldes con causa*, Colección Montesinos, Santo Domingo, Biblioteca Nacional, 1986, pp. 124-5.
57 Megenney, W., *Africa en Santo Domingo: su herencia lingüística*, Santo Domingo, Museo del Hombre Dominicano/Academia de Ciencias de la República Dominicana, 1990, p. 233.
58 Julián, R. (ed.), *Cuentos orales de origen africanos*, Cuadernos del CENDIA, vol. 312, no. 10, Santo Domingo, Editora de la UASD, 1982, p. 10.
59 Deive, C.E., 'La herencia africana en la cultura dominicana actual', *Ensayos sobre cultura dominicana*, Santo Domingo, Fundación Cultural Dominicana/Museo del Hombre Dominicano, 1989, pp. 133-5.
60 Deive, C.E., *Vodu y magia en Santo Domingo*, Santo Domingo, Fundación Cultural Dominicana, 3rd edn, 1992, pp. 171-4, 182-3.
61 Ibid., p. 17.
62 Ibid., p. 211.
63 Davis, M.E., *La otra ciencia: el vodu dominicano como religión y medicina populares*, Santo Domingo, Editora Universitaria UASD, 1987, pp. 423, 221-3.
64 Ibid., pp. 194-5.
65 Tejeda Ortiz, D., Sánchez Martínez, F. and Mella Mejía, C., *Religiosidad popular dominicana y psiquiatría*, Santo Domingo, 1993, pp. 31-2.
66 Rosenberg, J., *El Gagá: religión y sociedad de un culto dominicano*, Santo Domingo, Editora Universitaria UASD, 1979, pp. 17, 31.
67 Ibid., p. 17.
68 Del Monte, F.M., 'Cantos dominicanos', *Poesía popular dominicana*, ed. E. Rodríguez Demorizi, Santiago, UCMM, 3rd edn, 1979 p. 246; Deive, op. cit., *Vodu y magia*, p. 163.
69 Deive, op. cit., *Vodu y magia*, p. 164.
70 Ibid., p. 186.
71 Rodríguez Demorizi, E., 'Contra el vodú', *La Nación*, 16 August 1945.
72 Peña Gómez, J.F. and Alvarez Bogaert, F., *Anatomía del fraude electoral: testimonio preliminar*, Santo Domingo, Acuerdo de Santo Domingo, 1994.
73 Moya Pons, op. cit., *The Dominican Republic*, p. 443.
74 Guzmán, D.J., 'Raza y lenguage en el Cibao', *Eme-Eme: Estudios*

Dominicanos, no. 11, 1974, pp. 37-40.
75   Hughes, L., *Selected Poems*, New York, Vintage Books, 1974, p. 158.
76   Balaguer, J., *La isla al revés: Haití y el destino dominicano*, Santo Domingo, Librería Dominicana, 2nd edn, 1984, pp. 45, 97-8, 211.

Select bibliography

'Antihaitianismo', *Enciclopedia dominicana*, 3rd edn, 1988, vol. 1, pp. 64-71.
Báez Evertsz, F., *Braceros haitianos en la República Dominicana*, Santo Domingo, Instituto Dominicano de Investigaciones Sociales, 1986.
Bosch, J., *Composición social dominicana* , Santo Domingo, Alfa y Omega, 15th edn, 1986.
Bryan, P.E., 'The question of labor in the sugar industry of the Dominican Republic in the nineteenth and twentieth centuries', in Moreno Fraginals, Moya Pons and Engerman, op. cit., pp. 235-51.
Cassá, R., *Historia social y económica de la República Dominicana*, vol. 1, Santo Domingo, Editora Alfa y Omega, 1992.
Cocco de Filippis, D. (ed.), *From Desolation to Compromise: Bilingual Anthology of the Poetry of Aída Cartagena Portalatín*, trans. E.J. Robinett, Santo Domingo, Taller, 1988.
De la Gándara, J., *Anexión y guerra de Santo Domingo*, Santo Domingo, Editora Santo Domingo, 1975.
Deive, C.E., *Vodu y magia en Santo Domingo*, Santo Domingo, Fundación Cultural Dominicana, 3rd edn, 1992.
Deive, C.E., *Los guerrileros negros: esclavos fugitivos y cimarrones en Santo Domingo*, Santo Domingo, Fundación Cultural Dominicana, 1989.
Deive, C.E., *La esclavitud del negro en Santo Domingo (1492-1844)*, 2 vols, Santo Domingo, Museo del Hombre Dominicano, 1980.
Del Castillo, J., 'The formation of the Dominican sugar industry: from competition to monopoly, from national semiproletariat to foreign proletariat', in Moreno Fraginals, Moya Pons and Engerman, op. cit., pp. 215-34.
Díaz Quiñones, A., 'Pedro Henríquez Ureña: modernidad, diáspora y construcción de identidades', *Modernización e identidades sociales*, ed. G. Giménez and R. Pozas H., Mexico City, Universidad Nacional Autónoma de México, 1994, pp. 59-117.
'Esclavitud', *Enciclopedia Dominicana*, 3rd, edn, 1988, vol. 3, pp. 71-83.
Ferreras, R.A., *Negros*, vol. 4, Serie Media Isla, Santo Domingo, Editorial del Nordeste, 1983.
Franco, F. J., *Historia del pueblo dominicano*, vol. 1, Santo Domingo, Instituto del Libro, 1992.
Franco, F.J., *Los negros, los mulatos y la nación dominicana*, Santo Domingo, Editora Nacional, 7th edn, 1984.
García, J.G., *Compendio de la historia de Santo Domingo*, vol. 1, Santo Domingo, Publicaciones ¡Ahora! C. por A., 4th edn, 1986.
'Gómez Horacio, Maximiliano', *Enciclopedia Dominicana*, 3rd edn, 1988, vol. 3, pp. 226-8.

Gúzman, D.J., 'Raza y lenguage en el Cibao', *Eme-Eme: Estudios Domini-canos*, no. 11, 1974, pp. 3-45.

Henríquez Ureña, P., *La utopía de América*, ed. A. Rama and R. Gutiérrez Girardot, Caracas, Biblioteca Ayacucho, 1978.

Julián, R. (ed.), *Cuentos orales de origen africanos*, Cuadernos del CENDIA, vol. 312, no. 10, Santo Domingo, Editora de la UASD, 1982.

Lemoine, M., *Sucre amer: esclaves aujourd'hui dans les Caraïbes*, Paris, Nouvelle Societé des Editions, 1981.

'Liborio-liborismo', *Enciclopedia Dominicana*, 3rd edn, 1986, vol. 4, pp. 248-65.

Malagón Barceló, J. (ed.), *Código Negro Carolino (1784)*, Santo Domingo, Taller, 1974.

Mateo, A.L., *Mito y cultura en la era de Trujillo*, Santo Domingo, Librería La Trinitaria/Instituto del Libro, 1993.

Megenney, W., *Africa en Santo Domingo: su herencia lingüística*, Santo Domingo, Museo del Hombre Dominicano/Academia de Ciencias de la República Dominicana, 1990.

Mir, P., *Tres leyendas de colores*, Santo Domingo, Taller, 3rd edn,1984.

Moreau de Saint-Méry, M.L.E., *Descripción de la parte española de la isla de Santo Domingo*, trans. C. Armando Rodríguez, Ciudad Trujillo, Editora Montalvo, 1944.

Moreno Fraginals, M., Moya Pons, F. and Engerman, S.L. (eds), *Between Slavery and Free Labor: The Spanish-Speaking Caribbean in the Nineteenth Century*, Baltimore, MD, and London, Johns Hopkins University Press, 1985.

Mota Acosta, J.C., *Los cocolos en Santo Domingo*, Santo Domingo, Editorial La Gaviota, 1977.

Moya Pons, F. (ed.), *El batey: estudio socioeconómico de los bateyes del Consejo Estatal del Azúcar*, Santo Domingo, Fondo para el Avance de las Ciencias Sociales, 1986.

Moya Pons, F., *The Dominican Republic: A National History*, New York, Hispaniola Books, 1994.

Moya Pons, F., *Manual de historia dominicana*, Santo Domingo, Caribbean Publishers, 9th edn, 1992

Moya Pons, F., 'The land question in Haiti and Santo Domingo: the sociopolitical context of the transition from slavery to free labour, 1801-1843', in Moreno Fraginals, Moya Pons and Engerman, op. cit., pp. 181-214.

Ortiz Puig, J.A., *Emigración de libertos norteamericanos a Puerto Plata en la primera mitad del siglo XIX: la iglesia metodista Wesleyana*, Santo Domingo, Editora Alfa y Omega, 1978.

Plant, R., *Sugar and Modern Slavery: A Tale of Two Countries*, London and Atlantic Highlands, NJ, Zed Books, 1987.

Torres-Saillant, S., 'Dominican literature and its criticism: anatomy of a troubled identity', in A.J. Arnold (ed.), *A History of Literature in the Caribbean*, vol. 1, Amsterdam and Philadelphia, PA, John Benjamins, 1994, pp. 49-64.

6

PUERTO RICO

Kelvin A. Santiago-Valles

P uerto Ricans have a checkered and largely unwritten history that crystallized in the nineteenth century, directly affecting racial taxonomies, attitudes and identities in ways that have persisted up till today. 'Blackness' and anyone kindred to it are usually designated and experienced as 'strange', 'exotic' and/or 'suspicious'. More than any formal claim to explicit 'ethnic' uniqueness, those few Puerto Ricans who define themselves as 'black' or 'dark-mulatto' do so because they live at a socially inferior distance from light mulattos and whites in or from the island, from US–European Americans and from other lighter-skinned Latin American and Caribbean peoples.[1]

Few Puerto Ricans of African descent explicitly identify as such,[2] particularly among the labouring-poor masses, in spite, or perhaps because, of a long past of discrimination and a present of brutal, and covertly racist, police persecution.

Historical background

Similar to some other Latin American countries since the conquest, there were as many as sixteen – and in a few cases even more – different racial categories in Puerto Rico.[3] Nineteenth-century census figures for the local population, however, list only three main racial classifications: *blanco, mulato* and *negro*. Grouped together, the latter two categories, often known as *pardos* and/or *morenos*, fluctuated between 56 per cent (1820) and 38 per cent (1899) of Puerto Rico's inhabitants. Five decades after the US colonial regime replaced Spanish rule, the island's combined non-white population had declined officially to 23 per cent (1950).[4] This was the last time the colonial government – local or federal – formally used racial categories within Puerto Rico.

As elsewhere in Latin America and the Caribbean, greater income, influence and education could and can transform the darker-skinned into lighter-skinned persons. As US anthropologist Raymond Scheele concluded in his early 1950s study of prominent families in the island: 'an individual is "whiter" in proportion to his wealth. Anyone who is accepted into the upper class is considered non-Negro, despite his physical appearance.'[5]

Although the island's labourers come from all races, the 'native' propertied and educated classes tend to be exclusively white. They are still entrusted with varying degrees of control over the principal political organizations, financial resources and local government authority of the colonial order. Within the colonizers' racial categories, however, even rich *criollo* or Creole whites cannot escape being classified as racially inferior, together with the rest of the 'native' population.[6]

Slavery was, of course, the most salient historical factor behind this first taxonomy. Until its abolition in 1873, slavery predominated on the sugar-cane coast and in the lowland valleys. Although captives had also worked in lesser numbers in the coffee- and tobacco-producing hill country, there was no necessary correspondence between these slave concentrations and the settlement patterns of *pardos libres* ('free coloureds').[7] *Pardos libres* or *trigueños* (literally 'wheat hued') tended to settle in the central mountain range where most Puerto Ricans (mainly peasants) lived until well into the mid-twentieth century.

From the sixteenth to late eighteenth centuries, important segments of this peasantry have been of mixed racial heritage: maroons (of both sexes) settled and intermingled with fugitive galley prisoners, former soldiers and the minute remnants of the aboriginal population. Yet, until the 1940s and like most of the Creole-white rural population, many non-white hill tenants or non-white peasants migrating to the mountain valley towns tended to differentiate themselves from the coastal population – whom they saw as more identifiably 'African' – by, among other things, attempting to pass for 'white' or 'near white'.[8]

During the 1930s and 1940s these racial transmutations were canonized within official cultural memory and historiography when renowned native intellectuals affirmed that 'the Spanish race' had prevailed in Puerto Rico because it had weakened and assimilated all other races. For example, in 1937 the philologist Augusto Malaret remarked that Puerto Rico was the 'whitest of all the Antilles', because the African component within the island's general culture and gene pool was insignificant and overwhelmingly negative.[9] From the 1950s to the 1970s other prominent scholars echoed this same viewpoint.[10] In 1988 the colonial governor of the island (as usual, a white propertied Creole) declared in an official visit to Madrid that given 'our people's ... common Hispanic roots' African contributions to Puerto Rico's culture were 'a mere rhetorical identification'.[11]

Between the 1940s and the 1960s several island scholars challenged such views. Historian Tomás Blanco argued that in 1942 only about 40 per cent of the island's population could be considered mostly white. And in 1965 sociologist Juan Rodríguez Cruz found that the amount of racial mixing in Puerto Rico probably reached as much as 70 per cent of the population.[12]

Furthermore, the entire national-cultural palimpsest, on which Puerto Ricanness was being inscribed and reinscribed, massively continued to bear the distinct, historical emblems of African ways and meanings. Such is the case of the copious and profound Africanisms (inflexion, morphosyntax, vocabulary) of Puerto Rican spoken Spanish developed by the overwhelming majority of the island's inhabitants, who, ironically, still perceived themselves as 'white' or 'near white'. Similarly emblematic yet contradictory examples may be found in the various musico-folkloric genres (such as the *bomba, plena, seis* and *danza*) created and adopted by this very same population over the preceding four centuries.[13]

Current socio-economic context

Like other peripheral areas under US capitalist hegemony, post-war Puerto Rico went from agro-monoculture to being a light-industry enclave for cheap factory labour. The appeal of low-waged but better educated labour was enhanced by urban-based industrial programmes and increased public services in Puerto-Rico which coincided with labour shortages in the US north-east. This resulted in large-scale migratory movements and demographic dislocations between 1940 and 1970: from countryside to city within Puerto Rico, and from the island to the United States. The entire process was compounded by an expanded official culture (Creole and North American) of rapidly spreading schooling, radio, print media and television.

Between the mid-1960s and the late 1970s light-industry factories began being unevenly displaced by high-tech, capital-intensive plants, coinciding with massive waves of social unrest. The shift towards capital-intensive industry accelerated with the expansion of new state social control measures. Despite the fiscal constraints of the following decade, such regulatory measures have continued unevenly during the 1980s and early 1990s.

On one side of the social divide stood the heirs of the previous Creole elites – again, almost completely white and light-mulatto: (a) the junior partners of the new US corporate investors and the upper strata of the rapidly expanding state bureaucracy; and (b) an overlapping ensemble of highly skilled professionals, technicians, and/or managerial personnel spreading across all economic sectors. However restricted, the offspring of the old black or dark-mulatto intelligentsia also found a niche within this technocracy. This transition almost exclusively applied to non-white male professionals and/or bureaucrats, their female counterparts being primarily limited to professions with less prestige (such as public schoolteachers, social workers and nurses) and academia. Such burgeoning and gender-specific social mobility was inclined to estrange the upper reaches of this non-white middle stratum from their racial kin among the new indigent majorities.

On the other side rose a more socially and racially heterogeneous, much younger and, by the late-1960s, no longer rural populace, comprising two-thirds of Puerto Rico's population. Though still below poverty level, this labouring mass was more literate and media conscious, and had higher social expectations than its predecessors. Most now lived in the public housing estates (called *caseríos* or *residenciales*), as well as in the shanty towns and working-class suburbs that along with older, sometimes semi-rural, *pardo libre* communities were collectively known as *barrios*. All were rapidly being absorbed by the urban sprawl.

This socio-racial amalgam is still composed of: (a) a nucleus of unskilled industrial workers whose initial growth ended by the mid-1970s when capital-intensive industry expanded; (b) a larger and unstable fusion of impoverished minor professionals, semi-skilled clerical employees, unskilled wage workers and/or independent labourers in all service sectors; overlapping with (c), a swelling, formally non-employed sub-proletariat. People of colour, especially young men, appear to be overrepresented among many of these social sectors – the sub-proletariat, in particular.

Between 1950 and 1990 men continued to comprise most of the employed population, but their employment rates plummeted during this period as those of women labourers steadily rose. Official unemployment rates oscillated between 15 per cent and 30 per cent (both sexes) at this time, while everything indicates that it has been mainly male labourers who increasingly were not even bothering to look for jobs in the official labour market. The proportion of officially non-employed people climbed from a little less than a third of the entire population in 1950 to almost half in 1985. As in the rest of the post-war Caribbean, these were the elements involved in most social strife since the late 1960s: wildcat strikes (1968-73), squatters' movements (1966-72, 1979-83), riots, youth vagrancy, social violence, theft and the uneven rejection of traditional party loyalties.[14]

Political affiliations and struggles for equality

Transforming the colony's population and broadening the reach of institutional culture entailed a corresponding metamorphosis in the island's electorate. Although the pro-US-commonwealth Partido Popular Democrático (PPD) was the chief proponent of the post-war transformation, the rural-based PPD did not reap its electoral benefits: it failed to grasp the novel traits of the emergent impoverished majorities – both social and racial. Local election results still depended on how Puerto Rico's elite secured the support of impoverished native majorities. However, winning elections depended less on the Creole-white and light-mulatto mountain peasantry than on the darker, more predominantly urban *barrios* attracting impoverished rural folk.

At the same time, the new non-white middle stratum focused more on the remnants of the older, more formal patterns of socio-racial discrimination than on the concerns of most *gente de color*. Between the 1950s and early 1970s racial justice efforts in Puerto Rico usually reflected the middle-class background, careerist aspirations and masculinism of the black or dark-mulatto, and mostly male, leadership of such struggles. Historically and among the general population, women of colour were the ones who placed and continue to place the highest value on obtaining a profession as a way of counterbalancing the existing racial discrimination.[15] Nevertheless, the gender imbalances within these struggles for racial equality might explain why among the few educated, well-known island blacks and dark-mulattos it was primarily the men who reached prominence within political and public circles in Puerto Rico.

The colony's newly created Civil Rights Committee (subsequently the Civil Rights Commission) investigated recurring but more isolated cases of straightforward racism in fraternities, private academies, professional schools, elite sports and some high-profile jobs. Although the 1959 committee report confirmed the persistence of explicit bigotry in Puerto Rico, it did not issue any recommendations, a futile exercise that was repeated by legislative boards a few years later.[16] Perhaps the most scholarly, thorough and astounding – in its civic honesty – was the Civil Rights Commission's 1972 study and report prepared by Eduardo Seda Bonilla.[17] As before, all of these findings fell largely on deaf ears within government circles because the more blatant, older and traditional examples of racism had more or less disappeared, however slowly.

Between the 1970s and early 1990s this middle-class stratum

of colour and its white supporters have fostered and created varied 'culturalist' expressions of 'black affirmation'. Examples include university symposiums, literary presentations, modern dance performances, sculpture and graphic arts exhibitions. A few 'culturalist' efforts have attempted to bridge the gap between the black or dark-mulatto intelligentsia and the cultural production and social concerns of the *gente de color* in the *barrios*.[18]

Several young, black and dark-mulatto women in Puerto Rico have distinguished themselves in this type of activity: among them, Mayra Santos Febres, Ana I. Rivera Lassens, Rayda Cotto, Celia M. Romano and Marie Ramos Rosado. The fact that most middle-class women of colour on the island were excluded from the traditional political prominence and technocratic high-profile jobs might account for their apparent overrepresentation within 'black-affirmation' academic pursuits, arts and literature. Some of these women have organized themselves into the Unión de Mujeres Puertorriqueñas Negras. Several of them both promoted and participated in the Primer Encuentro de Mujeres Negras de Latinoamérica y del Caribe (First Meeting of Black Women from Latin America and the Carribean), held in Santo Domingo in July 1992.[19]

Meanwhile, the destitute majorities became alienated from the PPD administration because of coercive urban renewal programmes, spreading police intervention, expanding but decaying public services, rising social hopes and increased social imbalances. By the mid-1960s the more racially mixed urban poor became disaffected from the political party system in general and from the governing PPD in particular. This explains their tendency to support new political formations and play off one mainstream colonialist party against another, and to participate in the growing social unrest.

The prime beneficiary of the post-war social transformations was the new, pro-US-statehood and neo-populist Partido Nuevo Progresista (PNP) organized during the mid-1960s. After the PPD's landslide victories of 1952-64, this party and the PNP have practically alternated (1968-92) in controlling the colony's local administration, each time winning by scant margins. PNP rhetoric opportunistically emphasizes the mobilization of the indigent urban masses. It has successfully equated the erasure of all social (and racial?) inequalities in Puerto Rico with the transformation of the island into a state of the US federal union, which explains the PNP slogan: 'Statehood is for the poor!'

New settlement patterns and old solidarities

There is still a tendency to identify the multiracial population in the shanty towns, *caseríos*, deteriorating labouring-poor suburbs and the adjacent semi-rural localities with being of African descent. Despite existing governmental reforms, this demographic distribution was confirmed in the 1950s by, among other things, the Caplow, Stryker and Wallace urban sociology research on the colony's capital city. The study found that the beachfront, tourist and high-class districts 'had by far the lowest proportion of non-whites' in 1950, while 'the new suburbs, not yet urbanized' – where the poorest warrens were located – 'had the highest'. The authors concluded: 'Segregation by color, although not unknown in San Juan, occurs by blocks or by neighborhoods.' By the 1960s and early 1970s anthropologist Helen Safa observed that even the poor themselves 'tend to associate black and poor'.[20]

Social services and public infrastructures deteriorated between the 1960s and the 1980s, while sources of legal income (particularly factory jobs) shrank. This indigent urban mass thus reinstituted older forms of cooperation within new and more socio-racially mixed (predominantly mulatto) patterns of communal reciprocity. Safa says that exchanges of 'labor and skills in the repair and improvement of their homes' comprise 'one of the main avenues of cooperation among men in the shantytown' and the principal compensation assumes 'the form of food and drink and, of course, the expectation that these favors will be reciprocated'. According to the US anthropologist: 'The few possessions shantytown families own are usually shared with others.' These are gender-specific patterns of solidarity: 'Women borrow small articles like cups of sugar or electric irons, while men exchange tools and cooperate in the repair of their homes.' Such patterns are also age-graded: 'Even food is shared. Some old

1 Woodcarving depicting slavery in Olinda, Brazil.

CARLOS REYES/ANDES PRESS AGENCY

2 Street performance of Capoeira, Salvador, Bahia, Brazil.

JULIO ETCHART/REPORTAGE

3 Craft worker, Bahia, Brazil.
LORRY SALCEDO

4 Fiesta da Boa Viagen, Salvador de Bahia, Brazil.   LORRY SALCEDO

5 Family and friends mourning over coffin of teenager killed by death squads in Recife, Brazil. CARLOS REYES/ANDES PRESS AGENCY

6 Mining camp, Colombia, 1960s. NINA DE FRIEDEMANN

11 Dance of the liberation of the slaves, Havana, Cuba.

12 Twin older women in Havana, Cuba.

13 Low-paid electronics workers for US company, La Romana, Dominican Republic.

14 Protest by people whose homes were bulldozed in preparation for the 1992 quincentenary, Santo Domingo, Dominican Republic.

15 Ten-year-old Haitian sugar-cane cutter, Tamayo, Dominican Republic.

16 Women's meeting, Padre Las Casas, Dominican Republic.

men living alone in the shantytown depend almost completely on neighboring families for their meals, for which they contribute nothing.'[21]

There is still a dearth of even the most basic research specifically focusing on black and dark-mulatto island 'natives'. One of the few recent studies suggests that it is mainly older poor women living in historically *pardo libre*, semi-rural communities who fare the worst. These non-white women interviewees reported, however, that race (rather than age) was the greatest factor in determining the substandard quality of their lives.[22]

Roy Bryce-Laporte's 1968 investigation of former slum residents shows that reciprocal aid practices accompanied these impoverished people when they were resettled to *caseríos* and/or to labouring-poor suburbs. Such networks of solidarity included 'mutual economic and protective assistance, visiting and confidential exchanges, care in times of sickness and emergency', in addition to 'disciplining of children, borrowing and sharing, and decision-making on some subjects of common concern'. Practices of this sort linked each family or community participant within a lattice of interdependent relationships so dense that, in order to 'understand how individual members or individual units survived, it was necessary to know how they related to other units and operations of and within the network'.[23]

Musical creation

Islanders of African descent profoundly influenced Puerto Rican music, which stemmed directly from the Cuban–Puerto Rican–US–Africa–American cultural fusions of the interwar period. Subsequently, this process was decisively marked by the huge Puerto Rican migration to the United States (1940-70), by both the post-1959 Cuban migrations and the mid-1970s Dominican migrations to Puerto Rico, and by the subsequent cyclical flows of Puerto Rican labour between the island and the US mainland. This was how the *mambo*, big band and new *plena* waves of the 1950s and early 1960s engendered the *salsa* wave of the late 1960s to the present, as well as the *merengue* and rap waves of the 1980s and 1990s.

Musical excellence in composition and/or interpretation were gateways out of poverty and discrimination on the island and in the US ghettos, but primarily for male *salseros*. And of these musicians, few had formal training, most of them coming from the slums and *barrios* of New York City or San Juan. Puerto Ricans in general, and island black and dark-mulatto men in particular, were the main songwriters, performers and vocalists of the principal *salsa* bands on the United States–Caribbean circuit of the 1970s-80s. One of the factors making this an almost exclusively male-dominated art form and means of social mobility was the variously stringent interdiction on having women playing the drums – the most prominent instruments in all Afro-Hispanic–Caribbean musical genres.[24]

Many of these Puerto Rican musicians, particularly men of colour, never completely deserted their roots. Sometimes it was a conscious effort to remain 'authentic', mining these US ghetto and island urban indigent spaces for inspiration and feedback. At other times it was a matter of giving back to these communities, and to relatives and neighbourhood friends, some of the recognition given to their children. However, these *barrios* were also the last refuge of the once successful *salsa* musician crushed by unfair recording contracts, drugs and/or the criminal justice system.[25]

There have been other ways in which this urban music has personified the growing social and racial polarization among island Puerto Ricans. The violent clashes at concerts and in the streets and school lots between US (white) rock music advocates (known as *rockeros*) and *salsa* fans (known as *cocolos*) during the late 1970s to mid-1980s illustrate this. Historically, in the Spanish-speaking Caribbean, *cocolo* is one of several derogatory terms used for people of African descent. In contemporary Puerto Rico, *cocolos* are the mostly non-white adolescents and young adults from the *barrios* of Puerto Rico and the US mainland. The *rockeros*, instead, comprise primarily white, middle-class and rich youths, the children of the island's Creole elites.

The criminalization of subsistence activities

This period also witnessed an increase in the criminalization of survival practices (collective and individual) among the more non-white destitute majorities in urban, suburban and semi-rural settlements. Kurt Back's 1962 social psychology study of *caserío* occupants in Puerto Rico indicates that 'the residents frequently tapped power lines and hence did not have to pay for utilities' and that, in general, those interviewed 'mentioned a great amount of extralegal activity'.[26] In the early 1980s British historian Raymond Carr commented: 'The social alienation of the lumpenproletariat, of which disadvantaged blacks constitute a significant section, is expressed ... in deviance and deliquency.'[27] Regulated or not by non-legal and informal social control mechanisms, these are the social class, racial and geographical spaces officially identified with illicit drug sales, squatting, resisting police evictions, participating in unreported incomes, shootouts, the underground lottery, and so on.[28]

To a great extent, the key issue is not whether crime statistics are quantitatively higher among the urban poor in general and among its growing *gente de color* elements in particular. I agree with Stuart Hall *et al.* when, in the case of the United Kingdom during this period, they remark:

> *Black youth are clearly involved in some petty and street crime in these areas, and the proportion involved may well be higher than it was a decade earlier ... the question is not, precisely, how many, but why? What is the meaning, the significance, the historical context of this fact? This crime index cannot be isolated from other related indices if we really wish to unravel this puzzle. When examined in context, these various indices point to a critical intersection between black crime, black labour and the deteriorating situation in the black areas. Even these must be contextualised, by setting them in their proper framework: the economic, social and political crisis into which the society is receding.*[29]

The local mass media and the Creole intelligentsia (of all political stripes, formally anti-colonialist or not) have failed to see the structural logic – however disturbing – and much less the racial undertones, of this explosive social polarization. Instead, they have issued copious alarmist writings diagnosing such behaviour as the 'growing disease' of 'a community against itself'.[30] Few realize that the expansion of subaltern literacy levels and access to the mass media have been in direct contrast to the waning access to the growing social wealth created on the island among the dispossessed native majorities.

These illegalities should be understood as a response to the burgeoning of gross and frequently (though tacitly) acknowledged racially specific social inequalities. One of the injustices that has provoked considerable resistance among the destitute masses is the land-use policy of the colonial government, both local and federal, which has in turn been fuelled by the activities of corporate speculators and greedy developers. Increasingly, such schemes have placed residents in older, *pardo libre* communities outside the law, while at the same time forcing a growing number of poor urban families to unlawfully seize unused stretches of land, because these labourers are unable to afford legal housing: in both cases forced evictions are the ultimate official threat and/or actual practice. There have already been several notorious instances of this type of 'cautionary tale', where the local police have brutally crushed the resistance of predominantly black or dark-mulatto indigent residents. In 1980 a black labouring-poor mother, Adolfina Villanueva, was gunned down by patrolmen while she defied an eviction in the Medianía Alta sector of the maroon municipality of Loíza. The Villa sin Miedo squatter settlement, in whose organization poor women once again had a leading role, was razed by anti-riot platoons during a police assault and shootout two years later.[31]

Another outstanding example of criminalized responses to existing social inequalities stems from the local wage market's declining capacity to even attract, much less absorb, the growing numbers of mostly destitute, more racially mixed (that is, non-white) and disproportionately male youths. A case in point is the underground or informal economy. In Puerto Rico, unlike its US counterpart, illegal economic activity predominantly involves young men. They are the ones primarily absorbed by these burgeoning, now vital and volatile sources of income, whose most profitable endeavours are the distribution of controlled chemical substances, stolen goods in general and firearms in particular.

Such activities, in turn, have been closely associated with factors which have negatively affected post-war patterns of community solidarity, especially among increasingly mulatto, urban and indigent sectors. On the one hand, there is the increasingly perilous but lucrative nature of these leading, but by no means exclusive, sectors of the underground economy. On the other hand, there is the characteristically macho bravado of the male youth gangs operating both within and outside penal and juvenile institutions and fighting to control illicit operations at a neighbourhood level. Although drawing on patterns of traditional machismo prevalent in Puerto Rico's society as a whole and in dispossessed urban areas in particular, such vicious competition, to some extent, has strained the community and family networks that the island's illegal subsistence practices have historically depended on for protection, regulation and support. This situation has undoubtedly informed the rising rates of local and domestic violence in general, especially violence against women, within the *barrios*. A few of the gangs – the *ñetas* being the prime example – have attempted to counteract some of this social cannibalism by enforcing strict autonomous controls against indiscriminate violence.[32]

From the late 1970s to the early 1980s the estimated volume of the underground economy oscillated between US $3.5 and $4 billion, or more than a quarter of the island's gross national product. Puerto Rico's illegal economic activities seem to be 50 per cent to 100 per cent larger than their US equivalents and involved at least 500,000 island labourers during the 1980s. This amounted to a little over half of Puerto Rico's active labour force – almost 25 per cent of the entire population of employment age, both sexes.[33]

Government officials and advisers admit that unlawful practices such as the underground economy greatly weaken the hold of legal structures (local and federal) over the impoverished urban majorities in Puerto Rico.[34] In 1986 the consciously mulatto Puerto Rican writer and social critic José Luis González reached similar conclusions, but from an opposing historical perspective. 'Puerto Rico is undoubtedly living ... a state of insurgency,' he says. But the Creole-white elites mistake 'this insurgency ... for a simple rise in delinquency'. For González, the 'state of insurgency' is escalating into a veritable – and racialized – civil war

> whose real nature will be eminently social *because this war will involve a confrontation, not only between socioeconomic interests, but also between the cultural interests of the two contending sectors within Puerto Rican society. Add to this the racial ingredient of the conflict and one can see that the current and seemingly inconsequential strife between 'cocolos' and 'rockeros' is only a preview of a historical and much more serious confrontation.*[35]

The racialization of crime

Consequently and similar to what was happening in Great Britain during the mid-1970s, in Puerto Rico at this time (as in the United States) there was a

> *synchronization of the race and class aspects of the [economic] crisis. Policing* the blacks *threatened to mesh with the problem of policing* the poor *and policing* the unemployed: *all three were concentrated in precisely the same urban areas – a fact which of course provided that element of geographical homogeneity ... The on-going problem of policing the blacks had become, for all practical purposes, synonymous with the wider problem of* policing the crisis.[36]

In Puerto Rico this racialization was being executed by the Creole institutions directly administering the colony and responsible for maintaining law and order.

But how can this be officially documented, given the absence of regular census statistics on Puerto Rico's racial subdivisions since 1950? One analytical alternative is to examine the island police force's continuing use of racial (or colour) taxonomies as part of its regular criminal and/or delinquent identification procedures. Nevertheless, practically all of the criminological studies performed during this period (by Puerto Ricans or not) have simply omitted any reference to,[37] or have explicitly disclaimed the pertinence of,[38] the police's race and/or colour identification system.

The 1988 Nevarez-Muñiz and Wolfgang juvenile delinquency study, of a 1970 cohort in the San Juan Greater Metropolitan Area, is one rare example to the contrary. Despite repeated disavowals and unlike similar work from the 1950s to the present, the authors cite and use the explicitly racial classifications employed by the police, courts and social services themselves: *blanco, trigueño* and *negro*. Within their already defined delinquent cluster, these groupings were 54 per cent *blanco*, 38 per cent *trigueño* and 8 per cent *negro*.[39]

The study reflects the received official Creole perception that those living in island *barrios* – black males in particular – were more inclined to be classified as criminals and delinquents. But, although Nevarez-Muñiz and Wolfgang would want it otherwise, they give ample proof of how punitive agencies on the island have singled out black and dark-mulatto poor urban young males for a disproportionate amount of police identification and persecution.

According to this study:[40] *Negros* supposedly had almost twice the recidivism rates of *blancos*. More than twice as many male *negros* became delinquents by age 14 than their *trigueño* and *blanco* counterparts. Among male juveniles, *negros* were seen as more apt to commit severe crimes – particularly violent crimes (44 per cent) – versus 36 per cent of all *trigueños* and 32 per cent of all *blancos*. *Negros* were also reported as having the highest rates of illicit drug use.

Hence male adolescent *negros* were more likely to be referred to the courts (72 per cent) than *trigueños* (68 per cent) or *blancos* (61 per cent). As the court system issued much harsher sentences to recidivists than to first-time juvenile offenders, *negros* were more prone to be locked up within juvenile detention centres or psychiatric units (14 per cent) than *trigueños* (11 per cent) and *blancos* (5 per cent).

Although young women only made up 17 per cent of all those classified as delinquents (both sexes), the non-white members of the female population were also disproportionately identified as criminals, similarly to their male (*negro* and *trigueño*) counterparts.

In this sense, between the 1970s and early 1990s Puerto Rico saw what Stuart Hall *et al.* have called a 'synchronization' of race, poverty and unemployment, 'all three' being 'concentrated in precisely the same urban areas'. Meanwhile, policing has expanded on a much larger scale and with far more serious results. Since early 1993 the colony's PNP governor has mobilized the militia reserve units of the US Army (or National Guard) in order to carry out joint police raids and to regularly patrol the public housing projects and poor working-class suburbs. The troop deployment has transformed these areas into militarily occupied zones, formally and indefinitely under a state of siege.[41]

Such practices suggest that, as the electoral base of Creole-white officialdom continues to be partly composed of the urban, non-white, destitute and unemployed masses, then the local elite cannot revive the openly racist discourses of the early twentieth century. Yet, because the crisis has to be policed and as the already mentioned race-slums-unemployment-crime 'synchronization' still exists, then being of African descent continues to be the absent referent of how this 'geographical homogeneity' is both imagined and regulated.

Mass responses to the racialization of crime

As in the past, impoverished populations on the island have reproduced racist inscriptions of social 'threat'. With the enormous influx of Dominican workers (legal and undocumented) into Puerto Rico since the mid-1970s, this mass-based racism has also meant perceiving Dominicans – who tend to be darker-skinned than most Puerto Ricans – as members of an 'inferior race'. Such practices have gone from mistaking black and dark-mulatto Puerto Ricans for Dominicans (and sometimes provoking the arrest of the former for failing to produce the 'appropriate immigration papers') to graffiti calling for the murder of Dominicans residing in Puerto Rico.[42]

Young, impoverished Puerto Rican *gente de color*, unlike their black British counterparts, have not produced the island equivalent of an openly 'ethnically distinct class fraction' from the

1970s to the early 1990s. Instead of any explicit and frank 'ethnic consciousness' in its principal forms of organization, the latter mainly form bands or gangs outspokenly identified with the localities where certain individuals reside or are confined – namely, the group leaders of these 'young black school-leavers ... most exposed to the winds of unemployment'. Such was the case of specific Río Piedras *caseríos* such as the 'Manuel A. Pérez' clique; San Juan's former La Princesa jail where the legendary dark-mulatto convict, martyred social bandit and prisoners' rights activist Carlos Torres Iriarte (a.k.a. Carlos La Sombra) organized the *ñetas* or Asociación de Confinados (Convicts' Association) and later the state penitentiary – one of their multiple current strongholds; public housing projects in Ponce where the Avispas operated; or entire urban centres such as the Mayagüez band whose name corresponds to that of the third largest city on the island; and so on.[43]

Yet there may be also a paradoxical undercurrent of self-identification locating these *barrios* and/or detention units themselves as distinct, Puerto Rican *negro* and/or *trigueño* spaces. The groundwork for such a consciousness is partially being laid by the media coverage and police intervention described above. Perhaps more importantly, though, such self-identification seems to be emerging – since the late 1960s and early 1970s – with the growing overlapping of two processes. On the one hand, there are the illegal survival practices of these impoverished youths in island cities and US ghettos. On the other hand, there are the unevenly explicit Africanist–Antillean and Afro–US–Latino musico-cultural expressions (*salsa, merengue,* new *bomba-plena,* rap/hip-hop), as well as the partially candid Afro-Caribbean mix of semi-religious initiations and habitual rituals (Santería, *espiritismo, palo-mayombe*). Both the music and the rituals are extremely popular among the urban poor in general and the gangs in particular; they even have pockets of adherents among the island's middle strata.[44] This trend continues unabated, although it has not assumed openly self-conscious expressions.

Conclusions

The Creole historian and Jesuit priest Fernando Picó, in a 1988 study of one *pardo libre barrio*, remarked that today island officialdom and the propertied and/or educated minorities 'continue believing that their problem is drugs and crime and not the existing social conflicts resulting from racial discrimination and unequal opportunities'.[45] As the bleak conditions of the island's growing and predominantly mulatto poor merges with the socioeconomic predicament of the destitute majorities, solving one problem cannot be separated from solving the other. This cannot be done without confronting the penury, racist policing and socio-cultural undervaluation being endured and resisted (however paradoxically) by these subordinated populations.

Notes

1 E.g. Barbosa, J.C., *El problema de razas*, San Juan, Imprenta Venezuela, 1937, pp. 19-21; Rosario, J.C. and Carrión, J., 'Problemas sociales: el negro: Haití-Estados Unidos-Puerto Rico', *Boletín de la UPR*, vol. 10, no. 2, 1939, pp. 127-34; Picó, I., 'Entrevista de *La Hora*: el racismo en Puerto Rico', *La Hora*, 8 September 1972, pp. 10-11; Santos, M., 'A veces miro mi vida', *Diálogo*, October 1993, p. 42
2 E.g. Romano, C.M., 'Yo no soy negra', *Piso 13*, vol. 1, no. 4, 1992, p. 3.
3 Anonymous, 'El Jíbaro', in J.P. Morales (ed.), *Misceláneas históricas*, San Juan, Tipografía La Correspondencia de Puerto Rico, 1924, pp. 51-4; originally published in *Almanaque de aguinaldo*, 1876.
4 US War Department, *Report on the Census of Porto Rico 1899*, Washington, DC, Government Printing Office, 1900, pp. 57-8; Zelinsky, W., 'III. The Negro population geography of Cuba and Puerto Rico', *Journal of Negro History*, vol. 34, no. 2, 1949, p.211; US Census Bureau, *Seventeenth Census of the United States; Printed Report No. 53: Puerto Rico*, Washington, DC, Government Printing Office, 1951, p. 8.
5 Scheele, R., 'The prominent families of Puerto Rico', in R.H. Steward (ed.), *The People of Puerto Rico*, Urbana, IL, University of Illinois Press, 1956, p. 425
6 Sereno, R., 'Cryptomelanism: a study of color relations and personal insecurity in Puerto Rico', *Psychiatry*, vol. 10, no. 3, 1947, pp. 265, 268; Santiago-Valles, K., *'Subject People' and Colonial Discourses: Economic Transformation and Social Disorder in Puerto Rico, 1898-1947*, Albany, NY, State University of New York Press, 1994.
7 Zelinsky, op. cit., p. 214; Picó, F., *Vivir en Caimito*, Río Piedras, Ediciones Huracán, 1988, pp. 118-19.
8 Manners, R.A., 'Tabara: subcultures of a tobacco and mixed crops

municipality', in R.H. Stewart (ed.), *The People of Puerto Rico*, Urbana, IL, University of Illinois, 1956, pp. 129, 164; Wolf, E., 'San José: subcultures of a "traditional" coffee municipality', ibid., pp. 227, 238, 258; Whitten, N.E. Jr and Torres, A., 'Blackness in the Americas', *Report on the Americas: The Black Americas 1492-1992*, North American Congress on Latin America, vol. 25, no. 4, 1992, p. 21.

9   Malaret, A., *Vocabulario de Puerto Rico*, San Juan, Imprenta Venezuela, 1937, pp. 15, 20. See also Cadilla de Martínez, M., *La poesía popular en Puerto Rico*, Madrid, Universidad de Madrid, 1933, p. 4; Pedreira, A., *Insularismo*, Río Piedras, Editorial Edil, 1971, p. 35.

10 E.g. Babín, M.T., *Panorama de la cultura puertorriqueña*, New York, Las Américas Publishing Co., 1958, p. 121; Figueroa, L., *Breve historia de Puerto Rico*, vol. 1, Río Piedras, Editorial Edil, 1971, p. 15.

11 Quoted in Flores, J., 'Cortijo's revenge', *Centro*, vol. 3, no. 2, 1991, p. 11.

12 Blanco, T., *El prejuicio racial en Puerto Rico*, San Juan, Editorial Biblioteca de Autores Puertorriqueños, 1942, pp. 51-9; Rodríguez Cruz, J., 'Las relaciones raciales en Puerto Rico', *Revista de Ciencias Sociales*, vol. 9, no. 4, 1965, p. 381.

13 Alvarez Nazario, L.M., *El elemento afronegroide en el español de Puerto Rico*, San Juan, Instituto de Cultura Puertorriqueña, 1974; López Cruz, F., *La música folklórica de Puerto Rico*, Sharon, CT, Troutman Press, 1967, pp. 47-122.

14 Ríos, P., 'Export-oriented industrialization and the demand for female labor: Puerto Rican women in the manufacturing sector, 1952-1980', in E. Meléndez and E. Meléndez (eds), *Colonial Dilemma*, Boston, MA, South End Press, 1993, pp. 89-102; Silvestrini, B., *Violencia y criminalidad en Puerto Rico, 1898-1973*, Río Piedras, Editorial Universitaria, 1980, pp. 113-32; Anderson, R., 'The party system: change or stagnation?', in J.Heine (ed.), *Time for Decision*, Lanham, MD, North-South Publishing, 1983, pp. 3-26; Silén, J.A., *Apuntes: para una historia del movimiento obrero puertorriqueño*, Río Piedras, Editorial Cultural, 1978, pp. 163-200; Cotto, L., 'The Rescate movement: an alternative way of doing politics', in Mélendez and Mélendez, op. cit., pp. 119-30; Ferracuti, F. et al., *Delinquents and Nondelinquents in the Puerto Rican Slum Culture*, Columbus, OH, Ohio State University Press, 1975.

15 Quesada, P. and Rivera Ramos, A.N., 'La satisfacción de vida de la mujer envejeciente puertorriqueña blanca y negra en dos areas geográficas de Puerto Rico', in A.N. Rivera Ramos (ed.), *La mujer puertorriqueña: investigaciones psico-sociales*, Río Piedras, Editorial Edil, 1991, p.127.

16 Comité del Gobernador para el Estudio de los Derechos Civiles en Puerto Rico, *Informe al honorable gobernador*, San Juan, 1959; 'Viewpoint', *San Juan Star*, 23 December 1969, p. 34; Zenón Cruz, I., *Narciso descubre su trasero: el negro en la cultura puertorriqueña*, vol. 1, Humacao, Editorial Furidi, 1974, pp. 166-9, 176, 182-3, 194-5, 220-2, 234-6.

17 Seda Bonilla, E., 'El prejuico racial', in *La cultural política en Puerto*

Rico, Universidad de Puerto Rico, Centro de Investigaciones Sociales, 1972, pp. 103-89.

18   Monclova Vázquez, H., 'Julio Axel Landrón: en dos tiempos', *Claridad*, 5-11 November 1993, p. 19; López, R., 'Africa en el balcón y su cultura religiosa de paso por la universidad', *Diálogo*, April 1994, pp. 48-9; Routte-Gomez, E., 'Wood cutter carves own niche for black dignity', *San Juan Star-Venue*, 26 September 1993, p. 3; López, R., 'La ocupación de los ritos en manos de Daniel Lind', *Diálogo*, December 1992, p. 49; Fiet, L., 'Notas hacia un teatro cultural', *Claridad*, 10-16 September 1993, p. 26; 'Bomba y plena para rato', *Diálogo*, March 1994, pp. 20-1; Ortíz Luquis, R., 'Adolfina: un proyecto con su nombre', *Claridad*, 8-14 February 1991, p. 15.

19   De la Calabó, M., 'Entre sonera y sonero', *Claridad*, 19-25 January 1993, p. 29; de la Calabó, M.,'Testimonio de Año Nuevo', *Claridad*, 11-17 January 1990, p. 27; 'Carnaval de Pasión', *Claridad*, 4-10 June 1993, p. 44; Cotto, R., 'La mujer negra en la música folklórica y popular en Puerto Rico', *Claridad*, 25 September-1 October 1992, p. 25.

20   Caplow, T., Stryker, S. and Wallace, S.E., *The Urban Experience*, Totowa, NJ, Bedminster Press, 1964, pp. 48, 191; Safa, H.I., *The Urban Poor in Puerto Rico*, New York, Holt, Rinehart & Winston, 1974, p. 69.

21   Safa, op. cit., p. 17.

22   Quesada and Rivera Ramos, op. cit., p. 125.

23   Bryce-Laporte, R.S., 'Family adaptation of relocated slum dwellers in Puerto Rico: implications for urban research and development', *Journal of Developing Areas*, no. 2, July 1968, p. 534.

24   Special monographic issue on *salsa* in J. Roberts (ed.), *BMI: The Many Worlds of Music*, no. 3, 1986, pp. 32-9; Zenón Cruz, op. cit., pp. 318-24; Cotto, op. cit., p. 25.

25   Brenes, R.L., 'A puerta cerrada con Ismael Rivera', *Centro*, vol. 3, no. 2, 1991, pp. 56-61; Monclova Vázquez, H., '"Yo no estoy para jugar. Mejor me quito": entrevista a Roberto Rohena', *Claridad*, 6-12 May 1994, pp. 22-3; Rodríguez Juliá, E., *El entierro de Cortijo*, Río Piedras, Ediciones Huracán, 1983.

26   Back, K., *Slums, Projects and People*, Durham, NC, Duke University Press, 1962, pp. 9-10, 32.

27   Carr, R.C., *Puerto Rico: A Colonial Experiment*, New York, Vintage Books, 1984, p. 248.

28   Safa, op. cit., pp. 28-9, 41-56, 64-6, 81-6; Picó, op. cit., pp. 85, 133-58; Otero, R., 'Yo soy de Canales: entrevista a Cruz Rivera', *Piso 13*, vol. 1, no. 1, 1992, pp. 2-3; Osorio, I., 'Hablan los jóvenes del caserío', *Diálogo*, August 1993, pp. 16, 18; Centeno, D., 'Un llamado a valorar la opinión de los residentes', *Diálogo*, September 1993, p. 14; Cotto, op. cit.

29   Hall, S. et al., *Policing the Crisis*, London, Macmillan Press, 1978, p. 338.

30   E.g. Rodríguez, W., 'Puerto Rico: sociedad enferma – salud mental, gran serie no. 1', *El Nuevo Día*, 27 October 1977, p. 3; Silva de Bonilla, R., 'Un análisis de la violencia, el crimen y los criminales:

anatomía de un quehacer ideológico de los científicos sociales en Puerto Rico', *Revista del Colegio de Abogados*, vol. 42, no. 2, 1981, pp. 127-38; 'La criminalidad: síntoma de una crisis profunda', *Pensamiento Crítico-Documentos*, separatta, vol. 9, no. 49, 1986; Rivera Lugo, C. and Guttiérrez, P., 'Puerto Rico, Puerto Pobre: los senderos de la desintegración social o el camino de la esperanza', *Diálogo*, February 1993, pp. 16-17; Colón Martínez, N., 'Consenso frente a la criminalidad', *Claridad*, 28 January-3 February 1994, p. 11.

31 O'Reilly, P., '"Town without fear": making the land their own', *No Middle Ground*, no. 3-4, 1984, pp. 72-6; Brentlinger, J., *Villa sin miedo ¡presente!*, Claves Latinoamericanas, Mexico, 1989; Del Valle, S., 'Vecinos de Loíza enfrentan desahucio', *Claridad*, 31 December 1993-6 January 1994, p. 4; Archilla Rivera, M., 'Expropiación de las Picúas: legislatura defiende a los ricos', *Claridad*, 29 April-5 May 1994, p. 3.

32 López, R., 'Una vuelta al punto: el negocio y la cultura de la drogas al detal', *Diálogo*, February 1993, pp. 14-15; Pico, op. cit., pp. 133-158; Knudsen, D.G., '"Que nadie se entre": la esposa maltratada en Puerto Rico', in Y. Azize Vargas (ed.), *La mujer en Puerto Rico*, Río Piedras, Ediciones Huracán, 1987, pp. 139-54; Picó, F., *El día menos pensado: historia de los presidiarios en Puerto Rico (1793-1993)*, Río Piedras, Ediciones Huracán, 1994, pp. 152-4.

33 Russell, T., '"Underground economy": here is a huge activity', *Caribbean Business*, 21 April 1982, pp. 1-2; Stewart, J.R., 'Notes on the underground economy in Puerto Rico', *Puerto Rico Business Review*, vol. 9, no. 4, 1984, pp. 23-30; Junta de Planificación, *Informe económico al gobernador*, San Juan, Oficina del Gobernador, 1987, p. A-1.

34 Stewart, op. cit., p. 30.

35 González, J.L., *Nueva visita al cuarto piso*, Madrid, Libros del Flamboyán, 1986, pp. 46, 114.

36 Hall et al., op. cit., p. 332.

37 E.g. Vales, P. et al., *Patrones de criminalidad en Puerto Rico*, Río Piedras, 1982; Silvestrini, op. cit.; Peterson, J., *Evaluación de la estadística criminal de la policía de Puerto Rico: años 1969-70 a 1973-74*, San Juan, Departamento de Justicia, 1974; Vales, P. (ed.), *Justicia juvenil y la prevención de la delincuenca en Puerto Rico*, San Juan, Oficina del Gobernador, 1987.

38 E.g. Ferracuti et al., op. cit., p. 126.

39 Nevarez-Muñiz, D. and Wolfgang, M., *Delincuencia juvenil en Puerto Rico: cohorte de personas nacidas en 1970*, San Juan, Senado de Puerto Rico, November 1988, pp. 38-9, 41, 49, 83.

40 Ibid., pp. 39, 41-2, 43, 44, 50, 83-4, 87, 94, 96-7, 99, 154, 177-8, 183, 219, 222-3, 224, 226-7, 229-30, 265-6.

41 Archilla Rivera, M.Y., 'Guerra contra los pobres y militarización del país', *Claridad*, 5-11 February 1993, p. 4; Picó, F., 'Criminalidad y violencia: mano dura contra la mano dura', *Diálogo*, February 1993, pp. 12-13; del Castillo, N., 'Militarización de los caseríos', *El Diario*, 24 June 1993, p. 18; Picó, F., 'Crisis de autoridad y la autoridad por

la fuerza', *Diálogo*, August 1993, pp. 16, 18; Martínez, A., 'Una
división especial para vigilar los residenciales', *El Nuevo Día*, 1 June
1994, p.15.

42 Vélez, J., 'La "border patrol"', *Claridad*, 11 November 1993, p. 40;
Guadalupe, R., 'Del graffiti como medio de expresión racista', *Claridad*, 22-28 July 1994, p. 24.

43 Hall et al., op. cit., p 331; Picó, op. cit., pp. 151-3.

44 Muller, K.C., 'Santeria', *Sunday San Juan Star Magazine*, 22 May 1983,
pp. 2-3; Flores, J., 'Rappin', writin', & breakin'', *Centro*, vol. 2, no. 3,
1988, pp. 34-41; Fernández, W., 'Sepia del Bajo Mundo: música al
compás de La Perla', *Avance*, vol. 2, no. 75, 24-31 December 1975, pp.
24-31; Nurse Allende, L., 'Los Pleneros de la 23 Abajo: creando un
nuevo concepto de la plena y la bomba', *Hómines*, vol. 6, no. 1, 1982,
pp. 251-5; Rivera, R.Z., 'Rap music in Puerto Rico: mass consumption
or social resistance?', *Centro*, vol. 5, no. 1, 1992-3, pp. 52-65; Alegría
Pons, J.F., 'Aspectos de la religiosidad popular en Puerto Rico', *Claridad*, 27 December-2 January 1992, pp. 16-17; 'Latin empire: Puerto
rap', *Centro*, vol. 3, no. 2, 1991, pp. 77-85; Cámara, D., 'Las inicia-
ciones rituales de Palo Monte o Mayombe como fuentes de
conocimiento y evolución humana', *Africanías*, no. 7, 1991, pp. 3-4.

45 Picó, op. cit., p. 14.

Additional bibliography

A.G., 'Batacumbele', *Hómines*, vol. 6, no. 1-2, 1982, pp. 256-8.

Alvarez, L.M. et al., *La tercera raíz: presencia africana en Puerto Rico*, San
Juan, Centro de Estudios de la Realidad Puertorriqueña and Instituto
de Cultura Puertorriqueña, May-October 1992.

Blum, J., 'Problems of salsa research', *Ethnomusicology*, vol. 22, no. 1,
1978, pp. 137-49.

Díaz Quiñones, A., 'Tomás Blanco: racismo, historia y esclavitud', in T.
Blanco (ed.), *El prejuicio racial en Puerto Rico*, Río Piedras, Ediciones
Huracán, 1985, pp. 15-83.

Duany, J., 'Popular music in Puerto Rico: toward an anthropology of
salsa', *Latin American Music Review*, vol. 5, no. 2, 1984, pp. 186-216.

Dufrasne González, E., 'Al rescate de la africanía religiosa', *Claridad*, 1-7
April 1994, pp. 14, 31.

Encarnación, A.M., 'La aportación negra a nuestra cultura ¿adscripción
retórica?', *Claridad*, 31 July-6 August 1992, pp. 26-7.

Ginorio, A.B. and Berry, P.C., 'Measuring Puerto Ricans' perceptions of
racial characteristics', *Proceedings: 80th Annual Convention, APA*, American Psychological Association, 1972, pp. 287-8.

González, J.L., *El país de cuatro pisos y otros ensayos*, Río Piedras, Ediciones
Huracán, 1980.

Gordon, M.W., 'Race patterns and prejudice in Puerto Rico', *American
Sociological Review*, vol. 14, no.1, 1949, pp. 294-301.

*Informe general: primer encuentro del mujeres negras de Latinoamérica y del
Caribe*, mimeo, 1992.

Lewis, G.K., *Puerto Rico: libertad y poder en el Caribe*, Río Piedras, Editorial Edil, 1969.

Lewis, G.K., 'Caribbean society and culture', in A. Calderón Cruz (ed.), *Problemas del Caribe contemporaneo / Problems of the Contemporary Caribbean*, Río Piedras, Instituto de Estudios del Caribe, Universidad de Puerto Rico, 1979, pp. 5-16.

Mathews, T., 'La cuestión de color en Puerto Rico', discussion paper, Río Piedras, Facultad de Ciencias Sociales, Universidad de Puerto Rico, 1970.

Montalvo del Valle, J.V., 'Estudio psico-etnográfico de la música "salsa" en Puerto Rico', MA thesis, Río Piedras, Universidad de Puerto Rico, 1978.

Padró, D. and Rossó, M.L., *Proclama a los puertorriqueños sobre la cuestión de color*, mimeo manifesto, Río Piedras, Facultad de Ciencias Sociales, Universidad de Puerto Rico, 4 May 1972.

Rodríguez, H., '¿Debe la salsa representarnos internacionalmente?', *Claridad*, 12-18 June 1992, p. 18.

Sagrera, M., *Racismo y política en Puerto Rico*, Río Piedras, Editorial Edil, 1973

Siegel, M., 'Race attitudes in Puerto Rico', *Phylon*, vol. 14, no. 2, 1953, pp. 163-78.

Tumin, T. and Feldman, A., *Social Class and Social Change in Puerto Rico*, Princeton, NJ, Princeton University Press, 1961.

Ungerleider Kepler, D.I., 'Fiestas afro-borinicanas y cambio social en Puerto Rico: el caso de Loíza', MA thesis, Escuela Nacional de Antropología e Historia, Mexico, 1982.

Velázquez, I., 'From Africa with feeling', *Sunday San Juan Star Magazine*, 17 June 1984, pp. 2-3.

7
MEXICO AND CENTRAL AMERICA

MEXICO

Jameelah S. Muhammad

The African presence in Mexico is a subject often denied, but people of African descent have influenced every aspect of Mexican life, culture and history.[1] They participated in its discovery and conquest, exploring unknown territories and establishing communication between the indigenous peoples and the Spanish. For example, Esteban el Negro ('Steven the Black'), a Moor, explored northern Mexico, including Texas and New Mexico, and later found the legendary city of Cibola. Black people were also crucial to the early development of Mexico's economy, making it the most successful in colonial Spanish America, and they had a leading role in the War of Independence. Black people maintained a high profile in the ranks of Mexico's revolutionary forces.

Africans made important contributions to Mexican folk tales, religion, medicinal practices, cooking styles and, most notably, music and dance. The best example of this influence is the hit song, 'La Bamba', popularized in 1988 by the Mexican-American group Los Lobos. In Mexico, this song was sung as early as 1683 by black people from Veracruz. The *bamba* is also a traditional dance. Bamba or Mbamba is the name of an ethnic group in Angola who arrived in Mexico via the slave port of Veracruz in the seventeenth century. According to J.A. Rogers, among the many prominent Mexicans of African ancestry was the muralist and painter Diego Rivera.

In spite of this impressive historical, social and cultural legacy, however, Afro-Mexicans exist today as a marginalized group. They are, arguably, the least represented and most oppressed of all Mexico's ethnic groups, and have yet to enter the mainstream and be recognized as full citizens.

Historical background

Precise figures for the number of Africans brought into Mexico are difficult to come by. Many were brought in illegally, and unknown numbers of people died during the journey or escaped to the mountains upon coming. It is estimated that between the coming of Hernán Cortés in 1519 and the start of Mexico's War of Independence in 1810 more than 500,000 Africans were brought to Mexico. Their numbers increased so rapidly during the early years of the colony that the Spanish authorities feared a black uprising. In the late sixteenth and early seventeenth centuries Mexico employed more enslaved Africans than any other country in the Americas. Most came from West Africa, although people were also brought from Central and East Africa. *Ladinos* – Africans born and hispanized in the Caribbean, Spain and Portugal[2] – entered the country through the ports of Acapulco, Veracruz, Campeche and Pánuco.

Africans traditionally were skilled labourers in colonial Mexico. Their expertise was needed in the silver mines of Zacatecas, Taxco, Guanajuato, Durango and Pachuca, and on the sugar plantations of the Valle de Orizaba and Morelos. In many colonial cities they built roads and bridges, and it is thought that Mexico's cathedrals were, in some cases, built and designed by black people. Their labour was needed in the *obrajes* (textile factories) of Puebla, Michoacán, Mexico City and Oaxaca. They worked on the cattle ranches and dived for pearls on the coast in the pearl fisheries, a highly dangerous activity during which many of them drowned. Many served in domestic capacities, too.

Spaniards such as Bartolomé de las Casas suggested that Africans were needed to replace the *indio*, who was being exterminated at the alarming rate of 4 million within the first twelve years of the conquest. As early as 1511 Africans were said to be able to do the work of four indigenous people and were therefore considered four times more profitable. Their presence was indispensable in the mines and the sugar plantations of the colonial period. Mexico City, along with Lima in Peru, became the largest and wealthiest city in colonial Spanish America.

During this period, Mexico's African population always exceeded the European. According to the writer Aguirre Beltrán, in the sixteenth century black Mexicans constituted 71 per cent of the non-indigenous population, while the Spanish represented the remainder.[3] By the eighteenth century the number of African and mulatto Mexicans had declined to about 65 per cent of the non-indigenous population. However, Afro-Mexicans represented only about 2 per cent of the total national population, while white people represented less than 1 per cent; the native population was a massive 98 per cent.

Despite the fact that a large number of Africans had entered Mexico, as early as the late 1740s their numbers had declined due to several factors. In the sixteenth century the main cause of death for the Afro-Mexican population was European diseases like yellow fever, tuberculosis and syphilis. Death in the sugar-cane fields and in the silver mines was also very common among black workers. Moreover, much of the decrease can be attributed to the Spanish American concept of *blanqueamiento* (whitening of the races). It was legally and socially beneficial for Afro-Mexicans to mix with either indigenous people or the Spanish. Black women who married Hispanic men improved their social status and that of their children. Despite the many efforts by non-black Mexicans to restrict relations between African and indigenous people, black men often had sexual relationships with indigenous women, largely because black women were unavailable to them. During much of the colonial period, black women represented less than 10 per cent of the immigrant population. They served primarily as cooks and maids for the Spanish, and many became their concubines. It was a general rule to admit more men than women to Mexico, resulting in a ratio of black men to black women of about three to one.

Legally, the progeny of a black man and an indigenous woman was a free child; that of two black slaves was always a slave child.

As time went on, most of the non-indigenous population of colonial Mexico came to be the offspring of miscegenation between Africans and indigenous people. This mixture was known as *jarocho* ('wild pig'), *chino* or *lobo* ('wolf'), depending on the dominant features.

When black men were allowed to marry black women, this was almost always done violently and against the will of one or both parties. Slave owners married off enslaved black people and mulattos as soon as their age would allow, to procure children. The Catholic Church mandated that such couples see each other only on Saturday nights. Some slave owners forbad them to sleep in the same bed. This and other injustices led Afro-Mexican men to escape to *palenques* (armed settlements of escaped slaves). Here the uneven sex ratio caused many former slaves to kidnap indigenous women and force them into what were called *casamientos de monte* (mountain marriages). In some cases, indigenous women willingly became the sexual partners of black and mulatto men.

Mountain marriage is still an acceptable practice today in the Afro-Mexican community of Cuajinicuilapa, Guerrero State. When the groom describes his victory he proudly boasts, 'Me la robé' ('I stole her'); when the woman talks about her adventure she confesses, 'Me jullí' ('I got married').[4] Later, the town gossips about the event, saying, 'Se jullieron al monte' ('They got married in the mountains'). This is not real kidnap but a voluntary agreement between the bride and groom. Nor do they actually go to the mountain. The family of the bride is compensated for its loss.

The introduction of women in the *palenques* changed them demographically. Children began to appear, making the men less mobile. The men became more concerned with family responsibilities such as farming than with fighting and protecting themselves against the Spanish. 'Throughout the colonial period many *palenque* settlements in Veracruz died evolutionary deaths as restless unattached male runaways became village husbands and fathers.'[5] The former maroon (escaped slave) community of Yanga became racially and ethnically indistinguishable from other settlements that dotted the area, after a few generations.[6] The people of Yanga have now lost their identity as a black community.

Oppression, struggle and independence

Africans and mulattos were perceived in a negative way, perhaps in order to justify the brutal oppression to which they were routinely subjected. The Spanish described them as 'vicious people', 'naturally evil', of a 'bad race', bellicose and bestial. Such prejuidice was reflected in the way in which they treated them. In an effort to maintain their own alleged purity of blood, to ensure their superior status and to relegate black people to the lowest rung of the social ladder, in the seventeenth century the Spanish established a social system based on an elaborate colour bar. This caste system, prevalent throughout Latin America, controlled all aspects of life for Afro-Mexicans. Every person of African or indigenous ancestry was denied rights to education, and was not allowed to bear arms, to travel freely at night, to wear jewellery or silk, and in many cases to marry. Black people were not accepted in ecclesiastical orders. For those who violated these oppressive colonial laws, the punishment was as excessive and merciless as castration, maiming and disfigurement. Some black and mulatto slaves were branded with the slave owner's name. One of the cruellest and most widespread forms of physical punishment was a practice known as *pringar,* dropping hot pork fat or pitch melted over a large candle onto the victim's skin.[7] When a group of maroons were caught during the uprising of 1536, they were beheaded; their heads were later exhibited in Mexico City's Plaza Mayor as an example to others.

African resistance to slavery and oppression in Mexico began immediately after the institution was established. Aguirre Beltrán points out that more than 2,000 black people, approximately one-tenth of the black population, had escaped from their Spanish masters. They fled to the mountains and other remote areas of the country and later established *palenques.* The isolation of these *palenques* offered sanctuary to maroons and also preserved elements of African tradition. The best-known Mexican *palenque* still in existence is Yanga, although most of its Afro-Mexican inhabitants have relocated to the neighbouring town of Mata Clara.

In Mexico, black revolutionaries first offered emancipation to slaves during the War of Independence. Known as the poor peo-

ple's champion, Vicente Guerrero, also known as El Negro Guer-
rero, who would later become Mexico's second President, and
General José María Morelos both played a significant part in win-
ning Mexico's independence from Spain. The Mexican states of
Guerrero and Morelos were named in honour of these war heroes.
Other black people in leadership positions during the War of
Independence included the pure African Juan del Carmen, Juan
Bautista, Francisco Gómez and José María Alegre. Some historians
point out that it was the *ejército moreno* (dark army) of Father
Hidalgo that launched the independence struggle.

One of the reasons why black people were so involved in the
War of Independence was because they were fighting, not only for
national liberation, but also to end the institution of slavery and
the caste system that supported ethnic segregation and discrimination. It was a duty of every citizen of the colony to serve in the
military, a responsibility that many white people evaded. However, free black people (those who had obtained their freedom
through manumission) joined the cause that promised them full
liberty. As early as the eighteenth century troops of free black people were protecting the major cities of colonial Mexico. By 1770
Afro-Mexican militia began to appear, such as the company of *pardos* and *morenos* in Veracruz. However, even though these people
served in the military they did not enjoy full citizenship rights.

It was during Guerrero's presidency in 1829 that slavery was
officially abolished. Two years earlier, segregation laws had been
abolished and new laws passed that prohibited the Catholic
Church from using race designations in church records. Guerrero,
Morelos and other revolutionaries had developed nationalist
views. They wanted all the people of the nation to think in terms
of nationality and not race. Those who had been referred to by the
Spanish as *mestizo, mulato, negro* and *indio* now demanded to be
called Mexicans. Children born after independence were recorded
simply as Mexicans rather than as *negro, indio*, and so on. As a consequence, Afro-Mexicans moved further away from an African
identity, and studies of black life in the post-colonial period suffer
from the absence of ethnic identifications.

Population, demography and ethnic identity

The Mexican government does not nowadays collect data by ethnic group. The last census to do so was in 1810, when black people represented 10.2 per cent of the Mexican population. A 1950 estimate revealed that the Afro-Mexican population was about 5.1 per cent of the national total, half of what it had been at the time of independence.[8] Because of the high level of miscegenation, mostly between indigenous people and Hispanics, the African genetic pool diminished over time. To a large extent, this was official policy, as it was throughout Latin America, expressed in the now highly suspect phrase *mejorar la raza* (improve the race). This is a process by which African ancestry is 'diluted' by racial mixing. The idea was to mix the races to form a homogeneous group, the mythical 'cosmic race', an ideology perpetuated by many Mexican intellectuals. The twentieth-century philosopher José Vasconcelos, for example, preached this ideology.

Historically, Mexicans of African descent were considered the most undesirable group with which to miscegenate; African features were spoken of as 'abominable'. Many Afro-Mexicans tried to 'pass' the colour line into the European group if possible, or into the indigenous group. During the late colonial period, people of indigenous or African descent were allowed to buy the title of *blanco*. Such was the case for José María Morelos y Pavón, one of the heroic figures of the Mexican independence struggle. He was of African descent, but was described on his birth certificate as a *criollo* (a white person of Spanish origin). However, for *negros atezados* (very dark black people) and *negros retintos* ('double-dyed' black people) this was impossible.

The current number of Afro-Mexicans is not known. However, Miriam Jiménez Román, from New York's Schomburg Center for Research in Black Culture, estimates that '75 per cent of the population of Mexico has some African ancestry due to the pervasiveness and the extension of the African throughout Mexico'. The *1994 Britannica Yearbook* estimates that African descendants constitute 0.5 per cent of Mexicans – that is, 474,000 identifiable Afro-Mexicans among 94 million. This low estimate is partially due to the conflict over how 'black' is defined.

Mexico has tried to 'dilute' its dark population by discouraging – and in the case of the former dictator Porfirio Díaz by banning – immigration of people of African descent and encouraging immigration of European peoples, promising them jobs and economic stability.

Neither a single authority nor consistent data exist on the question of black demographics in Mexico. Historically, the Afro-Mexican population was concentrated on the coasts: on the Costa Chica in the western states of Guerrero and Oaxaca, and in the eastern states of Tabasco and Veracruz, where black people have remained living in and around the former slave ports. People of African descent also inhabit the northern deserts of the states of Coahuila, Zacatecas and Sinaloa; and they reportedly live in the southern states of Yucatán and Quintana Roo, where they represent 10 per cent of the province.[9] A further Afro-Mexican community, settled in the northern state of Coahuila, owes its origins to North American slaves who escaped during the seventeenth century and later cohabitated and intermarried with Seminole Native Americans. Today, their descendants have a society and culture of mixed African and Native American heritage.

Interestingly, many historically black communities along the Atlantic coast of Mexico bear names of African regions or make reference to people of African ancestry. Along the coast are towns called Angola, Guinea, Mozambique and Cerro del Congo or Congo Hill. Other settlements are named in recognition of the various African ethnic groups that came, such as La Mandinga, El Mocambo, La Matamba and El Monzongo; or they bear names such as El Mulato, La Mulata, El Negro and Juan Mulato. Some town names simply indicate maroon territories, such as Cimarrón and Palenque. There are also Afro-Mexican communities named after black liberators who fought against the Spanish. The town of San Lorenzo de los Negros was later named Yanga, after the African-born prince who after forty years of fighting the Spanish won sovereignty for his people, while Mandinga y Matosa was named after the maroon leader Francisco de la Matosa.

While many Afro-Mexicans lack a clear consciousness of their African heritage, some do not. The term *mestizo* (mixed) is never used to refer to Afro-Mexicans but is reserved exclusively for indigenous–Hispanic Mexicans. People of visible African ancestry are called *moreno* (brown), a euphemism that evolved after the War of Independence and replaced the malicious term *negro,* which dated from the slave trade.

The term *negro* evokes much discomfort among Afro-Mexicans and is avoided. In response to use of this word, Afro-Mexicans of Costa Chica say: 'Los negros son solo los burros, nosotros somos "prietos"' ('Negroes are donkeys, we are dark'). People in this community refer to their group as the *negrada* or the *negradita.* Members of this community who are of mixed Spanish and African origin, and who in colonial Mexico would have been called *mulatos blancos* and *mulatos lobos,* are known as *blanquitos* (little whites), because of the lightness of their skin and their less obvious African features. *Blanquitos* are the most privileged group in the community, generally occupying middle-stratum positions such as clerks. The *negros puros* – people with strong African features – are called *cuculustes.* According to local people, such individuals are the most discriminated against of this community. While the inhabitants of some Afro-Mexican coastal communities seem to associate negroid physical features with negative personal stereotypes, in other towns of the region such as the community of San Nicolás residents adopt such African names as Angola, Congo and Nigeria in proud recognition of their African ancestry.

Socio-economic condition and cultural forms

Only one detailed study is known to have been made of an Afro-Mexican community. In 1946 the Afro-Mexican scholar Gonzalo Aguirre Beltrán investigated the predominantly black town of Cuajinicuilapa in the state of Guerrero. But research on contemporary social conditions in Mexico tends to exclude black communities completely. Within the past decade, however, concerned anthropologists and others have visited Afro-Mexican communities, describing them as impoverished and marginalized. Illiteracy is common, and opportunities for education are scarce; school facilities are inadequate. In these communities residents have received little or no assistance from the government. Many towns lack such basic facilities as sewerage, drainage, potable water and paved streets.

According to data collected by Aguirre Beltrán in the 1940s, the town of Cuajinicuilapa became accessible only in 1965, when a highway was constructed; the first school was established only in 1940; the local businesses are owned entirely by the few upper-class white people. As a result of the agrarian reforms of 1910, black people work primarily on *ejidos* (communally owned estates) cultivating beans, corn, peppers and sesame seeds – their primary cash crop; others make a living by selling bread and other items, especially near tourist resorts like Acapulco. In the 1940s both the infant mortality rate and the number of women who died in childbirth were extremely high in the town due to the lack of doctors and medical facilities. Children under 4 died at an alarming rate, representing 45 per cent of the total deaths in the municipality. Half of the children born in Cuajinicuilapa did not live to the age of 5. Epilepsy, diarrhoea and fever were the major killers.

More recent evidence comes from the neighbouring Afro-Mexican town of San Nicolás. Here the schoolteachers, administrators, doctors and nurses are non-black and come from other parts of the country. Interestingly, however, all political matters are handled exclusively by Afro-Mexicans. The following observations and comments were made by Gwendolyn Twillie, chair of the Theatre Arts/Dance Department at the University of Arkansas at Little Rock, USA, during her brief stay in San Nicolás:

> *The houses along the dusty dirt roads are of three types: mud and sticks with dirt floors and tin roofs; brick; and the less common adobe houses of mud and sticks covered with plastic. The typical kitchen is a lean-to made of sticks with a tin roof. No bathrooms were observed. The houses are sparsely furnished – a hammock, two chairs and rope beds being standard. Those families fortunate enough to have refrigerators use them to store soft drinks for resale. A sign with soft drink logos nailed to the outside of a house is not only an advertisement, it is a status symbol proclaiming that that family owns a refrigerator.*
>
> *The day begins very early for the people of San Nicolás. Women wash, do other household chores, tend to the children, and bake pan (a type of sweet bread). Most of the men farm. In addition to*

corn, sesame seeds, chillies, jamaica beans, rice, watermelon, papaya, lemons, oranges and cacao are also grown. A few men own livestock, and some money is made through the sale of cattle and goats. Some of the men own small camionetas (small trucks), and they earn money by picking up passengers. It is commonplace for the women and girls to transport goods by carrying them on their heads. They work very hard and there is little time for leisure.

There are not enough teachers. The classrooms are crowded; there are few books and virtually no supplies. Children were observed using rulers made from paper to measure the diagram of a town square in shared textbooks. An interview with the principal of one of the three primary schools and a third-grade teacher revealed that most of the students do not finish secondary school. There is not a great deal of interest in school, except for the units on the conversion of dollars to pesos. Most of the students plan to go to the United States to work. They do not mind entering the country illegally to work in the fields. According to the principal, a recent survey revealed that 13 out of every 100 people from the state of Guerrero go to the United States to work.

The average Mexican lives in poverty, but the people of San Nicolás are poorer than average. The stark poverty is humbling. Many of the children appear to be malnourished. Their bloated abdomens and knobby knees are sure signs of malnutrition ...

Mexicans generally do not have much to say that is complimentary about the people of San Nicolás. Mexicans often declare: 'You should not go there, the people are bad. They will rob you. They will kill you. They are on drugs.' These statements are typical from Guadalajara to Acapulco and beyond. The people of San Nicolás do not deserve the wholesale derogatory comments that are made about them as a people. They have the same hopes, dreams and desires of other human beings. They want a cleaner town. They want better roads. They want a drainage system. They want a better life and they deserve it. Yet, although the people experience these deplorable circumstances, the author cannot help but sadly conclude that the people of San Nicolás could not sense that they deserve better. All they know or have been taught is destitution, slavery, and that they are a despicable people.[10]

Several factors have contributed to Afro-Mexicans' loss of cultural identity: the achievements of Mexico's African peoples have not been acknowledged; unlike the indigenous population, they lost many of their traditions during the upheavals of their enslavement; and as we have seen, their integration into the dominant society has been relentlessly brutal. Even so, Afro-Mexicans have managed to preserve a degree of African identity. In particular, they have successfully retained their musical styles. The musicologist Rolando Pérez Fernández has observed that traditional Mexican music 'is fundamentally the result of the transculturation between the Spanish and the blacks'. Traditional Mexican music finds its origin in the states that were heavily populated by black people: southern Jalisco, Michoacán, Guerrero, Oaxaca and, along the Pacific coast, Huasteco, Tabasco, Veracruz and northern Puebla. Each state has contributed a *son* (sound) or style of its own, narrating stories of love and conflict. Some popular *sones* are La Morena, La Negra and El Maracumbe. These styles are similar to many Afro-Caribbean and African musical forms. Other musical forms attributed to Afro-Mexicans are dances like the *jarabe*, the *chilena*, the *gusto* and the *zapateo*. These dances were once prohibited by the colonial administration but today are considered the model of Mexican folklore. Various African-style drums and the marimba (originating in the Congo) are widely used.

Another cultural form common among Mexico's black community is the *corrido*. *Corridos* are narrations in the first or third person by a *corridista* who witnessed a particular event. The themes are historical and revolutionary as well as tragedies of love and death. The *corrido* is usually recited or sung in an Afro-Mexican dialect. Popular along the Costa Chica of Mexico, these poems illustrate occurrences in everyday life. Since 1990 black communities of the Costa Chica have held annual competitions where *corridistas* compete against one another. Also, such narratives as 'The Rabbit and the Coyote' are as popular in the black communities of Mexico as they are among Afro-Americans elsewhere in the region.

Since the colonial era, the Dance of the Devil has been unique among Afro-Mexicans of the Costa Chica community, a tradition that was practised and preserved in the maroon communities. In the ceremony, men dress up in old tattered clothes and wear a horse mask. The Devil is represented by a man dressed in women's clothing. The participants dance traditional African dances throughout the night. Catholic deities, beliefs and rites are mingled with African ones. This dance is performed during Carnival, Kings' Day, Corpus Christi Day and the Day of the Dead. Aguirre Beltrán discovered that many religious beliefs and practices in this community, such as the cohabitation of dead relatives and family, and possession by ancestral gods and spirits, have their origin in the Congo and Guinea.

The language of Afro-Mexicans is sometimes said to be 'unintelligible Spanish'. In his study of the Afro-Mexicans of Cuajinicuilapa, Aguirre Beltrán noted that the Spanish spoken by many black Mexicans is similar to that of other areas in Latin America where people of African descent predominate. This unique Spanish dialect, which is rhythmic and rich in metaphor, developed because maroon communities were isolated from the rest of the country.

Other cultural traditions that speak of African influence include the carrying of babies on the hip and of objects on the head, which are common practices among Afro-Mexicans, and the building of *redondos* – homes made in a circular pattern, with reed walls and conical thatched roofs – throughout the Costa Chica. Both these African practices have been adopted by the indigenous people who also live in the region. Certain culinary techniques and foods have also been popularized by Afro-Mexicans, such as *mondongo* (pig intestines).

Discrimination and gender stereotypes

To date, no major study on Mexican race relations has been done; until recently the subject was kept out of national debate. When racism is talked about in Mexico, it is assumed to be racism against indigenous people, not against people of African ancestry. In Mexico it is argued that there is no discrimination, because there are no black people to discriminate against. Yet contemporary Afro-Mexicans are discriminated against for the same reasons that applied during the colonial period – for their alleged inferiority and skin colour. During the colonial era, they represented the bottom of the social scale, and they have remained there ever since.

Racism against black people in Mexico is subtle. Although legal segregation of blacks from whites no longer exists, there is a clear distinction between the life of an Afro-Mexican and that of a *mestizo* member of the oppressive, dominant group. Ironically, in May 1992 the former President of Mexico, Carlos Salinas de Gortari, and the Mayor of Mexico City invited leaders of several Afro-American studies programmes across the United States to the country, in an effort to bridge a perceived gap between Mexico and the Afro-American community in the USA. No such efforts have been made regarding Mexico's own black population.

Despite Salinas's claim that Mexico has successfully assimilated its black population, the only assimilation that has taken place is linguistic and, to some extent, biological. There is no general acceptance of the African ethnic and cultural element in the national heritage. Mexico, like other Latin American countries, identifies itself as a nation of *mestizos* – people of mixed indigenous and Spanish blood. Latin American historians claim that the 'discovery' of their region was an encounter of two worlds, the indigenous and the Spanish, a notion fully endorsed by Mexican academia. While many Mexicans boast about their Spanish relatives, rarely will one admit to having a black grandparent.

Afro-Mexicans have not assimilated, which explains their absence from such institutions as universities, hospitals and the government. While few black people occupy positions of authority, it is relatively common for them to excel in such stereotypical roles as athletes and entertainers. Their primary sources of income, however, are fishing, farming and domestic work. The popular Mexican saying 'Work hard like a nigger to live like a white' aptly illustrates the situation.

Since the beginning of Spanish domination, people of African origin have been portrayed in popular culture in a range of insulting stereotypes. Today they are depicted in the most distorted way on television, and especially in comic books which many Mexicans seem to enjoy. The popular biweekly comic book *Memín Pinguín* is one example of how black people are negatively portrayed; it features a carricature of a young Afro-Hispanic boy who is constantly bullied because of his physicial 'ugligness'.[11] Afro-Mexicans appear on national television almost always in such stereotypical roles as maids and entertainers.

Specific information concerning the condition of black women in Mexico is non-existent. However, the manner in which they are portrayed in Mexican popular culture provides an idea of some of the problems they encounter. Afro-Mexican women generally work as cooks, maids and domestics. Like black men, they are viewed as objects of servitude – overweight, uneducated, illiterate and poor, and speakers of unintelligible Spanish. Yet black women in Mexico cannot seem to escape the myth of being oversexed. Many historians write about Spanish men's desire to have African women as their concubines. In this way, the black woman's body has become a commodity. She was known as a prostitute in major colonial cities like Puebla City and Mexico City. At one point in history the words *negra* and 'prostitute' were synonymous. This image has persisted, and is routinely depicted in Mexican comic books.

The agenda for change

Afro-Mexicans have begun to mobilize for social change and economic development. Their primary focus is teaching black pride and improving the social and human rights status of all Afro-Mexicans. One of the earliest manifestations of this process of recovery occurred in 1932 in the state of Veracruz, when the descendants of maroons pressured the Mexican government to change the name of the town of San Lorenzo de los Negros to Yanga in honour of the Muslim maroon leader. Yanga's achievements included founding the first free town of maroons in Spanish America – something about which the average Mexican is never taught. Carnival here is now held almost exclusively to pay tribute to Yanga, the Liberator. This annual event acts as a celebration of African identity and culture. In an effort to build links between Africans and Mexicans of African descent, relationships have been established between the Embassy of the Ivory Coast and the municipality of Yanga since 1988.

Despite such initiatives, and regardless of the major role that

Afro-Mexicans had in the liberation of Mexico, their participation in the development of the nation and the countless other contributions they made to Mexican society, the general attitude towards black people in Mexico remains racist. They have yet to achieve political or social equality. Skin colour has remained an indicator of social position. The few black professionals encountered in Mexico tend to be Africans, African-Americans or Haitians, most of whom are employed in their respective embassies.

Afro-Mexicans lack recognition, representation, leadership and participation in the political, economic and educational institutions of their country. While indigenous groups have received national as well as international attention and support, Afro-Mexican voices have largely gone unheard. To live up to its claim of racial democracy, Mexican society must deal with its own racism and begin to accept its black population by viewing and projecting Afro-Mexicans in a positive light, and by illustrating their contribution to society in school textbooks and academic studies and by other means. This can be achieved by promoting Mexico as a tri-ethnic society as opposed to the mythical country of *mestizos* for which so much has been claimed. The production and circulation of negative images of black people in the media and popular culture should be brought to an end. Funds should be made available to improve the impoverished communities where most Afro-Mexicans live. Finally the culture, way of life and socio-economic conditions of the many silent black communities in Mexico should be studied and included in national analyses and reports, to combat the present ignorance and injustice.

Notes

1 In 1939, in the state of Veracruz, many giant heads displaying negroid features and carved from a single block of basalt, were unearthed. The creators of these sculptures, the Olmecs, were one of the most influential cultures of ancient Mexico. Other terracotta artefacts suggesting a pre-Columbian African connection were also found. See van Sertima, I., *They Came before Colombus: The African Presence in Ancient America*, New York, Random House, 1976.

2 Many Moors (black Muslims) who were expelled from Spain in 1492 were enslaved and taken to Mexico. Spain as a rule prohibited this introduction of Muslims.

3 Aguirre Beltrán, G., *La población negra de Méjico: estudio etnohistórico*, Xalapa, Universidad Veracruzana, 1989, p. 180.
4 The verb *juller* seems to be peculiar to this communtity, as it does not exist in Spanish dictionaries. It can mean 'to elope', 'to run off and get married'.
5 Carroll, P.J., *Blacks in Colonial Veracruz: Race, Ethnicity and Regional Development*, Austin, TX, University of Texas, 1991, p. 91.
6 Ibid., p. 92.
7 Palmer, C.A., *Slaves of the White God: Blacks in Mexico, 1570-1650*, London, Harvard University Press, 1976, p. 50.
8 No census seeking information on ethnic origin was permitted until 1921. But between 1930 and 1940 matrimonial licence forms stipulated that the applicant must indicate his or her race; see Rout, L.B. Jr, *The African Experience in Spanish America: 1502 to the Present Day*, Cambridge, Cambridge University Press, 1976, p. 280.
9 Black people were taken to the state of Yucatán to construct the railways; see Aguirre Beltrán, G., *Cuijla: esbozo etnográfico de un pueblo negro*, Mexico City, Fondo de Cultura Económica, 1985, p. 220.
10 Twillie, G., unpublished description of San Nicolás, 1991, reproduced with the author's permission.
11 The Organization of Africans in the Americas, based in Washington, DC, has recovered many Mexican artefacts, media and advertising images, publications and artworks depicting black people negatively.

Select bibliography

'Afro-Mexican names: a trail of history and kinship', *Conexoes*, Michigan State University, no. 2, 1994, pp. 1-5.
Aguirre Beltrán, G., *Cuijla: esbozo etnográfico de un pueblo negro*, Mexico City, Fondo de Cultura Económica, 1985.
Aguirre Beltrán, G., 'Medicina negra', in *Medicina y magia*, Mexico City, Instituto Nacional Indegenista, 2nd edn, 1973, pp. 55-72.
Aguirre Beltrán, G., *La población negra de Méjico: estudio étnohistórico*, Xalapa, Universidad Veracruzana, 1989.
Alamán, L., *Historia de Méjico, desde primeros movimientos que preparon su independencia en el año de 1808 hasta la epoca presente*, vol. 5, Lara, 1849.
Bonfil Batalla, G., *Méjico profundo: una civilización negada*, Mexico City, Grijalbo, 1990.
'Callate burrita prieta: poética afromestiza', *El Garabato*, Unidad Regional Guerrero, Dirección General de Culturas Populares, 1992, pp. 9-12.
Cancionero del primero encuentro regional de corridistas de la Costa Chica de Guerrero, Guerrero, Unidad Regional Guerrero, 1990.
Carrol, P.J., *Blacks in Colonial Veracruz: Race, Ethnicity and Regional Development*, Austin, TX, University of Texas, 1991.
Cruz Carretera, S., *El carnaval en Yanga: notas y commentarios sobre una fiesta de la negritud*, Veracruz, Culturas Populares Unidad Regional Centro de Veracruz, 1990.

Fleming, M.M., 'African legacy', *Hispanic,* January/February 1994, pp. 86-92.

Gleaton, A., *Africa's Legacy in Mexico,* Washington, DC, Smithsonian Institution Traveling Exhibition Service, 1993.

'Indigenas, mestizos, y afromestizos de Guerrero', *El Garabato,* Unidad Regional Guerrero, Dirección General de Culturas Populares, 1992, pp. 27-33.

Iturriaga, J.E., *La estructura social y cultural de Méjico,* Mexico City, Fondo de Cultura Económica, 1951.

Moedano, G., 'Danzas y bailes en recuerdo de los muertos', *Bailetomanía: el mundo de la danza,* vol. 1, no. 2, 1981, pp. 26-33.

Moedano, G., 'El estudio de las tradiciones orales y musicales de los afro-mestizos de Méjico', *Antropología e Historia,* vol. 3, no. 31, 1980.

Naveda Chavez-Hita, A., *Esclavos negros en las haciendas azucareras de Cordoba, Veracruz, 1690-1830,* Veracruz, Universidad Veracruzana, 1987.

'Negro resistance to Spanish rule in colonial Mexico', *Journal of Negro History,* Vol. LII, no. 2, 1986.

Palmer, C.A., *Slaves of the White God: Blacks in Mexico, 1570-1650,* London, Harvard University Press, 1976.

Parkes, H.B., *A History of Mexico,* Boston, MA, Mifflin, 1966.

Pérez Fernández, R., *La música afromestiza mexicana,* Veracruz, Universidad Veracruzana, 1990.

Rout, L.B. Jr, *The African Experience in Spanish America: 1502 to the Present Day,* Cambridge, Cambridge University Press, 1976.

Twillie, G., 'Contributions of enslaved Africans', *Journal of Black Studies,* vol. 25, no. 4, 1995, pp. 420-30.

NICARAGUA

Jane Freeland

Strictly speaking, Nicaragua has three Afro-Latin American ethnic groups, all concentrated in the Caribbean Coast region.[1] The Creoles descend from African slaves imported from the Caribbean and their white English masters. The Black Caribs or Garífuna[2] descend from escaped slaves and indigenous Caribs and Arawaks of the Antilles, and the Miskitu from escaped slaves and indigenous peoples of the 'Mosquito Coast' of Nicaragua and Honduras. Yet while the Garífuna are proudly Afro-Latin American, the Miskitu identify themselves as indigenous, and will not be dealt with here.[3]

The 36,000 Creoles are the third largest of the six ethnic groups of the Coast, 12.14 per cent of the regional and about 0.9 per cent of the national population. The majority live in the urban settlements of what is now the South Atlantic Autonomous Region (RAAS).[4] Smaller groups live in the towns of the North Atlantic Autonomous Region (RAAN), and there are migrant populations in Managua and in the United States. The Garífuna number just 3,068, only 1.02 per cent of the regional and 0.04 per cent of the national population. They chiefly inhabit two small villages, Orinoco and La Fe, on the shores of Pearl Lagoon north of Bluefields, and are scattered in other lagoon-bank villages, and in Bluefields.

Uniquely in Central America, both groups have recently experienced a socialist revolution which made minority rights a central issue. Each made different demands of the revolution, rooted in their historical experience, and gained rights unique to the Americas, which are now again in jeopardy.

The Creoles: dual colonization and identity[5]

The Atlantic Coast has always been physically and politically isolated from the rest of Nicaragua. Multi-ethnic, multilingual and Protestant, with strong Anglo-American affinities since the arrival of English settlers in the seventeenth century, it is incorporated into a typically Central American state, dominated by Spanish-speaking, Roman Catholic *mestizo* descendants of indigenous peoples and the Spanish who colonized Nicaragua's Pacific Coast region in the sixteenth century.[6]

Nicaragua's dual colonization created a tradition of hostile relations between the two resulting societies, which was exploited and exaggerated in the competition between 'Anglo' and 'Hispanic' powers for control of this strategic territory. Ethnic identity was shaped by this competition and the interventions it triggered: from Britain, North America and the Nicaraguan state itself. Each power favoured different ethnic groups, giving them space to develop but altering their relationships with the others, creating the complex inter-ethnic hierarchy observable on the coast today, and the Creoles' place within it.

Britain set the pattern in the seventeenth century by forming a strategic alliance with the indigenous Miskitu of the coast against their common enemy, the Spanish, and ruling the territory indirectly through a Miskitu chief recognised as 'King' of Mosquitia. British settlers imported African slaves, who occupied the bottom of the ethnic hierarchy created by this alliance. As in other slave societies, slave masters and slaves interbred, and their offspring formed an elite group within the slave population. When Britain vacated the coast in 1787, many of this group inherited economic and political roles previously occupied by the British, and formed independent communities which became the Creole centres of today.

Their advance was checked when Britain returned in 1845 to fill the power vacuum following independence from Spain, declaring Mosquitia a British protectorate. Nevertheless, political, economic and cultural changes in the nineteenth century enabled the Creoles to move up the ethnic hierarchy until they replaced the Miskitu as most favoured group.

From 1849 Moravian missionaries evangelized first Creoles and later Miskitu and other indigenous peoples. Mission schools taught literacy in English, strengthening links with English-based culture. Educated Creoles were trained as 'native helpers' to the white missionaries, and later as ministers, gaining authority over other ethnic groups as the Moravian Church became influential, politically and economically as well as spiritually.

Following independence from Spain (1838), Nicaraguan nationalism, backed by United States expansionism, gradually forced Britain out of the Coast, ending the special relationship with the Miskitu. To protect Miskitu rights, a US-style 'Mosquito Reserve' was created (1860), but its constitution limited the Miskitu chief's powers, giving control to an advisory council dominated by Creoles.

Between the 1880s and the 1950s US companies increasingly penetrated the Atlantic Coast economy, exploiting its resources in independent enclaves. Here, the Creoles' English-based education qualified them for clerical and middle management positions, while *mestizo* immigrants, casual indigenous wage-workers and unskilled black labour from the Caribbean did the heavy labour. As Afro-Caribbean immigration increased, a class/colour distinction developed that persisted well into the twentieth century, between 'Negroes' – black, predominantly Anglican and Baptist immigrants – and Creoles – older-established, lighter-skinned, Moravian professionals, independent farmers and fisherfolk. Gradually, 'Negroes' assimilated 'upwards', and all Afro-Caribbean *costeños* called themselves 'Creoles' to mark their associations with the Anglo culture and to distinguish themselves from the indigenous groups. By the 1890s Creoles were firmly in the ascendancy, in the church, the Mosquito Reserve and the enclave labour hierarchy. However, their authority, which depended on the presence of an external power, was short-lived.

In 1893 Pacific Coast politics brought to power the Liberal President Zelaya, determined to 'reincorporate' the reserve into the Nicaraguan state. Creoles fought hard to defend their autonomy but were defeated by US-backed government forces and stripped of their leadership roles. *Mestizos* ousted Creoles from government and administration; Spanish replaced English as the region's official language; teaching in other languages was forbidden. Designed to create national unity, these policies fuelled hostility to 'the Spaniards', particularly among Creoles. Frustrated by governments they considered inefficient, corrupt and culturally inferior, Creoles backed repeated coups and uprisings,

confirming *mestizo* perceptions of the Coast as a hotbed of seces-
sionism. Yet despite their support, when a 1909 Conservative
coup deposed Zelaya, neither the region's autonomy nor the
Creoles' place in its government were restored. Even their status
in the labour hierarchy of the enclaves slowly declined as US
companies withdrew.

Modern Creole identity

Creoles perceived themselves first regionally, as *costeños*, then ethnically, as Creoles. Their identity interwove class and ethnic elements and was inseparable from their position in an observable
ethnic hierarchy. At the time of the Sandinista victory (1979),
Creoles still considered themselves the elite of this hierarchy,
blocked only by *mestizo* domination from leading political and
administrative positions. They still dominated the Protestant
churches, and retained a share of white collar jobs disproportionate to their numbers,[7] accepting only reluctantly the non-skilled
or agricultural jobs associated with indigenous groups and *mestizo*
peasants. Education was the key to this status.

Other critical markers of identity were contact with English-
speaking culture, sometimes through higher education in the
United States, and a lifestyle based on the imported goods made
available through the US enclaves. As enclave work declined,
Creoles took to 'shipping out' as crew on US boats, or migrated,
first to the towns, then to Managua or the USA. Most Creole
families could rely on dollar remittances to supplement their
earnings and maintain their status.

To break into *mestizo*-dominated jobs, Creoles must assimilate
towards *mestizo* culture, at the cost of ethnic allegiances, the last
cultural markers to be shed being Protestant religious affiliations[8]
and creole-English speech. Such sacrifices were less urgent on the
Coast, where the lifestyles of Creole and *mestizo* elites borrow
elements from each other. But in the Pacific region, Creoles
would explain away their English speech by claiming to be Puerto Ricans, rather than be identified as Nicaraguan *negros*.

Creole women occupied a similar middle ground, enjoying
more freedom than women of other groups. They retained

rights, originating in the African family, to sexual pleasure and the negotiation of important family decisions. Creole history had given greater economic power to men, and Moravianism emphasized women's housewifely role. Nevertheless, Moravian education was open to women, who were encouraged towards careers in nursing or teaching, or to work as secretaries or accountants. Unmarried Creole women contributed to the family income with waged work, while mothers and grandmothers took charge of the household. Male migration left many female-headed Creole families, often with children of various fathers.

Attitudes to language mirrored the Creoles' self-image. Dominance in the ethnic hierarchy had long depended on command of Standard English, yet this became increasingly difficult to acquire and maintain. When Spanish displaced English as the school language, English became just another curriculum subject. As the companies withdrew, there was less call for Standard English and less contact with native-speakers. By the time of the revolution, it was spoken fluently only by an older minority, educated in Protestant Church schools by North Americans or US-educated Nicaraguans who rejected creole as 'broken' or 'bad English'. Most Creoles internalized these values: 'It was put into our mind that a person that speaks Standard English is ... well-prepared ... we all time look at that person with certain respect.'[9] Such linguistic and cultural alienation is common throughout the Caribbean. Here, it was complicated by the age-old hostility between Anglo and Hispanic cultures.

Political activity

Most Creoles were apolitical. At school, 'they no tell you nothing about politics'; parents warned: 'politics, watch out, don't get in that thing'.[10] Those who did followed two distinct tendencies, broadly corresponding to the 'Creole' and 'black' identities.

The 'Creoles' acted as *costeños* in the interests of the region, forming pragmatic alliances with *mestizo* national parties to negotiate better conditions for the Coast and leadership positions for themselves. At the time of the revolution this tendency was represented by the Organization for the Progress of the

Coast (OPROCO), founded in the 1960s, and including 'most of ... the worthwhile civic and political minded Creoles'. It promoted several ambitious but ultimately abortive projects, aimed at integrating the coast with the national economy. OPROCO died in 1979 of 'internal strife and rivalry among some of its leaders, and ... fear and mistrust of the Sandinista Revolution'.[11] The second tendency took a more ethnic, 'black nationalist' stance. In the 1920s Marcus Garvey's ideas travelled to Nicaragua with 'Negro' immigrants. A Nicaraguan branch of the United Negro Improvement Association (UNIA) attracted Creole and black men and women in large numbers. However, it drew Moravian disapproval as 'anti-white'. When Garvey's direct influence waned, the movement petered out.

Black consciousness resurfaced in the 1970s. The training of black churchmen abroad began to emphasize cultural sensitivity and the ideas of Martin Luther King. Sailors brought home Jamaican reggae music which sparked youthful interest in Rastafarianism. These influences coalesced in 1977 in the Southern Indigenous and Caribbean Community (SICC). Mainly a cultural movement, it also linked younger Creoles with community memories of Garveyism and Creole resistance struggles. Some even advocated affiliation to the Black Power movement, but SICC's activities remained relatively parochial. Few Creoles were willing to call themselves 'black' or, worse, *negro* in Spanish, still a powerful insult that lumped them indiscriminately with other minorities.

Ethnic rights and revolution

The Sandinista National Liberation Front (FSLN) came to power in 1979 with pledges never before made by a Nicaraguan government, to 'end racial discrimination' and 'encourage the flowering of the local cultural values of the region'.[12] Yet their first encounter with the Coast was an explosive clash of opposing interpretations.

Sandinista class-based ideology had little room for ethnicity. 'Culture' meant only its non-material expressions – language and beliefs – not their material and political foundations.[13] While demands for a literacy crusade in local languages were under-standably 'ethnic', claims to economic and political self-determi-nation were not. Racial inequality, the product of capitalist 'divide and rule' practices in the US enclaves and the Somoza state, would be 'eliminated' by 'integrating' the coast into an egalitarian economic system. Ethnic-based political activity would duly 'mature' into class-consciousness.[14]

Costeños saw it differently. The enclave times were 'golden days', with company stores stuffed with products 'from out', and good wages.[15] North Americans were benefactors; US-staffed Protestant churches had provided most of the social services on the coast and still set the prevailing apolitical, anti-communist ideology. The enclaves had practised racial segregation, but *costeños* associated racism more easily with 'Spaniards' from the Pacific, and 'integration' with annexation.

The USA armed one disaffected group, the Miskitu, to fight against the 'communist' revolution. Between 1981 and 1983, as the Miskitu struggle merged with the counter-revolutionary war, it eclipsed the needs of other groups. Indeed, all Sandinista–ethnic conflict is still viewed in terms of this struggle.

Yet Creoles presented the revolution with a different chal-lenge. The Miskitu made their claims through an apparently popular organization, in the communitarian discourse of international indigenism, which the Sandinistas initially found sympathetic. Creoles were barely mobilized and had no compa-rable associations. Although they claimed rights as an ethnic minority, the Sandinistas' perspective on discrimination picked up only their class implications.

For Creoles, 'the economic crisis was an ethnic crisis too'.[16] Sandinista economic policies, designed to reduce inequality and economic dependency, undermined Creole status in the ethnic hierarchy, and therefore their identity. Exchange and import controls reduced the flow of dollars and culturally significant imported goods; jobs arising from economic development plans were uncongenial. Yet to the Sandinistas, Creole complaints seemed like pleas for 'bourgeois' privilege cloaked in ethnicist language. Creoles expected recognition of their talents, but San-dinista distrust gave key posts to *mestizo* technicians and administrators from the Pacific. SICC was passed over and a Miskitu organization legitimated as official representative of all the minorities, with a seat in the Council of State held by a Miskitu.

In late 1980 Creole discontent exploded when Cuban 'atheist communist' teachers and technicians arrived in Bluefields to take 'our kind of jobs'. SICC organized strikes and demonstrations which escalated into the first ethnic violence of the revolution, which was forcibly repressed by the government, amid accusations of racist abuse.

This explosion opened a space for negotiation with more pragmatic Creole leaders. Where there were tangible gains, the FSLN gained support. So the Literacy Crusade (1981), run in Standard English by local educators, mobilized young people and seemed to fulfil Creoles hopes of reviving English-based education, until the war brought it to an abrupt close. Creole representation in leading posts improved. By 1985 they held 54 per cent of senior economic and administrative posts compared with 26 per cent in 1979, though they remained underrepresented in politically sensitive organizations.

However, a socialist economy strangled by war and US embargo could never meet Creole economic demands. Few took up arms. 'We Creoles ... don't like to fight. We want to live in Christianity.'[17] Passive resistance, adaptation or migration were the Creole style. Even so, in the 1984 elections the FSLN won 56 per cent of the Creole vote, compared with 67 per cent nationally.[18]

The 'autonomy process'

In 1984 the government began to seek a political solution to ethnic conflict, through the 'autonomy process', a three-year 'literacy programme in autonomy' for both government and *costeños*.[19] Guided by a National Autonomy Commission of elected representatives from each ethnic group, 'popular promoters' led detailed consultations in communities, workplaces and schools. Dialogue between ethnic groups, including *mestizos*, began to develop ethnic pride and break down ethnocentrism. In Tomás Borge's phrase, autonomy was 'proved before it was approved', through peace negotiations, amnesty for *costeño* fighters, locally

managed development projects and bilingual-bicultural education programmes in the region's three languages.

Out of this debate the 1987 Atlantic Coast Autonomy Law was
forged, and its principles incorporated into the 1987 constitution. Based in a concept of multi-ethnic nationality new to the
Americas, it gave people dual rights as Nicaraguans and as self-
defined members of ethnic groups. To the cultural rights already
recognized by the Sandinistas, it added economic rights – to
land, trade, influence and a share in the exploitation of natural
resources – and political representation through independently
financed Autonomous Regional Councils. Lacking the input of
grass-roots organizations like those which mobilized indigenous
Nicaraguans in ethnic conflict and reconciliation, the Creole
process was rather top-down and focused on the end product.
Creoles in the communities reacted with 'wait and see' scepti-
cism. Consequently, the actual devolution of political control
became so important that when Hurricane Joan (October 1988)
forced the postponement of regional elections, there was real
danger that 'the disaster of the hurricane could be converted
into the disaster of our autonomy'.[20]

Nevertheless, especially through its 'practical proofs', the
process stimulated new pride in the Creole identity. Black
Nicaraguans became visible beyond the coast, in diplomatic mis-
sions to Africa and the UN, and, for the first time in this cradle
of the national game, starred in the national baseball league and
the national team.

At the same time, Creoles' relationship with their black
African and white Anglo heritages was hotly debated. Argument
surfaced first around the bilingual programme, launched in primary schools in 1985. The Moravian-led educational establishment conceived it as a way-stage towards restoring the tradition
of English education; children could speak creole in class, teaching materials would reflect creole realities, but ultimately, Standard English would 'overcome' creole. To younger radicals this
was a 'surrender to cultural domination by historic oppressors';
creole should not be a mere stepping stone, but celebrated as the
authentic language of black Nicaraguans.[21] From the practice of
bilingual education, understanding grew about the roles of both

languages. Outside school, poets found their voice in creole, or the vibrant creole-Spanish mix typical of creole talk.[22]

Similar oppositions crystallized around cultural revival, crucial to a group who 'don't know much about ourselves because ... nothing has really been left that we can go back to and say ... these are some of the artifacts ... [or] the writings'.[23] A Centre for Popular Culture revived the traditional Palo de Mayo (Maypole) festival to welcome the rainy season, reclaiming its erotic, African elements from Managua's fashionable nightclubs as the core of 'Mayo Ya' (May Now), a festival of arts linking Creoles with their Caribbean roots. While for some, this revival 'hardly went beyond the folkloric', partisans of the staider 'Puritan conservative' version resented its celebration of the 'vulgar and obscene'.[24]

As Regional Council elections approached, these currents expressed themselves in new projections of the 'black internationalist' and the 'pragmatic Creole' political traditions. The 'black' tendency, revitalized by the revolution, campaigned on the FSLN ticket, with a vision of autonomy as freedom from internal and external colonization, based in an identity proud of both heritages. The 'pragmatic Creole' tendency, heirs to OPRO-CO's developmentalist assumptions and class/ethnic ambivalences, campaigned as the regional version of the National Opposition Union coalition (UNO), appealing to disparate, unmobilized anti-Sandinista resentment and nostalgia for the 'golden days' of capitalist prosperity. In the absence of effective Creole grass-roots organizations, no specifically regional party formed to challenge the FSLN view of autonomy.

Creoles in power

Ostensibly, autonomous government gives Creoles the leadership role they craved. They have a strength beyond their numbers in the RAAS Council, taking key posts on its executive board in both the 1990 and 1994 elections. Yet they have been unable to advance either regional or ethnic rights. Responsibility for much of this failure lies with Managua. Regional Council elections were finally held in February 1990, at the same time as the national elections which defeated the Sandinistas. So instead of cutting their political teeth with a government committed to consolidating the autonomy process, councils faced hostility to its very principles.[25] Besides, the FSLN had left key aspects of the Autonomy Law, such as the relative powers of central, regional and local government, and the mechanisms for controlling the Coast's resources, to be discussed and defined with the new Regional Councils: 'It didn't cross our minds that we were going to lose the election ... so we were careless.'[26]

The Chamorro government took advantage of these ambiguities, paying lip-service to autonomy while reinterpreting it as an innocuous form of local government. Central control was reasserted through a Managua-based Regional Development Institute (INDERA) that usurped the functions, and the funding, of the Regional Councils. Unilateral concessions gave designated foreign companies free rein over Coast resources, with risible returns of profits to the region. Councils rendered impotent by lack of finance were forced to confront central government on first principles.

Creole capacity to lead effective opposition to these abuses was undermined by their own contradictions. In both Regional Council and National Assembly elections in the RAAS, most Creoles had voted anti-Sandinista, against war, socialist austerity and the *panyas* (Spaniards). Regional results mirrored national ones: UNO, the party of central government, controlled the council and its executive board, while the FSLN fumed in opposition.[27] Paradoxically, this vote handed power to those most ambiguous about autonomy and least willing to confront central government, since they shared its class and sectoral interests. Although there were some early cross-party alliances, to defend the bilingual programme, for instance, class, party and personal enmities, with Creoles in a leading role, paralysed council activity, playing into central government's hands.

Meanwhile, economic conditions deteriorated. By 1994 unemployment had topped 80 per cent; infrastructure destroyed by war and Hurricane Joan was still unrepaired; crime and drug abuse were mounting. Yet, with 'their' government malfunctioning, ordinary Creoles had even less say than before autonomy.

Their councillors, especially from the anti-Sandinista benches, were inexpert at representing their constituents. The projects intended to 'prove' autonomy on the ground had withered for lack of financial support. Small wonder, then, that 'where ... Indians would stand out and demand their rights ... Creoles ... just sit around and grumble ... within the group.'[28]

The Garífuna: resistance and assimilation

The Garífuna entered the Atlantic Coast ethnic hierarchy in the mid-nineteenth century. In the 1830s Honduran Garífuna had fought, and lost, with the royalists against Morazán's Liberal land reforms. Fearing reprisals, they fled northwards into Guatemala and Belize and south into Nicaragua. Initially, they worked as seasonal loggers in the US-owned mahogany camps, establishing permanent settlements between 1881 and 1913.

Hard-working and reliable, they earned positions of responsibility in the enclave hierarchy beyond their 'proper station' as black immigrants, provoking jealousy and hostility towards their 'strange' language and customs. Creoles bracketed them with indigenous peoples as 'pagans'; Miskitu rejected them as rivals. Their Catholic allegiances set them further apart, especially when in 1913 the government authorized Capuchin missionary work which rivalled that of the Moravians.

Garífuna resistance to this hostility took strength from their culture. Their cult of the ancestors linked present trials to their long history of persecution, and as they buried their dead in Nicaraguan soil, attached them to their new territory. Traffic and trade up and down the coast maintained contact with other Central American Garífuna. Their language, in regular use as late as 1953, further cemented their group identity.

This identity came under threat when depression followed the decline of the foreign enclaves. In the open labour market 'the Garífuna people ... was look upon as ... the least people', in Creole parlance, 'the cow's tail',[29] and were forced to depend on subsistence agriculture, traditionally women's contribution to family income. To keep afloat, they assimilated, linguistically and culturally, to the dominant Creole culture, migrated to Bluefields and married outside the community. By 1980 there were even non-Garífuna living in Garífuna villages. 'No one under 34 converses in the language; no one in the previous generation speaks it regularly ... the last ancestor ritual [*dugu*, or *walagallo* in Nicaragua] took place seven years ago ... and no more Garífuna dances are held.'[30]

The Garífuna and the revolution

Unlike other *costeño* minorities, the Garífuna quickly perceived how the revolution could benefit their survival and development. The prospect of legal land titles under the 1981 Agrarian Reform Law promised to resolve long-standing struggles over land rights with neighbouring Creole and Miskitu communities. Under the Autonomy Law, 'so long you could get your education and you could understand ... you was equal like everybody ... people start studying and ... lift our self-esteem'.[31] The Garífuna formed a strategic alliance with the Sandinistas, remained loyal to them throughout, and still vote strongly for the FSLN.[32]

This alliance, like others in their history, proved costly. In 1983-4 Garífuna communities suffered *contra* attacks, forcing La Fe people to flee to Orinoco and Bluefields. In 1985 Orinoco became a Sandinista army base. Young Garífuna did their military service alongside Sandinista soldiers, interpreting it as part of their historic struggle 'to keep our land and to stop the foreigner from coming to take our riches'.[33]

Garífuna loyalty was rewarded under the 'autonomy process'. In 1986 Orinoco became the centre of an autonomy pilot project with foreign NGO assistance. During the 1981 Literacy Crusade a Belizean Garífuna volunteer working in Orinoco had rekindled interest in the culture, teaching the children a few words of Garífuna. (His plan to continue this work with a trained team from Belize was foiled by the outbreak of counter-revolutionary war.) The autonomy process continued this cultural revival. The *walagallo* ceremony was revitalized, first as folklore, for the Mayo Ya festivals in the 1980s. More authentically, in the 1987 Mayo Ya, it united Honduran and Nicaraguan Garífuna to effect a successful cure, and led to agreements to hold ongoing exchanges.

The Garífuna since 1990

Garífuna are now shunned by other *costeños* because they supported 'Pacific Coast people who had strange ideas and were communists'.[34] Their interests were not well represented by the polarized first Regional Council, especially since their constituency did not return a Garífuna candidate. The election of a trusted FSLN candidate from Orinoco in 1994 may improve matters.

In today's work-hungry conditions, envy of former Sandinista favour translates into discrimination, forcing Garífuna back to their subsistence economy, to the poorest *barrios* of Bluefields, and the bottom of the ethnic hierarchy. Little remains of the prosperity visible during the autonomy process, nor of the NGO 'community' projects, designed with too little understanding of the family basis of Garífuna economic activity and reciprocity.

The displacement of war, study in Bluefields and abroad and the drug economy and culture which have swept the coast since 1990 have all disrupted Garífuna life. Young people question the old identity; their parents worry about how to reintegrate them. The revolution left a strong sense of Garífuna pride, but uncertainty as to how it should be expressed.

Land remains their economic and symbolic base, around which the people of Orinoco recently rallied to defeat government attempts to sell their rainforest hinterland. But many feel that they are 'incomplete Garífuna', disconnected from the body of their culture, and even from the ancestors, by their ignorance of the Garífuna language. The *walagallo*, which integrates Belizean and Honduran Garífuna scattered in the United States with their home communities, evokes great ambivalence here. Many doubt its validity. Some young people are interested in reviving it; older ones fear they will debase it 'just for fun'. Others dream of re-establishing links with the mainstream by continuing the language revival begun during the revolution.

Without their central unifying ritual or language, other cultural signs risk becoming matters of individual family custom, disconnected from the system that gives them coherence. Grandmother-headed families, for instance, maintain strong links with their ancestors. Garífuna men evoked both God and family spirits before battles against the *contra*. Women still maintain and pass on traditional Afro-Catholic birth and funeral practices, and women and men are still skilled in traditional medicine, which enjoys NGO support, such as Christian Medical Action's workshops for midwives and health leaders.[35]

Conclusions and recommendations

Many Creole gains from the autonomy process still hold, though the constant need to defend them hinders further advance. Social mobility is no longer systematically blocked; the pressure to assimilate to *mestizo* culture has been removed. When they complain of discrimination, it is as *costeños*, vis-à-vis Pacific Coast society; they have lost their new-found visibility beyond the coast, in sport and diplomacy. The important revival of cultural identity has lost momentum with the demise of the Popular Cultural Centres; Mayo Ya and oral history research are again dormant, although recently a new Culture for Autonomy group has opened a popular arts centre with Swedish NGO backing.

English/Spanish bilingual-intercultural education has been pushed up to sixth grade by determined Creole teams. Nevertheless, every year sees exhausting appeals against centrally imposed cuts. Technical training depends on foreign NGO assistance, although the Ministry of Education is now beginning to take more responsibility. Planning problems would surely lessen if education and other social services were devolved to the region. The Autonomy Law provides unambiguously for this; its realization is a matter of political will. However, in the current polarized climate, it could become a political football.

The Garífuna have lost most from the change of government. They suffer overt discrimination for their ethnic differences and their Sandinista loyalties. Their land rights are unresolved and under attack, their reality underrepresented in public fora and education. To strengthen their voice, they need support to reactivate the links with their mainstream culture established during the revolution. What form these should take is for the Garífuna to decide, with good support. If language revival is the goal, for instance, it might be worth considering family exchanges involving all generations, to ensure learning of authentic community language, since school-based revival from such a low base is rarely successful.

The Autonomy Law, appealed to by both groups as 'a virtual legal Bible',[36] permits too many interpretations to be an effective weapon against abuses. Nor will its symbolic power last long if it fails to produce lasting change in the lives of ordinary *costeños*. Central government must urgently complete its *reglamentación* (detailed elaboration), defining with Regional Councils the limits of their powers. It must also tackle the conflict between its own free market policies and the law's stipulation of state and regional management, by at least regulating firms exploiting Atlantic Coast resources. Otherwise, the region will again be powerless to defend itself against over-exploitation, a particular threat to the Garífuna.

Since such positive government action seems unlikely, *costeños* must take autonomy into their own hands. Creoles, having probably gained most from Nicaragua's revolutionary autonomy process, have a particular part to play. Yet there is a danger that, as discrimination against them recedes, they will become lost in intra-group factionalism, forgetting their relationship to the whole multi-ethnic complex. 'The black community has to make an intense effort to understand itself. And that can only come after it understands the Miskitu, the Sumu, the Rama and the Spanish-speaking people.'[37] This is particularly relevant to the Garífuna, significantly unrecognized in this list, and overtly discriminated against by Creoles.

The current economic situation also distracts Creoles from this *concientización* (awareness raising). Migration and 'shipping out' on tourist cruisers are still prevalent, and the artificial prosperity of dollar remittances maintains Creole dominance in the socio-economic hierarchy. At the same time, those not so protected sink, with the whole economy, into increasing poverty. Some even abandon traditional prestige jobs in teaching and the Moravian Church to earn more 'selling ice creams and bananas from home', or go into domestic service,[38] coming into new competition with more pushy *mestizos*.

Recently, there have been promising efforts, largely by NGOs, to reactivate the autonomy process at grass-roots level. The Creole-led Foundation for Atlantic Coast Development, in collaboration with Nicaraguan and Honduran Human Rights Commissions, has sponsored 'Human, Civic and Autonomous Rights Commissions' which train local autonomous rights activists within a broad human rights framework. In July 1994 a Swedish-financed Atlantic Coast Autonomy Development Office initiated monthly training workshops for councillors. At the party level, a new Creole-led Authentic Autonomy Movement won two seats in the 1994 council elections, on a platform of unity around regional plans based on community development.[39]

In March 1995 the University of the Autonomous Regions of the Atlantic Coast began its first foundation year. A long-cherished dream of Creole educators, it aims to create and keep within the region the critical mass of trained human resources necessary for genuinely autonomous development. It, too, will have to survive on foreign aid.

Indeed, too many key ingredients of autonomous development are kept afloat on NGO assistance. Although invaluable, it is necessarily short-term and fragmentary, unable to provide the economic base the autonomy process needs. Nevertheless, if it comes in sufficient quantity and is *costeño*-controlled, it could have important advantages by allowing a localized and relatively depoliticized version of the autonomy process to continue.

Women, especially Creoles, seem happier to organize in this less politicized atmosphere. Many still prefer to work through church groupings in practical economic activities that do not openly challenge traditional gender roles. Others are becoming prominent in the Human Rights Commissions. A women's movement launched in 1988 appealed to a common *costeña* identity, creating awareness of shared interests across ethnic divides. Latterly, the interaction of gendered and ethnic discrimination has become an issue, especially in the public sphere, and in 1994 a new Afro-Caribbean women's group formed to focus specifically on Creole women's experience. At a more formal level, nine of the forty-five seats in the 1990 RAAN Council went to women, two to Creoles, and in the RAAS five out of forty-five, two to Creoles. These far-from-proportional figures were sustained in 1994. In the RAAN a Creole woman, Alta Hooker, has played a key part in consensus-building, first as second secretary to the council's executive board and, since 1994, as its president.

'If [autonomy] succeeds, it will set indigenous and other ethnic struggles ahead by twenty-five years. If it fails, or is made to fail, it will set those struggles back just as far.'[40] Despite government hostility and internal contradictions, it must be defended, locally, nationally and internationally, as the best guarantee of Creole and Garífuna minority rights, and as an example to other Central American states.

Notes

1 The terms 'ethnic group', 'indigenous people', 'people', 'nation' and even 'minority' all became sensitive during the Sandinista revolution. I adopt the usage of 'ethnic group/community' agreed for the Nicaraguan constitution (1987) and the Atlantic Coast Autonomy Law (1987). All these groups use *'costeño'* (Coast people) to refer to their regional identity.

2 Both names derive from the Carib word for the group and its language. 'Carib' is used by English-speaking members, and 'Garífuna' by Spanish-speakers. The Nicaraguan group favours 'Garífuna', even when speaking English, to signal the ethnic pride gained in the revolution.

3 For a comparison of Miskitu and Garífuna histories, see Dunbar Ortiz, R., *The Indians of the Americas: Human Rights and Self-Determination*, London, Zed Books, 1984, p. 261.

4 Population figures from Union of Small Farmers (UNAG), 'Consulta a mujeres campesinas, indígenas y negras' (mimeo), August 1994. The British called this region the 'Mosquito Coast' or 'Mosquitia'; it became 'Zelaya Province' on annexation into the Nicaraguan state, and 'Special Zones I and II' under the Sandinistas. *Costeños* themselves chose its current names, during the development of the Autonomy Law (1987).

5 See Dunbar Ortiz, op. cit.; Freeland, J., *A Special Place in History: The Atlantic Coast in the Nicaraguan Revolution*; London, Nicaragua Solidarity Campaign/War on Want, 1988; Gordon, E.T., 'History, identity, consciousness and evolution: Afro-Nicaraguans and the Nicaraguan revolution', *Ethnic Groups and the Nation State: The Case of the Atlantic Coast in Nicaragua*, Stockholm, University of Stockholm, 1987; Smith, H., 'Redefining national identity', in *Nicaragua: Self-Determination and Survival*, Boulder, CO, Pluto Press, 1993; Vilas, C.M., *State, Class and Ethnicity in Nicaragua: Capitalist Modernization*

and Revolutionary Change on the Atlantic Coast, Boulder, CO, Lynne Rienner, 1989.

6 According to Germán Romero in *Wani: Revista del Caribe Nicaragüense*, no. 13, 1992, '*mestizo* Nicaragua' is a nationalist myth which omits a third ethnic ingredient: mulatto slaves of African origin, who by the eighteenth century constituted a significant proportion of the Nicaraguan population. On emancipation, they had a key role as soldiers and militiamen in suppressing Pacific Coast indigenous rebellions and fending off attack by Atlantic Coast indigenous peoples. *Mestizo* society tried to hide or disguise their presence, and by the nineteenth century they were fully assimilated.

7 A 1985 survey of ethnicity and social class in the working-age population of Bluefields, cited in Gordon, op. cit., p. 161, classified 53% of Creoles as 'middle class'; 8% as 'elite' bourgeoisie or top state officials; 32% as 'lower classes'; 7% as unemployed. All further survey data are from this source, unless otherwise stated.

8 In 1985, 11% of Bluefields Creoles were Catholics, 49% Moravians and 34% of other Protestant denominations.

9 Sidney Francis, Creole project worker and poet, interview with author, Bluefields 1989.

10 Johnny Hodgson, Creole Autonomy Commission coordinator, interview with author, Bluefields 1994.

11 Sujo Wilson, H., 'Brief historical notes on the origin and political behaviour of the Afro-Nicaraguans of the Caribbean Coast of Nicaragua', presented at the Second Seminar of the Association of Black Nicaraguans held at the Moravian College, Bluefields, Nicaragua, September 1989 (mimeo). Sujo was one of the founder members of OPROCO. See also Vernooy, R., *Starting All Over Again: Making and Remaking a Living on the Atlantic Coast of Nicaragua*, Wageningen, Netherlands, Landbouwuniversiteit te Wageningen, 1992, pp. 257-61.

12 FSLN, *Historic Programme* , quoted in Vilas, C.M., 'Revolutionary change and multi-ethnic regions: the Sandinista revolution and the Atlantic Coast', in CIDCA/University of Stockholm, op. cit., p. 70.

13 Vilas, op. cit., *State, Class and Ethnicity*, p. 191.

14 Dunbar Ortiz, op. cit., pp. 75-109, compares class-based and ethnicist analyses of ethnic rights, pointing out the 'virtual denial of discussion' in the Americas until relatively recently.

15 Sujo Wilson, H., 'Historia oral de Bluefields', *Wani: Revista del Caribe Nicaragüense* , 1991, p. 25.

16 Creole FSLN Commander Lumberto Campbell, quoted in *Pensamiento Propio*, no. 17, 1987.

17 Betty Jordan, Creole trader, interviewed by Vernooy, op. cit., p. 178.

18 Butler, J., 'La costa votó: los costeños y las elecciones', *Wani: Revista del Caribe Nicaragüense*, no. 2-3, 1985, pp. 27-31.

19 Conversation with Ray Hooker, then National Assembly deputy for the south, and Creole representative in the Autonomy Commission. See English translations of the Autonomy Law and the relevant constitutional clauses, in Freeland, op. cit., Appendices I and II, and

accounts of the consultation process and analyses of the law in Vilas, op. cit., *State, Class and Ethnicity*, pp. 170-84, and Gurdián, G., 'Autonomy rights, national unity and national liberation: the autonomy project of the Sandinista popular revolution on the Atlantic Caribbean Coast of Nicaragua', in CIDCA/Stockholm, op. cit., pp. 171-89.

20 Johnny Hodgson, quoted in *Barricada International*, 19 January 1989, p. 13.

21 Yih, K. and Slate; A., 'Bilingualism on the Atlantic Coast: where did it come from and where is it going? (Special Zone II)', *Wani: Revista del Caribe Nicaragüense*, no. 2-3, 1985, p. 26.

22 See e.g. June Beer's poems, quoted in her obituary, *Wani: Revista del Caribe Nicaragüense*, no. 5, 1986, pp. 36-9; 'Tres poemas de Carlos Rigby', *Wani: Revista del Caribe Nicaragüense*, no. 8, 1990, pp 52-9; and Hurtubise, J., 'Poesia en inglés criollo nicaragüense', *Wani: Revista del Caribe Nicaragüense*, no. 16, 1995, pp. 43-56.

23 Faran Dometz, Moravian leader and former head of the Moravian College, interview with author, Bluefields, September 1994.

24 Savery, W.E., 'Una crónica social orquestada', *Wani: Revista del Caribe Nicaragüense*, no. 4, 1986, p. 43; Sujo, H., 'Palo de Mayo, todos los olores del mundo', *Wani: Revista del Caribe Nicaragüense*, no. 11, 1991, p. 106.

25 Most parties in the ruling National Opposition Union (UNO) coalition voted against the Autonomy Law in the National Assembly in 1987.

26 Hugo Sujo, losing FSLN candidate and former member of the Autonomy Commission, interview with author, Bluefields, March 1991.

27 This pattern recurred in the 1994 Regional Council elections; though support passed to a modern version of Somoza's party, the Constitutional Liberal Party (PLC), it campaigned on the same 'golden days' nostalgia. See 'Nicaragua's Caribbean Coast: new government, old problems', *Envío*, vol. 13, no. 155, 1994, pp. 33-43

28 Faran Dometz, interview with author, Bluefields 1994.

29 Fermín González, sixth grade teacher, during discussion with parents and teachers, Orinoco primary school, 1994; and José Idiáquez, interview with author, Managua, 1994.

30 Davidson, W.V., 'The Garífuna of Pearl Lagoon: ethnohistory of an Afro-American enclave in Nicaragua', *Ethnohistory*, vol. 27, no. 1, 1980, pp. 41-3.

31 See note 29.

32 In the 1984 presidential elections 65% of the main Garífuna communities voted FSLN (compared with 67% nationally). In 1990, 50% of Garífuna voted FSLN (compared with a regional average of 33% and a national average of 40%). In the 1994 regional elections, 90% of the Orinoco vote went to the FSLN candidate. See notes 18 and 27.

33 Interview with Freddy Guerra, Orinoco, in Idiáquez, op. cit., p. 187.

34 See note 33.

35 On birth practices and traditional medicine, see Idiáquez, op. cit., pp. 23-69; on funeral customs, ibid., pp. 127-45.

36 Ray Hooker, opening address to Second Symposium on Autonomy, 4-7 November 1991, quoted in *Envío*, vol. 10, no. 125, 1991, p. 17.
37 Interview with Ray Hooker, Bluefields, 1986, transcript kindly supplied by Duncan Campbell (Latin America Bureau).
38 Miss Patricia, primary school teacher, in a women's workshop organized by the small farmers' union UNAG, Vernooy, op. cit., quoted in UNAG, op. cit., p.16.
39 MAAC is a political projection of the Association of Black Caribbeans formed in 1989.
40 Member of the Autonomy Commission, quoted in 'Separatism to autonomy', *Envío*, April 1989, p. 41.

Select bibliography

CIDCA/University of Stockholm Development Study Unit (eds), *Ethnic Groups and the Nation State: The Case of the Atlantic Coast in Nicaragua*, Stockholm, University of Stockholm, 1987.

Davidson, W.V., 'The Garífuna of Pearl Lagoon: ethnohistory of an Afro-American enclave in Nicaragua', *Ethnohistory*, vol. 127, no. 1, 1980, pp. 31-47.

Dunbar Ortiz, R., *Indians of the Americas: Human Rights and Self-Determination*, London, Zed Books, 1984.

Ford, P., *Tekkin a Waalk along the Miskito Coast*, London, Flamingo, 1993.

Freeland, J., *A Special Place in History: The Atlantic Coast in the Nicaraguan Revolution*, London, Nicaragua Solidarity Campaign/War on Want, 1988.

Gordon, E.T., 'History, identity, consciousness and revolution: Afro-Nicaraguans and the Nicaraguan revolution', in CIDCA/University of Stockholm, op. cit., pp. 135-68, and 'Comments' by Buvollen, H.P., ibid., pp. 169-70.

Idiáquez, J. SJ, *El culto a los ancestros en la cosmovisión de los Garífunas de Nicaragua*, Managua, Instituto Histórico Centroamericano, 1994.

Smith, H., 'Redefining national identity', in H. Smith, *Nicaragua: Self-Determination and Survival*, Boulder, CO, Pluto Press, 1993, Chapter 9.

Vilas, C.M., *State, Class and Ethnicity in Nicaragua: Capitalist Modernization and Revolutionary Change on the Atlantic Coast*, Boulder, CO, and London, Lynne Rienner, 1989.

PANAMA

Darién J. Davis

Afro-Panamanians – Panamanians of African descent – have played a key role in the development of the Panamanian nation. That contribution, however, is not always acknowledged or recognized. The purpose of this section is to present a coherent picture of the status of Afro-Panamanians in contemporary Panamanian society. Given the scarcity of official documents and empirical data relating to Afro-Panamanians, and the various (skin-colour) classifications used in Panama to divide and separate people of African descent, this task is a difficult one. Despite these difficulties, however, this section will attempt to answer three basic questions: Who are the Afro-Panamanians? What are the problems they face in Panamanian society? And what measures have they taken as a group to combat those problems? In order to answer these questions, it is necessary to begin with a brief examination of Panama's historical and geographical importance.

Background

Bordered by both the Atlantic and the Pacific oceans, the Panamanian isthmus, some 75,517 square miles, unites North and South America. Panama's economic, political and social history has been influenced, if not dominated, by its strategic geographical position. Rodrigo de Bastides landed on the isthmus in 1501, accompanied by Vasco Nuñez de Balboa and Juan de Costa. Following their arrival, Panama almost immediately became an intercontinental crossroads and a centre for the launching of expeditions to South America.[1] The Spaniards also considered building a waterway to speed the transport of treasures, personnel and cargo across the isthmus. Not until 15 August 1914 did the United States complete what had been a Spanish dream: the Panama Canal.

The canal fundamentally changed the Panamanian way of life. Before 1903 Panama was a province of the Republic of Colombia.

In 1902 the United States Congress authorized President Roosevelt to acquire land from the Colombian government to build an inter-oceanic canal in the rebellious province of Panama. One year later, the Republic of Panama, assisted by the United States (which gained sovereignty over a ten-mile-wide strip along the canal), proclaimed independence from Colombia. Since then the United States has had a significant role in Panamanian politics.

Demographics and race relations

US and other foreign investment in Panama has had a profound effect on the country's demographics. Three main ethnic groups constituted colonial Panamanian society: indigenous peoples,[2] Spaniards and Africans who accompanied the Spaniards as servants or slaves. While the abolition of the slave trade slowed the flow of people of African descent to many of the Latin American republics, in Panama this was not the case. In the 1820s small groups of workers from the Caribbean islands travelled to work on construction projects in northern Panama.[3] Migrations continued throughout the nineteenth century for the construction of the Panama railroad, and for the cultivation of crops on the expanding commercial agricultural enterprises in the coastal regions.

Virtually all countries in Central America received migrants from the Caribbean islands and in some cases even from Asia. This migration changed the demographics in the region, spawning a new and vibrant Afro-Caribbean culture. Today, West Indian Afro-Creoles constitute a large percentage, and in some cases the majority, of the population in the coastal regions of Belize, Honduras, Guatemala, Nicaragua and Panama.

The construction of the Panama Canal spurred the second migration of labourers, the majority of whom made Panama their home. The canal builders considered Caribbean workers ideal because they understood the language of the overseers and had no roots on the isthmus to support a campaign for worker rights.[4] In the 1870s, when France won the contract to build the canal under the direction of Ferdinand de Lesseps, almost 20,000 migrants arrived from the Caribbean, particularly from Jamaica and Barbados. The vast majority were of African descent. When the USA took over from the French, over three-quarters of the workforce came from the British West Indies. The Caribbean population at first settled in the Canal Zone areas such as Colón City, but by the 1930s this migration had changed significantly the demographics of Panama City.

Panamanians have often approached the Caribbean presence with trepidation. On the one hand, Panamanians proudly proclaim themselves a nation in which people of all backgrounds coexist harmoniously. But Panamanians are also anxious to preserve their Hispanic heritage in the face of US domination and they have systematically rejected all foreign influences. Xenophobia prompted President Anulfo Arias Madrid to deny citizenship to children born in Panama of West Indian descent, and to include a provision to this effect in the 1940 constitution. Despite the 1946 constitution which revoked this injustice, West Indian black people continued to face prejudice and discrimination.

According to John and Mavis Biesans: 'the most virulent attacks against the Antillian threat have coincided with periods of economic depression and unemployment'.[5] Discrimination, however, is not based solely on economics, nor is it based entirely on race. After all, not all Afro-Panamanians are of West Indian descent. Part of a wider history of discrimination against people of African descent, the discrimination against Afro-Caribbeans is exacerbated by nationalism and xenophobia. Nationalism arises, in part, as a defence against the overwhelming US dominance in Panamanian affairs.

Panamanians – who, like most Latin Americans, have inherited European aesthetic values – often denigrate 'blackness' and exalt what is 'white'. In addition, Panamanian nationalism, based on *mestizaje*, or the idea that Panama is a nation of mixed-race people, has denied West Indian contributions to national culture and society and stymied native 'black consciousness'. Furthermore, Panamanian nationalism attempts to co-opt black people born in Panama while encouraging West Indians to identify with Hispanic values. Thus the Panamanians' social hierarchy has racial and cultural underpinnings.

Panamanians often attempt to distinguish West Indian black

people (*antillanos* or *chombos*) from Panamanian black people who predate the Caribbean migration, the *negros nativos*. Language often assists in this separation. For Panamanians the *chombos* are *negro* or 'black', while *nativos* are often called *morenos*, a euphemism for 'black'. These distinctions are mitigated by class considerations and personal relationships. The term *moreno* may also be used to describe black people held in high esteem. Thus, while many Afro-Panamanians face prejudice owing to their race or cultural background, black people are not legally prohibited from ascending the Panamanian social hierarchy. Moreover, West Indian black people who speak Spanish and appropriate the symbols of Panamanian nationalism are found at all levels of government and business.

One *antillano* from Colón, the second largest city in Panama, commented on the complexity of Panamanian racism:

> *There is a prejudice against us because we speak English, but rich Panamanians send their children to American schools to learn English. We are discriminated against, not because they think that we are inferior, but because they resent blacks being here. Panamanians are strange. They speak bad about you, but then they treat you like friends.*[6]

Another West Indian settler who eventually returned to the islands compared race relations in the US-run Canal Zone with race relations in the Panamanian territory: 'In the zone, white North Americans didn't socialize with us. Everything was totally segregated. When we passed into Panamanian territory, you always heard of stories of prejudice, but we never experienced it. Panamanians were horrified at the US system.'[7]

While Panamanians often distinguished *negros nativos* from *antillanos*, North Americans did not. One *nativo* reported that 'to the Americans, a black was a black, no matter where you came from'.[8] Since many Panamanians are of mixed heritage, US segregation policies instituted in the Canal Zone prior to the 1960s treated Panamanians as black people.

Common discrimination did not motivate *nativos* and *antillanos* to consolidate a consciousness until the 1980s, however. *Antillanos* suffered a series of injustices which the *nativos* escaped. While all Panamanians have constitutionally defined civil rights, the rights of *antillanos* were always questioned, even for second- and third-generation *antillanos* who had no other home but Panama.

The 1970s represented a crucial period in Panamanian nationhood. Panamanian Chief of State Omar Torrijos and US President Jimmy Carter revised the 1903 Hays–Bunau–Varilla Treaty which had given the USA jurisdiction over the Panama Canal and the Canal Zone in perpetuity. A more encompassing nationalism, coupled with a desire for sovereignty, brought Panamanians of all backgrounds together, including Afro-Panamanians and those of West Indian descent. Although 1990 population statistics indicate that, of the 2.5 million Panamanians, about 12 to 14 per cent are of West Indian descent, a vast majority of them have spoken Spanish as a first language since the 1960s and they identify with their new Hispanic heritage. But many of them cherish their Caribbean roots. Third- and fourth-generation Antillians who speak Spanish also speak English. While most Panamanians are Roman Catholic, West Indians are predominantly Protestant (Anglican or Methodist).

Minority rights and the 1989-90 invasion

Many Panamanian scholars and writers believe that, as assimilation increases, tensions between black people and white people will decrease. While this may be partly true, the theory fails to recognize that Panamanian politics and economy are dominated by a small elite who scorn the popular classes which include black, *mestizo* and *mulato* sectors. The Panamanian oligarchy's opposition to ex-strongman Manuel Noriega, who is of mixed racial heritage, for example, had racial overtones. Unfortunately, the 1989 invasion, which, according to US officials, aimed to remove Noriega, was disastrous for the poor and black communities.[9]

Shortly after midnight on 20 December 1989, the US military southern command, under Commander General Maxwell Thurman, led the most extensive military exercise ever to take place on Panamanian soil. Codenamed *Operation Just Cause*, the invasion began with a downpour of artillery fire on several targets in densely populated urban areas. It did not come to an end until the arrest of General Manuel Noriega on 3 January 1990. In the interim, many poor Panamanian communities were completely destroyed. Many of the communities hardest hit were in the city of Colón; others were the neighbourhoods of San Miguelito, Panama Viejo and El Chorillo in Panama City. An estimated 20,000 Panamanians lost their homes, more than 2,000 died, and many more 'disappeared'.[10]

While members of particular ethnic groups were not specifically singled out during the invasion, the poor neighbourhoods that suffered were disproportionately inhabited by Panamanians of African descent. US detention of many of the community leaders such as the labour leader Mauro Murillo and Balbina Herrera de Periñón, the mayor of San Miguelito, infuriated many Afro-Panamanians.[11] In the aftermath, the US military temporarily moved those left homeless into makeshift refugee camps at Albroock Air Station, under the auspices of the Panamanian Red Cross. Five years later, many were still without homes and jobs. The psychological wounds have been immeasurable.

Despite the travesties of the invasion, many Panamanians emerged afterwards to organize their communities. Several grass-roots movements continue to protest against the invasion and to demand both information and retribution. The president of the Afro-Panamanian Refugee Committee, Ashton Bancroft, for example, vehemently protested against invasion abuses, while attempting to organize the victims. Olga Mejía of the National Human Rights Commission and Isabel Corro of the Association of the Dead continue to search for information on the 'disappeared'. Other human rights and local groups have joined in to help rebuild community morale.[12]

The invasion, which was condemned by the United Nations and many Latin American countries, instigated an unprecedented level of human rights abuses in Panama. Throughout the 1980s human rights violations by the security forces and other paramilitary groups reached unparalleled heights. As in other Latin American nations, those who have suffered most have been poor black people. The 1948 Universal Declaration of Human Rights clearly states that no one shall be the object of arbitrary interferences in his/her private life, family or otherwise, yet community, grass-roots and labour leaders were consistently harassed. The documentary film *The Panama Deception* (1992) illustrates the extent to which the black and *mestizo* communities were devastated by the invasion. Panama has yet to recover.[13]

Education

The 1989-90 US invasion only exacerbated Panama's already existing problems. Public services such as health and education are in desperate need of restructuring. Although Panamanians as a whole are more literate and better educated than many of their Latin American neighbours (literacy is approximately 89 per cent, for example),[14] multicultural education has yet to be systematically introduced in a land which prides itself on being *mestizo*. The African presence and its contribution to Panamanian history and culture are largely ignored or overlooked in the standard textbooks used by private and public schools. *Quiero Aprender*, a national publication which is used for teaching Spanish to children, for example, mentions black people only briefly. There is no mention of Afro-Caribbeans, even in reference to the building of the canal.[15]

Labour, social and ethnic movements

Despite their absence from textbooks and official statistics, Afro-Panamanians continue to have significant roles in education at all levels, in grass-roots community efforts and in labour unions. Many Afro-Panamanians have also returned to the Caribbean or have moved to the United States (New York being one of the preferred destinations).

Today, information on Afro-Panamanians is often hard to unearth. This may be due to the fact that Afro-Panamanians often organize around issues which may not seem to be motivated exclusively by race, such as labour issues or community development. Moreover, the Panamanian mainstream media are uncomfortable discussing ethnic issues openly, and so many events often go unnoticed. Furthermore, Afro-Panamanian consciousness continues to be inhibited by three major obstacles: nationalism; the division between *antillanos* and *nativos*; and a social hierarchy based in part on skin colour, which allows a select number of blacks and mulattos to ascend unhindered into the dominant *mestizo* culture.

Since the 1960s, however, Afro-Panamanians have become more and more aware of the advantages of unity. Although *antillanos* continue to lead the movement, Afro-Panamanians figure prominently in many of the labour unions, for example. The National Centre of Panamanian Workers (CNTP), in particular, has supported Afro-Panamanian endeavours. This association stems in part from the CNTP's historical link with the People's Party, which became an important force among the United Fruit farmworkers, many of whom were West Indian.[16]

In the 1980s Afro-Panamanian activists organized a series of national congresses to discuss issues of race and ethnicity. These encounters marked a turning point in the consciousness movement, as *nativos*, *antillanos* and various Panamanian officials, as well as representatives of several indigenous groups, participated. Bringing together popular and neighbourhood organizations, intellectuals, students and government officials, the congresses, which commenced in 1981, created a dialogue on issues crucial to Panamanian society, including Afro-Panamanians' contribution to national culture, workers' rights, interethnic relations, the immigration of Afro-Panamanians to the United States and the international fight against racial discrimination and apartheid.[17]

As a result of these encounters, Afro-Panamanians committed themselves to a series of resolutions, promising to intensify studies on Afro-Panamanian contributions to national culture. Today, most Afro-Panamanians agree on the importance of recognizing the African and Caribbean contribution to the nation, and educating Panamanians in this subject. Panamanians of West Indian descent, in particular, continue to recognize the contribution of pan-African leaders such as Marcus Garvey to the lives of Panamanian workers.[18] Garvey is only one among a pantheon of black leaders who influenced the Panamanian labour and black consciousness movements.[19]

Afro-Panamanians continue to forge a sense of community through education, coupled with direct denunciations of acts of discrimination and prejudice. The first congress highlighted the treatment of black musicians in the National Symphonic Orchestra under Eduardo Charpentier de Castro. According to Afro-Panamanian activists, denouncing specific incidents allowed them to publicize socially unacceptable behaviour and thus raise the consciousness of all Panamanians. It also helped to create a network and forum to which Afro-Panamanians could turn.

Afro-Panamanians joined with other human rights activists and forged solidarity with indigenous groups. Together with the Kunas, Guaymíes and the Chocoes, for example, they requested that the government return lands and demarcate them carefully to assure indigenous people of a livelihood, limit tourism within those territories and permit indigenous people to take charge of tourism in their areas.[20]

Owing to the large presence of West Indians in the ranks of the Afro-Panamanian movement, the vision of the movement remains international, with strong contacts with pan-Africanists throughout the Caribbean and in the United States. Afro-Panamanians consistently and publicly condemned apartheid in South Africa before the election of Nelson Mandela as state President in the spring of 1994. They have also publicly endorsed a wide array of international political candidates.[21]

Afro-Panamanian women have had significant roles throughout these struggles. In the early 1900s, when the canal builders brought over approximately 31,000 official workers, the vast majority were men. Unofficially, however, more than 160,000 men and women migrated, and the Panamanian authorities were very 'flexible' in their documentation. The canal authorities initially attempted to solve this imbalance by allowing in a number of single women, especially from the French Caribbean.[22] Eventually, West Indian women entered Panama as family members, since the canal authorities believed that families encouraged stability and worker reliability. By the time the canal had been completed, the ratio between men and women had stabilized. Immigrant women participated in the workforce in a variety of capacities, from washer women and cooks to clerics and secretaries. Today, Afro-Panamanian women remain active in both the formal and the informal economy, although unemployment is generally higher among women than men. When women do participate in the labour force, they tend to receive lower salaries than men, but this is not peculiar to Panama.

Afro-Panamanian women such as Graciela Dixon have an active role in the movement. Ironically, mainstream Panamanian mores, characterized by machismo, often minimize Latin women's participation. The West Indian heritage, while not free of machismo, has historically seen a greater participation of women in all aspects of society. Often Panamanians of non-Caribbean background express dismay at the involvement of West Indian women in social movements, misinterpreting their presence as an indication of loose morals. The irony of this is that strong religious values among the West Indian Protestants impose a stricter code of conduct than that of their Catholic counterparts.[23]

Prospects for the future

The 1989-90 invasion stymied popular mobilization on many levels; Afro-Panamanian mobilization was among them. Indeed, the activities of Afro-Panamanian leaders and activists after the invasion illustrate the wider non-racial activities of community-building inherent in their struggle. Activists continue their protest through demonstrations, while collecting and disseminating information on the invasion and its devastation, and helping the refugees and homeless.

Several forums continue to serve the community in all of these endeavours. The Centro de Estudios Afro-Panameños (Center for Afro-Panamanian Studies) serves as an archive for information. Activists and professionals at the University of Panama have also been instrumental in acquiring information on Afro-Panamanians.

Panama is only now beginning to emerge from the severe economic and political problems generated by the invasion. Rates of both unemployment and crime remain high, and the economy is not generating sufficient jobs to absorb those coming on to the labour market. The recent Haitian refugee crisis underscores the relationship between social and ethnic tensions and nationalism. Panamanians protested vehemently against the arrival of Haitian 'boat people' from the US naval base at Guantanamo, arguing that they resented the USA using Panama to solve its problems. Former President Guillermo Endara himself recognized that these protests were ethnically and linguistically influenced (Haitians speak creole). After all, Cuban immigrants from Guantanamo were not greeted in this manner.[24]

The 1994 election of President Pérez Balladares of the Democratic Revolutionary Party (PRD) signals an era of reconciliation. Founded by ex-President Omar Torrijos, and later serving the interest of General Noriega in the 1980s, the PRD is beginning to reshape itself by returning to its populist roots. Within this new political framework civil rights for all will be safeguarded only when Panamanians deepen their understanding of the contribution that all ethnic groups have made to the creation of modern Panama. Afro-Panamanians, in particular, must recognize that opposition to discrimination and racism is a political affirmation independent of their cultural background. As in most Latin American countries, however, issues of race and ethnicity are interrelated with issues of class, and serious economic programmes and changes in education are essential for the future.[25]

Notes

1 Arauz, Dr C.A., 'La presencia negro en el Panamá colonial', *La Prensa*, 13 February 1991, pp. 2-11.
2 Indigenous peoples account for almost 7% of the Panamanian population and are by no means a monolithic group. Major groups include the Kuna, the Guaymí and the Terraba.
3 Conniff, M., *Black Labor on a White Canal 1904-1981*, Philadelphia, PA, University of Pittsburgh Press, 1981, p. 16.
4 Many migrants from the French-speaking islands also travelled to the isthmus to work on the canal, but their numbers were relatively small.
5 Biesans, J. and Biesans, M., *Panamá y su pueblo*, Mexico City, Editorial Letras, 1962, p. 176.
6 Interview with the author, Colón, Panama, July 1991.
7 Interview with the author, Nassau, Bahamas, October 1991.
8 Interview with the author, Colón, Panama, July 1991.
9 El Chorillo and San Miguelito, two of the poorest neighbourhoods in Panama and predominantly black, were particularly devastated.

10 Figures of casualties vary from the low US Department of State estimates of 300 to those reported by human rights groups and the
Catholic Church, of more than 500. The Panamanian Committee on
Human Rights pegs the number at 556; Xavier Gorostiaga, S.J.,
'¿Después de la invasión a Panamá que sigue?', *Tareas*, no. 74, 1990,
p. 89, quotes a figure of 2,500, while other groups report figures of close
to 4,000; Beluce, O., *La verdad sobre la invasión*, Panama, Centro de
Estudios Latinoamericanos, 1991, p. 102; see also 'Economía e invasión:
las perspectivas de la economía panameña', *Tareas*, no. 74, 1990, p. 40.
11 During interviews conducted in the summer of 1990, many Afro-
Panamanians expressed a sense of tragedy at this treatment. Many
Panamanians of all walks of life who criticized the operation's outcome none the less expressed the need for US involvement.
12 Beluce, op. cit., pp. 109, 120.
13 Baillou, C., 'Groups rally to support victims of Panama', *Amsterdam
News*, New York, 6 January 1990, p. 9; James, J., 'US policy in Panama', *Race and Class*, vol. 32, no. 1, pp. 17-32.
14 UNESCO, *Statistical Summary*, 1987.
15 Ortega, H., 'Racismo en los textos escolares', *Diálogo Social*, vol. XVI,
no. 155, 1983, pp. 16-23; see also Ortega, H., 'Racismo: el indígena
en los textos escolares, *Diálogo Social*, vol. XVII, no. 167, 1984.
16 Maloney, G., *El canal de Panama y los trabajadores antillanos*, Panama
City, Ediciones Formato, 1989, pp. 16-20.
17 Among the organizers of the congresses were Graciela Dixon,
Woodrow Bryan, George Priestly, George Fisher, Luis Anderson (president, First Congress), Joseph Dixon, Harley James Mitchell, Gerado
Maloney, Luther Thomas and Eugenio Barrera.
18 *Primer congreso del negro panameño*, memorias, Panama City, Impreso-
ra de la Nación, p. 26.
19 Among the various Afro-Panamanian role models is Dr Diógenes Dedeño
Cenci, rector of the first Department of Afro-Panamanian Studies.
20 *Primer congreso del negro panameño*, op. cit., p. 44.
21 Afro-Panamanians have publicly supported Salin Salem Salim in
Tanzania, for example.
22 Conniff, op. cit., p. 29; interview with Gerardo Maloney, July 1991,
University of Panama, Panama City. For a good fictional text which
examines the role of women from the French Caribbean in Panama,
see Condé, M., *Tree of Life*, New York, Ballantine, 1992.
23 *Primer congreso del negro panameño*, op. cit., p. 30.
24 BBC Monitoring Service, Latin America, 9 July 1994.
25 Wilkinson, T., 'The ghosts of Panama's past haunt elections, spook-
ing some observers', *Los Angeles Times*, Home Edition, Part A, 10
May 1994, p. 4.

Select bibliography

Arosemena, J., 'Los panameños negros descendientes de antillanos. ¿Un
caso de marginalidad social?', *Tarea*, no. 3, 1975, pp. 51-78.

Birmingham-Pokorny, E.D., 'The emergence of the new Afro-Hispanic women in Carlos Guillermo Wilson's *Cuentos del negro cubena Chombo*', *Journal of Caribbean Studies*, vol. 8, no. 3, 1991-2, pp. 123-9.

Castro, C., 'Estado y movilización étnia en Panama', *Estudios Sociales Centroamericanos*, no. 48, 1988, pp. 115-24.

Connif, M.L., *Black Labor on a White Canal 1904-1981*, Philadelphia, PA, University of Pittsburgh Press, 1981.

Lipski, J., 'The Negros Congos of Panama: Afro-Creole language and culture', *Journal of Black Studies*, vol. 16, no. 4, 1986, pp. 409-28.

Nelson, G., 'Old glory', *Village Voice*, vol. 35, 30 January 1990, p. 22.

Maloney, G., 'El grupo antillano en el proceso político panameño', *Tarea*, no. 33, 1975, pp. 12-26.

Millet, R., 'Looking beyond the invasion: a review of recent books on Panama', *Journal of Inter-American Studies and World Affairs*, vol. 35, 1993, pp. 151-70.

Priestly, G., 'Étnia, clase y cuestión nacional en Panama: análisis de estudios recientes', *Tarea*, no. 67, 1987, pp. 35-62.

Ramaga, P.V., 'Relativity of the minority concept', *Human Rights Quarterly*, vol. 14, 1992, pp. 104-19.

Smith, M.G., 'Some problems with minority concepts and a solution', *Ethnic and Racial Studies*, vol. 10, 1987, pp. 341-62.

Weterman, G., *Los inmigrantes antillanos en Panamá*, Panama City, Instituto Nacional de Cultura, 1980.

Williams, A., 'La mujer negra y su insersión en la sociedad panameña', *Tarea*, no. 57, 1984, pp. 83-90.

COSTA RICA

Kathleen Sawyers Royal and Franklin Perry

M ost Afro-Costa Ricans live on the Atlantic Coast of the country and are ethnically and culturally closer to the English-speaking Caribbean than to Afro-Hispanic communities of much of Latin America. Mainly descended from West Indian migrant workers, they traditionally kept themselves apart from the majority population. In recent decades this separateness has begun to dissolve, along with their strong sense of cultural identity. While there have been some improvements in their socio-economic status, the community still faces significant problems of poverty and disadvantage.

First arrivals

Official accounts of Costa Rican history do not record it, but Africans first entered Costa Rica at the very start of the European conquest in 1502. A few accompanied Columbus when he arrived on the east coast in September of that year.[1] By 1707 the Spaniards had begun to ship Africans into Costa Rica as a substitute for indigenous labour. Many slaves were put to work on the cacao plantations that supported the colony's economy. Costa Rica also supplied slaves to other Spanish American countries.[2] Records from the period show that the slaves included women.

Over the next 250 years it is thought that sizeable numbers of people of African origin came from the Caribbean islands to settle on the eastern, Atlantic Coast. Elsewhere, growing numbers of maroons (escaped slaves) lived in the more isolated areas.

Black workers of Limón

To facilitate the growing trade in coffee with Europe, an eastern seaport and a railway connecting it to the rest of the country were needed in the Atlantic coastal region, soon to be officially

215

designated as Limón Province. In 1870 Tomás Guardia, the country's President, obtained a loan from the British government to build a railway, and the construction of the first warehouse at Port Limón began on 15 November 1871.

Due to the perceived urgency of the construction work, foreign labourers were brought in. A report from 20 December 1872 reads: 'Today, at 2 p.m., the schooner *Lizzie* of 117 tons arrived ... carrying 7 men and 123 workers for the railroad. Included are 3 women.' Most of the new migrant workers were Afro-Caribbeans. While many came directly from the islands, especially Jamaica, others travelled up the coast from what was then part of Colombia and would become Panama, where they had been working for the French canal project. Thus began a pattern of migration between the Caribbean, Panama and Limón that would persist for decades.

Caribbean workers were recruited through a subcontracting system using overseers, which meant that proper employment contracts were not drawn up.[3] Pay was low, and the climate and conditions were harsh, with swamps, mosquitoes and prolonged rains. Many of the early migrant labourers died, despite the widely held belief that they had adjusted to the tropics.

The Keith brothers, who were contracted to build the railway, introduced the commercial cultivation of bananas beside the railway tracks. Jamaicans rather than Hispanic Costa Ricans were preferred for this work, because they had previous experience of banana cultivation and because they spoke English and were therefore considered loyal to the British Crown and the US-run company. When the French canal project collapsed in 1887, more Afro-Caribbeans came to Costa Rica in search of employment.

With the introduction of banana growing, the black workforce once more demonstrated its versatility. Canal builders turned railway builders and operators now also became farmers. The Keiths' company grew not only bananas but also cacao, sugarcane and, further inland, coffee.

The primary concern of the migrant workers was to make some money and then return to their home islands. But although their labour on the railway and plantations sustained much of the national economy, their wages remained meagre. Few, if any, earned enough to re-establish family ties, and the threat of unemployment and poverty was ever present. Return to the islands was little more than a dream.

In 1899 the Keiths merged their plantation enterprise with the Boston Fruit Company to form the United Fruit Company. Between them, the United Fruit Company and the Keiths' Northern Railway Company ran Limón for their own advantage, controlling the province's railways, docks, steamships and land. United Fruit continued to rent hundreds of acres of national land, tax free. The company built and ran housing, supply stores, medical facilities, churches and schools, determining the distribution of settlements along the railway route.

Ethnic relations and racism

By the early twentieth century Limón Province had a resident Caribbean population of many thousands, most of whom were single men, living as temporary residents. Despite their homesickness, the Afro-Limonenses came to form a permanent colony. They remained closer to the Caribbean, especially Jamaica, than to the host country in their speech, dress, food and way of doing business among themselves.[4]

In any case, Limón and its population remained largely isolated from the rest of the country, despite the railway. Few Afro-Costa Ricans ever travelled to San José, the capital – a distance of 103 miles, under each one of which, it was said, lay the body of an immigrant worker.

Tension existed between labourers and overseers, between black workers and native Costa Ricans, and even between the older Jamaicans and subsequent arrivals of younger Caribbean men. In general, the native Costa Ricans did not like having the Afro-Caribbeans in their midst; they spoke a different language, were Protestant rather than Catholic and had a different way of life. The immigrants did not trust the host population either. Seeing themselves as temporary inhabitants only, the Afro-Caribbeans kept apart. Most could not speak Spanish and had no wish to learn it, regarding Spanish culture as inferior to that of

Britain. Those who had children did not want them educated among the Spanish-speakers, whom they despised, preferring private schools instead.

During the 1920s and 1930s disaster struck Limón in the shape of various diseases attacking the banana plants. The United Fruit Company gradually abandoned its operations there, leaving behind its workforce. The company signed new agreements with the Costa Rican authorities and switched to the Pacific coast instead.

A ban was soon issued by Congress on any person of colour dwelling or seeking a job in the new company enclave to the west – on the grounds that jobs were needed for the Pacific coastal dwellers. (Racist legislation such as this has often been passed in Latin America. El Salvador did not until recently grant permanent residence to black people. Ironically, the few Afro-Americans in El Salvador are usually US diplomats.)

Many of the formerly subcontracted black labour force set up as small-scale independent growers of bananas, cacao and hemp on land vacated by the company. Others migrated to the larger towns, initiating a gradual process of cultural adaptation.[5]

Yet for numerous others unemployment, hunger and despair took hold. Significant numbers of the second generation of black Costa Ricans, ironically calling themselves 'Nowhereans', saw themselves as neither British, Jamaican nor Costa Rican. Although born in the country, none of them were legally its citizens. The United Fruit Company, the railway company, the Costa Rican government, the British consulate in Limón and the Jamaican government appeared to have washed their hands of them.

It was not until 1949, when a new constitution was drawn up after the civil war – in which many Afro-Costa Ricans fought with honour – that the former Caribbean islanders obtained full Costa Rican citizenship. The indigenous peoples of Costa Rica living in the same province would have to wait even longer.

Migration and the Afro-Costa Rican family

After the collapse of the east coast banana economy, and with discrimination still practised, if unofficially, large numbers of the 'Nowherean' generation of Afro-Costa Rican men – and some women – were forced to seek employment elsewhere. Many went to Panama in search of contract work; others went to sea, working for the shipping companies that plied the Caribbean and western Atlantic.

Migration for the Afro-Costa Ricans was thus a strategy for economic survival. But it was also a means of self-improvement, because migrant workers sent money to those who remained behind, helping them to become home-owners rather than tenants. In particular, with the 'ship-outs', as those who went to sea were called, black families achieved some upward economic and social mobility, often with ownership of small parcels of land or the start-up of a small business. Most of the men who signed up with the shipping companies had no qualifications, but a small percentage were professionals who had not been able to find work in Costa Rica.

The shipping companies obliged the men to serve at sea for eight to ten consecutive months, so there was relatively little time left to spend with their families. As a result, women came to head many an Afro-Costa Rican household.

In keeping with a good deal of Afro-American culture, Afro-Costa Rican families were, and remain, extended rather than nuclear. This bears out the traditional African saying that it takes a village to educate a child, which, some have argued, owes its origins to pre-colonial African culture. The idea that children belong to the community, regardless of origin, has persisted.

One of the basic distinguishing features of Afro-Costa Rican families today is that they have depended on internal informal support systems to a greater extent than Hispanic Costa Rican families. This applies even to the most progressive and upwardly mobile black families. Flexible household structures have enabled families to maintain stability. A readiness to absorb kin and other individuals in need of food, clothing and shelter has been an important factor in the collective survival of economic hardship.

Nevertheless, among those Afro-Costa Ricans who sought to establish a Western-style nuclear family, the migration process was sometimes immensely damaging. The men often established new families abroad, which undermined their ties with spouses and children left behind.

In addition to the periodic booms and slumps that attracted Afro-Costa Ricans to Panama or to sea, in the 1960s many black Limonese women went to the United States as domestic workers in Brooklyn and the Bronx. Their children, left in the care of grandmothers, aunts, other relatives and friends, could not have survived without the support of extended family.

Multi-ethnicity outside Limón

In Limón the Afro-Costa Ricans have remained recognizably a separate community; but elsewhere in the country considerable ethnic mixing has taken place. There are few government data, and official recording of ethnic identities ceased in the 1950s. However, most Costa Ricans today are thought to be partly African by descent as a result of intermixing with Africans brought over by the Spanish.

In the pre-industrial period there were several *pueblas* (non-white reservations, both urban and rural) in central and north-western Costa Rica where indigenous and black people lived. It was also a common custom for upper-class Hispanic men, including clergy, to take young slave women as concubines, producing mixed-race 'godchildren' who would carry their fathers' surname.

Difficulties with social integration sometimes occurred when former slaves bought their freedom or were granted it by their masters and began to work for themselves, notably in the former capital city of Cartago, inland from Limón. The white community of Cartago, headed by the city governor, would not countenance this social mobility of former slaves and confined black people to a *puebla*. This site is still a landmark in Cartago, a short distance from the Basilica de Nuestra Señora de Los Angeles, the black Virgin patron saint of the country.

Garveyism

In 1909 the Jamaican-born Marcus Garvey (1887-1940) made the first of several visits to Limón. Observing the deplorable working conditions on the banana plantations, he determined to dedicate his life to the Afro-American struggle. His public lectures helped Afro-Costa Ricans become more aware of their social conditions and problems. Increasingly a figure of international standing, he established one of the first branches of his Universal Negro Improvement Association (UNIA) in the country.

Under Garvey's leadership, significant numbers of Afro-Costa Ricans came to feel that they had more in common with the inhabitants of Bluefields in Nicaragua and of the Atlantic coast of Panama than with those of San José or London. The phrases 'We is we' and 'We is one people' became common parlance.

The influence of Garveyism was in many ways short-lived. Most young black people today see themselves as Costa Ricans first and foremost. And Garvey's legacy is sometimes considered to have been an impediment to black integration into the Hispanic Costa Rican labour movement.[6] Nevertheless, Afro-Costa Rican civic leaders such as Quince Duncan, Eulalia Bernard, Jocelyn and Kathleen Sawyers, Delroy Baston and Headly Hall were inspired by his message. And, over the years, UNIA-inspired lodges, burial schemes, churches, clubs and other community institutions have provided communal defences against poverty and hunger.

During the 1940s and 1950s these institutions were of considerable importance to the Afro-Limonenses, serving as centres of culture, recreation, spiritual guidance, education and self-help. In recent decades their role has declined, because of the growth of state welfare provision.

Today's reality

The Afro-Costa Rican population, perhaps 2 per cent of the national total, is still concentrated in Limón Province. An estimated third of the population of Limón city and the immediate vicinity – about 20,000 people in all – is Afro-American; and the total Afro-Costa Rican population of the province is probably more than three times that figure.[7] The last time that the national census included ethnic origin, in 1950, 91 per cent of Afro-Costa Ricans lived in Limón Province, with most of the remaining 9 per cent in San José Province.

Limón city might seem an anomaly compared with the rest of Costa Rica, because even today its character more closely resembles that of other Central American Caribbean ports. Spain generally neglected the Atlantic coast, while the influence of the British and their Jamaican subjects was strong. English and its offshoot dialects were, and remain, the *lingua franca* of a western Caribbean coastal belt that is home to some 500,000 inhabitants.

Contemporary Afro-Costa Ricans have retained many of the customs of their grandparents, although with modifications and adaptations. They are still closer to Afro-Caribbeans in outlook, culture, beliefs and language than to the rest of the country.

Yet there are differences. The older Afro-Costa Ricans had little more than basic education. Most attended parish schools provided by the churches, or the UNIA, or by individual teachers. Most had a 'trade' and learned some music and the history and geography of Jamaica and Britain, but nothing about Costa Rica. This has changed. Younger generations have had better opportunities than their forebears, and they enjoy full citizenship rights. They have full access to education and they can, in theory, work and live wherever they wish in the country.

Third-generation Afro-Costa Ricans are, in effect, bicultural. Their children go mainly to schools where Spanish is the first language, although most still speak and understand an English-based Limón creole popularly called Mek-a-Tell-Yu.[8]

In fact, Afro-Costa Ricans have a tradition of literacy that belies their difficult circumstances. Most of the earlier migrant workers arrived knowing how to 'read, write and cypher', and they sent their children to school no matter what. An estimated 97 per cent of black Costa Ricans can read and write, and they are generally highly educated.

The rather meagre opportunities available for self-improvement have not been neglected. There is hardly a field that Afro-Costa Ricans have not entered, but nursing, teaching and entertainment are the traditional occupations at which they work, and significant numbers of men still go to sea. Since 1949 Afro-Costa Ricans have taken part in national politics, largely through membership of the Partido Liberación Nacional. There have been perhaps two dozen black members of parliament and governors, as well as one black cabinet minister.

Economically, however, the position has not changed radically. Afro-Costa Ricans no longer suffer the severe hardships of earlier decades, but many black families still live in poverty, and only a small minority have enjoyed what might be called social or financial success. It remains the case that both Afro-Costa Ricans and the country's indigenous inhabitants have always lived in the poorest, most marginal parts of the country, and they continue to do so. They experience unemployment, poverty and substandard housing disproportionately. Despite official denials and excuses, the inequality remains plain to see.

Notes

We thank Donald Duncan, Fernando Hall, Delia McDonald and Mario Symes, interviews with whom helped in the writing of this chapter.

1 See Meléndez, C. and Duncan, Q., *El negro en Costa Rica*, San José, Editorial Costa Rica, 1977.
2 Interview with Delia McDonald.
3 See Echeverri-Gent, E., 'Forgotten workers: British West Indians and the early days of the banana industry in Costa Rica and Honduras', *Journal of Latin American Studies*, vol. 24, pt 2, 1992, pp. 275-308.
4 See Olien, M.D., 'The adaptation of West Indian blacks to North American and Hispanic culture in Costa Rica', in A.M. Pescattello (ed.), *Old Roots in New Lands: Historical and Anthropological Perspectives in Black Experience in the Americas*, Westport, CT, Greenwood Press, 1977, pp. 132-53.
5 Ibid.
6 See Purcell, T.W., *Banana Fallout: Class, Color and Culture among West Indians in Costa Rica*, Los Angeles, CA, Center for Afro-American Studies, University of California, 1993.
7 Ministerio de Economía Industria y Comercio, Dirección General de Estadística y Censos, 1984.
8 Herzfeld, A., 'The Creoles of Costa Rica and Panama', in J. Holm (ed.), *Central American English*, Heidelberg, Groos, 1983, pp. 131-49.

Select bibliography

Herzfeld, A., 'The Creoles of Costa Rica and Panama', in J. Holm (ed.), *Central American English*, Heidelberg, Groos, 1983, pp. 131-49.
Meléndez, C. and Duncan, Q., *El negro en Costa Rica*, San José, Editorial Costa Rica, 1977.
Purcell, T.W., *Banana Fallout: Class, Color and Culture among West Indians in Costa Rica*, Los Angeles, CA, Center for Afro-American Studies, University of California, 1993.
Stewart, W., *Keith y Costa Rica*, San José, Editorial Costa Rica, 1976.

BELIZE

Debbie Ewens

Belize, formerly British Honduras, is unique among the nations of Central America. It is the isthmus's only black nation; English is its official language; and its political history and development have been closely tied to Britain. This geopolitical peculiarity, and the country's isolation from other former British colonies (Jamaica is 600 miles away), have helped shape the destiny of its people.

Belize's population is composed mainly of Creoles (people of predominantly African descent), Spanish-speaking *mestizos* and a smaller number of Garífuna (Afro-Carib people). Numerically, the Creoles were long in the ascendant, occupying a central position with regard to the identity of their nation, a situation which was very different from the marginalized status of most Afro-Hispanic communities of the region. Recent growth of the Hispanic community, however, as a result of the movement of refugees and of population expansion, has introduced new tensions.

Early history

Belize was first settled by British sailors or loggers in 1638. It developed as an ambiguous bastion of British presence in a Spanish-dominated region supported by slave labour. British colonialism in the Belize settlement was 'created through confrontation and conflict'.[1] Settlement was established for the sole purpose of exploitation of the forests, and it has been said that Belize represents 'a classic example of colonial exploitation of taking away and not giving back'.

Almost from the beginning, Spain and Britain fought for ownership of the territory, and most treaties between the colonial powers included a clause on Belize. Yet this apparent importance was deceptive, because the country was of little political concern to either power. It was not until 1862, 224 years after the first settlers arrived, that the British Crown found it convenient to declare the territory a British colony, administratively linked to Jamaica. Until that time 'Belize offered an interesting study in primitive and spontaneous government set up without the sanction of the Crown, one that is unique and altogether anomalous in the story of the acquisition and development of Britain's colonial empire.'[2]

If Britain had misgivings as to the political status of the colony, it had no doubts about its economic value. Belize was a major producer of logwood at a time when the dye extracted from this wood was valuable to Europe. The lucrative trade in this species of timber, and later in mahogany, determined the foundation of the settlement and its retention in the late eighteenth century when conquest by Spanish invaders seemed inevitable.

African slaves are thought to have been brought to Belize from diverse origins, and the political climate of hesitation and inaction gave their descendants the opportunity to live in an informal atmosphere, in many ways unsupervised. The dispute between the two world powers over ownership disallowed any legal form of government in the settlement, and this limited the legal structures that could be created. Such a situation favoured slavery but permitted a pattern of legal improvisation, unlike in the more formalized Spanish colonies in Central America. Besides this, legal restrictions in Belize prevented the establishment of haciendas and impeded the development of agriculture.

While not benevolent, and comprising all the components of slavery elsewhere in the Americas, slavery in Belize had some differences. Chief among these was a measure of respect that the slave owners were forced to show towards their charges, due to the intense and arduous nature of the logging work undertaken, the isolation of the camps, the proximity of the Spanish and the economic value of the slaves themselves.

Restricted economic and political activity, an improvised social system and an uncertain economic future may appear unenviable. Yet these factors, with the formal ending of slavery in the 1830s, favoured the evolutionary development of Afro-Belizean society. The situation was further aided by the early reduction in numbers of the white population. At the dawn of the nineteenth century people of colour represented 75 per cent of the settlement's inhabitants. The Belize settlers from Britain tended to be men of low status who often could not obtain British brides. This allowed for an open and accepted relationship between white men and women of colour which quickly created an energetic and confident multiracial society.

By the 1820s the Creole population had grown demographically and economically strong, and two-thirds of the land was in its possession by the middle of the century. The wealthiest Creole landowners converted land to cash and educated their children in Britain, allowing them to achieve an elite status that no one had envisaged.

Meanwhile, the way of life of the majority of Afro-Belizeans developed largely out of the forest economy. Men would spend months working at the isolated logging camps, while women remained at home in villages and towns, caring for their children, baking bread or taking in laundry to make up for the lack of income. During seasonal breaks, the men would return, often to spend on drink what little money they had earned.

African and other cultural influences

Belize had a 'selective' immigration policy that unwittingly kept away influences that had the potential to change the emerging Afro-Belizean society and culture. Black people were brought directly from Africa rather than via Jamaica, which secured the continuity of African culture in the settlement. For example, *obeah*, a form of witchcraft of African origin, was criminalized and made punishable by death in 1791, yet the practice persisted well into the nineteenth century.

Belize Town, the cradle of Creole development, has been called an 'overgrown village' whose unusual pattern of settlement 'seems to have had particular consequences for the persistence and change of aspects of the African cultural heritage'.[3] Though an 'urban village', Belize Town was home to a growing multi-ethnic population and the seat of central government.

The construction of Government House, the court house, the Belize hospital and the Anglican cathedral laid the foundations for a socio-political edifice that would accommodate the original

Maya, white settlers and the various strata of African and Creole peoples. Along with the development of infrastructure came the gradual implantation of African culture among all sections of the population, including white people. A new and hybrid Belizean culture developed as a result.

A mid-nineteenth-century description of the conduct of wakes before the end of slavery shows how Belizean culture had become a blend of West African, European and Creole elements. It can be assumed that slave owners were of British ethnic origin:

If a slave owner died, all his dependants and friends came together to be feasted; and the wife or mistress and her children prepared the house and provided provisions and plenty of ardent spirits. The corpse, dressed in its best clothes, was laid upon a bed ... Cards, dice, backgammon, with strong drink and spiced wine, helped to beguile its watches ... In the negro yard below, the sheck'ka *and the drum 'proclaimed the sport, the song, the dance' ... [of] different African nations and creoles ... [T]he corpse was carried in the morning to the churchyard, the coffin being borne by labourers, who ... used to run up and down the streets ... with their burden, knocking at some door or doors ... contending with the spirit who opposed the interment of the body. At length some well-known friend came forward, speaking soothingly to the dead ... They then moved all together towards the grave, and the* sheck'ka's *jingle, the voice of song and latterly the funeral service of the Established Church were mingled together.*[4]

Vivacity at wakes remains common to all ethnic groups in Belize.

There were other influences too. The *Honduras Almanac* of 1830 states: 'It is not rare to meet with black persons who possess an utter aversion to spirituous liquors, and can by no means be prevailed upon to taste a beverage in which they know anything of the sort to be a component part.'[5] This suggests an Islamic element in the cultural mix.

Accounts of Christmas holidays from the nineteenth century give further evidence of the 'creolization' process:

[On] the morning of Christmas-day ... members of the several African tribes, again met together after a long separation, now

form themselves into different groups, and nothing can more forcibly denote their respective casts of national character than their music, songs and dances ... The endurance of the negroes during the period of their holidays, which usually last a week, is incredible. Few of them are known to take any portion of rest.[6]

Such festivities were marked by the use of drums, costume and dance rivalry and other features common to many Afro-American cultures. The creole dialect and Anancy stories of Belize are also remnants of African culture. Creole became the *lingua franca* of Belize and penetrated every ethnic stratum.

Social and political change

Belize entered the twentieth century with many of the historical factors that had contributed to its anomalous position still in place. The creolization process was an established fact. The presence of British political culture was a crucial component of Belizean social stability and formal Afro-Belizean equality, in a region where violent upheavals were common and black communities were frequently oppressed.

By the 1900s the Creole population had waged a successful struggle for political power, in which labour movements and black organizations had played a part. Theoretically, at least, they have retained since that time access to all social and political institutions in the country, and in this sense Belize has been presented as a prototype for social justice and equality for Central America's communities of colour.

Demographically, the white population had shrunk through net emigration and interbreeding, and it was the Creoles who began agitating for social change. The climate was right for political activism. Afro-Belizean men received a rude awakening in the West Indian Regiment of the British Army, where they discovered a hate-filled racism. Discrimination existed in Belize, but as soldiers the men experienced a level of bigotry previously unknown to them.

Despite the gradual establishment of social services, poverty continued to dominate the lives of most Belizeans of all ethnic groups. Plantation agriculture had developed, but steady jobs remained beyond the reach of much of the population, with the economy still primarily dependent on the export of timber and other forest products. The rise of the Creole population was, however, assisted by British commissions of inquiry that reported on conditions in the colony; the Moyne Commission into social and economic conditions was of particular importance. Outspoken comments were made concerning the stark poverty of the population, and the deplorable labour conditions. This helped create a liberal atmosphere in which Afro-Belizeans could assert their social and political rights.

Trade unionism, legal reform, democracy and self-government came strongly together in a political agenda that placed power directly in the hands of the Creole majority and cemented the political future of Afro-Belizean involvement in the political arena. At length such efforts bore fruit in the post-war Colonial Development and Welfare Act, which facilitated economic and social improvements.

Persisting problems

In recent decades the ethnic composition of Belize has been transformed. Dramatic change followed Hurricane Hattie in 1961, in whose wake large numbers of Belizeans began to migrate to the United States. Whereas the 1980 census found that 40 per cent of the country's inhabitants were Afro-Belizean and 33 per cent *mestizo*, Creole emigration and the immigration of *mestizos* from other parts of Central America, mainly as peasant farmers, had resulted by 1991 in *mestizos* constituting 41 per cent of the population, with the Creole proportion in decline. This shift towards a more Spanish-speaking population has considerable implications for the country's future and is already a source of friction.

Although the Creoles were, until recently, numerically predominant, they were not an absolute majority of the population. Inter-ethnic prejudice, stereotyping and discrimination have continued to exist, if not in any institutionalized form. Overall, the lasting effects of colonialism have tended to favour people with lighter skins, who are disproportionately represented among the wealthy and powerful. Garífuna, on the other hand, were traditionally discriminated against in Belize and demonized by some as having occult abilities or cannibalistic tendencies. The colonial heritage and a long history of inequalities, which used to define and solidify ethnic boundaries, is now reinforced by the pervasive influence of US economic and cultural domination; this has been referred to as the 'imperial succession'.[7]

Poverty remains the essential fact of life for most Belizeans, particularly for dark-skinned Creoles. Weekly earnings average between US $25 and $50, while a basic weekly food basket costs about $60. The 1991 census put the rate of unemployment at 20 per cent, and youth unemployment is 43 per cent in Belize City. Only 31 per cent of young Belizeans in the 15-19 age group have paid work, while 70 per cent of the country's adult women have never earned a wage.

Housing conditions in Belize City have long been a major signifier of poverty. In 1995 the capital still has areas where makeshift houses of one or two rooms accommodate families of six and upward and are reached by 'London Bridges' spanning mosquito-infested swamps. Single motherhood and unemployment prevent the renting of better homes. Sanitation and clean water are not as problematic as they were twenty years ago. But even so, the 1991 census showed that 38 per cent of households in the capital obtained drinking water from public pipes; and in 1990 it was estimated that only 43 per cent had adequate sanitation.

Malnutrition, parasites and respiratory tract disease continue to be among the chief causes of death among Belizean children. Essential proteins and vitamins are in short supply. Belize is only now beginning to experiment with fresh milk, having relied for years on the condensed variety. The daily diet remains based on the traditional staples of yam, cassava, rice and corn. Health care for most Belizeans also bears the seal of poverty. It is commonly said that in Belize the best health care available is second-rate. A new central public hospital is currently being built for Belize City, but it will reportedly have less bed space than the old facility, which is rumoured to be marked down for conversion into a private hospital. This suggests that, although government policy embraces free medical care, the new reality is that the population will be forced to pay for the service.

National literacy is estimated at about 70 per cent, with some 20 per cent of the population classified as semi-literate and 9 per cent as illiterate. An estimated 11 per cent of children never attend primary school, and 46 per cent do not complete their primary education. Belize's education process places strong emphasis on academic achievement, and almost no vocational, technical, creative or artistic studies are available. UNICEF has reported that three-quarters of all teachers who sit the annual teachers' college entrance exams fail. According to the Ministry of Education, only 47 per cent of the teachers in Belize primary schools in 1991-2 were fully trained.

Many youngsters work in the informal economy instead of going to school. Income-generating activities of boys include selling newspapers, cutting grass, cleaning yards, selling bottles, shoe shining, delivery and, in some cases, begging, stealing and peddling drugs. Girls, as reported by UNICEF, work as 'baby-sitters, domestics, shop assistants and prostitutes'.[8] Children who sell or deliver drugs make an average of about US $40 per sale. Many working children contribute much-needed money to the household budget.

In recent times, increasing numbers of women have moved out from the home into paid employment. Yet traditional conceptions of wifely obedience are still potent, and the majority of the female population remains essentially passive. A few semi-official women's organizations operate in such fields as domestic violence and child abuse.

It is estimated that 60,000 Belizeans – one-third of the population – live today in the United States. This trend has resulted in considerable damage to family and community life. It also represents a classic case of the 'brain drain' from South to North, because those who leave the country are among the best educated. The 1991 census indicated that as many as 47 per cent of emigrants, but only 20 per cent of immigrants aged 15-34, had reached secondary education or higher.

Social problems such as single parenthood, teen pregnancy, crime, drugs, HIV/AIDS, gang violence and dysfunctional families disproportionately affect people low on the socio-economic ladder, and hence are a significant reality in the contemporary lives of Creole Belizeans. Political activity among Belizeans tends to be on a non-ethnic basis, although fears have been expressed that a form of politics based more on ethnic groupings might emerge in the future. The late 1960s saw the development of the United Black Association for Development among the Creoles, modelled partly on the US Black Power movement. Maya and Garífuna ethnic groupings have also emerged, although none of these organizations is explicitly political.

Facing the future

Belize is a country with a young and rapidly growing population, half of whom are under 18 years of age. An increasing number of Afro-Belizeans are youths with insecure family backgrounds – children of poverty and often victims of abuse and neglect. UNICEF has stated: 'The healthy family structure in Belize is at risk, as are healthy, egalitarian economic conditions.'[9] Projections indicate that by 2015 the potential labour force will increase significantly in both percentage and absolute terms, creating an even greater demand for employment opportunities. Many Creoles now express anxiety that lighter-skinned *mestizos* are moving ahead of them in socio-economic terms. Thus, physical appearance continues to correlate with socio-economic position, although there is no formal racial discrimination in Belizean life.

Despite issues of ethnicity, however, Belize's major problems, which threaten its stability, are mainly non-racial and non-ethnic. They centre on the country's severe case of economic dependency and indebtedness, which is likely to become worse under the impact of the recently concluded North American Free Trade Agreement. Much of the economy is under foreign, in particular US, control.

So Afro-Belizeans continue to evolve, not in a country of 'multiracial harmony', but in a society of multiracial tensions. For most Belizeans of all ethnic groups, poverty, low educational attainment, few opportunities for economic advancement or social mobility, and political weakness are the dominant experience. 'Without major economic developments, it is unlikely that any significant shifts will take place in the relations of class, race and ethnicity in the social structure.'[10] Future prospects for Creole Belizeans, as for most of their compatriots, seem likely to hinge on whether a greater measure of economic justice is obtainable for majority populations, both generally between South and North, and within the countries of the South.

Notes

1 Bolland, O.N., *Colonialism and Resistance in Belize*, Belize City, Cubola, 1988.
2 Grant, C.H., *The Making of Modern Belize*, Cambridge, Cambridge University Press, 1976.
3 Bolland, op. cit.
4 Quoted ibid., p. 76.
5 Quoted ibid.
6 Quoted ibid., p. 78.
7 Grant, op. cit., p. 123.
8 Anti-Slavery Society, *Children in Especially Difficult Circumstances*, two reports for UNICEF: *The Exploitation of Child Labour*, London, 1984, and *The Sexual Exploitation of Children*, London, 1985.
9 UNICEF.
10 Bolland, op. cit., p. 52.

Select bibliography

Bolland, O.N., *Colonialism and Resistance in Belize*, Belize City, Cubola, 1988.
Grant, C.H., *The Making of Modern Belize*, Cambridge, Cambridge University Press, 1976.

HONDURAS

Rachel Sieder

Nearly all black Hondurans belong to the Garífuna Afro-Carib population group, which currently numbers some 98,000 people. In Honduras the experience of the Garífuna has been largely one of marginalization and disadvantage. Issues of communal land rights, and access to and protection of natural resources, have been a particular concern for the Garífuna community. While there are significant Garífuna populations in the country's capital, Tegucigalpa, and in the northern cities of San Pedro Sula, La Ceiba, Puerto Cortés and El Progreso, most Garífuna are located on the Atlantic Coast, distributed among some forty-three towns and villages from Masca in the Department of Cortés to Playaplaya in the eastern-most Department of Gracias a Dios. Garífuna populations also live on the Belizean coast, in the coastal town of Livingstone in Guatemala and in the Atlantic region of Nicaragua. Beyond Central America, there are sizeable Garífuna populations in the United States, in particular in New Orleans, Miami and Los Angeles.

Origins and history

The origins of the Garífuna remain the subject of considerable controversy, but it is now generally agreed that they are the descendants of African and Carib populations from the Antillean islands of St Vincent and Dominica. Following the shipwreck of two Spanish slave-ships in the mid-seventeenth century, the surviving slaves are said to have taken refuge on St Vincent, where they mixed with the local Carib population, forming maroon (free slave) communities in the north-east. The indigenous origin of much of the Garífunas' economic and cultural universe is observable today in the manner in which Garífuna women cultivate and prepare yucca, used to make *casabe* (cassava), and also in certain linguistic traits.

In 1775 the British conquered St Vincent and evicted the Garífuna in order to take over their fertile lands. War between the colonial forces and the Garífuna ensued, and in 1797 the surviving Garífuna, some 3,000 to 5,000, were expelled and taken to the island of Roatán, off the Caribbean coast of Honduras. With this forced deportation of the Garífuna, the English aimed to rid themselves of a rebellious population and cause problems for their imperial rival, Spain, which controlled the territory of Honduras. Many of the Garífuna died *en route* of disease. The survivors subsequently populated the sparsely inhabited coastal region of mainland Honduras.

The Garífuna were often recruited as local militia by the Spanish during English incursions on the coast. However, the friendly relations between the Miskitu (allies of the British) and the Garífuna periodically aroused Spanish suspicions against the latter. It was only the heroic defence in 1820 of the port of Trujillo by Garífuna soldiers against a British attack which secured a series of privileges for the Garífuna, ratified in the first post-independence constitution in 1825.

During the first half of the nineteenth century, in common with many indigenous populations in Central America, the Garífuna allied themselves with Conservative forces against the Liberal reformers. The eventual defeat of the Conservatives in the mid-nineteenth century occasioned an exodus of Garífuna from Honduras to the Atlantic Coast of Nicaragua. This pattern of war and expulsion has dominated the historical memory of the Garífuna:

> *If you look closely you will see that we have always had a history of danger. We were always persecuted, the powerful always wanted to humiliate us, they always wanted to take away the land of our ancestors. Fighting with our weapons, we have always escaped to the mountains and we have always defended ourselves from the bad spirits.*[1]

Religion as resistance

During the late nineteenth century the evangelizing work of the Catholic Church began to have an impact on the Garífuna, and since the Second World War the influence of evangelical Protestant sects has increased significantly. Most Garífuna would describe themselves as Catholic, yet their religious rituals represent a syncretism between Catholicism and prior belief systems. As one Garífuna elder stated: 'We Garífuna believe in God and in the spirits of our dead, and we will continue to be Catholics. This is our Garífuna tradition.'[2]

Garífuna conceptions of the world combine indigenous and African elements and are centred on ancestor cults. The Garífunas' philosophical-religious system is known as *dugu* or *walagallo* and in some respects compares with the voodoo system practised in Haiti. The idea of *gubida*, or ancestral spirit possession, continues to have a central role in Garífuna religious practices; possession of an individual is considered an illness, and *gubida* is used to explain periods of illness or abnormal behaviour. The condition is officially diagnosed by a shaman (male or female) who enters a trance to consult with the spirits of the dead. The dead are believed to be able to communicate their wishes through the dreams of their living family members experiencing *gubida*. Ritual offerings to appease the ancestral spirits include food and drink, together with animal sacrifice, and (in the case of the more elaborate *dugu* ceremony) trances and spirit possession are common. In the case of death, Catholic mass and wake are observed, together with Garífuna rituals which include songs, dance and traditional drum music. Many African influences can be seen in dance styles – including the *punta*, now popular throughout Honduras, oral traditions, forms of drum-playing and animal sacrifice. According to Honduran anthropologist Ramón Rivas, out-migration together with remittances of dollars from family members living in the United States appear to have increased the frequency and elegance of traditional religious ceremonies among the Garífuna.[3]

Garífuna religious practices, conceived of as a collective struggle against death and illness, constitute a focus of resistance against ethnic and class oppression. José Idiáquez notes that the role of ancestors in the collective historical struggles of the Garífuna is of central importance, and it is this, he argues, together with their ability to absorb new cultural aspects into religious practices, which lends particular stability to the Garífunas' ethnic identity.[4]

Languages

Most Garífuna speak Spanish and Garífuna. The linguistic origins of Garífuna may remain in dispute – researchers claiming it to be a mixture of other languages, including Arawak, French, Yoruba, Swahili and Bantu – but it is a central part of Garífuna ethnic identity:

> *For us Garífuna, the defence of our language has always been very important. Many people have made fun of our language and the same thing happened to our ancestors. But they were never shamed by this. We speak our Garífuna language, we pray and sing in Garífuna. This is why it's important that the teachers who educate our children should be Garífuna, so that the children can learn Garífuna and our religious beliefs. Our religious beliefs and language are an important part of our culture and our Garífuna tradition and we have to defend them in the same way that our ancestors did.*[5]

The establishment during the last two years of a National Council for Bilingual Education, financed by the international community, has considerably strengthened Garífuna demands for use of their language in local schools.[6]

Socio-economic position

The main economic activities among the Garífuna are subsistence agriculture (yucca, plantains, beans, rice and maize) and fishing. However, unemployment and under-employment are high – affecting over 80 per cent of the population – and men tend to emigrate periodically outside their communities in search of work, reinforcing the traditional matriarchal structure of Garífuna families. Skill specialization is uncommon among the Garífuna and they are particularly disadvantaged in the national job market. Some 72 per cent of the Garífuna population is illiterate or semi-literate.[7] Migration to the United States in search of work has increased in recent decades.

In a country where some 70 per cent of the population lives below the official poverty line, the Garífuna are one of the most disadvantaged sectors. Socio-economic indicators show that 62 per cent of Garífuna children up to the age of 12 display signs of malnutrition; and malnutrition affects up to 78 per cent of children below 12 years of age in the most isolated departments of Colón and Gracias a Dios.[8] In recent years, conflict over land, particularly in the area around Trujillo and Limón, has become acute. Politicians, military officers and large cattle-ranchers have illegally expropriated Garífuna communal lands. For example, in the Sico Valley, Limón, military officers with interests in the agro-export of African palm have come into conflict with Garífuna groups.[9] Additional pressure on scarce land resources comes from increased migration from the interior, and clashes have occurred with landless peasants who have occupied Garífuna plots. There has also been conflict over fishing rights, with Garífuna in the Cayo de Cocinos being denied access to their traditional fishing areas by private capital interests anxious to develop 'eco-tourism' projects.[10]

Some Garífuna leaders have traditionally been co-opted into the traditional, clientelist political parties (Liberal and Nationalist) and have failed adequately to represent the Garífuna as a whole. However, others have been elected as local mayors and have concentrated on addressing the community demands. For example, in Limón, Garífuna mayor Lombardo Lacayo has commissioned a survey to establish the legal status of lands in the municipality as a first step towards recovering Garífuna communal lands which have been illegally expropriated.[11]

Strategies for recovery

The oldest Garífuna organization, the Organización Fraternal Negra Hondureña (OFRANEH), works together with the *patronatos* in local communities but enjoys little legitimacy and has been beset by internal organizational problems since it was founded in 1984. OFRANEH has sponsored workshops and local theatre to educate the public about Garífuna origins and culture. Such efforts, together with the international success of the National Garífuna Ballet (which performs a stage version of the *walagallo*) and also of the popular group Banda Blanca – who along with other groups have popularized *punta* music – have helped to 'nationalize' Garífuna culture throughout Honduras.

However, they have arguably done little directly to improve the position of the Garífuna.

More radical Garífuna organization in Honduras has grown in recent years. Garífuna are now working together with other indigenous groups in the Consejo Asesor Hondureño para el Desarrollo de las Étnias Autóctonas to highlight the encroachment on indigenous lands. In July 1994 an unprecedented demonstration by Honduran indigenous groups occurred in the form of a protest march (or 'indigenous pilgrimage' as it was called by the organizers) converging on the capital, Tegucigalpa. Some 3,000 indigenous activists, including Garífuna groups, camped outside the Legislative Assembly for five days. Their demands included respect for indigenous rights, environmental protection measures and the release of indigenous leaders jailed in land disputes. The programme also included demands for the return of communal lands to the Garífuna and a thirty-year ban on logging throughout the country. The indigenous groups were strongly supported by progressive elements of the Catholic Church throughout the country, and many priests joined the protest.

The protesters' demands were positively met by the newly inaugurated government of Carlos Roberto Reina; on 14 July an emergency commission was set up including the ministers of culture and health, the director of the agrarian reform institute, the transport minister and a representative of Congress to attend to the indigenous groups' demands. The government has already cancelled some logging concessions in Lempira and Intibucá and seems to be committed to taking positive action on the question of indigenous rights, including the implementation of ILO Convention 169. Garífuna have joined forces with other ethnic groups, such as the Lenca, and the non-governmental Committee for the Defence of Human Rights to lobby the government for full implementation of the ILO Convention. Subsequent to the march in July 1994, Garífuna groups have met in Iriona, Colón and other areas to discuss the land problems affecting them. However, powerful local interests will continue to intimidate Garífuna activists, and further conflict over land is likely.

Conclusion

Garífuna traditions of struggle and their collective religious beliefs and practices have lent stability to the group's identity. Demands for autonomous political participation have increased in recent years, but advances in this respect have been slow and piecemeal in nature. The centrality of Garífuna demands for respect of patrimonial land rights has strengthened their linkages with other ethnic groups in Honduras and their bargaining position vis-à-vis the government, which, although broadly in favour, in principle, of respect for indigenous rights, has yet to prove its commitment to enforcing those rights in practice.

Notes

1   Interview with school teacher Javier Sierra, Cristales *barrio*, Trujillo, Honduras, cited in Idiáquez, J. SJ, *El culto a los ancestros en la cosmovisión religiosa de los Garífunas de Nicaragua*, Managua, UCA, 1994, p. 167.
2   Interview with Don Francisco Guiti, Cristales *barrio*, Trujillo, Honduras, cited ibid., p. 156.
3   Rivas, R., *Pueblas indígenas y Garífuna de Honduras*, Tegucigalpa, Guaymuras, 1993, p. 286.
4   See Idiáquez, op. cit. An example of this ability to absorb new cultural elements is given by González, who in 1984 noted that Garífuna in one Honduran village had incorporated jazz-blues musical accompaniment into their funeral rituals. She speculates that this is probably a result of large numbers of Honduran Garífuna having lived in New Orleans over the past generation; González, N.L., *Sojourners of the Caribbean: Ethnogenesis and Ethnohistory of the Garífuna*, Chicago, IL, University of Illinois, 1988, p. 79.
5   Interview with school teacher Javier Sierra, Santa Fé, Trujillo, Honduras, cited in Idiáquez, op. cit., p. 158.
6   Interview with Ramón Custodio, president of the non-governmental Committee for the Defence of Human Rights in Honduras, London, 19 March 1995.
7   Rivas, op. cit., p. 279.
8   Ibid., pp. 276, 279.
9   Interview with Ramón Custodio, op. cit., 19 March 1995.
10 Ibid.
11 Ibid.

Select bibliography

Beauçage, P., 'Economic anthropology of the Black Carib of Honduras', PhD dissertation, University of London, 1970.

González, N.L., *Sojourners of the Caribbean: Ethnogenesis and Ethnohistory of the Garífuna*, Chicago, IL, University of Illinois, 1988.

Idiáquez, J. SJ, *El culto a los ancestros en la cosmovisión religiosa de los Garífunas de Nicaragua*, Managua, UCA, 1994.

Rivas, R., *Pueblos indígenas y Garífuna de Honduras*, Tegucigalpa, Guaymuras, 1993.

8

VENEZUELA

Eduardo Bermúdez and María Matilde Suárez

The historical contribution of people of African ancestry to Venezuelan society is different from that in many other Latin American countries. Over the centuries Afro-Venezuelan ethnicity has become so intermixed with other elements in the nation, through an unusual degree of physical and cultural merging, that the African heritage can be largely perceived as defining, not a black presence, but a Venezuelan one. Yet, while Venezuela may represent the nearest that the region comes to a genuine 'racial democracy', and in formal terms there is little or no racism, Afro-Venezuelans are generally among the poorest and most marginalized sectors of society, and few of them join the ranks of the wealthy and influential.

Slave economy and slave society

The first African slaves arrived in Venezuela, part of the Spanish colony of New Granada, during the opening decades of the six-teenth century. As throughout Latin America, these slaves were referred to as *conquistadores*, because they had been born in Spain and joined the conquest of the Americas and the indigenous populations. Employed especially in land clearance, road build-ing and the construction of towns, they participated in the con-quest because their masters had promised that, once their task was fulfilled, they and their children would be granted freedom, and they would be exempted from paying taxes.

During the same period New Granada also witnessed the arrival of so-called *bozales* ('wild people') – Africans brought against their will to work in the mines or in the exploitation of pearls. But unlike in other Spanish American colonies, such as Peru and Mexico, where mining enjoyed a great boom and hence created a high demand for unskilled labour, in Venezuela this exploitation did not require very large numbers of slaves to be imported. Thus between 1500 and 1530 some 2,400 slaves were brought to Venezuela from Cape Verde and Guinea to work in the mines. Between 1536 and 1550 an additional 2,600 arrived. By the end of the sixteenth century the black slave population – comprising *conquistadores*, *bozales* and those from other origins – amounted to about 13,100 individuals, accounting for 6 per cent of the slaves taken to the Spanish American colonies during the century.

Throughout the seventeenth century, when mining came to an end in Venezuela, a major change occurred in the colonial economy. With slavery as its foundations, large-scale cocoa farming for export developed. The colonial estate was the basic production unit. The agricultural slave economy in Venezuela differed from that in the nearby Caribbean colonies in several ways.

First, until the second half of the seventeenth century administration of the lands conquered in Venezuela, as well as initial control over the slave trade, was entrusted to the Catholic Church by the Spanish Crown. Besides their evangelizing activity, priests had an active economic role. They used several measures of social control, such as the *Black Code*, which determined the duties and rights of slave owners, punishments, trade in and sale of slaves, the work that African slaves shared with indigenous people, and Catholic religious observances. They were also in charge of administering charitable activities and supervised the settlements where Christian doctrine was taught.

The development of an agricultural economy in Venezuela led to a significant change in the possession and use of land. The Spanish Crown – represented by the Church, as sole owner of the conquered territories – encouraged the development of legal forms that benefited the *conquistadores*. Through grants and other arrangements landownership gradually became privatized. As a mercantile economy emerged in private ownership, the

Church lost the hegemony that it had enjoyed during the first 150 years of the conquest. There was now less evangelization, and priests became more restrained when dealing with the Africans in their midst. So much so that, faced with the precarious economic situation of the Church, the clergy offered slaves the possibility of creating their own holy societies and brotherhoods, thus contributing to the maintenance of the Church under a fiscal regime that taxed the right of assembly.

The second distinctive feature of slave society in this region was the massive import of slaves to Venezuela during the first two decades of the eighteenth century, when the cocoa plantation economy was at its height. Finding the trade in African slaves expensive, Venezuelan landowners bought their slaves in the Caribbean. During this century 70,000 slaves were imported to the territory, 18 per cent of the estimated 390,000 captives brought to all the Spanish American colonies in this period.[1] These new arrivals were mostly Caribbean-born *ladinos* (Spanish-speakers) who had already been baptized.

The eighteenth-century newcomers included artisans, tanners, masons, skilled farmers and traditional healers and sorcerers. Many had held positions in churches or slave societies. Others were captured fugitives and rebels who were bought, despite the risks of rebellion, by Venezuelan landowners because of their pressing need for labour to develop the cocoa plantations. Yet other slaves were referred to as *mala entrada* (illegal entry) by the colonial authorities, because they were smuggled secretly into the country in an attempt to evade taxes and regulations. It has been estimated that *mala entrada* slaves accounted for 20 per cent of the total number imported during the century to the Province of Venezuela.[2]

The third significant aspect of Venezuelan slave society was that the slave population developed a way of life characterized by very weak forms of control on the part of their masters. The vast territory of the central valleys and states, where cocoa cultivation thrived on a huge scale, had no important urban centres that could control or ensure effective surveillance over the slaves. The need for manual labour led landowners to create arrangements for settling the workforce within the boundaries of the estate, granting slaves *conucos* – plots of land where they could build their houses, cultivate subsistence crops and enjoy their own communal life.

This guaranteed landowners the labour force they required while at the same time minimizing maintenance costs, because the slaves were largely self-sufficient. Over time, such provision developed into a pattern of land use that was not substantially different from one based on free workers. The social organization of production on Venezuelan colonial estates, then, did not rest on the strict and vigilant rule of masters over slaves, but rather involved a relation of common dependence.

The slave population also experienced an unusual degree of freedom by participating in certain activities related to the organizational structure of the colonial estate. The almost permanent absence of the landowners was generally filled by an African who had been picked out by the owner as able to manage and influence the remaining slaves. African individuals were in this way appointed as heads of work-crews and leaders of work-groups, and generally allowed to exert authority over their peers.

It was practically impossible for Venezuelan landowners to control the behaviour of their slaves. They never sought to regulate their religious conduct, as the Church had done; and there was, in any case, immense diversity on the estates, because slaves were imported without taking into account their religious practices or social status. Most of the cocoa haciendas founded in Venezuela did not have a church, although some had a small private chapel, built of clay and straw, in honour of the owner's patron saints. Priests were rarely seen; contact with them might occur only through a pastoral visit or with the celebration of a saint's day in a nearby town that had a church where slaves from the hacienda could attend mass. The lack of close religious supervision also resulted from the dispersion of the plantations in vast areas of jungle and from the seasonal nature of cocoa cultivation. Thus the black workforce was largely left alone to continue with its own religious activities, to increase the productivity of its *conucos* and to trade crops clandestinely.

By the end of the eighteenth century and the first half of the nineteenth, Venezuelan slave traders had resorted to a new practice in order to reduce prices. Black people born in the country were now bought and sold on the domestic market. Between 1780 and 1850 this internal trade was controlled by a group of local slave traders known as *negreros criollos*. They had their haciendas in the central states and the coastal areas near Caracas, the capital city. By about 1800, 99.5 per cent of the slaves traded by these Creole businessmen were *mulatos* (people of mixed Afro-Hispanic parentage, also known as *pardos*) and *zambos* (part African, part indigenous) born in the country. The importing of slaves from elsewhere dropped drastically; during the nineteenth century only 2,343 slaves were brought into Venezuela, out of about 20,000 arriving in the Spanish American colonies.[3]

It is therefore possible to identify in Venezuela a slave trade that comprises three consecutive historical periods. The first phase, from 1500 to 1600, was characterized by the arrival of black Castilian-born *conquistadores* who helped the Spaniards subdue the indigenous peoples and the land, and large numbers of *bozales* from Africa. The second period, from 1700 to 1780, was marked by the massive import of *ladino* slaves from other colonies of the Americas and the Caribbean to labour on the cocoa haciendas of the central valleys and states. During the third stage, between 1780 and 1850, domestic trade in *criollo* slaves born in the country was dominant.

Overall, the limited introduction of African slaves, the predominance of *ladinos* from other colonies and the inter-regional trade in people born and raised in the country made the Venezuelan slave regime unusually heterogeneous and very different from what prevailed in other colonies, where the origin of slaves was more uniform. This was a significant determining feature of a colonial society that was divided strictly into castes whose membership depended on skin colour, 'purity of blood', family origins and material wealth.

Caste in colonial Venezuela

From 1750 to 1810 Venezuelan society appears to have been sharply polarized between two social groups: the upper classes, consisting of the Hispanic whites and Creoles, who held political and economic power; and the lower classes, a combination of black people, whites and indigenous people. Yet already the degree of racial blending was unusually complex and deep. The wide variety of race mixture in modern Venezuela has been attributed to the fact that during the early colonial period there was a shortage of white women and the Spaniards had no objection to sexual relations with black women.[4]

Although contact between white and black peoples implied a master–slave relationship, white children were brought up with no prejudice against dark skin; on the contrary, upper-class infants had black nurses, and white people retained fondness for, and trust in, the black people who had helped raise them. As well as breastfeeding, black nursemaids passed on African-derived oral folklore to their young white charges. Sons and daughters of the ruling class thus carried the imprint of Afro-Venezuelan influence in their traits of tenderness and affection, excessive gesticulation, modes of speech and remembered lullabies. Young white males frequently learned the ways of physical love from black women of the household or the estate, and close friendships between an upper-class white youth and the *prieto* (dark) son or daughter of slaves were common.

Venezuelans of the colonial period, no matter how white-skinned, had at least a trace of African ethnicity in their gestures and habits. People of mixed parentage – *mestizos, zambos* and *mulatos* – cross-bred with others of different origins, making still more complex the ethnic composition of the Venezuelan population. This gave rise to an extraordinary assortment of terms used to describe people's ethnic identities: *mulato prieto, zambo prieto, castizo* ('pure'), *morisco* (Moorish), *torna-atrás, sambayos, barcinos, coyotes, chinos, ahí te estas, tente en el aire, no te entiendo,* and so on.[5]

Despite the ethnic complexity, however, socio-economic roles were often rigid and static. Free *pardos, mulatos* and *negros* carried out menial and subservient tasks. They were also small traders and artisans and formed part of the new urban mass of labourers, along with *blancos de orilla* – marginal whites supposedly of mulatto origin. Members of lower castes were excluded from participation in political institutions, universities and the clergy. But they could join the militias, in which many earned their freedom.

While Hispanic white people of the landowning caste held political power, other white people born in the Americas and *blancos de orilla* increasingly identified themselves with the aspirations of the *pardos* and jointly participated with mulattos and *zambos* in the struggles that started to take place by the end of the eighteenth century. Thus, white people joined people of colour in a wave of uprisings and revolts against slavery and the caste structure that kept them socially oppressed.

Rebellion, independence, abolition

With growing demand from European markets, the early eighteenth century witnessed an increase in cocoa production on the Venezuelan colonial haciendas. This in turn brought about growth in the income and wealth of the estates. Besides the slaves, free labourers were now hired to work the land. With a greater pool of labour to draw from, and more productive land needed, it became less expensive to hire paid workers than to set aside land for slaves to live on and cultivate for themselves. Landowners thus began to take back from black and mixed-race slaves the *conucos* that they had acquired over the generations. Also, through the gradual replacement of slaves with free labourers for agricultural work, social conflicts were further deepened.

This increasingly gave rise to a wave of rebellions and to slaves absconding to the mountains and the rainforest, where they sought to protect themselves against the abuses of their masters. Escaped Afro-Venezuelan slaves settled in *cimarroneras* and, more frequently as time went on, in *cumbes*. *Cimarroneras* (from *cimarrón*, a runaway slave) were temporary mountain camps or settlements, where the fugitives organized the smuggling of cocoa and planned their armed revolts and surprise attacks. *Cumbes* were more permanent towns, also located far from the haciendas, mainly in the jungles, whose inhabitants worked the land and raised animals.

The presence of large numbers of *criollos* and *ladinos* in the country, many of them fugitives from the Caribbean, often awakened to French ideals of freedom and equality, further spurred on the social conflicts that Venezuela experienced during the eighteenth century. The *ladinos* were good soldiers and led countless outbreaks of rebellion. Between 1721 and 1795 no less than seventy slave revolts took place. One of these, in 1795, led by the *zambo* José Leonardo Chirinos in the Mountains of Coro, is considered to have been among the key events that brought about Venezuelan independence.[6]

At this time, too, the brotherhoods and religious societies in which Afro-Venezuelan slaves developed strong bonds of mutual solidarity came to prominence. These societies were often the main centres of rebellion against the slave owners, a fact that led the authorities to try to suppress them when the War of Independence erupted at the end of the eighteenth century.

This war continued until 1830, when Venezuela finally separated from Colombia, in union with which it had overthrown Spanish rule some years earlier. The colonial haciendas were seriously affected by this long-drawn-out conflict. Infrastructure – both buildings and cultivated land – was destroyed; the organized production of cocoa and the slaves' own production of food crops on their *conucos* were severely disrupted. Afro-Venezuelans participated in this war on both sides, as allies of the Spanish royalists or of the patriots. The opposing sides offered them liberty and the recovery of their lands as soon as the struggle was over. Many slaves, however, continued to grow their crops on vacant uncultivated land under a very precarious form of land tenure, while others plundered and burned the property of their masters.

El Liberador, Simón Bolívar, understood the economic and social aspirations of Venezuela's black and mixed-race population:

Legal equality is not enough for the spirit of the people. They want total and absolute equality, both in public and in domestic affairs. Later, they will want a pardocracy, which is their natural and sole inclination, so as to later exterminate the privileged class.[7]

When the war was over and the Republic of Venezuela was established in 1830, changes were made with respect to the legal condition of the slaves. By 1810 the Supreme Council had enacted a decree that prohibited international slave trafficking, although this measure was not far-reaching. In 1821 the Law of Freedom of the Wombs, or Law of Manumission, was enacted, stating that henceforth children born of slaves would be free. Likewise, owners of haciendas were obliged to educate, dress and feed the slaves. A fund was created for the progressive liberation of slaves via boards of manumission. With the slaves divided into factions, with the high number of deaths resulting from the war, and with implementation of legal measures to benefit the slaves, slavery had started on a process of natural extinction, a change paralleled by an increase in the number of free paid labourers.

By the time that the Law of the Abolition of Slavery was enacted on 24 March 1854, slavery had all but disappeared in Venezuela. The law rendered formal what was already a de facto situation and legally consolidated the transition from manumission to paid labour. Abolition therefore brought about few significant social traumas. It was not the result of a principle of political ethics, but rather the consequence of a purely economic phenomenon during the closing decades of the colonial period that gradually demanded new social relations of production.

The road to equality

In the first national constitution, enacted by the Congress of the new Venezuelan Republic on 22 September 1830, the nation was declared to be made up of all Venezuelans, whether by birth or naturalization, assembled under a pact of political association. All citizens would share the same rights and duties. Yet, in fact, the new republic was an oligarchy with a centralist government supported by a conservative commercially oriented bourgeoisie living in Caracas, which had emerged during the military campaigns as war suppliers and as a result of land expropriations. Rich landowners of the interior of the country, by contrast, enjoyed only limited political participation and lacked power.

Venezuela's contrasting political tendencies of the period can be expressed as centralism and federalism, and these two trends led to confrontations between the two dominant groups between 1858 and 1863, during the country's civil war, known as the Federal War. This conflict resulted from an intellectual movement that emerged in the rural areas and advocated open war against centralism and the commercial bourgeoisie. Its leaders – from the military and owners of haciendas, allied to many of the peasants – demanded abolition of the death penalty, the perpetual prohibition of slavery and universal suffrage based on the principle of alternating administrations. During the Federal War, armed bands of ex-slaves, who had slogans such as 'Death to whites!', fought to set up a republic of mulattos, *zambos* and indigenous people.

Venezuela's civil war was not a struggle of hegemonic classes for political power, but rather a renewed attempt to merge two social and ethnic realities: on the one hand, white people; on the other, the *mestizos* and black people of agrarian Venezuela. The war created a social storm that eradicated both the regime of castes and the ethnic conflict that had been inherent since colonial times.

At the outbreak of the Federal War in 1858, the constitution was amended with a new article that explicitly stated: 'Slavery is definitely abolished in Venezuela and all the slaves living in its territory are declared free.'[8] The idea of equality was further developed among guarantees set forth in 1881: 'All must be judged under the same laws and subject to the same duties, services and contributions.'[9]

Eighty years later, in 1961, after a decade of dictatorship, Venezuela enacted a new constitution. Here it was clearly provided for that all Venezuelans, with no distinction as to sex, age, social class or ethnic origin, would be ruled according to principles of 'human dignity ... maintaining social and legal equality without discrimination on account of race, sex, creed or social condition'.[10] The modern constitution also states, among individual rights, that 'No discrimination derived from race, sex, creed or social condition will be allowed' (article 61).

With all forms of discrimination prohibited by legislation, and following the destruction during the Federal War of social barriers based on caste, modern Venezuela offers little opportunity for the development of racism. But, as we shall see, weaker forms of ethnically motivated social discrimination and rejection have persisted.

Ethnicity and identity

Recent research concerning descendants of Africans in Latin America has frequently centred on processes of ethnic reintegration or re-encounter. This refers to the way people sharing a similar African background culture, who were separated violently from their groups of origin during the process of enslavement, later regained a degree of ethnic consciousness and identity in new autonomous communities in the Americas.[11] It has been argued that this process of ethnic reintegration may have originated in relationships between deck companions on the slave ships.[12] Or it may have arisen from the operation of a form of collective memory, maintained when people performed traditional rites and practices that helped reintegrate the group.[13] Many studies have pointed out the degree to which identifiably African beliefs, values and customs survived the Atlantic crossing and the upheavals and disruption of the slave experience.[14]

Magico-religious beliefs and practices were a key feature of the survival of African culture in Venezuela, with a diversity that owed much to the presence of large numbers of *ladino* slaves imported from the Caribbean and of *criollo* slaves, born and traded locally. This cultural heterogeneity was augmented by indigenous influence and by the teachings of the Catholic Church. Yet, although during the colonial period there was a powerful process of Afro-Venezuelan identity formation, by the early nineteenth century this ethnic development had all but come to a halt.

From the seventeenth century until the early nineteenth, religion had a socio-political role in fostering the emergence of a community of individuals who exercised their identity via subjective values and beliefs that were shared by the group. Thus, Afro-Venezuelan religious practices acted as codes that enabled their adherents to differentiate themselves from outsiders and set common cultural boundaries.[15] During the years of uprisings and formation of *cumbes* and *cimarroneras*, a new Afro-Venezuelan ethnicity developed secretly in the societies and religious brotherhoods, as well as in the hamlets where fugitive slaves congregated.

The struggle to defend their freedom led to the growth of

groups that could maintain autonomy. Thus, out of a total lack of economic and political institutions, a new way of life emerged, characterized by religious beliefs and practices adapted as ethical and moral mechanisms for the regulation of social relations. The *cumbes*, with their sense of spiritual solidarity, and the religious societies, with their commitment to mutual help, filled the void that Afro-Venezuelans experienced due to the absence of their own secular institutions, and helped them forge collective identities.

However, the practice of ethnicity and the creation of ethnic groups in Venezuela were interrupted in the later eighteenth and early nineteenth centuries. Many of the societies and religious brotherhoods were eliminated, seen by the authorities as the source of uprisings and rebellion. The abolition of slavery encouraged ascending socio-economic mobility. The secularization of national society, the participation of black people in the War of Independence, the progress of Western medicine and, more than anything else, the expropriation of lands and the usurpation of economic and social freedoms that the black population had acquired through their own forms of social organization – all these processes halted the process of ethnogenesis, bringing to an end the consolidation of ethnic groups among people of African descent.

As in much of Latin America, too, *blanqueamiento* (whitening) has played a part in undermining the formation of a distinct Afro-Venezuelan identity. In the case of Venezuela, whitening since colonial times has been a way for people of African slave ancestry to take up the role of the white person. Historically, people of colour who were appointed to prominent positions often became the main oppressors of their black brothers and sisters. Under the plantation system it was the black foreman who, in the absence of the landowner, had to denounce the theft of cocoa and impose punishment on slaves who tried to escape.

Also, when slaves joined the ranks of the royalist or patriot militias in the War of Independence, enticed by the promise of freedom and land, many went on to take advantage of this by confiscating haciendas and exploiting slave labourers for their own benefit. By the turn of the twentieth century, Afro-Venezuelans accounted for 20 per cent of owners of haciendas in the cocoa-growing Barlovento region.[16] Today most black landowners are wholesalers who reap large profits through making loans to small cultivators to guarantee the purchase of their best crops.

This combination of forces has resulted in the situation whereby in contemporary Venezuela people of African ancestry do not constitute a stable or distinctive ethnic group or minority.

Immigration from the Caribbean

Besides the original importation of slaves to work the cocoa plantations of the colonial haciendas of the central states, other influences of an African origin have had an impact on Venezuela's population. These influences are historically related to the opening in 1860 of the gold-mines of El Callao, in the state of Bolívar, in the south of the country.

Gold exploitation was begun by a French company that hired English-speaking workers and technicians from the nearby islands of Trinidad, Aruba and St Thomas. Forty years later the El Callao vein was exhausted and the company went bankrupt. However, many descendants of these Afro-Caribbean workers stayed in the area as independent miners, or started to farm the land and trade in commodities. They generally kept in contact with their home islands, thereby consolidating both the English language and their traditions.

When oil and iron exploitation was begun by North American companies in the eastern states of Venezuela during the 1930s, many Afro-Caribbeans found new job opportunities there. Children and grandchildren of these immigrants were educated at the excellent schools that were set up in the oilfields. Many learned technical crafts, while others gained entrance to universities, going on to graduate as engineers, geologists and administrators.

The Antilleans, as they are known, of El Callao tend to be conservative, and many of them have gained access to positions of influence and power. As Pollack-Eltz writes:

The traditions of the Antilleans reflect the traditions of the English bourgeoisie. They attend the Anglican church and they have

*their own clubs, where tea parties are offered. They regard them-
selves as indeed superior to the* criollos *who arrived after them
and work in the fields or in the mines.*[17]

For such people the African past is of little significance; they perceive their traditions and culture as solely Caribbean.[18] This
applies, for example, to their style of food. They eat calalu, a dish
based on codfish, and tarquery, a meat and curry recipe from
India that is very popular in Trinidad, and drink yinya bie and a
beverage called mabi that originally comes from Trinidad. Likewise, Antillean women prepare their own traditional 'gateau',
'dumpling' and bollos.

Until the second decade of this century Antilleans and their
descendants celebrated 1 August in commemoration of the day
when slaves were declared free in the British colonies. Nowadays
their most important holiday is Carnival. This tradition, brought
by the French, has been present in El Callao since the end of the
nineteenth century. Unlike Carnival in the Caribbean, which
now features the music of steel bands, the one in El Callao has
retained the original calypso drum music unchanged.

Antilleans have also settled in the Paria Peninsula, in the
state of Sucre. Most of them live in the towns of Guiria and
Irapa, close enough to Trinidad to facilitate close links and penetration of the English language and the gastronomy based on
curry and *quimbombo*.

Afro-Venezuelan family life

Among the rural Afro-Venezuelan population, families tend to be
large and to constitute the primary form of social organization.
The most characteristic domestic unit consists of husband, wife,
children and paternal or maternal grandparents. The family
accounts for the most important economic and emotional support for its members. Work is equally divided between men and
women, with men working throughout the year on their *conucos*
or in small businesses, and women participating in harvesting
but generally responsible for household chores.

Domestic groups can be matrifocal, such as when a man abandons the household to set up another home with a younger woman. Women who have been left in this way frequently call on their own mother or other close relatives to help them raise their children.

Family groups from the same town are often related to each other by consanguineous ties. This creates large networks of relatives that help satisfy collective needs and provide personal links with other settlements and with the national society.

Legal or common-law marriage takes place among Afro-Venezuelans when they are very young, with couples often remaining in the house of the husband's parents until they are able to move to their own home. Couples live together as long as they want, without needing to make their relationship legal.

Urban Afro-Venezuelan families are commonly the product of migration from the rural areas to the poorer areas of the large cities. Migrants from the same hamlet, town or region of the interior of the country may meet in the city and begin a family. Often it is young men with a basic level of schooling and knowledge of a craft who are the first to move to the cities; then, if they find a stable job, they sometimes go back to their home town or region to look for a wife or fiancée, and thus create a new family group in the city. However, more frequently they have relatives or friends from back home already living in the city and they look for a partner among that group, a process that helps build ties of solidarity among the urban population and leads to the growth of large extended families.

In the case of the poorer Afro-Venezuelans who live in the slum areas, the term 'family' is also a social and cultural marker that identifies them and differentiates them from people of different origin.

Religious beliefs and practices

We have seen that Afro-Venezuelan religious culture is the result of several influences. Descendants of black slaves preserved values, beliefs, rhythms and expressions of African origin. However, these influences have been integrated and amalgamated with Catholic rituals and indigenous traditions to such an extent that it is, at times, very difficult to define what is distinctly African, Spanish or indigenous.

The syncretic nature of the African-derived religion gave way in Venezuela to a Creole religion. The worship of Catholic saints, the presence on altars of the indigenous chieftain Guaicaipuro and the rhythm of African drums today comprise a structure of belief and ritual that appeals strongly to most poor urban and rural Afro-Venezuelans, who identify closely with it. The potency of an altar or the acceptance of a traditional healer from such places as Barlovento or Yaracuy lies in the balanced interaction of these three ethno-cultural influences.

No one can deny the persistence in Venezuela of African cultural elements. Yet to depict these traits as an essence of what is African would be to identify contemporary Afro-Venezuelan culture as folklore and to divorce current manifestations from their social context. The same applies to the indigenous influence. For example, in Birongo, a region of hamlets that can trace its origins back to a *cumbe* founded by escaped slaves, there is strong indigenous influence in the pharmacopoeia, in the forms of agriculture practised, in social organization and in hunting techniques; but it would be wrong to conclude that Birongo culture and society are indigenous.

One religious phenomenon that brings together Afro-Venezuelan communities with a notable unity of purpose is the vigils of the saints. This ritual can be traced back to the period of slavery in the haciendas of colonial times. The vigils were occasions of strong ethnic identification beyond the control of the slave owners and symbolized a personal commitment involving the offerer, their family and the community as a whole, much as they do today. The vigil is a celebration prepared for a saint, either in return for a favour related to health, protection, a good harvest or any other benefit, or as a petition. The offerer makes a promise and accepts a personal commitment to the saint, and the offerer's family takes a share of the responsibility that the celebration entails.

When the offerer and their close relatives invite others to the vigil, which is held in their house, they risk their prestige in the community. Hence they spare no expense in ensuring the success of the celebration. The vigil takes place among flowers, prayers, abundant alcohol and food, and with musicians to enliven the party. The guests – usually from the same town or neighbourhood – petition the saint with their own favours, while at the same time confirming their commitment to collective solidarity.

Another feature of the religious life of some predominantly Afro-Venezuelan towns is the 'dances of devils'. These occasions are organized by religious societies or brotherhoods for the day of Corpus Christi, in honour of the Blessed Eucharist. They can be traced back to origins among the white population, but the masks and forms of expression used are similar to those of the Bapende people of Zaire. The horns or sisal-root hairs hanging from the masks that determine hierarchy and leadership in the dance are clearly of African provenance.[19] The dances, which express gratitude, are believed to bring luck to the participants and to ensure the well-being of all members of the community.

Traditional African elements are marked in the Afro-Venezuelan celebration of saints. Festivities in honour of St John, St Peter and St Anthony, organized at the summer solstice, combine Catholic forms of worship with African-derived drum rhythms. In fact, similar celebrations, danced to the rhythm of drums, take place at the same time of year in West Africa. Yet most Afro-Venezuelans have little or no knowledge of the African origins of such ceremonies and regard them as something invented by their grandparents.

Now that some five centuries have elapsed, the secret religion of African slaves is practised quite openly. It is shared to some extent by more sophisticated members of the population professionals, business people, students and intellectuals, although many religious customs are maintained only by older people in rural areas and have little chance of being handed down to future generations. Though religion is no longer a marker of ethnic differences, it is still a powerful social force, and status is often acquired by holding positions in religious groups and societies.

World view and image-worship

The characteristic Afro-Venezuelan concept of the world assumes two coexisting but mutually opposing ideas. On the one hand, there is faith in God and in the Catholic saints, hence the need to follow a code of honour that demands respect, mutual help and compliance with rituals. This is held to be the path to the morally good. On the other hand, there is a strong sense of evil, centred on the Devil and on evil spirits – souls in purgatory, apparitions or ghosts. This sense of the sinister may include belief in occult powers that can bring harm to others, the practice of sorcery, lust, greed and feelings of vengefulness and envy.

Social relations among Afro-Venezuelan people are consequently often ruled by magico-religious beliefs and practices that generate social controls to regulate good and evil in human behaviour. Fear of envy plays a significant part in modifying social inequalities, restraining the unbridled overabundance of some and alleviating the extreme poverty of others, allowing those who are more affluent to come closer to those who are less so. Feelings of envy emerge when people compete for basic survival resources while being aware that others enjoy material wealth or social position. Its effects are feared as being destructive because those who are envious are thought capable of causing harm and diseases because of their evil minds; once unleashed, it is believed that the only defence against such forces is magic or religion.

In their daily activities, then, many Afro-Venezuelans attempt to balance the forces of good and those of evil, an equilibrium that is essential for life in a community. Similarly, their notion of disease is founded on the premise that health is a state of balance between cold and hot. A disease emerges when this balance is broken as a result of natural or mysterious causes. Natural causes are found in the environment; mysterious, magical or supernatural ones are the result of the bad wishes of others. Once a diagnosis has been specified, therapy is based on the use of plants, patented drugs or sorcery, and is aimed at eradicating the cause and restoring the adequate hot–cold levels that the body requires to be healthy.[20]

Health and disease are accordingly closely related and interdependent concepts, linked to the notion of the Hippocratic humours inherited from Spanish medical practices of colonial times. In general terms, Venezuelan peasants – even in those agricultural areas where no slaves were imported, such as the Andean region – base their explanations of common diseases on the belief that the cause is an imbalance of hot and cold in the body.

Popular medicine, magic and witchcraft are frequent cultural manifestations among peoples of African ancestry. Afro-Venezuelan witch doctors, like their counterparts in West Africa, not only cure disease but also solve emotional problems with the help of medicinal plants. Traditional medico-magical practices have reached the cities via rural–urban migration, and it has been shown that rich and poor Afro-Venezuelans equally resort to witch doctors and *curiosos*, or traditional healers. Professional people look to them for help when they are experiencing difficulties or want their future foretold.

The influence of Cuban image-worship, brought to Venezuela after the Cuban Revolution, and the penetration of Caribbean beliefs and cults have fostered more recently a multiplicity of ideas and beliefs that have strengthened the Afro-Venezuelan religious traditions. Image-worship is practised by both Cubans and Venezuelans in Venezuela. The 'seven African powers' or Yoruba deities invoked by worshippers are gradually replacing traditional deities – María Lionza, among them – and native spirits that are no longer as frequently manifest in the mediums of the spiritist centres. Image-worship is a devotion to, and a personal identification with, a saint. A person who wants to enter the cult will appoint a godfather. Through the help of God, the latter will show the person the correct path to sanctity. The saints keep the person from being a victim of what could harm them, such as alcohol, drugs or illicit sex. Image-worship is a spiritual belief that shapes the social behaviour of those who practise it, and they stand as an example in the process of transculturization where the indigenous, African and European elements have combined to create a new domestic Venezuelan religious culture. María Lionza (of Spanish origin), Negro Primero (of African origin) and Guaicaipuro (of indigenous origin) have combined themselves, via spiritism, to create a syncretic religion that appeals to large segments of the population.

Economic, social and political change

Until the 1920s Venezuela's national life took place in a predominantly rural environment. Demographic density was low; there were very few urban centres; and the economy was based on the export of coffee, cocoa, livestock and other commodities. When oil was discovered and exploited, a far-reaching change occurred in the economic, social, cultural and political life of the country. Oil brought with it fast money and rapid economic growth. Between 1936 and 1975 the national budget increased fifteenfold. A major wave of migration from the rural areas to the cities took place, reversing earlier patterns of settlement. Whereas in 1936 only 34.7 per cent of the population lived in urban areas, by 1971 the figure had risen to 78.4 per cent. Currently, towns and cities are home to eight out of every ten Venezuelans.

With the oil boom Venezuela grew rich enough to import whatever foodstuffs it needed and, in many respects, to follow consumption patterns typical of rich industrialized countries. With this came increasing homogeneity of social values and principles – based, perhaps undesirably, on easy wealth and respect for the wealthy. Simultaneously, a significant loss of traditional cultural values occurred. Social status came to be measured more narrowly in terms of material wealth, regardless of ethnic and cultural origins, which had previously been social markers.

However, alongside such changes were emerging social movements that led to the formation of political parties. This is the case of the 'generation of 1928', which produced the Revolutionary Party of Venezuela, the Communist Party of Venezuela and the Revolutionary Alliance of the Left, which in 1941 became the party known today as Acción Democrática.

The populist democratic political project implemented in 1961, after the end of the dictatorship, paved the way for Afro-Venezuelan political participation. Acción Democrática, with its social democratic philosophy, owes much of its vitality and strength to people of colour, who have found in politics in general, and in this party in particular, a useful mechanism for socio-economic progress. Acción Democrática developed into the party of the Venezuelan peasants and workers. Its leaders were professional politicians with limited formal education but who were deep-rooted in the population and influenced it greatly. 'Juan Bimba', the fictional archetype of the Venezuelan poor man, is the clear personification of Acción Democrática. Of peasant origins, he lives in the city and has access to decision-making processes and to important politicians via the 'party of the people'.

Acción Democrática took power nationally in 1959. Many Afro-Venezuelan leaders had taken up its message in the regions, and large numbers of them had gained political office. The party and its leadership had come to be strongly associated with Afro-Venezuelan ethnicity. Its leaders addressed the nation with a series of populist speeches that drew together an important mass of peasants and workers, giving them for the first time an effective political voice. The new government fostered widespread agrarian reform, and many Afro-Venezuelans, especially in rural areas, began to participate actively in the political life of the country. They were particularly active in the trade unions of the oil industry and in the state agrarian associations. Afro-Venezuelans are now prominent in public and official life. In the 1993 election, Acción Democrática fielded a black presidential candidate.

Further to the left, the Causa Radical party includes in its ranks many Afro-Venezuelan activists, including Aristúbolo Isturiz, Mayor of Caracas.

Despite such activism and political progress, however, the vast mass of Afro-Venezuelans possess only very limited possibilities of socio-economic advancement. Venezuelan society remains generally polarized between the wealth of a few and the poverty of the great majority, with only a relatively small middle class.

Self-perceptions and prospects

Most Afro-Venezuelans who work the land, such as those living in the Barlovento region and along other parts of the central coastline, openly reject suggestions of African ancestry and see themselves as *criollos*. They are not deeply attached to their land; many will readily sell their plots to outsiders. Unlike in Brazil,

Cuba or Colombia, the black rural population of Venezuela does not remember its origins. There is no continuity or bridge that unites them with Africa, and there are few if any intermediaries to preserve ancestral and traditional values and beliefs.

We must recall that the direct import of slaves to Venezuela from Africa ceased by the end of the sixteenth century, giving way to the massive transfer of *ladinos* from the Caribbean and to inter-regional trade in *criollos*. The African memory faded away. By contrast, in Brazil *pai de santos* – religious leaders familiar with ancestral African values and beliefs – may disown their people's history of slavery, but only as a deliberate strategy to revitalize the historical bridge between Brazil and Africa.[21] In Venezuela the black population has shown a strong tendency to forget or reject the African past, along with slavery, because both are seen as undermining an improved socio-economic condition.

Poor rural Afro-Venezuelans, then, while acknowledging their economic and social marginalization, do not see themselves as being linked with Africa. Likewise, the urban poor, predominantly people of colour but rarely blue-black, refer to themselves, not as *negro*, but as 'the people', 'the poor', 'working class' or 'marginal'.

The fact that Venezuela's dark-complexioned population disproportionately experiences low socio-economic status is not the result of racial discrimination. It is, rather, the consequence of economic processes working in an unfair and unbalanced society. Employment opportunities for the majority of poorly educated and poorly skilled Afro-Venezuelans are much the same as those for white people living under the same conditions. In downtown Caracas both white and black young adults from Barlovento work as police officers, security staff, watchmen or as the bodyguards of politicians and wealthy business people. Others sell lottery tickets, fast food and other products in street kiosks. Recently, people of colour from Santo Domingo, Trinidad and Colombia have arrived in the capital and in Maracaibo to work as domestic staff or as street fruit-sellers.

The educated Venezuelan middle class is made up of people of varying backgrounds and descent, including some whose physical appearance suggests a considerable degree of African ancestry. Among this segment of the population what matters is not skin colour but educational level, professional accomplishments, material aspirations and a desire to adapt to modern city living. In the case of upper-class Venezuelans, however, skin colour does have a significant role, especially in marriage. Selection of spouses is based primarily on levels of education and income, but it is unusual to see a black person marrying somebody who is white.

Yet the influence of African ethnicity still permeates the Venezuelan population in many ways. Afro-Venezuelan bands play at high-society parties. 'White' Venezuelan women are popularly considered to exhibit traces of African ancestry on the dance floor and in their approach to cooking. A common expression in Venezuela that suggests the country's unusually relaxed attitude to the phenomenon of race mixture is that there is 'a drop of coffee in the milk'.[22] Similarly, common terms of affection between lovers are *mi negra* and *mi negro*. We can conclude that the unusual degree to which Venezuela represents a genuine mixing of races and ethnicities has resulted in a conspicuous lack of racism in the society – a notably different situation from what prevails in other parts of Latin America.

Despite the absence of overt racism, however, there is a wide spectrum of stereotypes and social prejudices. As elsewhere in the region, Afro-Venezuelans are eroticized in popular art forms such as films and popularly considered to be 'natural' practitioners of sport and music. Their traditional cultural celebrations in the Barlovento region are a focus of folkloric interest. Yet black people rarely reach prominence in such high-status occupations as medicine, engineering and the diplomatic service.

In a society that is predominantly cross-bred and Creole, lacking in a self-consciously African ethnic minority origin, and where racial segregation is covert rather than overt, it is difficult to forecast the future of the black population. Venezuelans of African descent have contributed their captive and free labour, skills, religion and music to create a national society and culture, but the degree to which ethnic identities are mixed and integrated seems likely to lead to the eventual disappearance of a definable Afro-Venezuelan minority; future generations will perhaps all be *morenos pardos*.[23]

In the rural sector, where the black population predominates, accelerating rates of urbanization and tourist development are radically transforming the traditional economic structure, along with forms of land tenure and family groups. Little space remains for traditional Afro-Venezuelan cults, and the religious societies are losing their historical function as sources of mutual help and community solidarity. The drum dances, too, are declining in authenticity as they are exploited in an increasingly commercialized market of mass culture. Similarly, image-worship and witchcraft, although still powerful influences among the poor, are now exploited commercially, and tourists from Caracas visit houses of vigil or places where curing is being performed by incantation in the black towns of Barlovento and Aragua.

Efforts have been made, and are still being made, to preserve Afro-Venezuelan culture. As a result of government policies since 1968, offering a wide range of subsidies and scholarships for the development of popular culture, many Afro-Venezuelan drum, dance and theatre groups have become well known nationally and abroad. More recently, foundations for the defence of Afro-Venezuelan traditions have been established by university academics.

Nevertheless, for the majority of Afro-Venezuelans, the reality of survival is seen no longer to depend on tradition but to rest on new job opportunities offered by urban life. They generally do have an awareness of their poverty and marginality, but they see the remedy in terms of moving to the cities, becoming politically active and gaining access to the labour market.

In a sense their reinvention and adaption of traditional values and social forms to modern life represent a kind of cultural persistence. The Afro-Venezuelan poor of the urban slums are today tending to adopt new religious forms, such as charismatic groups, pentecostal sects and Afro-Cuban cults.

Afro-Venezuelan identity and culture, then, are likely to survive only as long as the process of assimilation and integration takes to complete itself. The probable final outcome is a multiracial society lacking distinct forms of ethnic awareness and, one hopes, enjoying a general acceptance of universal values and standards.

Notes

1 Brito Figueroa, F., *El problema tierra y esclavos en la historia de Venezuela*, Caracas, Ediciones de la Biblioteca de la Universidad Central de Venezuela, 1985.
2 Ibid.
3 Brito Figueroa, F., *Historia económica y social de Venezuela*, Caracas, Ediciones de la Biblioteca de la Universidad Central de Venezuela, 1984.
4 Pollack-Eltz, A., *La negritud en Venezuela*, Caracas, Cuadernos Lagoven, 1991.
5 Troconis de Veracochea, E., *Historia del Tocuyo colonial*, Caracas, Ediciones de la Biblioteca de la Universidad Central de Venezuela, History Series X, 1984, p. 269.
6 Magallanes, M.V., *Historia política de Venezuela*, Caracas, Ediciones de la Biblioteca de la Universidad Central de Venezuela, 1990.
7 Bolívar, S., 'Carta a Francisco de Paula Santander', 1825, quoted in Brito Figueroa, op. cit., *El problema tierra*, p. 114.
8 National Constitution, article no. 13, 1858, in A.R. Brewer-Carias, *Las constituciones nacionales*, San Cristóbal and Caracas, Coordination of the Centre of Constitutional Studies of Spain and the Catholic University of Tachira, 1985, p. 384.
9 National Constitution, Title III, article no. 15, 1881, ibid., p. 489.
10 Constitution of the Republic of Venezuela, 1983.
11 Friedemann, N. de, 'Huellas de Africanía en Colombia: nuevos escenarios de investigación', paper presented at the International Conference on the African Presence in the Caribbean, Institute of Caribbean Studies, Recinto de Río Piedras, San Juan, Puerto Rico, 6-11 September 1989; Mintz, S. and Price, R., *An Anthropological Approach to the Afro-American Past: A Caribbean Perspective*, Philadelphia, PA, ISHU, 1976; Bonfil Batalla, G., 'La teoría del control cultural en el estudio de los procesos étnicos', in *Anthropology Yearbook*, Brasilia, University of Brasilia, 1986.
12 Mintz and Price, op. cit.
13 Bonfil Batalla, op. cit.
14 E.g. Bastide, R., *Projimo y el extraño: el encuentro de las civilizaciones*, Buenos Aires, Amorrortu Editores SCA Luca, 1973; Bateson, G., *Steps to an Ecology of Mind*, New York, Ballantine, 1972; Friedemann, op. cit.
15 Barth, F., *Los grupos étnicos y sus fronteras*, Mexico City, Fondo de Cultura Económica, 2nd edn, 1976.
16 National Cocoa Fund, *La producción de cacao en el estado Miranda*, Caracas, Ediciones Foncacao, 1989.
17 Pollak-Eltz, op. cit., p. 80.
18 Ibid.
19 Ibid.
20 Guerra, F. 'Casualidad de las enfermedades en Birongo: un análisis del sistema conceptual', MSc dissertation, Caracas, Center for Advanced Studies, Venezuelan Institute of Scientific Research, 1981.

21 Carvalho, J.J., 'La fuerza de la nostalgia: el concepto de tiempo histórico en los cultos Afrobrasileños tradicionales', *Research Art Studies*, Caracas, Andres Bello Catholic University, School of Arts and Education, no. 20, 1988, pp. 194-7.
22. Hence the title of the classic study by Wright, W.R., *Café con Leche: Race, Class and National Image in Venezuela*, Austin, TX, University of Texas Press, 1990.
23 Moreno Gomez, L., *País pardo*, Caracas, Editorial Cromotip, 1987.

Select bibliography

Bastide, R., *Projimo y el extraño: el encuentro de las civilizaciones*, Buenos Aires, Amorrortu Editores, 1973.

Bateson, G., *Steps to an Ecology of Mind*, New York, Ballantine, 1972.

Bonfil Batalla, G., 'La teoría del control cultural en el estudio de los procesos étnicos', *Anthropology Yearbook*, Brasilia, University of Brasilia, 1986.

Brito Figueroa, F., *Historia económica y social de Venezuela*, Caracas, Ediciones de la Biblioteca de la Universidad Central de Venezuela, 1984.

Brito Figueroa, F., *El problema tierras y esclavos en la historia de Venezuela*, Caracas, Ediciones de la Biblioteca de la Universidad Central de Venezuela, 1985.

Carvalho, J.J., 'La fuerza de la nostalgia: el concepto de tiempo histórico en los cultos Afrobrasileños tradicionales', *Research Art Studies*, Caracas, Andrés Bello Catholic University, School of Arts and Education, no. 20, 1988, pp. 194-7.

Friedemann, N. de, 'Huellas de Africanía en Colombia: nuevos escenarios de investigación', paper presented to the International Conference on the African Presence in the Caribbean, Institute of Caribbean Studies, Recinto de Río Piedras, San Juan, Puerto Rico, 6-11 September 1989.

Guerra, F., 'Casualidad de las enfermedades en Birongo: un análisis del sistema conceptual', MSc dissertation, Caracas, Center for Advanced Studies, Venezuelan Institute of Scientific Research, 1981.

Mintz, S. and Price, R., *An Anthropological Approach to the Afro-American Past: A Caribbean Perspective*, Philadelphia, PA, ISHU, 1976.

Moreno Gomez, L., *País pardo*, Caracas, Editorial Cromotip, 1987.

National Cocoa Fund, *La producción de cacao en el estado Miranda*, Caracas, Ediciones Foncacao, 1989.

Oficina Central de Estadística e Informática, 'General census of population and housing: general demographic characteristics', *El censo 90 en Venezuela*, Caracas.

Pollack-Eltz, A., *La negritud en Venezuela*, Caracas, Cuadernos Lagoven, 1991.

Serbin, A. (ed.), *Geopolítica de las relaciones de Venezuela con el Caribe*, Caracas, Fundación Fondo Editorial Acta Científica, 1983.

Troconis de Veracochea, E., *Historia del Tocuyo colonial*, Caracas, Ediciones de la Biblioteca de la Universidad Central de Venezuela, History Series X, 1984.

Weber, M., *Economía y sociedad*, Mexico City, Fondo de Cultura Económica, 1981.

Wright, W.R., *Café con Leche: Race, Class and National Image in Venezuela*, Austin, TX, University of Texas Press, 1990.

9

PERU

José Luciano and Humberto Rodriguez Pastor
translated by Meagan Smith

Peruvians of African descent number an estimated 1.4 to 2.2 million, or between 6 and 10 per cent of the national population.[1] Despite belonging to a racial group whose contribution to the nation and its culture has been highly significant, most Afro-Peruvians experience poverty, marginalization and racism in their daily lives, and they tend collectively and individually to possess little sense of ethnic identity. There is also little recognition nationally that they constitute a community with particular problems and goals. In response, a number of Afro-Peruvian individuals and organizations have been working to build a social movement whose aim is the full achievement of equal rights.

Conquest and slavery

The first Africans who came to the region of the Inca empire now known as Peru were among the troops of Francisco Pizarro in 1527. They were not conquerors, but rather the conquered, taken by force from their homes and subjugated to the Spanish conquistadors. Many were valiant soldiers, although they fought not for a cause but rather to save their lives and those of their oppressors. Some of these Africans acted as interpreters between their fellows and the Spanish.

The indigenous Peruvians' perception of the first Africans to arrive in their country was clearly established at this time.

Although Afro-Peruvians had a different skin colour, they were seen as invaders, equal to white people; both took over the land and criticized the indigenous gods. Many years passed before this indigenous view of Afro-Peruvians began to change.

By 1540 the Spanish conquest of the Incas had been consolidated. The Viceroyalty of Peru and its Hispanic cities were built on what was left of the most important indigenous communities. With the establishment of the viceroyalty began the slow process of creating a new society; and thus Africans, being present, were incorporated into the economic, social, cultural and ethnic foundations of the new colony.

The colonial Spanish society that grew from the conquest combined two economic systems of production: indigenous servanthood and African slavery. Early in the viceroyalty almost the entire Afro-Peruvian population, some 93 per cent, was located on the coast, and close to 70 per cent of this population lived in Lima, the capital, and other urban areas. Slavery in Peru therefore took on a distinct urban and domestic character. Nevertheless, part of the Afro-Peruvian population was destined for agricultural work, on the new haciendas around the colonial cities.

Each Peruvian hacienda usually cultivated one main agricultural product, such as grapes, sugar-cane or cotton, which were the three chief European agricultural imports from the region. However, they also included other products destined for the colonial system, for sale in the surrounding cities or for their own consumption. These were not large plantations needing a great number of slaves; rather, the haciendas were typically quite small, each having an average of twenty to thirty slave labourers. Even so, a constant flow of African slaves was required. The Spanish conquest had annihilated most of the indigenous population along the coast, and so the importing of slaves was crucial for the functioning of the haciendas and the survival of colonial society.

Along with the urban and rural segments of the enslaved population, there were also a good number of Afro-Peruvians who lived freely, known as *libertos*.[2] These freed slaves accounted for no less than 30 per cent of the population of African descent and engaged in such urban activities as domestic service, construction and dock work in the ports.

At this time Peruvians of African ancestry constituted an important minority of between 8 and 10 per cent of the population of the viceroyalty. They were an essential component of the *mestizaje* (ethnic mixture through the birth of mixed-race children) of the national society.

Cultural contribution and assimilation

The French anthropologist Roger Mastidas wrote in his classic book *Las Américas negras*: 'African slave ships transported from Africa not only men, women and children but also their gods, their beliefs and customs.' Since the beginning of the arrival of Africans in the Americas, their culture has gradually been integrated into the cultural synthesis of the region.

An understanding of the true historical extent of the cultural contribution of Afro-Peruvians demands an awareness that methods of production, as well as artistic traditions, formed part of what they brought to the new society. For example, Afro-Peruvians participated in economic activities tied to commerce, transportation (by pack mule) and the provision of firewood, which were all indispensable aspects of city and rural life.

In the case of Peru, people of African descent not only provided invaluable physical labour but also contributed techniques and new skills to the development of coastal agriculture. Many of those who were brought in the seventeenth century came from self-sufficient tribes that possessed advanced skills in agriculture, metallurgy, craftsmanship and manufacturing. Among those brought as slaves were artists, musicians, oral historians and doctors. Some of these people had been exposed to Islam and knew how to read.

Due to Peru's geographical location on the far western coast of South America, the colony was not on a direct route from Africa. Consequently, the majority of Africans were brought from the Caribbean or from Brazil. This made the situation in Peru distinct in several ways: slaves were very expensive; Spain had no control over the slave trade in the area; and the slave ships that arrived tended to be few and far between. Besides, Africans who came to Peru were already somewhat used to European culture through their previous work or travels in other parts of the Americas. By the time they arrived in the colony they had largely lost touch with specific African ethnic identities and customs, and they more easily integrated into their new culture.

Afro-Peruvians played their part in the moulding of a unique national identity. In the cities especially, daily interactions and many similarities between people of African descent, indigenous people and *criollos* (Hispanic white people born in the Americas) favoured the creation of unique customs. A new popular religion was born through a merging of the religious beliefs and practices of the various groups, a striking example of which was the procession of the Señor de los Milagros.[3] Similarly, significant contributions were also made to the colloquial language, customs and culinary arts during the colonial and republican periods.

The influence of Afro-Peruvian women on the culinary arts and foods of Peru was exceptional, although most research tends to neglect this and to emphasize instead Afro-Peruvian cultural aspects, such as music and dance. The skills that women of African ancestry possessed permitted the elaboration of soups of variety and flavour that captured the attention of all. Traditionally, no table was considered well served if it did not include some dish made by an expert Afro-Peruvian cook. Yet the people who supplied this expertise went largely unrecognized among the wider population.

Aside from cooking directly for their masters, Afro-Peruvian women also sold food products in the street, excelling at the commercialization of food for the masses. Men also participated in the production and sale of some food products, especially sweets. *Vivenderas* (women food-vendors) and *pregoneros* (travelling street-sellers, usually men) spread the acceptance of, and taste for, delicious plates of African origin such as *anticucho bereber*, *chicha de terranova* (corn liquor), *sanguito ñaju del Congo* (a wheat-based dessert) and *choncholí* (tripe brochettes). Through the work of such women and men, Afro-Peruvian culinary traditions were spread throughout the cities. The possession of culinary abilities was also an important way of gaining employment and social mobility – and even a way to obtain freedom from slavery, as people could save their profits and buy their liberty.

The colonial regime established a strict social hierarchy that

17 Family living on contaminated land next to pharmaceutical plant, Manati, Puerto Rico.

18 Woman washing fish, Punta Maldonado, Guerrero, Mexico.

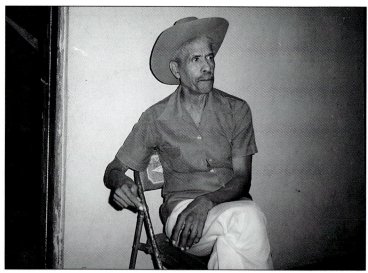

19 Don Miguel telling the myth of a ship with doors of gold that brought black people to the Mexican coast, San Nicolás, Guerrero, Mexico.

20 Children in school, Atlantic coast, Nicaragua.

21 Young Nicaraguans.

JANE FREELAND

22 Workers during the building of the Panama Canal, c.1910.

ANDES PRESS AGENCY

23 Shanty-town dwellers, Panama.   CARLOS REYES/ANDES PRESS AGENCY

24 Children, Colón, Panama.
CARLOS REYES/ANDES PRESS AGENCY

25 Thomas Simpson, a Belizean farmer.

26 Oscar Deleón, musician, Venezuela.

27 The Ballumbrosio family, keepers of Afro-Peruvian traditions,
El Carmen, Ica Province, Peru.   LORRY SALCEDO

28 Rural family, Chota Valley, Ecuador.

SOUTH AMERICAN PICTURES

29 Women of Sud Yungas Province, Bolivia.

30 Young man, Montevideo, Uruguay, 1949.

31 Jésus Vieira, Uruguayan trade union leader, 1962.

32 Carnival, Montevideo, Uruguay.

assigned to each group of people specific roles and functions. Nevertheless, Afro-Peruvians used all of the system's contradictions and all the resources in their reach to overcome barriers and obtain their longed-for freedom. Food was one of the activities through which they transmitted their values, beliefs and culture to the rest of society, and they effectively converted this resource into a form of resistance to slavery.

Most of the culinary practices and alimentary habits that stemmed from Afro-Peruvian communities had initially remained within the community. Many of the customs of this marginalized group were viewed by Hispanics as dangerous and lacking in value. As with their cooking and food traditions, many elements of Afro-Peruvian culture have slowly been recognized as part of the rich cultural identity of Peru, although this process is incomplete and still continues.

From rebellion to national independence

Active resistance to servitude and slavery was a permanent condition of life among both the indigenous population and people of African descent in Peru, usually occurring independently in each of the two groups. From the earliest years of the colony, in the 1540s, various acts of rebellion were reported; revolts, escapes, mutinies and insurrections were the principal forms of social protest during this era. However, Afro-Peruvian resistance was chiefly expressed in the flight of slaves and in the formation of *bandas de cimarrones* and *palenques*.[4]

For survival, runaway slaves relied on their own ingenuity and creativity and at times on the assistance and solidarity of their freed brothers and sisters. But in some cases *libertos* remained faithful to their former masters and would not help escaped slaves. Because of this ambiguity and the dangers for runaway slaves, this form of resistance never reached massive proportions.

In the central coastal region the best-known refuge for runaway slaves was El Palenque de Huachipa. Huachipa existed as a stronghold for escaped slaves for more than half a century, from 1712 to 1792, and its greatest leader was the well-known ex-slave Francisco Congo, also called Chavelilla.

On some occasions these African rebels created strong alliances with the indigenous population, such as that of the rebel Juan Santos Atahualpa and the indigenous chief Tupa Amaru in 1780. Their insurrection was the first to include the liberation of slaves as part of its demands.

The long struggle for freedom gradually combined with the *criollo* and *mestizo* struggle to liberate the cities from Spanish control. From the seventeenth to the beginning of the nineteenth centuries, then, the majority of urban insurrections included in their demands the freedom of Afro-Peruvians, who were usually well represented among the participants. Similarly, in the Cartagena and Intendencia of the Rio de la Plata Region (today Colombia and Argentina, respectively), the slaves quickly embraced the flags of independence that leaders such as Bolívar, Sucre and San Martín raised. Believing that the liberal ideas of the independence struggle would give them the freedom, equality and fraternity that for centuries had been denied to them, Afro-Peruvians played a decisive role in the battles of Junín and Ayacucho (1824). Here the Husare del Perú battalion, formed of *libertos*, slaves and *mestizos*, won a decisive victory that helped secure not only the independence of Peru but also that of the entire South American continent.

Socio-economic experience to 1950

The abolition of slavery in 1854 was, of course, an all-important event affecting the legal and social status of Afro-Peruvians. Yet abolition was not accompanied by the necessary changes in economic, social, political and cultural structures to create real conditions of liberty and equality. While some laws were passed in favour of their freedom, other legislation further restricted their rights.

Every aspect of society was undergoing transformation, although not always in a positive direction for Afro-Peruvians. Severe economic crises, particularly in the agricultural sector, worsened their situation as one of the most marginalized social groups. Moreover, external events also aggravated the inferior status of Afro-Peruvians. For example, the defeat of Peru and Bolivia by Chile in the War of the Pacific (1879-84) meant that the country lost important resources of guano (fertilizer from bird dung) and saltpetre, and it created social chaos which prevented the possibility of mobility and progress for Afro-Peruvians.

Peruvians of African ancestry continued to be seen by the rest of national society as inferior and dangerous, and their cultural practices were considered obscene. The mind-set of the epoch cast Afro-Peruvians in the role of victimizers instead of the victims they largely were, the guilty instead of the innocent. Due to this, the memory of slavery began to torment Afro-Peruvians themselves and not the Hispanics who had enslaved them.

At the beginning of the twentieth century the socio-economic situation of Afro-Peruvians did not differ significantly from that experienced in the previous colonial and republican periods. The *barrios* and *callejones* in urban areas and the *galpones* on the haciendas were the silent witnesses of the struggle for true liberty and equality, for the rediscovery of their roots and the affirmation of a free identity without any trace of racial discrimination.[5]

Unlike in many other parts of the Americas and the Caribbean, the majority of Afro-Hispanic people in Peru resided in the cities. The highest concentration was in Lima, and even today the capital claims nearly 60 per cent of the total Afro-Peruvian population. This was one of Lima's oldest-established communities. The majority of domestic servants in the capital were Afro-Peruvian men and women. Public transport, public and private security, the growing textile manufacturing industry and civil construction were areas where Afro-Peruvians were often employed, mostly in jobs not far removed from their previous work during slavery. These trades enjoyed little social prestige and offered few managerial opportunities; and racist stereotypes, considering Afro-Peruvians to be useful only for manual labour and not capable of intellectual work, were reinforced.

Daily urban life for Afro-Peruvians until relatively recently was lived chiefly at the workplace and in the *callejón*. Many *callejones* lacked even the minimum facilities for hygiene, with a single tap often shared between numerous households. The poor living conditions and lack of privacy in these dwellings led to a high level of disputes and conflicts among the inhabitants.

Nevertheless, the *callejón* was where urban popular culture took root and flourished. This urban popular culture was the authentic expression of the marginalized, the poor, the mass of unskilled workers whose daily labours allowed the economic structure of society to function. Out of this internal community culture emerged one stream that combined with indigenous, *mestizo* and white middle-class elements, giving rise to the *criollo* culture that represented Peruvian urban popular culture, one of the fundamental manifestations of Peruvian identity.

In the early twentieth century two social and cultural manifestations reflected the influence of Afro-Peruvians in Lima. The procession of the Señor de los Milagros, one of the most important religious activities in Peru, was originally an exclusively Afro-Peruvian tradition. In fact, although this ceremony has been practised since the eighteenth century, only recently has it gained its current national and international prominence. Today the Señor de los Milagros procession is considered one of the three most important religious events in all of Latin America.

Another significant contribution was the creation of the Club Alianza Lima, a sports organization that gradually became representative of the best football players in Peru. Although very different – one religious and the other pagan – both institutions expressed the major but largely unrecognized role of Afro-Peruvians in the social and cultural life of the capital.

Along the coastline, meanwhile, were small Afro-Peruvian rural communities. First sugar-cane cultivation, and later cotton on the haciendas, have traditionally provided the main economic activities for rural Afro-Peruvians. Domestic service on the haciendas also required sizeable numbers of black workers.

As in the city, rural Afro-Peruvians experienced the same harsh treatment and lack of social mobility as during the previous era of slavery. Persisting relations of dependence between farmworkers and landowners, and the survival of a *patron–peón* relationship that differed little from the master–slave tie, made it difficult for people to perceive that the situation had changed. Hacienda owners, although no longer masters of slaves, exercised strict control over the social and personal lives, as well as the working conditions, of their employees.

They acted as judges and representatives of the state, restricting the rights of their workers as citizens.

Abuse and low pay were the staple of everyday experience for Afro-Peruvians and their fellow indigenous, Asian and *mestizo* workers, making rural life generally even more brutal than life in the cities. Agricultural stagnation and abuse on the part of hacienda owners are two factors that explain the mass rural–urban migration that began in the 1950s. Nevertheless, in distinct areas along the coast there developed diverse expressions of Afro-Peruvian culture. Local particularities and variations occurred, depending on the degree of cultural interaction with the indigenous peoples and on the proximity and relationship with hacienda owners and other workers.

For many years it was assumed that the relationship between Afro-Peruvians and indigenous peoples was characterized by confrontation and conflict. Contributing to this idea was the sense of rivalry between the two groups in asserting which of them experienced the worst subjugation by the Spanish. Feelings of racial inferiority, resulting from the severe injustices of the colonial and post-colonial social system, created frustrations that were most easily expressed towards the other subordinated group, with each side trying to make the other weaker. This behaviour predominated in the urban environment, whose close living conditions and daily interactions were not characteristic of the rural zones.

Nevertheless, integration and alliance were also features of the Afro-Peruvian–indigenous relationship. As we have seen, from the beginning of Spanish colonization Afro-Peruvians and indigenous peoples united to fight for their liberty. After many years the racial and cultural mixture created strong bonds which gave rise to the well-known Peruvian saying: 'El que no tiene de inca, tiene de mandinga' (whoever does not have Incan ancestry has African ancestry).

However, given that all social power lay with the white classes, Afro-Peruvians were prompted to search, mainly through *mestizaje*, for routes of escape from the poverty and ethnic discrimination they suffered. The social condition most valued by both Afro-Peruvians and indigenous people was to be white, which implied not only skin colour but a higher social status. As a result, the rejection of roots in the search for social mobility and acceptance became standard among people of colour in Peru.

At the core of Afro-Peruvian community life was – and remains – the family, providing both biological reproduction and socio-cultural formation. The extended family persists as one of the strongest remnants of African traditions in Peru. Besides, the term 'family' traditionally identifies not only relatives by birth but also 'brothers and sisters of the race'. This all-encompassing vision of the family was nourished by communal experiences in the city *callejón* and hacienda *galpón*.

The role of the woman as the source of cohesion remains a fundamental element in the family configuration. Afro-Peruvian women's role, during the time of slavery, as both natural mother and caretaker of the master's children, created their special position as cultural transmitter and interpreter. Afro-Peruvian women remain agents of cultural transmission, proponents of Afro-Peruvian culture and the source of income for their families.

Changes since 1950

From the abolition of slavery until the second half of the present century, the general situation of Afro-Peruvians continued much as during the period of slavery. While abolition in 1854 signified a change of sorts, it did not end their marginalization and subordination. Afro-Peruvians remained second-class citizens and the poorest of the poor. Yet they developed processes of cultural and economic adaptation that were to create conditions for a new situation.

Beginning in the 1950s, Peruvian society experienced profound changes that modified the entire social fabric of the country. At this time Peru experienced the final crisis of its oligarchic system. National politics had previously been dominated by a small number of wealthy, powerful and often related families; but now a general process of democratization began which integrated new social groups into public life – not without conflict involving both the state itself and privileged groups within society.

The democratization of public and private life was accompanied by a significant extension of social services in the areas of health and education. This implied the possibility for the poorest people to receive health services and access to education, which could provide important links to social mobility. In addition, the cities underwent a rare period of growth beginning in the 1950s. Gradually such changes generated new challenges and conflicts for the Afro-Peruvian population.

Part of the result was a process of rebirth and reaffirmation of Afro-Peruvian culture. The enormous rural–urban migration of Afro-Peruvians at this time led to a fusion between country and city customs which created a new popular urban culture. Because of their relative isolation on the haciendas, rural Afro-Peruvians enriched the urban culture with many customs which had long been forgotten in the cities.

The 1950s and 1960s witnessed the appearance of Afro-Peruvian dance and theatre groups such as the Grupo Cumananá, founded by the brothers Victoria and Nicomedes Santa Cruz, and later in the 1970s the formation of Perú Negro. Dance and folklore groups provided the most frequent vehicle for cultural expression and affirmation, and within them several families such as the Vásquez, Campos, Santa Cruz and Azcue had important roles.

Not directly connected with the arts, but also a vital aspect of the new Afro-Peruvian movement, were the social groups which were established. In the 1960s the Grupo de los Melamodernos and the Grupo Harlem, influenced by the civil rights movement in the United States, formed with the intention of tracing their African roots. These groups brought together the few Afro-Peruvian professionals who worked in Lima – lawyers, academics and working-class intellectuals who sought to question the rigid hierarchical system that prevailed in Peru. Their lack of organization and of a vision free of racial prejudice slowly led to their isolation and eventual disappearance.

In the 1970s the Asociación Cultural de la Juventud Negra Peruana (ACEJUNEP) was founded with the goal of improving the quality of life for people of African descent. The ACEJUNEP was an important influence on young Afro-Peruvians in Lima and in nearby provinces. The search for their roots, the discovery of the culture that their parents had brought to the city in the 1950s and 1960s, and the need to create a future for themselves with conditions equal to those available to other young Peruvians led them to question the inequalities they faced and to propose approaches to overcome the problems of their community.

In spite of the merit of their motives, lack of support and solidarity on the part of other Afro-Peruvians, and of society in general, contributed to the failure of this initiative. Nevertheless, in the following years various former members of the ACEJUNEP went on to participate in other Afro-Peruvian organizations and projects.

During the 1980s the Instituto de Investigaciones Afro-Peruano (INAPE) was founded with the objective of carrying out diagnostic research regarding the collective situation of Afro-Peruvians and proposing practical alternatives for the solution of their problems. The INAPE developed research and outreach activities in universities and the media regarding the situation and experience of the Afro-Peruvian population. Its field research was oriented towards preserving and reviving the traditions and collective memory of rural Afro-Peruvians, and it made a study of the gender- and race-related problems faced by Afro-Peruvian women.

In 1984 the Movimiento Negro Francisco Congo was formed. This remains the best-known Afro-Peruvian organization that represents the interests and needs of the community. Associated with the movement, which owes its name to the hero Francisco Congo, are all those Peruvians who fight against racism and in the defence and promotion of Afro-Peruvian culture.

More recently, two other notable organizations have been established: the Agrupación Palenque, whose goal is to promote Afro-Peruvian culture, and the Asociación Pro-Derechos Humanos del Negro, whose objective is to fight racism and to provide legal services for men and women who require but cannot afford to pay for legal assistance. The Asociación in particular focuses on the field of human rights and seeks to promote the full exercise of civil and political rights for all members of the Afro-Peruvian community. It has also begun to organize projects and programmes oriented towards social development and the eradication of poverty.

In the past few years such Afro-Peruvian organizations have worked hard to consolidate their achievements and to develop affiliated groups in different parts of the country. Together they constitute a social movement whose principal goal is to defend the culture and the human rights of Afro-Peruvians, and to promote new forms of integration and relations with the rest of Peruvian society.

The great majority of the social demands of these organizations have never been recognized within the political system. Because of the legacy of the colonial and republican periods, when Peru was incapable of constructing a society formed of citizens equal before the law and equal in rights and responsibilities, the fight against racism has still not been embraced by the country's political parties. Some parties consider that the problems of Afro-Peruvians stem mainly from an inadequate distribution of wealth, while others see class divisions as the primary issue. No party has understood that Afro-Peruvians have collective needs that urgently demand creative solutions.

At the same time as the political parties have failed to understand their needs and aspirations, the parties' own vertical structures and hierarchies have made them unappealing to Afro-Peruvians. Thus Afro-Peruvian invisibility remains the most dominant form of political exclusion in Peru.

Future challenges

Afro-Peruvians currently confront several serious problems. First, extreme poverty affects the majority of Afro-Peruvians in the marginalized urban areas as well as in the countryside. In the urban context, poverty manifests itself in the large number of people who lack stable work and fair pay. Poverty is also reflected in the abysmal living conditions, and in the proliferation of social conflicts arising from drug addiction and alcoholism, both of which affect a significant number of Afro-Peruvians. In rural areas, the continuing crisis of agriculture has severe impacts on Afro-Peruvian households, which often have to provide for many members. In these areas practically no basic services or social programmes exist to meet their needs.

Secondly, Afro-Peruvians suffer from racism and from the propagation of ideas and stereotypes that accentuate their social exclusion. Racism in Peru is expressed on a daily basis in a subtle manner, through insults, mistrust and expressions of rejection, sentiments of superiority, and so on. Given the prevalence of such racist attitudes and behaviour, the subsequent lack of self-esteem and self-recognition on the part of Peruvians of African ancestry means that there is both a personal and a collective lack of identity, especially among the youth.

The third problem is the Peruvian state's ignorance and unawareness regarding the goals and problems of Afro-Peruvians. As a result of the false assumption of 'social and racial equality', the state is released of its responsibility to provide effective help and to involve itself in the collective solution of these problems. Peru's political parties have not incorporated the demands of Afro-Peruvians into their programmes; nor does there exist a national consensus on the need to combat racism.

The Peruvian media have not helped this situation; on the contrary, through advertising and television programmes media images tend to reinforce racist ideas and stereotypes that discriminate against Afro-Peruvian men and women.

In response to these challenges the Afro-Peruvian community needs to redouble its efforts to establish stronger and more effective organizations. Practical plans must be proposed to confront the community's problems, while Afro-Peruvians should also strive for more active participation in tackling the general issues that today face Peruvian society as a whole. The promotion of a democratic society and culture that respect the rights and equality of all citizens, regardless of ethno-cultural differences, is fundamental to the achievement of social well-being and the eradication of all types of mistreatment and discrimination.

Notes

1 Monge Oviedo, R., 'Are we or aren't we?', *Report on the Americas: The Black Americas 1492-1992*, North American Congress on Latin America, vol. 25, no. 4, 1992, p. 19.
2 *Liberto/a* referred to an African slave who obtained his or her liberty either by permission of the masters or by buying their freedom.

3 The Señor de los Milagros is an important religious procession that occurs in Lima every October.
4 *Bandas de cimarrones* were groups of slaves who escaped from the hacienda or from the control of their masters. *Palenques* were the refuges and hideouts where the escaped slaves lived.
5 The *callejón* was a brick building with a rush-thatched roof; it had a common entry whose interior was a central patio lined with rooms, which served as lodgings for a number of families. The *galpón* was a similar structure but located within the hacienda.

Select bibliography

Aguirre, C., *Agentes de su propia libertad: los esclavos de Lima y la desinte-gración de la esclavitud, 1821-1854*, Lima, Fondo Editorial, Pontificia Universidad Católica del Perú, 1993.

Bowser, F.P., *El esclavo africano en el Perú colonial, 1524-1650*, Mexico City, Siglo Veintiuno Editores, 1977.

Carneiro, E., *Guerra de las Palmares*, Mexico City, Fondo de Cultura Económica, 1946.

Centurión Vallejo, H., 'Esclavitud y manumisión de los negros en Trujil-lo', unpublished, Trujillo, 1974.

Couche, D., *Poder blanco y resistencia negra en el Perú*, Lima, Instituto Nacional de Cultura, 1975.

Espinoza, V., 'Cimarronaje y palenques en la costa central del Perú, 1700-1815', in *Primer seminario sobre poblaciones inmigrantes, Mayo 9 y 10, 1986*, vol. II, Lima, Consejo Nacional de Ciencia y Tecnología, pp. 29-42.

Freitas, D., *Palmares a guerra dos escravos*, Rio de Janeiro, Edicoes Graal, 4th edn, 1982.

Harth-Terre, E., *Negros e indios: un estamento social ignorado del Perú colo-nial*, Lima, Libreria Editorial Juan Mejía Baca, 1973.

Hunefeldt, C., 'Los negros en Lima', *Histórica*, Lima, vol. III, no. 1, 1979.

Hunefeldt, C., *Mujeres esclavitud, emociones y libertad, Lima 1800-1854*, Working Paper no. 24, Lima, Instituto de Estudios Peruanos, 1988.

Jacobsen, N., *The Development of Peru's Slave Population and its Importance for Coastal Agriculture*, Berkeley, CA, Graduate History Department, University of California, 1974.

Kapsoli, W., *Sublevaciones de esclavos en el Perú: s. XVIII*, Lima, Universidad Ricardo Palma, 1975.

Macera, P., 'Plantaciones azucareras en el Perú: 1821-1875', in *Trabajos de historia*, vol. 4, Lima, Instituto Nacional de Cultura, 1977, pp. 9-307.

Millones Santa Gades, L., *Minorías étnicas en el Perú*, Lima, Editorial Andina, 1973.

Price, R. (ed.), *Sociedades cimarronas: siglo XXI*, Barcelona, 1981.

Reyes Flores, A., *Esclavitud en Lima, 1800-1840*, Lima, Universidad Nacional Mayor de San Marcos, 1985.

Romero Pintado, F., *Safari africano y compraventa de esclavos para el Perú 1412-1818*, Lima, Instituto de Estudios Peruanos, Universidad San Cristóbal de Huamanga, 1994.

Santa Cruz, N., *La décima en el Perú*, Lima, Instituto de Estudios Peruanos, Lima, 1982.

Sotomayor, R.C. and Aranda de los Rios, R., *Sublevación de campesinos negros de Chincha 1879*, Lima, Universidad Nacional Mayor de San Marcos, 1979.

Trazegnies, F. de, *Ciriaco de Urtecho: litigante por amor – reflexiones sobre la polivalencia táctica del razonamiento jurídico*, Lima, Fondo Editorial, Pontificia Universidad Católica del Perú, 1981.

10

ECUADOR

Norman E. Whitten Jr and Diego Quiroga
with the assistance of P. Rafael Savoia

Negro, negro, renegrido,
negro, hermano del carbón,
negro de negros nacido,
negro ayer, mañana y hoy.
Algunos creen insultarme
gritándome mi color,
más yo mismo lo pregono
con orgullo frente al sol:
Negro he sido, negro soy,
negro vengo, negro voy,
negro bien negro nací
negro negro he de vivir,
y como negro morir.

Nelson Estupiñán Bass[1]

The Republic of Ecuador in western South America is a modern OPEC/NOPEC nation that won its independence from colonial rule in 1822 and became in 1830 El Ecuador (the Equator). Colombia lies to its north, and Peru to its east and south. Sustained ethnic clashes and, equally, sustained domination by a white minority are salient features of Ecuador's tumultuous history. Mainland Ecuador is divided into three parts: Coast, Sierra (or Andes) and Upper Amazonia (or Amazonian Region). Most of its 12 to 13 million people live in the Coast and Sierra. Ecuador is now, as it has been since at least the early nineteenth century, and perhaps since the six-teenth century, in the ongoing process of social reproduction and cultural transformation of strongly represented ethnic cate-gories that signify segments of its ever-expanding population.

To understand the dimensions of blackness in Ecuador, the three concepts of *indio* (Indian), *negro* (black) and *blanco* (white) must be explained. These concepts emerged in the Americas as the kingdom of Castile and Aragón forged a cultural hegemony of racial separation. The concept of 'race' (Spanish *raza*) itself emerged in European dictionaries at the time of the rapidly expanding racist hegemony in the Americas. The racialist struc-ture looks like this:

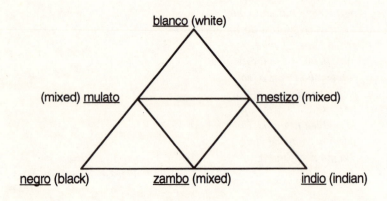

Ecuadorian social structure may be considered a class pyramid. An oligarchy, known in the upper classes as *la sociedad*, and internally as *gente de bién* (or *gente bién* – proper, 'right kind of' and, by extension, righteous people), constitutes the pinnacle of political power, economic control and social esteem. The *sociedad* is complemented by what we might call a new oli-garchy, whose position is a direct result of accumulated wealth.

All members of these oligarchies self-identify unconditionally, and are usually identified, as *blancos*. Ecuador has a significant middle class of professionals and business and service industries people who generally self-identify as *blanco*. The self-identifying phrase *buena familia* (good family) is today the most popular one among such people. It is from the elite, the educated upper and middle classes and the military that the concept of a united body of mixed people, *el mestizaje*, emanates. And it is among the elite, and educated upper and middle classes, that the rhetoric separating Ecuador's 'races' also emanates.

Farther down the class hierarchy we find people dependent for their livelihood on commercial transactions of varying scale, none of whom self-identify as *mestizo*, except under exceptional circumstances, but who are politely tagged with various labels meaning 'mixed' by those above them, or with the labels of the antipodes – *indio, negro* – when discourses reflect interaggregate or interpersonal anger signalling open conflict. Sometimes, under conditions of severe stress, those in superordinate positions use common associations for the ethnic antipodeal terminology – *salvaje*, meaning savage, or *alzado*, meaning out of control – in heated discussion reflecting social conflict. Upward mobility is conceived of by those in superordinate positions of power and wealth as a process often called *blanqueamiento*, or whitening, in Ecuador, as in Colombia and Venezuela (the cognate term in Brazilian Portuguese is *embranquecimento*). The processes of *mestizaje* are also often called by the vulgar term *cholificación* in Ecuador, as in Peru and Bolivia.

People represented by those in power as *negro*, on the one side, and *indio*, on the other, are thought to be the real social antipodes of class-status relationships. Whitten has noted elsewhere that, in power politics, indigenous leaders endeavour to move a discourse about the *indio* potential for revolt directly into the realm of the status-conscious rhetoric of the oligarchies.[2] Spokesmen and spokeswomen of the *negro* potential for insurrection aim their discourse of pending disorder at the middle levels of the class and status hierarchy.

When discourses of ethnic 'disorder' or 'revolt' reach the mass media all subtleties of ethnic categorization are dropped in favour of unified, pejorative representations of human beings. In this process synthetic, symbolic units of racialist ideology that emerged in the Americas soon after its European 'conquest' – *blanco, negro* and *indio* – bring forth a predicative link that carries the double act of assertion and denial.

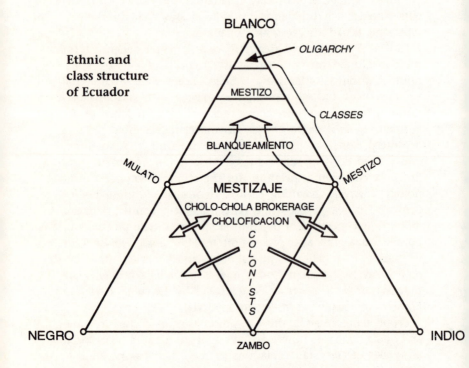

Ethnic and class structure of Ecuador

Historically, there are three rural streams of Africans who became part of Ecuador's dynamic black history: those who occupy the present Province of Esmeraldas in the north-west; those of Carchi and Imbabura in the northern Andes and western escarpments; and those of Loja in the south. Three urban streams also exist: those of Guayaquil, the largest city in

Ecuador; those of Quito, the nation's capital; and those of Ibarra, the north's urban distribution point. Black people have also emerged in virtually every area of Ecuador through its entire history. We treat the three rural regions briefly, and then comment on the rest of Ecuador.

Esmeraldas

Regional blackness as a force of self-liberation in Ecuador begins in Esmeraldas, and its origin occurs during a violent tropical storm and a movement of African rebellion. The documented history of Ecuador establishes the beginnings of Afro-Hispanic culture in what is now Esmeraldas, Ecuador, where a Spanish slaving ship ran aground in 1553. There a group of twenty-three Africans from the coast of Guinea, led by a black warrior named Antón, attacked the slavers and liberated themselves. Not long after, this group, together with other blacks entering the region, led by a *ladino* (Hispanicized black person) named Alonso de Illescas, came to dominate the region from northern Manabí north to what is now Barbacoas, Colombia. At this time (late sixteenth century) intermixture with indigenous peoples, to whom black people fled to establish their *palenques* (villages of self-liberated people – some fortified, some not), was such that their features were described as *zambo* (black–indigenous admixture), synonyms of which were *negro* (black) and *mulato* (mixed or hybrid black-white). Movement into Colombia by Africans was through Cartagena via the Cauca Valley, and through Panama and Pacific ports. The first black person there may have arrived with the pilot of Francisco Pizarro, Bartolomé Ruiz, on the Isla de Gallo in 1526.

There is evidence that the earliest influence on Afro-Hispanic culture in the region came from the Senegambian area of northwest Africa. Culturally, the influence of Bantu and Mande Africa (as seen in the music, especially the *currulao*) and of archaic Spain and North Africa (especially some funeral customs) predominates. By 1599 black people were clearly in charge of what was called 'La Republica de Zambos' or 'Zambo Republic'. *Zambo* refers to people of colour who are descendants of Native Americans and African-Americans. In that year a group of Zambo chiefdoms, said to represent 100,000 or more Zambo people of Esmeraldas, trekked to Quito to declare loyalty to Spain. An oil painting of these chiefs from the emerald land of the Zambo Republic is portrayed by the 'Indian artist' Adrián Sánchez Galgue; it is reportedly the earliest signed and dated painting from South America.

The Afro-Hispanic culture of the Pacific Lowlands of Ecuador and Colombia extends from Muisne in southern Esmeraldas Province, Ecuador, to the San Juan River, in Valle Department, Colombia. It is part of the greater 'Pacific Lowlands Culture Area' of Panama, Colombia and Ecuador. South of this area is a distinct Manabí culture region of Ecuador; north of the area is the Afro-American Chocó region of Colombia, with black culture shared with people of the Darién Province, Panama. East of the region are the interior Andean zones of Ecuador and Colombia. The Afro-Hispanic cultural region (which is predominant) is shared with Tchachela, Chachi and Awá (Coaquier) indigenous peoples of Ecuador, and with Awá, Waunam and Emberá native peoples of Colombia.

Spanish was the language of conquest in Ecuador and Colombia, and became the language – in stylized transformations – of black people of the Pacific Lowlands. Serious linguistic work remains to be undertaken on the dialect of stylized Spanish spoken in Afro-Latin American culture of this region.

Between 600,000 and 800,000 black people occupy this region, making it the densest population in the entire lowland rainforest tropics of the Americas. About 85 per cent of the population of the region shares Afro-Latin American culture. In Esmeraldas itself we estimate a figure of about 200,000 people, with the same percentage being black.

Carchi and Imbabura (the Chota–Mira Valley)

The regions of Carchi and Imbabura, with sizeable populations of black people, are located in deep valleys conducive to tropical and subtropical agriculture. Especially prominent in this racial topography is the Chota–Mira Valley (sometimes also known locally, regionally and nationally as Coangue). This area features excellent growing conditions for commercial agricultural products sought after by such urban areas as Ibarra and Quito, and is today served by modern bus lines. Black people live in the region drained by the Chota River, which runs into the Mira River that traverses the black lowlander culture of Ecuador and Colombia, and which, in its upper course, cuts across the Panamerican highway between the Colombian border and Ibarra, capital of Imbabura Province.

Members of this expanding black population cultivate small plots of one to five hectares, upon which a large variety of foodstuffs are grown for the urban markets, for smaller villages of northern Ecuador and for internal consumption. Such small farms, drained by irrigation ditches radiating from the Chota River, were long controlled by a few huge haciendas. After the Agrarian Reform Law of 1964 black yeomen shed the status of rural share croppers and entered a system of covert and overt conflict with the power wielders of the region. They also engaged in a system of geographic and upward socio-economic mobility as their populations continued to flow from the valley to Ibarra and Quito.

The early history of the Chota–Mira Valley and its affluents and hinterlands is summarized by various authors as one characterized by ongoing open conflict between conquerors and those they sought to vanquish and turn into serfs. Between 1550 and 1610 indigenous chiefdoms were broken down, black people began entering the area, from the coast and from the Andes, and a Spanish-dominated boom in such products as gold, cotton, corn and chickens took place, but with an awful social toll.[3] The wider span of dates given, 1550-1700, subsumes a period of indigenous secular exploitation by white and *mestizo* overseers and *hacendados*, followed by a Jesuit (Society of Jesus) solution to the indigenous–non-indigenous conflicts by the direct importation of African slaves (from Africa, Iberia, the Caribbean and Colombia). Other Catholic orders and secular organizations also imported slaves for plantations in the Chota–Mira Valley.

The Jesuits ran slave-based, productive and profitable plantations in the area, and found the military means to put down slave rebellions, from their entry in 1586 until their expulsion in 1740. The strategy of the Jesuits was to focus on sugar-cane production based on black slave labour. They also introduced European grapes to be made into wines and brandies for their own local consumption. Between 1776 and 1779 Colonel calculates the *piezas de indias* (a measure of labour based on what a strong man-slave could accomplish in one day) as 1,324 for eight sugar plantations.[4] In reading such figures one must keep in mind that, the weaker the slaves became, the more it took for them to constitute one *pieza*. A recent calculation by Nelson Estupiñán Bass (1990) for 1781 is that of 2,553 slaves in the valley, divided among ten haciendas.[5]

For their part, black people, free and slave, grew other commodities for their own consumption, and eventually for the growing markets in northern Ecuador for tropical and subtropical products: avocados, tomatoes, manioc (cassava), beans, sweet potatoes, anise, papaya, watermelon, citrus fruits, plantains, bananas, grapes, cotton, coca, fibres and other crops.[6] Flight from slavery to the west (Esmeraldas), south, to the large towns and small cities of colonial rule, and east to the Amazonian Region was common. Such acts of *cimarronaje* are not documented to any significant extent in Ecuador, but we need to keep the image of an expanding web of black people in Ecuador, through runaways and their routes, in mind.

Today the population of the Chota–Mira Valley is estimated at somewhere between 15,000 and 20,000 people, of whom 97 per cent or more share this regional black Ecuadorian culture.[7] We must stress here, however, that the out-migration of Afro-Chota peoples, who maintain webs of social relationships through sporadic contact with one another, is such that we should probably at least triple this figure when talking of people from the valley.

Loja

In Loja, southern Ecuador, Amazonian ecology winds its way through a low point in the Ecuadorian Andes. Indeed, in the *National Geographic* map of South America for 'Indian' cultures, Loja is given the status of 'Amazonia'. Into this rich land of native peoples came conquerors and their curate scribes. One of these, Don Juan de Salinas Loyola, on his march to the tropical forests to conquer the 'Jívaros' in 1557, had with him black slaves, one of whom saved his life when his canoe tipped over while trying to pass dangerous river rapids.[8] Later, in the famous (infamous) revolt of the 'Jívaro' in 1579 (usually reported as 1599), it now seems clear that black people constituted part of the insurgents, as did *mestizo* people. In other words, one of the first successful revolts in Ecuador's colonial history involved the multicultural union of indigenous Amazonian people, imported and/or self-liberated black people and emerging *mestizo* people.

The slaves brought to this region were primarily household servants and gold-miners. Black yeomen fanned out, especially along the Catamayo River, and black slaves were held in bondage as *piezas de indias* for killing work in the gold-mines. Many fled mining and forced agricultural labour to the adjacent tropical regions, where some engaged in placer gold-mining. In 1572 the lawyer Juan de Ovando described free and black people of the city of Loja as having a colour just like that of the people of Guinea, West Africa.[9] There seems to have been much genetic intermingling in this region, together with an inflow of black servants and slaves from Spain, Portugal, West Africa and Colombia. Throughout the colonial era black people inhabited the Catamayo River region and engaged in rural agriculture; they also resided in a black *barrio* of the capital of Loja, also named Loja. The black population during the colonial period numbered somewhere around 5,000.

In the late 1990s we do not encounter anything resembling the concentration of black people of Esmeraldas and the Chota–Mira Valley region in Loja. Out-migration and internal genetic intermingling have changed the complexion of the area, as has the routing of the small farmers of the Catamayo River system by such modernization strategies as the development of an airport there. The twin phenomena of 'development' and 'whitening' are well reported in the literature on blackness in Ecuador, as elsewhere where Afro-Latin Americans live.

Slaves from all of these areas of Ecuador were legally manumitted when what is now Ecuador became part of Gran Colombia in

1824 (Colombia manumitted its slaves in 1821). But in various areas of Ecuador manumission came at different times. It supposedly came by national decree in 1854, but slavery endured in some areas until the 1860s. Slaves were freed in Loja in 1837, but in Esmeraldas and the Chota–Mira Valley some bondage still existed, now called the system of *concertaje* (often called by the Quichua phrase *huasipungo* in the Chota–Mira region), right up to the 1890s.

Later arrivals

The history of blackness in what is now Ecuador up to the wars of liberation led by Simón Bolívar in the north and José de San Martín in the south is that of slavery and freedom existing side by side. From about 1600 through the early 1800s slaves were brought to Barbacoas, Colombia (just north of the free Zambo Republic in Ecuador), each year. About ten *negreros* (literally, 'black-bringing' ships; slavers) would arrive each year in this placer-gold-mining area, with slaves to replace those who had died and those who had fled to areas such as Esmeraldas or Chota–Mira.

In Esmeraldas Province, organizational forms of labour cooperation in raising food, exploiting forest, mangrove and sea, and panning for gold existed in remarkably similar forms in both free and slave communities. The primary cultural relationship from the sixteenth century through the twentieth is that of 'racial succession' whereby black people encroach on the cultural territories of indigenous people.

In Chota–Mira the oppression of the plantation system continued, as did out-migration and sustained conflicts between black people and their wealthy white oppressors. Such conflict continues in the late twentieth century. In Loja far more absorption of black people into the general population occurred, with 'racial succession' passing through generations. Also, it appears that the black people of Loja continued a pattern of out-migration.

Ibarra, Quito and Guayaquil

Probably less than 4 per cent of Ibarra is black; most of these people are from the Chota–Mira Valley and maintain their contact there. Ibarra is a residential area for black people, and it is also a springboard for migration to Quito. The concentration of the black population is found in the area of the major market and the railroad terminus. In Quito one finds from 50,000 to 60,000 black people, most of them from the Chota–Mira Valley. To this we could add about 10,000 people who might or might not be defined as black by Ecuadorian or other Latin American definitions. The neighbourhoods where concentrations of black people live and work are Batallón del Pueblo, Bastión Popular Aticucho, Roldós, Carapungo and Comité del Pueblo. But they are also scattered throughout the city.

Black people have been in Quito since Pedro de Alvarado, coming from Central America with a well-seasoned army, and Gonzalo Pizarro's troops from Peru moved north to conquer it in 1534. By 1535 Quito was a Spanish colonial city, the northern sector of the administrative area of Peru, with its centre in the port city of Lima. The truncation of the Inca empire was complete. The body was indigenous and black (and becoming *mestizo*), but the head was Spanish and white. Various streams of black people entered, left and stayed during its entire history. *Cimarronaje* was so prevalent in Quito that specific violent punishments (including mutilation, torture and death) for runaways were proclaimed there in 1548.

Guayaquil has a significant black population of which the largest concentration is in the *barrio* Cristo de Consuelo, with other concentrations in La Chala and La Marimba. More recent invasions of black people from Esmeraldas have resulted in black people throughout this city of more than 3 million.

Definition of the black minorities

Gente morena and *moreno* are the polite terms of reference and address in most of rural and urban Ecuador where aggregates of black people live. *Gente negra* (black people) is accepted in some areas, but is rejected in others if used by anyone not identified as black. *Afro-ecuatoriano* is an intellectual term now in favour, though it is pejorative if used colloquially. *Negro* is another intellectual term in vogue, but it is pejorative colloquially wherever black people live, when used by a non-black person. *Zambo* (indigenous–black admixture) is commonly used in black areas of Ecuador, and may or may not be pejorative if used by a non-black person. *Libre* – free in the sense of self-liberated – is not common south of the San Juan River, Colombia. It is the primary term in the Chocó north of the San Juan River and is known and sometimes used in Ecuador. On the coast, *costeño* is the primary ethnic designation for black Ecuadorians. All designations of black people are of foreign origin and designate the combination of blackness and territory. Colloquially, in Ecuador, *gente morena* (dark people) is polite usage, but intellectuals now stress the Spanish terms *negro* (black), *afro-ecuatoriano* or *afro-colombiano*, and more generally *afro-latinoamericano*.

The latter concept emerged in 1992 as nationalist ideologues stressed the Ibero-Latin American unity that excludes both blacks and indigenous people. Coincident with such stress, black leaders of movements of ethnic self-assertion came forth with the concept of *afro-latinoamericano* as an emergent idea of self-representation and self-identity for black intellectuals.

The etymology of *moreno* and *negro* seems to stem from the same root, the Latin diminutive of *maurus*, through Mozarabic and Castillian Spanish.[10] Today, however, dictionaries define *negro* as black and *moreno* as brown or brunet(te). None the less, *moreno* means black in Ecuador; it is not used to refer to people of lighter skin, or to brunet(te)s. It is used to refer to people of darker skin, or lesser status, than the speaker. In modern Ecuador the word *negro*, when used by non-black people, is pejorative, even though journalists and scholars have seized on it as the proper term for dark people. Although Ecuadorian intellectuals may disagree, if they have never lived with black people in Esmeraldas, the Chota–Mira Valley or Loja, the phrase *gente morena* is still the polite manner of speaking about dark people. One also hears *la raza morenita*, but this is not appreciated by black people, for it has a connotation of childlike and cute.

Mulato is also used for very light people; *zambo* refers to black–

indigenous mixing but has other usages. Such terms are normally used as adjectives, not nouns. Examples include *pueblo negro* (black people) or *comunidad negra* (black community). In the 1990s the representation *negro fino* (refined black) is used in Ecuador to differentiate black people who are educated and are white-collar employees from those who are not. *Mulato* is often used in journalism to refer to a distinguished poet or novelist who usually refers to himself or herself as *negro* or *negra*. Historically, *mulato* referred to affinity between someone who was 'wild' (such as an African or Native American) and 'civilized' (a white person). The etymology lies in ancient Mediterranean concepts of hybridity.[11] Because of this, European colonial writers avoided drawing attention to unions between African and indigenous peoples, and substituted the term *mulato* for *zambo*.[12]

The term *negro* has repercussions in politics that demonstrate the contextual nature of this important reference point. It has recently been claimed that Esmeraldas has never had a black political representative to the national Congress. Yet Jaime Hurtado González, for many years the socialist representative from Esmeraldas (who was also a presidential candidate on two occasions), would fit all the international and national criteria of 'blackness' and he was called, colloquially, in various parts of the nation, *El negro*. When confronted with such a perspective, however, black spokesmen and spokeswomen for blackness and for Esmeraldas as a black province say that he gave up his blackness by joining the power structure of Ecuador. Clearly, blackness represents more than mere skin colour to those who seek a regional and human dignity through deployment of the concept.

Black people in Ecuador draw specific attention to nouns, verbs, adjectives and adverbs involving double meanings of blackness. For example, the verb *negrear* (to blacken) is used socially to confer lesser status. To say that someone's life is *negreando* can mean the person is drifting towards crime, is becoming poorer or is heading towards states pejoratively associated with black people: lazy, dirty or ugly. By inference, of course, *negrear* and its derivatives and near cognates (*negar*, to negate) bring all such associations to bear on the stigmatized subject of the predication. *Negrear* can also mean to make someone 'disappear' as a social being of worth. For example, the verb is applied to people who have been promised a salary at one level, and then are actually given far less. Such a person is *tratado como negro*, 'treated like a black', or simply *negreado*, 'blackened'. To contest being treated in a disparaging way one may exclaim, '¡No mi negré!' which can be translated euphemistically as 'Don't deny me' or 'Don't look through or past me.' But literally it means, 'Don't treat me like a nigger!'

During a public lecture in Quito during the summer of 1993, Ms Sonya Catalina Charla offered this definition of blackness (translated from notes taken by N. Whitten): 'Who are we? We are black groups, we share history, we have our proper culture, and we have our dignity and our identity.' And she went on:

> *We are from Esmeraldas and from the Chota River Valley. We have distinct historical products that we know and understand. Where do we come from? We are from here. There were blacks with the conquerors, Alonso de Illescas freed us and we constituted the Republic of Zambos. We defend the liberty of the black people and indigenous people, just as did Antón from Cabo Verde in Africa, and Alonso de Illescas, the first Governor of Esmeraldas.*

She then moved briefly to the Chota–Mira area, which had another origin in slavery, but with whose people 'we are now one'. She spoke of Guayaquil, 'where the black people came as domestics and carpenters and where there are black communities today'.

Population size and demography

Population size and the demography of blackness in Ecuador are extremely difficult to estimate. There are no census categories to help us, and we must rely on the calculations of self-identifying black people who are working diligently on such subjects. The calculations usually proceed to take census figures from Esmeraldas and Chota–Mira, to assign a percentage to them that factors out non-black people, and then add the figures estimated for black people in Quito, the capital of the republic, and Guayaquil, the largest city on the Guayas River of the coast.

In the 31 July 1994 'Panorama' section of the conservative

Quito newspaper *El Comercio*, Renán Tadeo, from the parish of Concepción of Mira Canton, in Carchi, gives us the figure of 700,000 black people in Esmeraldas, Imbabura, Carchi, El Oro and Loja, including in these figures the urban populations of black people in and on the fringes of Quito and Guayaquil. P. Rafael Savoia, who directs the Centro Cultural Afro-Ecuatoriano in Quito, Guayaquil and Esmeraldas, confirms our impression that Tadeo offers a reasonably accurate estimate of Ecuador's black population. If we figure Ecuador's national population as 12 to 13 million, we have a population that is 6 to 7 per cent black. This is within the range of a 5 to 10 per cent black population often given in Ecuador's official statistics, and by the US State Department. The concentration of black people is in northern Ecuador in a square that encloses the Quito–Muisne–Colombian-border–Ibarra points of reference (provinces of Pichincha, Esmeraldas Carchi and Imbabura).

Cultural forms

Spanish is the language spoken by all black people in Ecuador. A different stylization of the language is spoken in Esmeraldas than in the Chota–Mira Valley. Black people in Quito and Guayaquil, as elsewhere, are stereotyped by the way they speak, and in many places they take pains to emulate the dialects of Spanish taken to be more prestigious in certain contexts. This leads, at times, some speakers of Esmeraldas to speak with some Italian inflections due to the long association with Comboniano priests, all of whom, until fairly recently, came from Italy. Some black people from Esmeraldas speak at least rudimentary Chachi, but it is not common for them to do so.

In the Amazonian Region there are black-skinned Quichua-speaking people within Canelos Quichua culture. Some came from the Pacific Lowlands three generations ago; others came westward from Brazil and Peru during the Amazon rubber boom. Recent migrations have resulted in a substantial proportion of black people in Lago Agrio, on the Agua Rico River.

Music is a cultural form by which black people are well known in Ecuador, and in which great pride is manifest. Black musical groups are now in demand for national and regional festivals of arts and music. In Esmeraldas and the Guayas Basin international music traditions spanning the African and American continents are enlivened by all sorts of informal and formal bands. Popular music such as *gaita, cumbia, merecumbea* and now *salsa* is ubiquitous.

In Esmeraldas, as in the Pacific Lowlands of Colombia north to the San Juan River, the marimba band, sometimes called *currulao*, is an ascendant cultural expression. Two men play the marimba. One of them, the *glosador*, or another man not playing the marimba, sings long songs, some of which are improvised, at least in part, while two women, *respondadoras*, 'answer' the singer. The female singers shake tube-rattles, called *guasá*, as two drummers accompany them on the *cununos*, which are cone-shaped drums like the Cuban 'conga drum'. The dominant beat of the marimba music is from two huge base drums, without snares, called *bombos*. The rhythms played are as African as any in the Americas, originating in the Bantu and Mande areas of West Africa.

The traditional marimba band assembles to play the music for a dance of respect (*baile de respecto*), which features a number of very different presentations, each with different rhythms, marimba melodies, *glosador* renditions and response patterns. This music and dance of respect are purely secular rituals. Powerful though these renditions are, no saints or spirits enter; the universe is restricted to respectful human interaction. Today, for national or regional festivals, the *bambuco* rhythm and dance predominate.

Another traditional music form of this area is played for the death of a child, *chigualo*, or for the festival to a saint, *arrullo*. This music is led and controlled by women, who shake maracas, and direct the rhythms of the two men playing the *cununo* and the one or more men playing the *bombo*. During the *chigualo*, the soul of the deceased child goes directly to heaven (*gloria*), bypassing purgatory. Saints and spirits may also enter from the heaven and other worlds, but those that would do harm to the celebrants are chased away by the sound of the *bombo*. Sometimes, such as during Easter festivals, an *arrullo* to a saint may be accompanied by a marimba band.

At the death of an adult an entirely different kind of music is sung. These are dirges sung by women in a style reminiscent of North African Muslim Hispanic style. Here songs are sung of the coming and going of demons and devils, as the soul of the deceased remains in the vicinity of the corpse. After nine days people again come together to sing final dirges and, essentially, dismiss the soul of the deceased to its fate in other worlds, purgatory, hell or heaven.

The most dramatic ceremony in Esmeraldas Province is that of the *tropa* (the troop or troops). This is a forceful enactment of the formation of a *palenque*, which was a village established by black people (or indigenous people) fleeing bondage. Such people were known as *cimarrones*. *La tropa* is enacted at Easter. Attendance at *la tropa* brings out-migrants from small villages such as Güimbí on the Santiago River back home from, especially, Guayaquil. Community ties are very important to many out-migrants, who spend considerable sums of money, and take two to three weeks out of their urban lives, to make their way up the coast of Ecuador, and thence upriver by launch, or by canoe, to attend.

La tropa ceremony begins in the fringes of the community as groups of soldiers run off in search of the lost Christ, but they find only the biblical thief, Barabas. They then march on the church and enter it and eventually enact the killing of Christ, his removal from the cross, the reign of the Devil, the bringing of the forest into the Catholic church of the *palenque*, the resurrection of Christ within the forest within the church, and the liberation of the people of the forest and of the church within the *palenque*.

The ubiquitous interest in globalization of their local culture manifest by black people in Ecuador was recently stimulated by a number of events that brought together black *esmeraldeños*, black people from the Chota–Mira Valley and musicians and performers from other countries, such as Cuba. One group, the Chigualeros, adapted their rhythms to *salsa* music, and introduced the marimba into the resulting dynamic renditions.

Two groups, led by Petita Palma and Segundo Quintero, have been experimenting with the globalization of their local and regional traditions for some time. A newer group, probably the most famous internationally, is Koral y Esmeralda ([Black] Coral and Emerald). Led by the dynamic *salsa* singer Carmen González, Koral y Esmeralda has played in Japan, including in its expanding repertoire the songs 'Perla Negra', 'Canoita' and 'Chocolate'. The group is also experimenting with a front-line instrumentation featuring trumpet, trombone and saxophone, while adapting rhythms, melodies and call–response patterns from *arrullo, chigualo* and *currulao*. 'This is what our ancestors told about,' say some young spokespeople for this dynamic international music.

The dominant musical form of the Chota–Mira Valley is *la bomba,* also called *la banda mocha.* Traditional instrumentation features a large single-head conical drum, called *bombo,* and smaller conga drums, called *redomblantes,* together with snare drums, maracas, guitars and sometimes other instrumentation, including flutes and panpipes. Couples dance *la bomba* with stylized steps and sing stylized songs, some of them improvised. At a point in some dances each woman puts a bottle on her head and dances in an attractive, undulating manner, without disturbing the bottle. New bands dedicated to *la bomba* have played in regional and national festivals, and there is interest in many sectors to merge creatively the Afro-Latin American beats and sounds of Chota–Mira and Esmeraldas.

The cosmology of black people of Esmeraldas reflects conjunctures of Catholicism and African religion that have fused and reconfigured from the mid-sixteenth century to the present. 'Dynamic' is an apt term for the religious beliefs and practices of this region of Ecuador. Other worlds exist on the sea and under, over and beyond it. The sea itself is a universe of spirits as well as a domain for visiting, travelling and shipping. Fear creatures, called *visiones* (visions, or images), are said to be encountered everywhere. Principal among them in most places are Tunda, a spiritual body-snatcher who is driven away by the sound of a base drum or shotgun, and Riviel, an especially dangerous ghost-ghoul who must be deposed by a shotgun or rifle. Other fear creatures specific to localities include 'the widow' (a masked flying witch), 'the headless man' and 'the living dead'.

This earth contains multiple entrances and exits to other worlds, including the site of a shrine to a saint, the locus of a funeral ritual for a child or an adult, and the cemetery. Heaven and purgatory seem to exist 'below' the sky; saints, spirits, virgins and souls of the dead come there, and souls of the dead depart from the earth to go there. Hell is set aside from purgatory and heaven; it is the locus of the Devil, demons and the souls and spirits of dead people who expired while 'hot' (that is, in a state of anger and conflict).

In the southern sector of Esmeraldas, in the area where black culture abuts the culture of the Manabí region, the cosmos is divided into two halves, called the *divino* and the *humano*. The former is the domain of the virgins and the saints (of colloquial Afro-Latin American Catholicism), and the latter is the domain of the Devil and of all the spirits and dangerous souls that can be appropriated to the Devil's domain. The domain of the *divino* is a plane of existence populated by a number of saints, including especially the Virgen del Carmen, San Antonio, Santa Rosa, El Niño Dios and La Mano Poderosa. Many people have shrines in their homes on which they light votive candles to the saints who protect them from diseases and other misfortunes. The domain of the *humano*, overseen by the Christian Devil, is the other plane of existence, populated by obscure figures such as the Anima Sola (soul by itself, lone soul) or El Mismísimo (the Devil himself).

Curanderas (female healers) and *brujos* (male sorcerers) are the active agents who draw from the domains of the *divino* and from the *humano*. *Curanderas* have special relationships with some saints and many of them are people who stand in for, or represent, particular saints. *Curanderas* use the power of the saints and virgins during their curing rituals. They heal illnesses such as evil eye, malignant air and magical fright. To cure patients of these afflictions, they recite secret prayers, light candles to the saints and virgins and use herbs whose names invoke the powers of important figures of the *divino*. *Brujos*, by contrast, are said to use the powers of the Devil to make people ill or infertile, or to destroy someone's business. Although most of such talk is in a 'he said, she said' mode of rumour and gossip, a *brujo* will sometimes actually admit to performing acts of malign magic.

At the academic–ecclesiastical congress Compromisos por un Nuevo Ecuador held in Quito during the summer of 1994, black spokeswoman Sonya Catalina Charla explained to an audience of more than 200 people the essence of black culture and black organization in Ecuador. Her first subject was economy. She noted with care that black people in Ecuador were not to be caught on the horns of the modernization-versus-subsistence dilemma. She said that black people knew, and scientific studies have documented, the remarkable economic adaptability of black cultures to both subsistence and market economies, the latter of which she called 'global'. They could take care of themselves when they needed to do so, and they could, and would, participate fully in modernization plans, if only they were not blocked from doing so by racist barriers. Drawing on the 'scientific genealogical' studies of Fernando Jurado Noboa, she noted the colour of Presidents past, and how an ancient 'gens' (line of descent) was recently described as *zambo*, or 'one-quarter black'. The 'gens' under discussion was that of Vicente Ramón Roca, early President of Ecuador.

Having warmed her audience with the slight allusion to blackness within an ideology of *mestizaje* in a class that should have been *blanco*, she defined clearly the cultural dimensions, called *la cultura* (in Spanish the definite article *la* before *cultura*, culture, elevates the concept to something high, refined and sophisticated).[13] The first of these was poetry, and she mentioned specifically Antonio Preciado Bedoya (see below), moving from the beauty of his work to the principles of blackness underscored in it. 'Black people have survived, and they know how to survive,' she said. She drew careful attention to the diverse skills with language which resulted from the mixing of people from various parts of Africa, and the subsequent elaborations and creative adjustments made by them and their descendants in Ecuador. Music also drew her attention, especially the marimba complex of Esmeraldas and that of the *bomba* in Chota–Mira. Finally, she turned to the strengths of black co-parentage (*compadrazgo*), to black family and to black community as structures of endurance, adaptation and creativity.

Literature, art and poetry

> Barrio de los negros
> de calles oscuras
> preñadas de espantos,
> que llevan, que asustan,
> que paran los pelos
> en noches sin luna
>
> Barrio encendido,
> de noche y de día,
> infierno moreno,
> envuelto en las llamas
> de son y alegría.

Antonio Preciado Bedoya[14]

Black intellectuals, often identifying with, and usually representatives of, Esmeraldas Province, have contributed substantially to Ecuadorian literature and to an international or global literature. Antonio Preciado Bedoya is one such prominent poet. Adalberto Ortiz, who wrote the internationally acclaimed novel *Juyungo* (1943), is another, though he has long resided outside of Ecuador. His subsequent book, *La entundada* (1971), presages recent professional ethnography of folklore and cosmology of Esmeraldas.[15] The prize-winning novels of Nelson Estupiñán Bass, *El ultimo río* (1966) and *Senderos brillantes* (1974), are required reading for learning about black culture in Esmeraldas, and his essay 'Apuntes sobre el negro de Esmeraldas en la literatura ecuatoriana' (1967) underscores themes currently salient in Ecuador. The book by Julio Estupiñán Tello, *El negro en Esmeraldas* (1967), skilfully blends history and lore animated by literary techniques.

Constance García Barrio reviews this literature and more.[16] She clearly identifies 'outsiders looking in' as a genre of literature *about* black people, and then, from the standpoint of black literature itself, identifies a number of themes, including 'slavery, and flight from it', 'folklore', 'daily life and customs', 'racial mixture–racial identity' and 'conflicts of culture'. Literature,

including novels, short stories and poems, is a critically important window through which to understand meanings of blackness. The black writers of Ecuador have contributed significantly
to this subject by drawing on local themes and understanding
their global dimensions.

Recent and present developments

On 30 January 1988, following some years of discussion, people
in Esmeraldas formed La Asociación de Negros del Ecuador
(ASONE – the Association of Ecuadorian Blacks). It included
black people from the urban areas of Guayaquil, Quito and Ibarra and from other cities in the Sierra and Coast, and from the
regions of Loja and Chota–Mira, as well as from Esmeraldas. One
of its principal themes was, and is, 'rescate de la dignidad
nacional', to 'rescue national dignity'. This rescue is of a dignity
that cannot exist while racism prevails. The movement is black
ethnic nationalist and it is also nation-state nationalist. It seeks
to 'minimize the Spanish yoke' that has held black, indigenous
and other peoples in check for a half-millennium. It seeks modernization of the economy while maintaining the skills of subsistence. Leaders currently prominent in ASONE, which is
intensively involved in reversing the ecological destruction
caused by lumber companies and shrimp farms, include Nel
Pimentel and Simón Estrada.

Another development reported by activist Renán Tadeo, a
researcher at the Centro Cultural Afro-Ecuatoriano, is significantly improved relationships between the black people of the Chota–
Mira Valley and those of Esmeraldas. Relationships between such
people were often characterized by suspicion and by various
forms of covert and overt conflict. The will to forge black unity in
Ecuador across economic, ecological and socio-political barriers is
strong, as is the movement, in some sectors, to unite indigenous
and black organizations. Countering this is the hiring by *hacendados* of black paramilitary bands to intimidate indigenous and
other people in the rural hinterlands in various parts of the
nation, including Imbabura and Carchi in particular.

According to Jacinto Fierro, who is from Borbón, in northern

Esmeraldas, opportunities for black people to advance their education in secondary schools and universities have increased significantly. The movements of musical groups, mentioned above, are important, and their incorporation of more and more aspects of selected global movements (such as *salsa*), while at the same time digging deeper for their own cultural roots by reference to the musical knowledge and skills of their living forebears, is obvious.

One form of racism in Ecuador today is that of ecological transformation to the benefit of non-black people, and to the disenfranchisement of black people. Since the majority of black people in Esmeraldas have been coded in economic schemes as living on 'uninhabited lands' (*tierras baldías*), they have long been targeted for displacement. In Esmeraldas today the rape of the forest is well under way; in some areas black and indigenous people clash, while in others they unite. The mangrove swamps, the most productive region for economic exploitation for subsistence and market economies for black people, are being systematically and completely destroyed by shrimp farmers, while the naval personnel responsible for protecting the swamps look on and do nothing.

There have been serious ethnic clashes in Ecuador over the past decade. In 1991 in San Lorenzo, Esmeraldas Province, black townsmen and townswomen stormed the naval base to protest against the torture and killing of a black man from Borbón; black lives were lost. News about such clashes is quickly suppressed, and very little is forthcoming from the media. In 1992 black people from Esmeraldas province joined indigenous peoples in a protest march from Puyo, in the Amazonian Region, to Quito. Later, black people from San Lorenzo vowed to initiate a black march from that port town to Quito, and they wanted the black Andeans of Imbabura and Carchi provinces to join them. As of May 1995, the march had not taken place, though the rhetoric of its imminence continues to surface. The rhetoric of the central government of Ecuador promises immediate repressive military action should such a march begin.

Black discourse at national levels stresses the positive powers of blackness, and the negative effects of white and *mestizo* exploitation and disenfranchisement of Afro-Latin American peoples of Ecuador.

Minorities and human rights in Ecuador

Ecuador is today governed by an ideology of *mestizaje*, which is itself driven by the spirit of *blanqueamiento* – ethnic, cultural and racial whitening. The concept of *mejor la raza* ('improve the race') has been important throughout Ecuador's history, and is stressed today as it was centuries ago. The current President, Sixto Durán Ballén, spoke of blackness and indigenization during his inaugural speech; this was only the second time that such an issue, including 'blackness', was raised at this important event. But unlike the first President to raise the issue of blackness, Jaime Roldós Aguilera, who spoke of Ecuadorian pluralism and pleaded for tolerance for all Ecuadorian people during his assumption of office in 1979, Durán Ballén stressed *mestizaje*.

For nation-state nationalists and developers, those who are black and indigenous constitute a 'problem' for the nation, one that can only be solved when people of colour and varied cultural practices and beliefs accept the elite-generated goals of ethnic and racial intermingling. Unfortunately, such alleged intermingling leaves black and indigenous peoples – who together constitute more than 30 per cent of the republic – at the antipodes of the ethnic spectrum, as illustrated at the beginning of this chapter.[17]

Ecuador is now being scrutinized by international agencies for alleged human rights violations. Data are not available on human rights activities, or lack thereof, vis-à-vis black people, and they are skimpy for indigenous people. However, the anecdotal and casual information available indicates significant prejudice of white and *mestizo* officials towards black people when any conflict of interest involving a black person and a non-black person occurs.

Gender issues and children

Black women clearly vie for position as domestic workers with indigenous women. That more and more Quito households have black maids is clear. Through a combination of domestic work for black women, and other sporadic work for black men, the black population of Quito has grown significantly over the past two decades, and upward mobility in that city is also obvious. In rural areas all children have access to schooling up to the sixth grade, but after that relatively few, though perhaps in increasing percentages, can move to higher levels of education. Men and women seem to have about an even chance of securing higher education. The military presents an opportunity for some black men to gain access to higher education, and through it to higher-paying positions.

Social movements and mobilizations

During the nationalist build-ups to the 1492-1992 quincentennial celebrations in Ecuador and Colombia, cultural images of a distinct 'Latin American–Iberian' unified identity became very important. The elite in these nations, who identify themselves as *blanco*, stressed that the national identity symbol should be that of *mestizaje* (racial intermingling) to emphasize Latin America's heritage in the 500th year since European 'discovery' and 'civilizing conquest' began. In direct opposition to this elite-sponsored nationalist identity emblem, black spokesmen and spokeswomen rejected 'Hispanic' (Iberian) designations and stressed 'Afro-Latin American culture' as their preferred designation. They also stressed the dynamics of racism built into *mestizaje* representations, and contested the use of such pejorative labels as 'darkening' to refer to socio-economic processes analogous to colours of skin and other physical features.

The concept of 'Afro-Latin American culture' emerged in Ecuador in 1992. It draws attention to the three emphases that characterize modern black people who maintain their dynamic and traditional lifestyles there: they are *of* 'Latin America'; they stem *from* Africa; and they *are* black. 'Latin American' in this context contrasts with 'Anglo-American', and 'Africa' contrasts with 'Iberian Europe'.

In Esmeraldas a small park has been established with the name of Mandela. There, every afternoon, black people gather informally to discuss the way in which blackness is perceived as inferior to whiteness. They undertake sophisticated analysis of language, talk, reference and representation. For example, they contest the phrase *mejor la raza* with another, *hacer valer la raza*. By this is meant that blackness, for black or dark people, is to be of worth, of value, and with this phrase they also call to account the discriminatory language of blackness presented daily to them through all media oriented towards 'whitening'. The principal contrast is that of the developers' *despreciar*, disrespect for their physical features and lifestyles, and the assertion of Afro-Ecuadorian leaders and speakers of the need for *respecto* (respect) for black people, their lifeways and viewpoints, if the nation-state of Ecuador is 'to rescue its national dignity'.

Use of language drawn from the domain of economics is common in the positive rhetoric of indigenous and black movements in Ecuador; it signals, among other things, that respect for the humanity of black and indigenous peoples, and the economic worth of such peoples, are inextricably bound together. This liberating figure of speech is amplified by expressions such as 'Do not accept any more terms [or terminologies] against our dignity and promote the belief in our intellectual capacity.'[18] This small park in Esmeraldas is emblematic of sites throughout Ecuador where small groups of black people gather to talk of their history, their present and their collective and individual fates and destinies in the futures of the various nation-states that make up the Americas.

Prospects for the future

The black population of Ecuador is expanding in numbers, diversifying in the sectors available for black enfranchisement and moving in search of new and better opportunities. Ties between black people in rural and urban areas are becoming stronger as the national infrastructure expands. A number of loosely articulated black movements dot the provinces of Esmeraldas and Imbabura–Carchi, and groups in Ibarra, Quito and Guayaquil engage the nationalist rhetoric of *mestizaje* with their international, national, regional and local discourses of *negritud* (blackness).

Racist barriers truncate movements, and localize them. Difficulties with access to funds for ideological and social mobilization for black people are many, in striking contrast to the pools of international money available to indigenous peoples. It is not clear whether human rights agencies are as interested in black problems as they are in those of some indigenous people. What black people have in Ecuador today they have taken for themselves, against astounding odds and adversities.

Black people say that research into their communities and cultures is lacking; international attention would be greatly appreciated. But little serious research is being done, in spite of the collaborative mood between local people of colour and international scholarship that could prevail.

There are three dimensions to affirmative blackness in Ecuador. The first is in the realm of globalization of interest and concern. Do people in Europe and the United States really listen to black voices from Ecuador? If so, do they respond positively as they do with indigenous movements and movements to 'save the rainforests'? We think not, although publication of this book is certainly a positive step towards the much needed globalization of information.

The second dimension is one of serious research in Afro-Latin American communities in the hemisphere. 'Community studies' are not in vogue in anthropology and sociology. But people live in communities, and it is there that they talk intensively to one another, and wish their voices to be heard. A call for serious studies in communities to see what, indeed, a *comunidad negra* is in the late twentieth century, and the twenty-first century, is essential. The world needs to know how people live, what they say, what they see, feel and seek in life and in afterlife.

The third dimension is developing access to opportunity so that people who live Afro-Latin American lives, whatever those lives may be, have greatly increased opportunities for formal education so that they, at last, can undertake studies of what they deem significant. This call for research and appreciation of black lifeways in Ecuador, as elsewhere, demands an integrated and creative cross-disciplinary approach that treats seriously the ethnography, history, literature and richness of culture of Afro-Latin American peoples everywhere. The Afro-Latin Americans of Ecuador are ready and willing to participate in multiple and creative ways in such an endeavour.

Acknowledgments

We could not have prepared this chapter without the sustained help and support of P. Rafael Savoia, Director of the Afro-Ecuadorian Cultural Center, Quito, Guayaquil and Esmeraldas, and his staff. Ana Rosa Menéndez also helped with the project that resulted in this chapter, at a preliminary stage. Our colleague at the University of Illinois at Urbana-Champaign, Dr Arlene Torres, read and commented on a draft of this chapter. We are responsible for any errors of commission and omission that may come to light in what we hope will be sustained future research.

Notes

1 Estupiñán Bass, N., 'Canción del niño negro y del incendio' ('Song of the black child and of the conflagration'), in *Canto negro por la luz: poemas para negros y blancos,* Esmeraldas, Casa de la Cultura Ecuatoriana, 1954, pp. 50, 53.

   Black, black, blackened
   black, brother of charcoal,
   black of blacks born,
   black yesterday, today and tomorrow,
   Some believe they insult me
   mocking my colour,
   but I myself proclaim it
   with pride in the face of the sun:
   Black I have been, black I am,
   black I come, black I go,
   black real black I was born,
   black black I must live,
   and as black must die.

2 Whitten, N.E. Jr, *Black Frontiersmen: Afro-Hispanic Culture of Ecuador and Colombia,* Prospect Heights, IL, Waveland Press, 4th edn, 1985.
3 E.g. Stutzman, R., *Black Highlanders: Racism and Ethnic Stratification in the Ecuadorian Sierra,* PhD thesis in anthropology, Washington University, St Louis – Ann Arbor, MI, University Microfilms, 1974; Colonel Feijóo, F., *El valle sangrieto,* Quito, Abya-Yala, 1991, p. 19.
4 Colonel, op. cit., pp. 88, 94.
5 *Hoy,* 25 March 1990.
6 See Peñaherrera de Costales, P. and Costales Samaniego, A., *Coangue o historia cultural y social de los negros del Chota y Salinas,* Llacta no. 7, Quito, Organo de Publicación Semestral de Instituto Ecuatoriano de Antropología y Geografía, 1959; Klump, K., 'Black traders of north highland Ecuador', in N.E. Whitten and J.F. Szwed (eds), *Afro-American Anthropology: Contemporary Perspectives,* New York, Free Press, 1970; Stutzman, op. cit.
7 Rafael Savoia, P., personal communication, November 1994.

8 Anda Aguirre, A., *Indios y negros bajo el dominio español en Loja*, Quito, Abya-Yala, 1993, p. 257.
9 Ibid., p. 258.
10 See Forbes, J.D., *Africans and Native Americans: The Language of Race and the Evolution of Red-Black Peoples*, Urbana, IL, University of Illinois Press, 2nd edn, 1993, pp. 67-8.
11 Ibid., pp. 131-3.
12 Ibid., pp. 93-238.
13 See Whitten, N.E. and Torres, A. (eds), *To Forge the Future in the Fires of the Past: Blackness in Latin America and the Caribbean*, New York, Carlson Publishing, 2 vols, 1995.
14 Preciado Bedoya, A., *Jolgorio [Joy]: Poems*, trans. M. Lewis, 1983, pp. 121-2:

Barrio of blacks
of dark streets
bursting with spooks
that carry off, that frighten,
that make hairs stand
on moonless nights

Inflamed barrio
by night and by day,
black hell
enveloped in the flames
of rhythm and happiness.

15 Quiroga, D., *Saints, Virgins and the Devil: Witchcraft, Magic and Healing in the Northern Coast of Ecuador*, PhD thesis in anthropology, University of Illinois at Urbana-Champaign – Ann Arbor, MI, University Microfilms, 1993.
16 In Whitten, N.E. Jr, *Cultural Transformations and Ethnicity in Modern Ecuador*, Urbana, IL, University of Illinois Press, 1981, pp. 535-62.
17 In January 1995 armed border conflict again erupted between Ecuador and Peru. Two salient images of savagery and barbarism in defence of the fatherland (*la patria*) appeared on national television. One of these depicted a 'Shuar' ('Jívaro') native person of the Cordillera de Condor holding a machete in his right hand, and a reduced head (monkey or human) aloft in his left hand. 'This is what I will do to Fujimori' (the President of Peru), read the subtitle to this violent imagery of jungle savagery. The other image was that of huge black men, all more than six feet tall, preparing for movement to the frontier, in 'dangerous Jívaro country'. The announcer explained that these black people were from Esmeraldas, and specially trained in guerrilla warfare near the Taura airforce base near Guayaquil. He proceeded to explain that black people were a 'race adapted to the jungle', that 'they fought naked from the waist up in the jungle'. The negative, racist imagery of savage (jungle-dwelling, head-taking Jívaro) and huge barbarian (jungle-dwelling, bare-chested, machete-wielding *cimarrón*) – both of which are rejected antipodes of Ecuadorian nationality during quotidian times – were

raised as hyper-positive symbols of nationalism in the defence of *la patria* in the liminal space of death and destruction wherein Ecuador was engaged in sustained armed struggle with its historic nation-state adversary.

18 See e.g. the magazine *Otra, 18* May 1990, p. 70.

Select bibliography and works cited

Anda Aguirre, A., *Indios y negros bajo el dominio español en Loja*, Quito, Abya-Yala, 1993.

Cabello Balboa, M., *Obras*, vol. 1, Quito, Editorial Ecuatoriana, 1945 [1583].

Colonel Feijóo, R., *El valle sangrieto*, Quito, Abya-Yala, 1991.

Estupiñán Bass, N., *Canto negro por la luz: poemas para negros y blancos*, Esmeraldas, Casa de la Cultura Ecuatoriana, 1954.

Estupiñán Bass, N., *El ultimo río*, Quito, Casa de la Cultura Ecuatoriana, 1966.

Estupiñán Bass, N., *Senderos brillantes*, Quito, Casa de la Cultura Ecuatoriana, 1974.

Forbes, J.D., *Africans and Native Americans: The Language of Race and the Evolution of Red-Black Peoples*, Urbana, IL, University of Illinois Press, 2nd edn, 1993 [1988].

García, J., *Cuentos y décimas afro-esmeraldeñas*, Quito, Abya-Yala, 2nd edn, 1988.

Girardi, G., *Los excluídos: ¿constrirán la nueva história? El movimiento indígena, negro, y popular*, Quito, Centro Cultural Afro-Ecuatoriano and Ediciones Nicarao, 1994.

Jurado Noboa, F., *Esclavitud en la costa pacífica: Iscuandé, Barbacoas, Tumaco y Esmeraldas, siglos XVI al XIX*, Quito, Centro Afro-Ecuatoriano, Corporación Ecuatoriana de 'Amigos de la Genealogía' (SAG) and Abya-Yala, 1990.

Ortiz, A., *Juyungo: historia de un negro, una isla, y otros negros*, Buenos Aires, Editorial Americalee, 1942.

Ortiz, A., *La entundada y cuentos variados*, Quito, Casa de la Cultura Ecuatoriana, 1971.

Ortiz, A. et al., *Antología de cuentos esmeraldeños*, Quito, Casa de la Cultura Ecuatoriana, 1960.

Peralta Rivera, G., *Los mecanismos del comercio negrero*, Lima, Kuntur Editores, 1990.

Peñaherrera de Costales, P. and Costales Samaniego, A., *Coangue o historia cultural y social de los negros del Chota y Salinas*, Llacta no. 7, Quito, Organo de Publicación Semestral de Instituto Ecuatoriano de Antropología y Geografía, 1959.

Quiroga, D., *Saints, Virgins and the Devil: Witchcraft, Magic, and Healing in the Northern Coast of Ecuador*, PhD thesis in anthropology, University of Illinois at Urbana-Champaign – Ann Arbor, MI, University Microfilms, 1993.

Rahier, J., *La décima: poesía oral negra del Ecuador*, Quito, Abya-Yala and Centro Cultural Afro-Ecuatoriana, n.d., c.1990.

Savoia, P.R. (ed.), *El negro en la historia: aportes para el conocimiento de las raíces en América Latina*, Quito, Centro Cultural Afro-Ecuatoriano, 1990.

Stutzman, R., *Black Highlanders: Racism and Ethnic Stratification in the Ecuadorian Sierra*, PhD thesis in anthropology, Washington University, St Louis – Ann Arbor, MI, University Microfilms, 1974.

Whitten, N.E. Jr, *Class, Kinship, and Power in an Ecuadorian Town: The Negroes of San Lorenzo*, Stanford, CA, Stanford University Press, 1965.

Whitten, N.E. Jr (ed.), *Cultural Transformations and Ethnicity in Modern Ecuador*, Urbana, IL, University of Illinois Press, 1981.

Whitten, N.E. Jr, *Sicuanga Runa: The Other Side of Development in Amazonian Ecuador*, Urbana, IL, University of Illinois Press, 1984.

Whitten, N.E. Jr, *Black Frontiersmen: Afro-Hispanic Culture of Ecuador and Colombia*, Prospect Heights, IL, Waveland Press, 4th edn, 1985 [1974].

Whitten, N.E. Jr, *Pioneros negros: la cultura afro-latinoamericana del Ecuador y de Colombia*, Quito, Centro Cultural Afro-Ecuatoriano, 1993.

Whitten, N.E. and Szwed, J.F. (eds), *Afro-American Anthropology: Contemporary Perspectives*, New York, Free Press, 1970.

Whitten, N.E. and Torres, A. (eds) *To Forge the Future in the Fires of the Past: Blackness in Latin America and the Caribbean*, New York, Carlson Publishing, 2 vols, 1995.

11
BOLIVIA AND URUGUAY

BOLIVIA

Alison Spedding

As in most of the New World, the origin of Bolivia's Afro-Latin minority lies in the colonial slave trade. Most of the ancestors of today's Afro-Bolivians arrived before independence (in 1825), and a considerable black minority was present in Bolivia throughout the colonial period. Due to the relatively open ethnic structures of local society, however, and the lack of a binary racial and ethnic classification or pronounced colour prejudice, they intermarried with both *criollos* (native-born 'white' people) and native Andeans. As a result, most Afro-Bolivians merged with the local population, and today there are only a few regions where a visible minority persists – above all, the provinces of Nor and Sud Yungas in the Department of La Paz.

Black people are usually referred to as *negros*; the term *afro-bolivianos* has appeared only in the past ten years with the birth of the black consciousness movement. Up to the middle of this century they might also have been referred to as *morenos*, although both these terms are also used to describe people of dark colouring due to indigenous descent. People who display some 'black' physical characteristics such as notably wavy hair (called *chiri* in Aymara) may be called *zambos* (black-indigenous 'mixed bloods'); very rarely they are called *mulatos*. Mixed marriages are common, and within the same family some children may look very black while others look purely indigenous. The Bolivian population in general, and particularly in Yungas, is very mixed, and it is equally common to find within one family some children who are pale-skinned and look quite European while others have classic indigenous features.

As a result, it is difficult to define exactly who should be considered Afro-Bolivian, and 'black' has not appeared as a census category in the modern era; thus, there are at present no figures on the actual number of Afro-Bolivians, although they have recently requested that they should be counted separately and are considering carrying out their own census. A casual (and probably too low) estimate based on personal observation in Yungas suggests that in the region there may be 10,000 or 15,000 individuals who look Afro-Bolivian and would be called *negros*, and many more of mixed blood; it is impossible to guess how many more there are in other parts of the country, especially in Santa Cruz, where black people have tended to migrate from Yungas.

History

The first Africans arrived in Bolivia in 1535 with the expedition of Diego de Almagro. By 1650 there were about 30,000 Africans in a total population of some 850,000 in the then Audience of Charcas; about 700,000 of the population were considered 'Indians' (the distinction between indigenous people and *mestizos* or other 'mixed-bloods' was, and is, based largely on language, dress, social class and general cultural characteristics – ethnicity rather than 'race' as such). At this time, most of these black people were slaves. Some are cited as *bozales* – that is, born in Africa, mostly in Angola or the Congo – but a large proportion were *criollos*, or Americas-born. The *bozales* were never sufficiently numerous to organize themselves into 'nations' according to origin, as occurred in Lima, Montevideo, Buenos Aires and various Brazilian cities. This, evidently, has much to do with the fact that today's Afro-Bolivians have adopted local Andean culture, including the Aymara language, and have not maintained a separate identity with respect to religion, for instance, although there are some indications that syncretic cults similar to those found in Brazil existed among urban black people in the eighteenth century.

At this time the majority of Afro-Bolivians were urban, house slaves or artisans. Their value rose in so far as they dominated certain specialized skills such as carpentry or fancy baking. They could purchase their liberty, but this was rare; it was more common for them to be freed in the owner's will. In the mining centre of Potosi, Afro-Bolivian slaves served in the Royal Mint – since they could be permanently shut up inside the mint, it was more convenient to employ them than free workers, who would have found it too easy to steal silver – but they never seem to have worked in the mines, which were staffed by indigenous labourers, forced (*mitayos*) or free. Some haciendas were also staffed by slave labourers, particularly in the Yungas, where the subtropical climate was considered more suitable for them, but their numbers were never very large. The most important Afro-Bolivian communities today correspond to colonial haciendas in Nor Yungas, such as Mururata, which appear to have been entirely staffed by slaves; in Sud Yungas the haciendas with slave labourers always included other *colonos* (labour tenants) of Altiplano origin, and these seem usually to have been in the majority.

A study written by a hacienda administrator, Francisco Xavier de Bergara, in 1805 explains why this was so. He calculated that, although black people did not receive *aculli* (coca-chewing breaks) as the indigenous people did, and thus worked longer hours, they cost money compared with the indigenous people, who were free. They had to be given medical treatment when they fell ill, and to be guarded and pursued if they ran away, in order not to lose the investment. The owner also had to feed and clothe them and pay for their weddings and funerals; the slaves did receive a small wage, but it seems that this did not cover their requirements, and they were not given usufruct plots as was the case with indigenous *colonos*. Although the slaves' offspring represented a profit, the owner lost the mother's labour during the last months of her pregnancy and the first months after giving birth, and the child started to work only at the age of 7. If the child died before this, as many did, it represented a total loss, and in reality it was cheaper to buy children than to 'breed' them.[1] The conclusion was that it was more profitable to staff the hacienda with indigenous *colonos* than to purchase slave labourers. Although Bergara does not mention this, Bolivia is also a long way from the ports (Lima, Buenos Aires) where the slaves arrived, whereas indigenous people were already 'on hand' in the Yungas. It is also significant that there were no large-scale haciendas cultivating export crops in Bolivia, and labour tenancy was more appropriate for haciendas which supplied only national markets.

The gradual process of liberation, and the end of the slave trade with Africa, reduced the numbers of slaves compared with those of free black people or 'mixed-bloods' in Bolivia before the legal abolition of slavery. In 1846, 27,941 black people were counted among a total of 1,373,896 inhabitants, of whom only 1,391 were still slaves. Their liberty was officially declared in 1851, with a limit of five years to allow the owner time to replace them. After this, 'blacks' as a separate category largely disappear from the historical record – something that is related to the general tendency to regard 'ethnicity' as a jural rather than an intrinsic category in Bolivia.[2] Once slaves no longer existed, 'blacks' faded out as a category, since slavery was regarded as the basic condition of their special status. It is not clear why urban Afro-Bolivians did not persist as a recognizable group into the twentieth century. Some suggest that after the end of slavery, or indeed before, they went to the Yungas to work on haciendas as free *colonos*, since the climate was more congenial to them than the chilly highlands where most Bolivian cities are located. The only known fact is that Nor and Sud Yungas are the regions where distinct Afro-Bolivian groups have persisted. Even here, only certain communities are known as partially or mainly Afro-Bolivian: in Nor Yungas, Mururata and Tocaña in the Coroico sector, and Calacala, Dorado Chico, Coscoma and Chillamani in Coripata; in Sud Yungas, Chicaloma, Villa Remedios, El Colpar, Naranjani and Thaco.

Afro-Bolivians in Yungas today

Notably, although observable physical characteristics do not generally have a principal role in Bolivian ethnic classification, in the case of *negros* they are indeed the distinguishing factor. Most

Afro-Bolivians have been assimilated into the local peasant culture, which is a version of the Aymara-speaking peasant culture of
the neighbouring Altiplano and valleys,[3] the place of origin of the
majority of Yungas dwellers. Like other Yungueños, most black
people are bilingual in Spanish and Aymara, and cultivate the
same crops (coca, coffee and oranges for sale, plus a variety of
taro, bananas, sweet cassava, and so on, for subsistence) using the
same methods. Afro-Bolivian women wear the same dress as
indigenous peasant women. This is typified by a wide, flounced
skirt known as a *pollera* and a bowler hat; they even twist their
hair into two tiny plaits joined by a tasselled band, just as the
indigenous women arrange their long straight hair in two plaits.
There are some black *yatiris* (wise people, *curanderos*) but their
religious practice (according to Jaime Salinas Lira, from Lasa, Sud
Yungas, whose grandfather was a black *yatiri*) shares the Catholic–
Andean syncretism of the rest of the population (divination in
coca, cult of mountains and other earth spirits, and so on). Likewise, Afro-Bolivian family structure is no different from that of
other Yungas peasant or small-town families. The 'matrifocal families' common in the Caribbean are not found here, and Afro-
Bolivian families follow the region's matrimonial customs,
involving the formal 'asking for the hand' of the bride and a visit
from the bridegroom's family to the bride's with gifts of coca and
alcohol, usually preceded by the elopement of the young couple
and followed by a legal marriage some years later, or not at all.

Distinguishing characteristics of Afro-Bolivians in Yungas,
apart from their appearance, are their surnames, which can at
times be identified as surnames of former slave-owning *hacienda-
dos*, and are distinct from the Andean or Spanish surnames of
the rest of the population. Typical Afro-Bolivian surnames are
Angola (evidently in this case the place of origin), Pinedo, Zavala
(two slave-owning families), Casisima and Arrascaita, although
other surnames such as Medina, Flores, Torrez and Peralta are
shared with other groups.

Coroico, Nor Yungas, seems to have had the largest concentration of pure-African slave haciendas owned by colonial Spanish
aristocrats, and this is the region where Afro-Bolivians have
maintained the most separate identity and rejected contact with

their indigenous neighbours. Here, it seems, they at least claim not to speak Aymara, although all the Afro-Bolivians in Arapata and Coripata (Nor Yungas) and Sud Yungas do. They speak a dialect of local Spanish with an accent and styles of expression different from those used by Aymara–Spanish bilingual speakers. The hacienda of Mururata maintained a 'black king' (*rey negro*) among its slaves, and later among its *colonos* after emancipation. This 'king' was reputed to be the descendant of an African prince brought there as a slave in 1600. The landowners provided him with a sceptre, cape and crown (supposed to have replaced more valuable originals sent over from Africa by his family); he was excused from the usual labour services, and at Easter and other festivals was carried in a litter by other Afro-Bolivians. He also performed a dance called the *zemba*, reputed to be of African origin, although old people earlier this century have claimed that in the past all black people used to do this dance. The last 'black king', Bonifacio Pinedo, died in the 1960s, but his grandson – who now lives in La Paz – has recently been named as his successor.

Music and dance are the other principal elements of Afro-Bolivian identity. The best-known dance is the *saya*, performed by men who play a series of drums of different sizes: the largest is the *bajo*, followed by the *caja*, the *requinto* and the smallest, the *quayingo* or *cachimba*. Each is beaten with a *jawq'aña* (the Aymara for 'to hit with a stick') in a different rhythm, accompanied by a ridged gourd called a *kuancha* or *rig'i rig'i* that is played with a stick and sounds like a washboard. A troupe of women accompany the men, dancing and singing in high voices. An older married woman leads them, and the men are led by a *caporal*, who wears bells on his legs and brandishes a whip as a sign of authority. Other Afro-Bolivian dances now forgotten or rarely seen are the *tundiqui* and the aforementioned *zemba*. Afro-Bolivians sing in styles different from those of the mainly indigenous communities, and on different occasions; in particular they sing at funerals. For instance, in Tocaña, there is a funeral song called the *mauchi*, with words in Spanish. This is sung on the way back from the cemetery and formally accompanied by a slow dance performed by a line of men and a line of women. The indigenous communities in Yungas do not sing on these occasions, except for a few Catholic or evangelical hymns (generally in Aymara) at the moment of burial, and they consider dancing taboo at funerals. Wedding songs in Spanish also have a place among the Afro-Bolivian communities.

Perhaps the major difference between Afro-Bolivians and the majority of the Yungas population is that the former have no relatives in the Altiplano or the upland valleys. As a result, they do not travel there either to visit or to exchange products from the different ecological zones; much less do they marry up there (it is more common for uplanders to marry down into Yungas). Although they do consume (for instance) salt fish from Lake Titicaca, they are known for their preference for traditional Yungas products such as *quineo k'asurata* (a type of banana peeled while green, sun-dried for a few days and eaten boiled), and seem to have little interest in Altiplano products such as *ch'uñu* (freeze-dried potatoes) which are much esteemed among Aymara-speakers. Their migration patterns are also different; while other Yungueños prefer to migrate to La Paz, there is a considerable current of Afro-Bolivian migration to the eastern lowland city of Santa Cruz. The reason given for this is that they find its hot climate more congenial than that of chilly La Paz, but the absence of kin connections in the highlands is no doubt an influential factor as well.

Relations between ethnic groups

The class position of Afro-Bolivians is the same as that of Aymara-speaking peasants and lower-class urban dwellers. Both are distinguished from middle- and upper-class *mistis/mestizos* or 'whites' (as already stated, these are class rather than racial terms; there are plenty of 'white' Aymara-speakers in the Yungas and elsewhere). Their problems relating to employment, education and the position of women and children are not significantly different from those of other Bolivians of the same class. In one sense they are more discriminated against; since indigenous people, *mestizos* and 'whites' in Bolivia are not defined by colour, it is possible for someone of indigenous origin to achieve social mobility through education and economic success, but Afro-Bolivians can never escape from their category – unless perhaps through intermarriage.

There is some social stereotyping relating to Afro-Bolivians. The middle classes tend to see them as more sociable, affectionate and lively than indigenous people. The historic association of *criollo* masters and African house slaves probably explains why Afro-Bolivian women are thought to be cleaner and more competent as domestic servants than Andean women, and also why Afro-Bolivians regard themselves as more 'refined' – that is, adjusted to *criollo* values – than Andeans. Afro-Bolivians are also thought to be lucky and to have curative powers. This is probably derived from Andean colour symbolism, which attributes superior nutritive and curative value to the meat, milk, blood, and so on, of a black animal compared with that of an animal of the same species but of another colour.

In Nor Yungas, particularly Coroico, Afro-Bolivians tend not to socialize or to intermarry much with others, but in Sud Yungas mixed marriages are common,[4] and at times preferred. In this region the Afro-Bolivians (at least until recently) have declined as a distinct group through intermarriage, and there are references to communities such as Miguillas which were 'black' in the early decades of this century but no longer have any Afro-Bolivian residents. Black women in particular are seen as attractive. This is perhaps a relic of slavery; slave status was matrilineal, and consequently slave owners tried to deter male slaves from marrying non-black people so as not to lose their offspring, whereas this would not have been a problem with a female slave. There is, however, no evidence at all of institutionalized hostility between Afro-Bolivians and others; and in cases of social conflict, now or in the past, Afro-Bolivians show solidarity with their class fellows regardless of ethnicity – as when they took part as musketeers in the Tupaj Katari indigenous uprising of 1780-2.

The new social movement

Despite some references to traditions of African descent in Muru-rata, Jaime Salinas reports that most of the Afro-Bolivians he knows in Yungas do not regard themselves as Africans – 'they thought they had always been Bolivians' – or recall anything about slavery. In the 1980s the few distinct Afro-Bolivian charac-teristics such as Spanish dialect or music were being abandoned in many communities; there is no evidence that institutions such as the organization of Afro-Bolivian men of the same gener-ation into groups called *categorías* (reported for Chicaloma in the 1960s)[5] have persisted into the present. The traditional *saya* such as that recorded by the folk group Los Payas in Naranjani in 1970 was rarely heard, except in a bowdlerized form performed by non-black people, with their faces painted and using congas instead of the correct instruments.

This trend has recently been reversed with its first impulse coming from the revival of the *saya* dance in the community of Tocaña, apparently at the instigation of a teacher in the Coroico high school. This troupe has had great success as the Saya Afrobo-liviana, and its members have become semi-professional perform-ers in La Paz and elsewhere. The success of this group provoked Afro-Bolivians in Chicaloma and El Colpar to dig out their old *saya* drums (which no one made any more) and form their own troupes, which they claim to be much more 'original' – that is, faithful to tradition – than the Tocaña group. It is certain that, although the Tocaña performers wear *polleras* and other items of traditional dress on stage, they wear Western styles for everyday use, and many of the women have adopted styles of international 'Afro-culture' such as corn rows or beads in their hair rather than the two plaits typical of Yungas black women.

The first 'meeting' (*encuentro*) of Afro-Bolivians in Yungas was held in 1992, followed by a second, and the third took place in Coripata, 22-24 September 1994. There is some competition between the less 'mixed' Coroico communities, who would like to assert a monopoly of Afro-Bolivian identity, and the other com-munities who are more integrated with their non-black neigh-bours. The main emphasis of these meetings so far has been music and dance – attempting to revive purer forms of the *saya* and combat 'folklorized' versions of it, which, they say, are merely the popular *caporal* dance with drums incorporated. Only recently has an interest in history and cultural tradition appeared within this incipient movement, made more difficult by the extreme paucity to date of published – or unpublished – material about the African presence in Bolivia.

The embryonic Afro-Bolivian social movement may be seen as part of a general ethnic resurgence currently taking place in Bolivia, focused particularly in ethnic minorities such as the Guarani-speakers and other small ethnic groups in the tropical lowlands. The recently established government department of ethnic affairs (*asuntos étnicos*) is conducting a census of these groups and intends to do the same with the Afro-Bolivians. There are plans to introduce bilingual education in Spanish and various indigenous languages. Other concerns are the establishment and defence of ethnic territories, and preventing their exploitation by loggers, cattle ranchers and others. These last, however, do not affect the Afro-Bolivians, and it seems likely that the movement will be primarily cultural and artistic.

The social and economic problems faced by Afro-Bolivians in Yungas – environmental deterioration, the low prices for agricultural produce, the US-sponsored demands for the eradication of coca cultivation, and so on – are shared with all the other inhabitants of the region and can best be confronted by participating in the existing regional organizations such as the Peasant Federation and the Association of Coca Producers. Attempts such as occurred in the community of Villa Barrientos, where the Afro-Bolivian inhabitants tried to organize their own peasant syndicate separately from non-blacks, proved counterproductive and have been abandoned. The peasant syndicate is the organ of local government in the countryside; each community syndicate is autonomous, but is affiliated to the provincial, departmental and national peasant federations. Likewise, any attempt to obtain special resources in health, education or other services, whether from the government or from non-governmental organizations, would be likely to provoke ethnic conflict and division where it does not at present exist.

The nascent movement, however, faces certain problems of organization. On the one hand, there is the aforementioned regionalism, whereby each of the scattered communities, and more particularly those from the Coroico sector, sees itself as *the* repository of Afro-Bolivian culture and tends to deny validity to the others. There is also a wish to avoid a 'folklorization' of the culture and its use for merely touristic or propagandist purposes. This was what happened with the recent crowning of a new 'black king'; it turned out to be no more than a publicity stunt staged by a middle-class non-black person to promote the hotel he had set up in the former hacienda house at Mururata. The local Afro-Bolivian community was not consulted or even invited to the event, and when representatives of the Afro-Bolivian movement later tried to contact the 'king' he showed no desire to take part in their activities.

On the other hand, there are considerable class differences between Afro-Bolivians, especially between those who live in cities and have salaried employment, and those who are peasant farmers in the countryside. The first group includes many members of the semi-professional Saya Afroboliviana, intellectuals and others, and is likely to provide potential leaders for the movement; rural Afro-Bolivians work in agriculture and have neither time nor resources for travelling, added to which they live in isolated communities where communications are poor, although they make the most effort to preserve Afro-Bolivian culture. At the same time, they are suspicious of the urban intellectuals, who – as previous experience has confirmed – obtain grants or finance in the name of the social movement but use the money for the consolidation of a new elite rather than for the benefit of the mass of poor Afro-Bolivians in the countryside.

At the 1994 *encuentro* the proposals of the urban participants focused on the creation of an office in La Paz with fax and telephone for communication with international organizations rather than on any idea of working with rural Afro-Bolivians, the vast majority of whom have so far taken no part in the movement. This is a dilemma faced by many of the new ethnic organizations, whose leaders tend to adopt a lifestyle increasingly divergent from that of the ethnic community they supposedly represent. The rural contingent objects to the fact that urban intellectuals are called upon to go to international conferences and speak in the name of their national ethnic community, although they have not been nominated to do so or in any way chosen by the people. The scattered settlements of the Afro-Bolivian population and the difficulty of communication in the countryside, however, make it difficult to combat this. It remains to be seen if the movement will achieve real grass-roots participation or if it will remain what it is at present – largely the concern of a small group of urban intellectuals.

Notes

1 This report is studied in full in Crespo, A., *Esclavos negros en Bolivia*, La Paz, Academia Nacional de Ciencias, 1977.
2 See Spedding, A., *Wachu wachu: cultivo de coca e identidad en los Yunkas de La Paz*, La Paz, COCAYAPU/CIPCA/HISBOL, 1994, for a general commentary on ethnicity in the Yungas, although black people are not discussed specifically. The only full historical treatment presently available concerning Afro-Bolivians up to the abolition of slavery is Crespo, op. cit., which includes the cited report by Bergara. Some references to blacks in Yungas between 1880 and 1930 can be found in Soux, M.L., *La coca liberal: producción y circulación a principios del siglo XX*, La Paz, COCAYAPU/CID, 1993.
3 It is common to find 'Aymara' used as the name of an ethnic group, in both academic literature and the Bolivian press, but in reality it is the name of a language and not an ethnic group. Speakers of this language, although mainly peasants or lower-class urbanites, are divided into various regional groups with different dialects and customs and do not generally regard themselves as a distinct group defined by language.
4 Leons, M.B., 'Race, ethnicity and political mobilization in the Andes', *American Ethnologist*, vol. 5, no. 3, 1978, estimates that for Chicaloma (Sud Yungas) in the 1960s, 22% of marriages were between blacks and non-blacks, and 37% of marriages involving blacks were to non-blacks.
5 Ibid.

Select bibliography

Crespo, A., *Esclavos negros en Bolivia*, La Paz, Academia Nacional de Ciencias, 1977.
Leons, M.B., 'Race, ethnicity and political mobilization in the Andes', *American Ethnologist*, vol. 5, no. 3, 1978.
Leons, W., 'Las relaciones étnicas de una comunidad multi-racial en los Yungas Bolivianos', *Estudios Andinos*, vol. 4, no. 2, 1975.

Mendoza, D., *El negro no es un color, es una saya*, La Paz, Gobierno Municipal de La Paz, 1993.

Pizarroso Cuenca, A., *La cultura negra en Bolivia*, La Paz, Ediciones ISLA, 1977.

Soux, M.L., *La coca liberal: producción y circulación a principios del siglo XX*, La Paz, COCAYAPU/CID, 1993.

Spedding, A., *Wachu wachu: cultivo de coca e identidad en los Yunkas de La Paz*, COCAYAPU/CIPCA/HISBOL, 1994. (Earlier English version available as 'Wachu wachu: coca cultivation and Aymara identity in the Yunkas of La Paz', PhD thesis, London School of Economics and Political Science, 1989.)

URUGUAY

Alejandrina da Luz

For a long time the Republic of Uruguay has had the dubious privilege of being self-defined as 'the American Switzerland'. The concept sounds exotic, considering that the country is located in South America and that it was colonized by Spaniards and some Portuguese. It bears little resemblance to Switzerland other than its geographical size. Yet this image has remained strong in the minds of many Uruguayans, denoting the kind of inter-ethnic or communal 'harmony' that the country is often said to have achieved. The reality is considerably different.

Colonial slavery

Integrated into the Viceroyalty of the River Plate in the colonial era, Uruguay had no large rural establishments like those elsewhere in South America which permitted the cultivation of cotton, coffee or sugar-cane. Cattle-breeding was the main activity in colonial times, employing relatively few people. Even after independence, most of the national territory was for some years devoted to pasture.

Montevideo, the capital city, founded as an alternative port to Buenos Aires, was, and remains, the biggest urban concentration in the country. Due to its favourable geographical location, it became the gateway to the greatest African slave contingent of the southern part of the colony. All kinds of transactions were carried out in this market and from here caravans with human cargo departed to far-away regions, such as the Viceroyalty of Peru.

Africans entered the Americas as human merchandise, mainly valued as a source of labour. However, in Montevideo, special attention was paid to the slaves' intelligence as well as to their skills and abilities, as they would be used in household tasks and in the care of human and material goods. The Montevidean ruling classes were notorious for their avoidance of mundane occupations: men used to choose government or business, and women religion, society or social gatherings. Care of infants, household duties, cooking and the general satisfaction of everyday domestic and family needs were left in the hands of Africans. In some cases, specially gifted men or female slaves became an extra source of income, for after completing their duties in their owners' homes, they were hired or sent to sell their products elsewhere. This especially applied to good cooks.

The first reactions against slavery took place during the nineteenth century, in Buenos Aires. As of the May Revolution (1910), slave imports were forbidden by a decree signed by Feliciano Antonio Chicana and Bernardino Rivadavia. The provision affected 'the illustrious people of the United Provinces of the River Plate' and was dated 9 April 1812. The same year, on 18 September, the Civic Regiment of Free Mulattos and Coloured People was created, with white officers. Nevertheless, the egalitarian intentions of the Buenos Aires junta rapidly failed in the face of opposition from economic interests, which argued that African liberation would lead to an irrecoverable loss of labour and productivity. The alternative was the Free Womb Act, introduced in Uruguay by José G. Artigas, following the steps taken by the Buenos Aires junta.

National independence and ethnic oppression

Created in 1828, the Republic of Uruguay proclaimed the equality of its inhabitants. Yet there existed two ethnic groups that disturbed the egalitarian harmony, making it difficult for the country's leaders to fulfil their hegemonic group project. These were the indigenous peoples and the Afro-Uruguayans.

The indigenous peoples had played a valuable part in the army of independence. Once the wars finished, they decided to settle close to the northern border of the country, by the River Cuareim. There they defended their communitarian organization, refusing to be assimilated as long as this meant submission. Thus, in 1831, during the first constitutional government, the ethnocide of the indigenous Uruguayans was carried out, led by Bernabé Rivera, the nephew of President Fructoso Rivera.

The situation of Uruguayans of African descent was different, due to their profound importance in the country's everyday life, and because they had already been displaced from their home-lands and had suffered ethnic fragmentation, in another time and on another continent. They did not constitute a real force of opposition, because they were not organized; they had stronger ties with their owners than among themselves. This was largely the result of the separation of slaves who came from the same African nation; during the early years slaves had to resort to their masters' language in order to communicate, because they were for-eigners to each other. Successive generations grew up with Spanish as their own language, and with the language they internalized the stereotypes of the dominant culture – that is, the image of the *negro* as dirty, marginalized and damned by God. To quote J. Hernández in his *Martín Fierro*: 'The Devil created Negroes to be hell's burnt sticks.' They accepted that 'white' meant good, digni-fied and Christian. As Uruguayan society evolved, these primary paradigms became more subtle and complex.

The Uruguayan state solved the 'Negro problem' by abolishing slavery on 12 December 1842. The process took approximately ten years, and only after 1852 can we say that there were no more slaves, as such, in the national territory. Officially, there was now no *alteridad* (perception of the other as different) in Uruguay. Afro-Uruguayans were thus notionally free and equal; but the ruling classes considered them to be people of little intel-lectual capacity, to be vicious and to have very bad working habits. This was made clear in a document sent by the Economic Administrative Junta of Minas in 1852 to the President of the Republic, Dr Juan Francisco Giró:

> *The freedom granted to coloured people previously slaves, putting them in the state opposite to the one they had before the war, has developed in them the spirit of independence that always accom-panies men, in such a way that it makes them insubordinate to any work in which they suffer a superior authority. This makes them lead a lazy life, fed by vices, whose consequences are always a burden on the country's authorities. To avoid the evil that may hence originate, the Junta asks the Government to control the*

service of coloured people in a way that is useful for them and for society in general.

The state replied to this and similar demands by passing a series of regulations, among which was one setting the times during which black people were allowed to circulate in the capital city. Those who violated the rule were sent to prison. Movements outside town were also limited. Besides white people, or those who could produce their employers' authorization, nobody was allowed to stroll in the countryside.

The first fifty years of 'freedom' represented a deterioration in African descendants' quality of life. Afro-Uruguayan men and women had different opportunities: while men could enrol in the army, women continued to work as domestic servants, in both the city and the countryside. Women's domestic work included acting as wet nurses, mainly in patrician families, and providing sexual services to young and not-so-young members of the family. This last activity – more common or not so hidden in rural areas – was also extended to ranch foremen, thus generating a large number of new mixed-race farm labourers. The situation inherited from colonial times reportedly continued unchanged. In very bad cultural and economic conditions, illiterate, and unknown to each other, many rural black women had few other survival strategies.

The coming of change: two communities

By the end of the nineteenth century, the situation had begun to change, in part because of an influx of slaves from Brazil. Uruguayan abolitionist policy represented a promise of freedom for the many Afro-Brazilian slaves who worked in the sugar mills across the border. These people looked for work in the new republic, bringing with them a new sense of self-determination which had a substantial influence on the building of a sense of community. Families started to form between the newcomers and Afro-Uruguayans.

Nationally, this was also a time of change, of increasing urbanization and social development. When in 1904 Aparicio Saravia's rebellion was crushed by the government of José Batlle y Ordóñez, the city secured its predominance over the country-side, as did the centre over the periphery. Afro-Uruguayans could not remain untouched by these events. In its haste to imitate European countries, and especially Switzerland, Batlle's government introduced measures that unintentionally included and benefited Uruguayans of African descent.

At about this time, the first steps in the direction of Afro-Uruguayan organization were taken. These occurred in a religious context as maids attended churches and took part in related activities with other women of their own ethnic background. Yet from the outset, Afro-Uruguayans were divided between the original black community of Montevideo and from the rural areas.

The Afro-Uruguayans of Montevideo had, almost from the beginning, their celebrations on the dates allowed by the colonial authorities. In these celebrations, still known as *llamadas* (drum calls), they reproduced African drum rhythms; starting from the four cardinal points, the drummers 'called each other' at sundown, until they gathered in a frantic and deafening march that ended by the sea that separated them from their lost land. Over the years, characters typical of Uruguayan society were added. Thus 'the old mother' dressed in lace and with a parasol imitates her white mistress; by her side, 'grandfather' in a dress-coat mocks his master, while 'the sweeper' renews the deeds of the African tribal wizard or 'witch doctor'. After liberation the Montevidean black community continued to live on the fringes of the city, in unsanitary wooden houses near the port. By the end of 1880 a fire had devastated this neighbourhood, and the inhabitants moved to *conventillos*, tenements where dozens of families lived together, sharing the bathroom and kitchen. These urban Afro-Uruguayans were not fond of their rural counterparts; paradoxically, they felt closer to white people.

Rural Afro-Uruguayan women, as mentioned already, began to organize through the churches. This rural community rejected all that embodied excesses and the violation of good manners. When members of this group began to migrate to the capital, differences between them and the Afro-Montevideans became evident. This migration, which lasted from the first decade of the century until approximately 1950, produced a new urban group of rural origin.

The people from this group, mainly descendants of slaves who had run away from Brazil, had – and still retain – an outstanding characteristic in common: high self-esteem. They did not deny their ethnic origins, and their aim was not to leave aside their African ethnicity but to conquer those places in society that had been exclusively white. Thus, the new urban community began to establish societies and clubs. They were great self-educators, learning from their employers, from priests and from army officers; every opportunity and every place were used for learning – kitchens and servants' rooms, chauffeurs' seats in politicians' cars, police station watch-rooms and janitors' rooms in public buildings. Education changed and strengthened them for their struggle.

Consolidation in Montevideo

The black population coming from Brazil settled mainly in the departments of Artigas, Rivera and Cerro Largo. Later, they moved to central and southern Uruguay, or in some cases to the western coastal zone. Meanwhile, Batlle's government introduced the country to industrialization; as factory chimneys changed the urban landscape, villages awoke to the need for abundant labour in the cities. Commission agents travelled through the interior of the country, offering jobs in Montevideo, unleashing a massive exodus from the rural areas.

Thus, the sons of servants, cooks and washerwomen boarded trains with no other luggage than a small cardboard suitcase, their Sunday clothes and a scribbled note of the name and address of the owner of the place where they would ask for work. Many also carried the addresses of friends, relatives and acquaintances who had made the trip before them and were now in work and 'very well off'. Those who knew how to read and write, and those who were strong and good at manual work, were rapidly absorbed by the port, warehouses, factories and workshops. Those with a better education or good contacts even became public servants as chauffeurs and janitors in public offices.

For rural Afro-Uruguayan women, the situation was different. Lacking independent mobility at this time, they would reach Montevideo only when their masters decided to move the entire household to the capital. The other way was to resort to the commission agent, who would hire them to a Montevidean family and loan them the train fare. They would have to repay both the debt for the ticket and the commission.

In their small-town and rural communities, Afro-Uruguayans had their own space, clearly defined by the church, the funeral parlour, the social clubs, and so on. Once they reached the capital city, problems arose. There were lines of separation between the 'white' and *negro* space in Montevideo, but while in some cases this was explicit, in others it was rather more subtle. Black people were generally alert to this situation, and in cases of doubt they retreated, keeping themselves apart. For newcomers, ignorance about Montevidean geography and homesickness often compounded the difficulties. For Afro-Uruguayans, however, the end-result was positive: a growing sense of solidarity and community.

For example, Praxedes B., one of the many black women who travelled as a child from Melo in Cerro Largo Province to Montevideo, on account of the commission agent, tells us:

> *In Melo there was a lady who, as soon as she learned that some girl was 'leaving for the city', used to knit her a bed jacket, bake her a bread and then take them to the train station. This, together with the little clothes we had, was the only thing we took ... The home where my mother and I came to was not bad, but they treated us as slaves ... One day while we were going shopping we met an acquaintance from Melo, whom my mother told about our situation, and she told her to go with her, that she would find us another home, and she took us walking to the house where she worked, which belonged to a very good family. They agreed to meet the following day in the same place, but my mother did not look up the address for she did not know how to read.*
>
> *The next day she quit the house where we were living. Holding me in one hand and the suitcase in the other, we left. My mother thought she could find her acquaintance's house, but when we*

started walking there were many streets ... and we walked and walked. I remember it was very hot, but my mother did not give up, and I was too small to realize the situation we were in. It was already afternoon when we met my mother's acquaintance, who was shopping around, and she took us to the new house, where my mother started working, and there they treated us very well. I could learn to sew, and there we were all right.

Not everybody was so lucky. In September 1924 Julieta Reyes, aged 16, a servant in a house in El Prado, died as a result of her master's punishments.

Afro-Montevideans had only limited opportunities for socializing during the first half of the century. Parties and balls were divided into three main groups: those of the aristocracy, those of the immigrant communities and those of the lower classes. The first and second categories naturally excluded black people, and no self-respecting Uruguayan would attend the third category; so the only alternative left was to found their own clubs. Thus arose such social centres as Sons of Melo, Sons of Asina, the Black Race Cultural Association, the Colonia Sport and Social Club, the New Life Social Centre, the Joy Entertainment Centre and the Glory Social Centre. Here friends and relatives could meet, encounters took place and couples were formed.

Politicization

In contrast to the Uruguayan immigrant community, Afro-Uruguayans were deeply concerned with national and international events. They had access to information by listening to their employers' conversations and to the radio. They held discussions at their clubs and associations, taking advice from those who were better educated. Among these unofficial community leaders were poets such as Pilar Barrios, journalists, graduate lawyers from the state university – such as Dr Betervide, who despite his degree worked as a porter – musicians such as Julián García Rondeau and artists such as Ramón A. Preya.

During these years, the magazine *Nuestra Raza* (Our Race)

(1929-50), an informative and cultural organ for the Afro-Uruguayan community, was always alert to the black condition in any part of the world. For example, in 1935 it reported the Italian invasion of Abyssinia, the indifference of the League of Nations and the danger of the fascist threat to world democracy.

Nationally, Afro-Uruguayans were greatly involved in the movement for workers' rights, which became increasingly politicized. At about this time the ban was lifted that had prevented Afro-Uruguayans from entering the movie industry; and black political activity reached its zenith with the foundation of the Black Autochthonous (that is, Native) Party, which lasted until 1941, when it fragmented. The party's literature is worth quoting for the light it sheds on the thinking of politicized Afro-Uruguayans at this time:

> *The Black Autochthonous Party ... is, above all, an eminently national party; although it has been founded to defend ... those interests relevant to black people, this does not mean that it will develop an essentially racial policy, since all those citizens of the country who support our ideals and are ready to cooperate with the task carried out will be admitted as members ... The Black Autochthonous Party will try as hard as possible to improve the social and cultural level of our race ... it will open libraries, organize cultural conferences and try to inculcate in their kind everything related to wisdom and the arts in all their expression.*
>
> *Brothers: The black race in Uruguay has started its way. The time has come to wake up and get rid of the torpor which imprisoned us ... and work hand in hand, heart and soul, gathering our efforts ... so that we will be able to tell the world that in this country, small in territory but big in history, and in its people's work, the black race has been constituted to meet one of its greatest desires: to get a real representative at the National Parliament, who will fight for the social improvement of the country, but at the same time will also speak for the interests of our race, whenever this may be necessary.*[1]

Nineteen forty-two was a year of intense political activity for the Afro-Uruguayan community as they fought against pro-Nazis at the local level and celebrated the centenary of the abolition of slavery in Uruguay. Poets, musicians, painters, workers, women and men – everybody worked at their clubs and associations, preparing for the celebrations. A national committee was formed, and the official commemoration was the unveiling of a monument to Manuel Antonio Ledesma (Ansina), who faithfully accompanied José Gervasio Artigas, the leader of the independence movement, until the latter's death in Paraguay. Dr Amézaga, President of the Republic, ministers and ambassadors took part in the event. If Afro-Uruguayans had a moment of splendour, it was surely the day of 12 December 1942, even if the official speeches ignored the ethnicity of the loyal black soldier while delivering their homage.

Earlier in the year the National Committee for the Commemoration of the Centenary of the Abolition of Slavery – linking a large number of individuals and organizations – issued the following statement:

Our country in general, and the black race in particular, will celebrate a date of extraordinary importance in the course of our citizen life in a free and independent country ... And today, one hundred years after [the abolition of slavery], which was an example in the continent, the black community in particular, together and joining the nation of which they are part, at the exact moment when a battle between civilization and barbarity is taking place, will assert their shining democratic faith ...

The Black Community National Committee for the Commemoration of the Abolition of Slavery Centenary, inspired by the aforementioned concepts and supported by the Black People's Cultural Association ... calls all the members of the black community to join us. We also call all the inhabitants of the country in order to make this initiative fostered by the black community a common initiative to all the people without any difference: from the most humble citizen to the most important ones, from the smallest progressive group to the highest magistrates, from the simplest cultural centres to the university staff.[3]

The women's section of the committee added its voice:

We want to express our recognition of those patriots who have proven to be great in both thought and action, banishing forever the evil privilege by means of which the so-called white people's civilization intended to humiliate us, thus depriving us of our human rights ... [A]ll human beings are equals before the law ... no one must be a victim of racism or social injustices. The black people are not part of a foreign community in Uruguay ... When the winds of betrayal and ambition blew in our country, the black heroes, with strength provided by the hatred of servitude, stood up on the ruins and fought magnificently ...

In these times of evil thoughts, the black race carries its democratic faith like a torch, to place it at the disposal of democracy ...

Our declaration is addressed to all Uruguayan women to make available in the most hidden places of the republic our voice of FREEDOM and JUSTICE.[3]

An identity lost?

Once the Second World War was over, there was a marked improvement in the purchasing power of the middle strata of Uruguayan society. The government's policy of free education at all levels allowed the children of hardly literate black workers to reach intermediate or university-level careers. But at the same time, a rapid process of *blanqueamiento* (whitening) took place. The non-discriminating 'colour-blindness' of the government's discourse and policies resulted not in equity but in a subtle form of racism, leading to self-discrimination among Afro-Uruguayans, against which no association or club can be formed and no accusation made.

Thus, 'invisibility' became official policy. As they grow up, young Afro-Uruguayans today will find that their nation's history records only one black person: the loyal soldier Ansina. There are no black writers in Uruguayan literature; only in the United States are there black musicians; and in painting, black people appear only on canvas. Dozens of Afro-Uruguayan writers, dramatists, painters, musicians, and so on, seem to have faded away.

The hegemonic discourse of our European-like culture favours the rapid loss of identity with regard to all that is alien. The formerly emerging Afro-Uruguayan community has fragmented as individuals have made personal advances in material and social terms, and as society has begun to open its doors. Discussion of the persistence of a subtle form of apartheid is considered to be in bad taste by most Uruguayans. Self-discrimination due to a lack of identity is considered a private matter – no one can intervene. Yet unofficial figures indicate that 75 per cent of Afro-Uruguayan women are still domestic workers, for example, and that most black children fail to finish high school.

Since the 1950s Afro-Uruguayan ethnic associations have disappeared at an alarming rate, and ignorance of the African heritage seems to be widespread. Of the earlier groupings, only the Uruguay Cultural and Social Association (ACSU) survives; this organization reappeared during the military dictatorship of 1973-84 as a 'free territory' for both black and white people.

The other notable black grouping, which has been set up much more recently, is Mundo Afro (Afro World),[4] and together the two organizations have fostered the appreciation of Afro-Uruguayan music and folk culture, at home and abroad. Both associations have problems, however; the ASCU lacks the necesary strength to unite the community, while Mundo Afro is weakened by its dependence on foreign donations.

Nevetheless, it is probably through self-help organizations that Afro-Uruguayan identity can best be reclaimed and the subtle but persistent forms of racism counteracted. Yet, until such efforts bear significantly more fruit, Afro-Uruguayans will remain largely invisible in the white people's universe, a world that denies black people's existence, even in its speech, for Afro-Uruguayans are not black, but 'coloured people'.

Notes

1 Partido Autóctono Negro, 'Estimado congénere', statement of principles and objectives, 1939, translation by A. da Luz.
2 Comité Nacional Pro-Conmemoración del Centenario de la Abolición de la Esclavitud, 'A la raza negra y al país', 1942, translation by A. da Luz.
3 Comité Nacional pro Festejos Centenario de la Abolición de la

Esclavitud, Sección Femenina, 'Las mujeres negras a sus hermanas de todo el país', 25 August 1942, translation by A. da Luz.

4 Editor's note: In 1992, the quincentenary of Columbus's landing in the Americas, Mundo Afro was active in the international campaign that drew attention to the 500-year history of racism and human rights violations on the continent. The organization has worked with black *barrio* dwellers, helping them improve their living standards and providing training in communication skills and leadership, making women and young people a special focus in its work. Mundo Afro states its aim as 'to discover the past in order to confront the racism hidden in the present' (*Latinamérica Press,* Lima, 20 February 1992, p. 7). In December 1994 Mundo Afro hosted in Montevideo a major conference on racism and xenophobia, which is described in the Postcript to the present book.

Select bibliography

Araujo Villagran, H., *Estoy orgulloso de mi país*, Montevideo, Sociedad Universal de Publicaciones, 1929.

Barran, J.P. and Nahum, B., *Historia rural del Uruguay Moderno, 1851-1855*, Montevideo, Ediciones de la Banda Oriental, vol. 1, 1967.

Barrios Pintos, A., *Los aborígenes del Uruguay: del hombre primitivo a los últimas charrúas*, Montevideo, Linardi y Risso, 1991.

Foucault, M., *Genealogía del racismo*, Madrid, Ediciones de la Piqueta, 1992.

Isola, E., *La ésclavitud en el Uruguay: desde sus comienzos hasta su extinción (1743-1852)*, Montevideo, Publicaciones de la Comisión Nacional de Homenaje del Sesquicentario de los Hechos Históricos de 1825, 1975.

Lozano Lerma, B.R., 'Una crítica a la sociedad occidental patriarcal y racista desde la perspectiva de la mujer negra', *Pasos*, Segunda Época, no. 42, 1992, pp. 11-21.

Pi Hugarte, R. and Vidart, D., *El legado de los inmigrante*, vol. 1, Montevideo, Nuesrat Tierra, 1969.

Rosenblat, R., *La población indígena y el mestizaje en América*, vol. 1, Buenos Aires, Ediciones Nova, 1954.

Sala de Touron, L. and Alonso Eloy, R., *El Uruguay comercial, pastoril y caudillesco*, vol. 1, Montevideo, Ediciones de la Banda Oriental, 1991.

Sans, M., 'Genética e historia: hacia una revisión de nuestra identidad como "país de inmigrantes"', in *Ediciones del quinto centenario*, vol. 1, Montevideo, Universidad de la República, 1992, pp. 19-42.

Varela, J.P. and Ramirez, C.M., *El destino nacional y la universidad polémica*, vol. 1, Montevideo, Colección de Clásicos Uruguayos 67, 1965.

Zea, L., *Discurso desde la marginación y la barbarie*, Barcelona, Anthropos, 1988.

CONCLUSIONS

Anani Dzidzienyo

I t is self-evident that specific historical, cultural, socio-economic and political conjunctions result in the emergence of different race relations patterns in the Americas. Brazil and the Caribbean countries, for example, differ significantly from Peru, where people of African descent are in a distinct minority and their position can be properly understood only in relation to a numerically dominant 'minority' of indigenous peoples. In the discussion of race relations, however, neither Latin America nor the United States occupies a position of privilege; fluidity, we now understand, requires some rethinking and re-evaluation in light of what we have come to learn about race relations orders and how they interface with orders of power and privilege. If fluidity or ambiguity resulted in the creation of greater manoeuvrability for individuals, it is by no means clear that such an option was maximally beneficial to groups seeking political action and organization.

The much admired non-contentiousness of race relations patterns in Latin America is beginning to seem rather less benign than it did, if only because of the relative silence of voices from 'below'. This is not, of course, to deny the presence of contrarian voices; the present volume contributes greatly to our knowledge of those Afro-Latin Americans who, over time and in various ways, and contrary to hegemonic ideologies that assign overriding significance to nationality (*not* race), have defined themselves as black and chosen actively to protest disadvantages directly attributable to their race and to propose remedial measures.

Peter Wade's insightful discussion of Colombian race relations posits that they can be understood only in the context of the

345

power relations involved. Indeed, it is precisely the dimension of power and its unequal distribution that frame race relations throughout the Americas.[1] That Afro-Latin Americans have consistently developed cultural initiatives in response to their predicament is testimony to their unwillingness to embrace victimhood. Yet those initiatives in no way address issues of political and economic power and representation, nor do they resolve the tension between actual power and symbolic power.

The most intractable problem for both the state and society in the matter of Afro-Latin Americans is how, for the first time in their collective history, to incorporate demands of non-dominant groups into the system of governance. What lessons or inferences they may draw from the experiences of the United States – which has known continually evolving public articulations of the presence of racial discrimination and the role of state and society in enforcing, modulating and abolishing that discrimination – are not easily predicted. But charges of Americanization and, implicitly, denationalization suggest that individual societies, eager to protect themselves against corrupting influences from extraneous sources, may well justify establishing a *cordon sanitaire*. Latin America's borders are permeable; thus the notion of the hermetic society, when applied specifically to Afro-Latin Americans, means, among other things, forcing a racial group to accept a narrowly conceived identity – that of nationality – while assiduously rejecting all external influences.

Given the dynamics of the real world, however, the predicament of Afro-Latin Americans may be defined as an issue of human rights. This reformulation of the issue effectively expands the conceptual and discursive parameters of the continuing discussion about race, allows for specific responses to specific situations and situates it in the context of debates and struggles that no state, and no society, will easily ignore. Yet if, as so often happens, the official response is mere lip-service, then little is to be gained; the issue of Afro-Latin America will simply languish under the rubric of a broader, more intractable problem.

The importance of this volume is that it raises the 'visibility' of Afro-Latin Americans from likely, and unlikely, parts of the region. All the countries covered here offer examples of the socio-economic and political deprivation of their black populations – a deprivation that suggests absence from national and regional power structures. What makes the problems of Afro-Latin Americans particularly tricky is that in the post-colonial period there has been no explicit legal exclusion of blacks from participation at various levels of society. A closer look, however, points to pervasive areas of exclusion, some intended, others not.

Complicating the issue is the very role of the law in defining and managing race relations in the region. A fundamental fact about Latin American polities has to be confronted and 'deconstructed'. This is that, in the absence of post-abolition legislation specifically targeting former slaves and their descendants, and in the absence of a tradition of compliance – either because such legal provisions do not exist or because the law has an ambiguous role in assuring equality of rights to all citizens – it is highly problematic to plunge headlong into recommending possible roles for the law when there has been no history of the law functioning in such a manner.

Issues of inclusion and exclusion

In any analysis of Latin American race relations, it is crucial to distinguish between dominant ideas articulated about national unity and race relations and oppositional ideas emerging from Afro-Latin American groups in a way that reflects their political heterogeneity. The role of historical memory cannot be overstated, especially in view of the fact that present-day activists are not necessarily concerned with political genealogies.

The issue of 'group' versus 'individual' rights is another problematic area. In the case of Brazil, for example, the thrust of post-abolition race relations and social mobility has been predicated upon 'individual mobility', as was the case during slavery. This emphasis on individual strategy resulted in the emergence of individuals of stellar quality whose removal from the group did not in any way reflect the general predicament of the group. The dominant society, with no small pride, often cites these 'honourable exceptions' as examples of the successful working of the model, though the group from which these individuals emerged might interpret their 'exceptionality' rather differently.

At what point in time does the paradigm shift its focus from individual to group? And what are the hurdles that advocates of group identity and group activism have to confront?

To explore such difficult questions, contributors to this volume have sought to investigate the historical formation of Latin American race relations patterns, and so to unravel the gap between professed ideals of unity and one-peopleness, on one hand, and deeply rooted patterns of exclusion of Afros from the political, socio-economic and educational centres of the polity, on the other. Here lies a fascinating contradiction: between the incorporation into the legitimate national arena of erstwhile African-derived religious, cultural and social traditions once considered societally or politically subversive because of their 'primitive' provenance, *and* the absence of a corresponding insertion of Afro-Latin Americans into areas and structures of power and privilege from which they have traditionally been excluded.

To put the issue provocatively: what have been the real rewards for Afro-Brazilians, for example, now that the dominant society, including exclusive hotels, serves *feijoada* and the whitest-looking Brazilians are practitioners of Candomblé? Has this legitimating of Afro-Brazilian traditions fundamentally altered the imbalance in power relations between Afro-Brazilians as a group and the dominant society? Is the dominant society thinking 'nationally, collectively' but continuing to act racially, exclusively?

Balancing historical, cultural and political realities

Is slavery still relevant? Yes and no. To argue that one cannot continue to talk back to slavery and its socio-racial economic structures to account for the conditions of Afro-Latin Americans does not mean that it *ipso facto* ceases to be relevant, especially in view of the images and roles linked to slavery. The archaism of slave relations and their supplanting by 'modernizing' economic and social relations have not resulted in the emergence of new societies in which status linked to slave origin has totally disappeared. The earlier optimistic expectations about the potential of class relations to undermine archaic socio-racial structures have not entirely materialized.

What is intriguing in this connection is the continuing hold of structures of power and prestige on Latin American societies, irrespective of the relative size of the 'white' population. Whether or not the societal push is to negate, or maintain distance from, blackness or to confine expressions of connection to blackness to the merely symbolic – particularly among those who are not identifiably black – the open articulation of pride in blackness is nowhere acceptable. Specific national permutations on 'relations to blackness' (positive or negative) can provide important insights.

If Dominicans, for example, cannot contemplate blackness without the historical 'spectre' of Haiti and its present-day consequences, collectively and individually, how, specifically, are black Dominicans affected? Does the designation *indio* resolve the problem for them? Do Dominicans of a darker hue constantly face the problem of being mistaken for closet Haitians? The interesting and even insightful notion that Dominican national identity makes sense only in relation to Haiti – to be Dominican is to be not Haitian – does not sufficiently explain the long-range consequences for individual Dominicans.

History, nationality and Afro-identity

The impressive presence of historical Africa in the cultural, religious, folkloric and culinary spheres, so richly documented in the preceding chapters, attests to the strength of both the original bearers of these forms and their descendants; it demonstrates, too, the ability of nations to absorb these legacies. To imagine or attempt to establish that from the time of their inception the incorporation of these traditions occurred in a linear fashion is to engage in selective historical evaluation. It is arguably the case that the very process of incorporation reveals certain basic contradictions in the relationship of the dominant society and its black population. Take, as examples, two definitive institutions in the cultural life of Brazil – Carnival and Candomblé. To survey either merely from the perspective of the past ten years is to ignore a complex history of repression of traditions that were of African provenance. That these institutions moved from the clandestine to the marginal to their present status as national institutions is indeed remarkable.

The real problem for Afro-Latin Americans is how successfully to juggle common nationality and the struggle to attain public legitimacy for Afro-identity. Legislation as a regulator of race relations in the post-colonial period can be only part of the solution, as blacks have not been excluded by law from full participation in the society. What is required is not a compilation of constitutional provisions as evidence of the role of law in guaranteeing rights. Given the interplay between (a) laws, customs, etiquette and publicly articulated views about the ideals of interracial harmony and (b) the reality of racial segmentation, not much would be gained by this. Afro-Latin Americans are already, indeed, full members of the 'nation'. How, therefore, can they structure their questions and demands in strictly legalistic terms? Can they challenge, or change through the mediation of the law, something that has been neither legal nor illegal? Does there exist anywhere in Latin America the modern-day equivalent of the system of customary law established in British colonial Africa – a body of traditional precepts and practices that, though unwritten, came to acquire the force of law?

Entry into government service, particularly the foreign service, as it affects Afro-Latin Americans offers an interesting challenge to the researcher. In Brazil one faces the sheer impossibility of finding anyone who will even acknowledge that race is a not insignificant factor in explaining the absence of blacks from the diplomatic service. Indeed, one even marvels at the sheer ingenuity of the rationalizations offered: to wit, nationality – Brazilianness – binds a multiracial society that enjoys exceptionally smooth relations among its many racial groups, which include a large number of people of mixed blood, and an absence of overt racial tensions. Nationality singularly and effectively eliminates the need for other identities, particularly those whose inherent volatility poses a threat to national unity. Here, too, one can look for comparisons with the exceptional cases of the United States and South Africa.

One commonly hears from non-Afro-Latin Americans perhaps overconfident denials that blacks – be they servants, soccer players, musicians – have any abiding interest in black issues or movements. They speak, too, of their access to Afro-derived religious and cultural institutions, remarkable for its ease when one considers the uneasy divisions of, say, North American society. But what of the Afros themselves – can one imagine a space in which they at times think and act independently of the overarching race-free, classless national identity? Given the power of that identity, all-inclusive yet respectful of implicitly racial privileges, it is not surprising that a certain caution prevails among blacks who in other systems or circumstances might choose to mobilize around race or Africanity.

It is encouraging to learn that Afro-Dominicans, for example, exhibit a reasonable degree of self-esteem in a negrophobic society. But we perhaps risk over-sentimentalization when we note that extensive racial mixing produces offspring who though visibly of different shades – one black, the other white – identify themselves as biological siblings.

Comparative perspectives

There is no evidence to suggest that significant numbers of people of African ancestry anywhere in the Americas actively contemplate voting with their feet. However unsatisfactory existing conditions for those of their kind, they tend not to abandon their home countries to seek other national identities. How to explain this? Afros undoubtedly derive some benefit from the flexible system of racial designations. In post-colonial Latin America blacks have not been the targets of physical lynchings and other racially motivated acts of violence. The *de facto* segregation of Panama's Canal Zone was never the norm in the rest of Latin America. Nor did exclusionary practices – in schools, in clubs, in residential area – enjoy the kind of legal sanction associated with racial segregation in the United States. Yet, as Abdias do Nascimento has consistently argued, 'lynching' has far deeper meaning than the actual physical act. There is a special case to be made for (re)conceptualizing the role of violence as a determinant of 'good' or 'bad' race relations. A recurrent refrain in his writings since the mid-1940s is that racial violence is multifaceted and extremely subtle. To deny access to structures of education, health and political participation, he observes, constitutes violent actions for those on the receiving end. Such a conceptualization of violence and its role in race relations has the potential of liberating our understanding of the Latin American situation.

The point speaks directly to comparisons between the United States and Latin America. Meaningful comparisons cannot be selectively applied to only the most conspicuous aspects of race relations, especially those regulated by the force of law. Nor can comparisons be magically terminated at some point in the 1950s when the world was left to wonder at images of National Guard troops escorting a little black girl to school in the US South to the taunts and jeers of whites. What happened after such shocking events is central to the comparison. Why, it needs to be asked, do institutions of higher learning in Latin America have so few black students, a paucity made even more astonishing when one compares their numbers with their counterparts in the United States? No amount of 'flexibility', 'smoothness' or 'lack of tension' in racial matters can adequately explain away what is clearly a problem.

In a widely discussed case the daughter of the governor of the state of Espirito Santo, an Afro-Brazilian, was denied entry to an elevator designated for use by residents of a high-rise apartment building and, presumably, their guests. The story, a characteristic example of what one observer has very aptly termed 'vertical apartheid', rings a familiar note to the many blacks who have themselves been assumed to be service personnel irrespective of their dress or demeanour. The governor's legal counsel chose not to argue the case on the basis of existing anti-racist legislation as they well understood the difficulties of successful prosecution in a legal climate where precedents are few and, perhaps even more important, the plaintiff bears the burden of proof. Lack of precedent here is linked to the conspicuous absence of multiracial civil rights organizations. The struggle for racial justice presupposes some notion of racial injustice; and as Latin American self-conceptions do not include that crucial notion, prominent multiracial organizations dedicated to racial justice are seen to be fundamentally oxymoronic and crass in their attempt to apply inappropriate North American racial paradigms to their societies.

Future examinations of present-day Afro-Latin Americans need to seek actively to extend the framework of the process to one that permits global comparison. That framework will have no *a priori* victors or successes contrasted with worst-possible cases; it will, one hopes, open the way for Afro-Latin Americans themselves to establish links with other peoples of African ancestry in transnational encounters much like the recent gathering in Uruguay discussed in the Postscript to this volume. The salient feature of these meetings is not the search for ready-made, all-purpose solutions; rather, it is the airing of reflections and histories that transcend individual cases.

A possible future research area would be, for example, inter- and intra-Dominican relations in communities outside the national territory. Do Dominicans in the United States hold steadfastly to the single commonality of Dominicanness, irrespective of race or colour? What happens when they come into contact with other Latin Americans whose socio-racial mix may not be so directly linked to a Haitian factor but whose societies none the less confer privilege, status and power on those who are of lighter hues? What happens when in the United States Dominicans and other Latin Americans confront the rigidly binary division of racial lines? But even this binarism is more complicated than it would appear.

Even more productive would be an exploration of both overt and covert differences, posing the question, Are there in fact certain *constants* in race relations throughout the Americas, constants implicit in oft-repeated phrases: 'money whitens'; 'in the other Americas an individual has a greater possibility to be whatever he or she chooses or desires'; 'there is certainly greater racial mixture in Latin America'; 'after all, we are all at least symbolically hybridized or mesticized'? What the literature lacks is an indepth comparative inquiry, across cultures, that does not give disproportionate credence to colonial nomenclatures, idealized expressions of nationhood or peoplehood that extol race mixture while ignoring the clearly colour-based rank order of preference.

No amount of verbal elegance – or money – can 'whiten' a Pelé, a Benedita da Silva or a Peña Gómez and still qualify as an accurate description of reality outside specific national contexts.

Emphasizing the particularity of national etiquettes matters precisely because national histories and cultural practices are never to be ignored. However, as soon as individuals or groups cross national boundaries, those etiquettes and practices, be they concrete or symbolic, cannot be maintained in their innocence or originality. Does the *indio* Dominican or the Brazilian *moreno* who insists on being so identified find that North Americans, say, or Europeans, or continental Africans accept these categorizations? Indeed, it would be highly instructive to record African responses to the application of these labels to large numbers of their own, not simply a minority of honourable exceptions.

In 1989 a popular women's programme on Venezuelan television discussed the question 'Is it punishment to be a black woman in Venezuela?' The participants – a well-known politician, a physician, a model and sibling athletes – offered a range of perspectives. In its modest way the programme sheds light on the discussion of race and gender in present-day Latin America. How interesting it would be to compare the programme with advocacy initiatives undertaken by, say, Afro-Brazilian women's organizations, together with examples drawn from other national groups.

Visibility, or non-invisibility, is a multifaceted and variable phenomenon. In Peru, where the salient divide is between the indigenous and the mesticized components of the population, any disadvantages associated with blackness pale in comparison to the individual and collective weight of those disadvantages endured by the majority indigenous population. What Peru does share with other Latin American countries is the privileging of whiteness. In this particular race relations universe a study of indigenous–Afro relations in specific situations, over the centuries, could well contribute to our understanding of comparative race relations. Similar work could be done on Ecuador.

On matters of race and colour the novice observer does well to tread lightly when approaching societies and systems such as those in Latin America. Non-whiteness and blackness, one quickly learns, are not interchangeable concepts; never assume blackness – determine, with delicacy, the individual's personal identification, which may not be consistent with that assigned him or her by others. For the Latin American, a similar challenge awaits in North America, say, or even continental Africa, where what is perceived as 'white' may very well be, to the person concerned, 'black'.

Looking to the future

'Revealing' the true number of blacks in specific societies, in an effort to establish their numerical majority, does not *ipso facto* translate into power-holding or even power sharing. Yet Afro-Latin Americans can bring to the study of comparative race relations their unique ability to interrogate Latin American paradigms both in theory and in practice. Those who in varying ways, and often in hostile conditions, struggle to be both true nationals and clear-eyed critics risk accusations of sullying the national image with imported ideas. Unlike their fellow nationals, they are oddly expected to limit their socio-political and even cultural thoughts and actions to approved ideals. The success of their struggle ultimately hinges on the legitimacy of a black perspective in national public discourse.

By focusing on the Afro-Latin American experience, then, this volume will, we hope, provide a real service. This will be to reopen the historical debate on comparative race relations in the Americas and to transcend the reductionism characteristic of earlier works that imposes a simple binarism – be it religion, history or culture – on what we now understand to be a complex reality. As we are confronted with the ever-increasing Latin Americanization of migrations to North America, the complexities and contradictions of each side's race relations become more fully exposed, making it possible to frame new questions and thus to avoid hackneyed explanations based on ideally constructed images rather than realities in which Latin Americans of African ancestry make themselves heard.

The battle to insert a politically active Afro-identity into the public discourse continues, and the authors of this book hope to have made a useful contribution to this struggle. In this context, 'no longer invisible' should be seen more in a political sense than in merely demographic, cultural or religious terms. It is not that politics and political participation are the sole definers; but without them the battle is only half won, and the fundamental role of power is not sufficiently accounted for or taken into consideration.

The country studies in this book point to the rich heritage of Afro-Latin America and to enduring similarities in the position of Afro-Latin Americans in their societies, particular national conditions and background notwithstanding. The Cuban example both fascinates and frustrates. The only Latin American country to confront racism publicly, Cuba has undertaken concrete measures to integrate Afro-Cubans into institutions and areas of Cuban life from which they were traditionally excluded. It cannot, however, be assumed that race or racial factors have become non-issues. In a period of worsening economic conditions the society is coping with extraordinary pressures that impact negatively on the kinds of initiatives from which Afro-Cubans have derived considerable benefit. The discussion of recent events in Colombia, especially the struggles of Afro-Colombians to attain fuller inclusion in the national polity and its institutions, points to prospects for renewed political participation. Belize, Honduras and Nicaragua reveal complexities related to their histories, and to specific permutations of language, culture and identity tied to the non-Hispanic Caribbean. And the inclusion here of the story of Afro-Bolivians, Afro-Mexicans and Afro-Uruguayans is in itself a noteworthy achievement; discussions of the Afro presence in Latin America will now have information, long missing from the literature, on countries that have, to date, been given little or no prominence or thought.

Of particular interest are the multiple meanings of Africa for Afro-Latin Americans. Nowhere in the Americas has there ever existed a unidimensionally positive image of Africa. It is to be hoped that this collection will generate interest in researching the general and specific consequences of African descent for Afro-Latin Americans.

Recommendations

This volume could well be the foundation for the development of a data bank that stores information on the history, culture, politics and education of Afro-Latin Americans. For emerging grass-roots non-governmental organizations the information provided would be invaluable in their struggle for legitimacy.

The book provides much useful information that could also serve as the scholarly base for film documentaries and other projects examining the history, culture and politics of the societies discussed here. By raising common issues it lays the groundwork for comparable transnational programmes and areas of cooperation.

Might one hope for a programme – sponsored, say, by UNESCO or the Organization of American States – that seeks not just to catalogue distinct historical events but, first and foremost, to identify and monitor (currency being of primary importance here) the intersections of history, economics, politics and culture among nations with populations of African descent? The African Diaspora Research Project based at Michigan State University serves as a useful model. That project has, *inter alia*, brought together scholars and graduate students who jointly explore interdisciplinary issues pertaining to the African diaspora. A good point of departure might be Norman Whitten's proposal for reactivating studies of Afro-Ecuadorian communities.

For scholars and non-specialists alike, a perennial problem in their search for information on Afro-Latin Americans is locating materials. This book, at the minimum, provides a source of recent provenance that is widely available, and as such, it will contribute mightily to what one hopes will be a move closer to centre stage for a much neglected group.

Africa and Afro-Latin America: reconnecting the two through mutual exchanges of learning and information would surely count as one of the more fruitful outcomes of any effort to shed light on Afro-Latin Americans. A cooperative research undertaking – involving perhaps UNESCO, the Organization of American States and the Organization of African Unity – would seek to collect oral histories, published texts, films, and the like, organize them thematically and disseminate them in both Africa and Latin America. Individual countries working cooperatively could initiate film and video projects. The challenge here would be to reach a broad audience nationally and transnationally.

Fundamental to any understanding of Afro-Latin Americans is, I believe, the question of Africa. Deeply embedded in centuries-old shame, the idea of this continent has a central, though rarely considered, role in the complex relations among its descendants in the diaspora and the larger societies in which they live. The real and imagined meanings of Africa in all its richness and contradictoriness beg to be contemplated not as aspects of a single phenomenon but as factors in the dynamic of Afro-Latin American life today.

Notes

1   Wade, P., *Blackness and Race Mixture: The Dynamics of Racial Identity in Colombia*, Baltimore, MD, Johns Hopkins University Press, 1993, p. 3.

Select bibliography

Barbalet, J.M., *Citizenship – Concepts in Social Thought: Rights, Struggle and Class Inequality*, Minneapolis, MN, University of Minnesota Press, 1988.

Castro, N.A., 'Inequalities in a racial paradise: labor opportunities among blacks and whites in Bahia, Brazil', *SPURS*, Massachusetts Institute of Technology, Spring 1994, pp. 6-8.

Dzidzienyo, A., 'Brazilian race relations studies: old problems, new ideas?', *Humboldt Journal of Social Relations*, vol. 19, no. 2, 1993, pp. 109-29.

Edwards, J., *Where Race Counts: The Morality of Racial Preference in Britain and America*, London and New York, Routledge, 1995.

Fiske, J., *Media Matters: Everyday Culture and Political Change*, Minneapolis, MN, and London, University of Minnesota Press, 1994.

Guimarães, A.S., 'Race, racism and groups of color in Brazil', unpublished paper, Atlanta, GA, Latin American Studies Association, March 1994.

Hall, J.A. and Ikenberry, G.J., *The State: Concepts in Social Thought*, Minneapolis, MN, University of Minnesota Press, 1989.

Hanchard, M., *Orpheus and Power: The Movimento Negro of Rio de Janeiro and São Paulo, Brazil, 1945-88*, Princeton, NJ, Princeton University Press, 1994.

Hellwig, D. (ed.), *African-American Reflections on Brazil's Racial Paradise*, Philadelphia, PA, Temple University Press, 1992.

Higginbotham, A.L. Jr, 'Seeking pluralism in judicial systems: the American experience and the South African challenge', *Duke Law Journal*, vol. 42, no. 5, 1993, pp. 1023-68.

Horne, G., *Reversing Discrimination: The Case for Affirmative Action*, New York, International Publishers, 1992.

Merelman, R.M., *Representing Black Culture: Racial Conflict and Cultural Politics in the United States*, New York and London, Routledge, 1995.

Nascimento, A. do and Larkin, E., *Africans in Brazil: A Pan-African Perspective*, Trenton, NJ, Africa World Press, 1992.

Oboler, S., *Ethnic Labels, Latino Lives: Politics of (Re)Presentation in the United States*, Minneapolis, MN, University of Minnesota Press, 1995.

Portocarrero, G., *Racismo y mestizaje*, Lima, Edición Maruja Martinez/Eduardo Cáceres, 1993.

Reichmann, R., 'Brazil's denial of race', *Report on the Americas: Brazil*, North American Congress on Latin America, vol. 27, no. 6, May/June 1995.

Winant, H., 'Rethinking race in Brazil', *Journal of Latin American Studies*, no. 24, 1992, pp. 173-92.

Xavier, A. and Pestana, M., 'Survival guide for blacks in Brazil', contribution to the Discussion of Racism in the Constitutional Revision supported by Geledés Black Women's Institute, São Paulo, Brazil, 1993.

POSTSCRIPT

Darién J. Davis

*No nos vamos a unir por ser personas negras, sino por
identificarnos con las obras de personas negras.*
Juan de Dios Mosquera, Moviemento Nacional Cimarrón,
Colombia

In cooperation we need to build bridges. We cannot do it alone.
Charles Mohan, employee association delegate,
United States

The chapters in this volume have aimed, in part, to shed light on the struggles of Afro-Latin Americans throughout the hemisphere. As is evident, Afro-Latin Americans have pursued a variety of strategies to confront racism and ignorance in their respective nations. Indeed, the national milieu has shaped the parameters of race relations in each country. At the same time, Afro-Latin American activists throughout the hemisphere are increasingly turning to international and hemispheric pan-African forums for support and exchange of ideas. Pan-African activities serve important political ends, while providing much-needed psychological and moral support to national movements. This Postscript seeks to evaluate attempts by Afro-Latin Americans to assert themselves internationally through the creation of pan-African liaisons in the Americas, taking as its main focus the recent international First Seminar on Xenophobia and Racism, in Montevideo, Uruguay, initiated in December 1994 by the Afro-Uruguayan organization Mundo Afro.

Pan-Africanism and Afro-Latin Americans[1]

Between 1900 and 1974 pan-Africanists organized six international conferences. African-Americans from the United States had a crucial role in these forums, and English-speaking black people initially appeared in the forefront. African-American W.E.B. Du Bois and Jamaican-born Marcus Garvey were early twentieth-century pan-Africanism's two most important figures. Du Bois toiled for self-reliance and integration; Garvey promoted self-determination and separatism. Both struggled for the promotion of black consciousness and dignity. Du Bois was involved in the organization of the pan-Africanist conferences for over forty years. The first such conference, in Paris in 1919, resulted in the indictment of imperialism and support for self-determination for African nations. At the next three conferences – 1921, 1923 and 1927 – colonialism in Africa remained the central focus.

The Fifth Pan-African Congress of 1944 produced a schism between Garveyites and followers of Du Bois, as new voices from Africa and the Caribbean emerged. While colonialism remained an important issue, Caribbean pan-Africanists such as C.L.R. James stressed the need for class analysis of racial problems. For the first time, the conference demanded the outright independence of Africa and the rights of all peoples throughout the African diaspora. Between the fifth and the sixth conferences a host of regional movements, particularly in Africa, the United States and the Caribbean, attained momentum. By the time of the Sixth Pan-African Conference in 1974 regional movements were on the rise in the Americas. Nationalist struggles and civil rights movements had emerged with specific national agendas, not always in step with international pan-Africanism.

Latin American pan-Africanists have long recognized Africa as the source of a shared experience, and have denounced European and North American imperialism in Africa, condemned racism and prejudice internationally, celebrated heroes of the African diaspora and forged links with groups and individuals abroad. Yet Afro-Latin American participation in the pan-Africanist movement has been historically weak. Language barriers have limited the participation of Spanish- and Portuguese-speaking activists, while socio-cultural, economic and political disenfranchisement often prohibited Afro-Latin Americans from creating strong national or international voices.

Language, for example, becomes a barrier when individuals throughout the diaspora are prohibited from meaningful discourse. Afro-Americans all over the continent speak and write in many languages, from *patois*, Papiamento and Garífuna to major European languages. Thus, international dialogue is often fractured by language group. In recent years the propagation of English as an unofficial *lingua franca* has facilitated dialogue among people involved in race consciousness and civil rights movements, but many grass-roots organizers do not have access to English classes, and many Latin Americans regard the prevalence of English as a form of cultural imperialism. Adoption of Spanish, however, does not solve the problem entirely, particularly, of course, for Brazilians.

While education and interpretation services slowly erode language barriers among Latin American pan-Africanists, other factors remain endemic. Political, economic and cultural underdevelopment greatly affect the ability of would-be pan-Africanists to participate in global forums. Although Afro-Latin Americans' political participation has never been explicitly restricted by race, slavery, disenfranchisement and economic deprivation have inhibited the growth of a coherent black middle–class.[2] Lower-income classes, in general, have less discretionary time to invest in national, much less international, enterprises. Moreover, lack of political access prohibits racial discrimination from becoming an agenda issue in favour of class inequalities.

The politics of racial identity represent the most formidable enemy of pan-Africanism. In the great majority of countries profiled in this book, *mestizaje*, miscegenation, nationalism and colour codes have inhibited solidarity among people of African descent within individual countries. In many such countries, race is seemingly unimportant, while colour has a more significant role in the social hierarchy. This colour consciousness, combined with fervent patriotism and nationalism, encourages identification with the nation rather than with extra-national entities. The apparently fluid colour line and theories of whitening thus together prohibit the development of a strong race consciousness. Yet, despite such difficulties, many Afro-Latin Americans have opposed national and social constructs which seek to make them 'invisible'.

Although race consciousness heightened in the post-Second World War era, the onslaught of military dictatorships in many Latin America countries further exacerbated the possible emergence of black movements in the 1960s and 1970s. With the return to liberal democratic governments in the 1980s and 1990s, however, national movements and organizations have blossomed. As a consequence, the Americas have witnessed an increase in international cooperation among people of the African diaspora, most notably the series of Congresses on Black Culture in the Americas.

Congresses on Black Culture in the Americas

The Congresses on Black Culture in the Americas, organized between 1977 and 1984, represented a rare success in pan-African organization. While participation came overwhelmingly from artists and intellectuals, the spirit of the conferences reflected a strong desire to forge solidarity among people of African descent throughout the diaspora.

Held in Cali, Colombia, in 1977 and sponsored by the Organization of American States in conjunction with the Fundación Colombiana de Investigaciones Folklóricas, the First Congress took pride in the fact that it represented the first hemispheric reflection on Afro-Americans by Afro-Americans. After an emotional opening, Afro-American delegates divided themselves among several working commissions to discuss: political ideas, religions, aesthetics and morals; socio-economic structures; art and technologies; and ethnicity, *mestizaje*, castes and classes. The commissions were united in their denunciation of all mechanisms of alienation aimed at people of African decent in the Americas. Delegates called for greater unity, while pledging to increase investigations of the historical importance of Africans in the creation of Latin American culture and to support struggles of liberation in Africa.[3]

The Second Congress on Black Culture in the Americas, in Panama City, Panama, in 1980, developed the theme of race and class. Delegates discussed issues under the broad theme of Cultural Identity of Blacks in the Americas. Sponsored by the Instituto Nacional de Cultura de Panama with the aid of the Centro de Estudios Afro-Panameños and the Patrimonio Histórico, four commissions were convened, along with round tables to discuss future strategies of cooperation. According to Congress President Gerado Maloney, two major achievements of the conference were the integration and incorporation of Afro-Americans from all regions of the Americas, including the English- and French-speaking Caribbean, and the conviction of all members of the inseparable relationship between ethnicity and class.[4]

The Third Congress, held in São Paulo, Brazil, in 1982, under the directorship of the Brazilian political activist Abdias do Nascimento, in conjunction with the Instituto de Pesquisa y Estudios Afro-Brasileiros, was more defiant in tone. The theme of this congress, African Diaspora: Political Consciousness and African Culture, reflected the growing political consciousness of Afro-American communities.[5] Increased black consciousness and politicization of black movements led to a more forceful condemnation of racist policies around the globe. Delegates declared solidarity with a number of national liberation movements, particularly in Africa and the Middle East. The conference passed motions of support for, and solidarity with, Namibia's SWAPO, South Africa's African National Congress and the Palestine Liberation Organization.[6] The conference also recognized the need to reach out to marginalized Afro-American communities and organizations in countries previously unrepresented in pan-African work. In particular, it was noted that Afro-Uruguayans were in danger of being further isolated from national life.

The Fourth Congress, initially planned for Paris, under the theme Afro-America and the European Community, instead took place in Quito, Ecuador, in 1984, focusing on Black Women in the Americas.

Since 1984 several regional meetings have drawn scholars, intellectuals and activists from around the hemisphere. The dream of a formal and permanent pan-African organization, however, is yet to be achieved. Funding and regional and national problems still plague national movements and make international coordination difficult. Besides, such international organizations have historically emphasized scholarship, art and intellectual concerns, rather than grass-roots activities. None the less pressures of economic and political globalization, and the collapse of Eastern European state socialism, make the need for international communication among African-Americans ever more urgent.

The First Seminar on Racism and Xenophobia, Montevideo, December 1994

The uneven development of the various Afro-Latin American movements, especially in regions not usually associated with people of African diaspora populations, such as the Southern Cone and the Andes, has made communication between many Afro-Latin American grass-roots movements difficult. With these constraints in mind, Mundo Afro of Uruguay announced its plans to host in December 1994 the First Seminar on Racism and Xenophobia in Montevideo.

In the event, the Uruguayan conference reflected, on the one hand, the development of pan-Africanism in the Americas; but, on the other hand, it illustrated the long and hard work ahead if the dream of an intercontinental organization is to be brought to fruition. Unlike previous meetings, Uruguay was largely anti-academic. Indeed, its US coordinator, Michael Franklin of the Organization of Africans in the Americas, stressed the problem-solving focus. While political awareness and activism have heightened over the years, activists and grass-roots organizers see the importance of establishing a rapport with international political and economic institutions, particularly in the United States. Partnerships with such institutions may provide valuable future contacts and access to funds as well as information, not to mention raising their own visibility internationally and thus nationally. Unfortunately grass-roots movements representing poor or disenfranchised minority groups often receive national attention only after they have obtained international recognition, particularly from the United States or the European Union.

The Montevideo Conference was, however, far more than an exercise in seeking visibility. Organizers and participants searched for a balance between grass-roots action and intellectual cooperation, with the long-term goal of educating the public.

For Afro-Uruguayans the conference was a crucial turning point in a long but slow civil rights struggle. Young and old Uruguayans turned out in support of platforms and ideas which would be of central importance to their communities. While participants were expected from all of the cultural and linguistic regions of the Americas, representatives and advocates of Afro-Latin Americans from the United States, Brazil, Uruguay, Argentina, Honduras, the Dominican Republic, Colombia, Peru and Cuba constituted the majority of the participants. The absence of major leaders from past conferences and community activists from many other Latin American communities was an indication of far-reaching structural problems which limit communication among Latin American nations. Many activists from Brazil, Central America and the Caribbean were not aware of the conference, for example. Indeed, there is no intercontinental database which registers the major movements or activists from each country, nor are there sufficient resources to ensure contact and follow-up.

Structural and political problems notwithstanding, Montevideo symbolized an important watershed in black consciousness within the region as delegates began to define, in the words of the official agenda, a Program for the Development of Black Latin America. In addition, major networking took place after the official presentations, in the lobbies, bars, cafés and restaurants. Personal contacts were made, and discussions held, between union leaders, representatives of women's groups, human rights and development workers, local campaigners and organizers, and other participants.

The Montevideo Conference: commissions and outcomes

The five commissions at Montevideo provided important frameworks for future cooperation and consideration. A brief description of the activities of each commission follows.[7]

Education, Culture and Communication. Delegates in this commission debated issues related to the educational reality and cultural rejuvenation of Afro-Americans, focusing particularly on proposals that would permit advances within black communities. The commission arrived at several long-term goals, including commitment to set up an inter-American communications network using fax and electronic mail. It was agreed that the inter-hemispheric network should be further divided into the three regions of North America, the Caribbean and Central America, and South America. Other resolutions included the creation of an intercontinental pressure group responsible for responding to events affecting black communities throughout the hemisphere and the promotion of educational programmes related to Africans.

Women and Society. Afro-Americans clearly understand the extra pressures that women face in their respective communities. This commission set out to develop economic alternatives to improve family income, to generate work and to improve the standard of living of black women around the hemisphere, while promoting the most efficient forms of social integration. The historical contributions of black women to American societies were discussed. That contribution, the session unanimously agreed, has been continually minimized and ignored. The illiteracy, pauperization and hardship that so many Afro-American women experience today is indicative of that neglect. High unemployment and rural–urban migration have led to problems of sexual exploitation, involuntary sterilization, lack of access to education and health services and a high incidence of AIDS. The lack of role models, multiplication of negative stereotypes and severe underrepresentation of women in the decision-making processes of non-governmental and governmental organizations and agencies further compound the problem. The commission agreed to pursue strategies to increase the visibility of Afro-American women and to guarantee their access to credit, education and health.

International Cooperation and Alternative Development. This commission listed its main aims as the generation of collective ideas for a quantitative and qualitative advancement of Afro-American communities in the third millennium. Participants also saw their role as helping to create a continental network of cooperation that would facilitate the sustainable development of Afro-American communities. Representatives from Latin America were particularly concerned to promote cooperative relationships with multinational corporations, non-governmental organizations and other international institutions; other delegates warned that relations with international organizations should be approached with caution. Most agreed that grass-roots movements should under no circumstances relinquish direction and control of their projects and communities to international financial institutions. Likewise, it was argued that cooperation among Latin American countries should take into account the relative development and potential of each national community. A representative from the international financial community warned that Afro-Americans cannot simply shun international lending institutions, because they need to become not just job seekers, but job creators. Two broad goals expressed by this commission, largely in agreement with proposals made by other commissions, were, first, to encourage black organizations to alert financial institutions to their plans for the development of black communities, and, second, to encourage and persuade financial institutions to direct funds towards black communities.

Political Strategies. Mundo Afro's vision of political strategies was decidedly long-term. After centuries of isolation, Afro-Latin Americans were looking at ways to consolidate and augment their political power. Delegates began their discussion with an eye towards stimulating initiatives with governments and private institutions which would lead to the further integration of black communities into national life. The development of strategies of cooperation, representation, information, promotion and technical aid for the interchange of information between the countries of Europe, the Americas and black Africa became the guiding aim. Many political strategies emerged, ranging from the theoretical and long-term to immediate activities for specific groups and communities. One general project united participants, however: the desire to develop an intercontinental network, based on regional commissions, with a continental directory comprising delegates from each Afro-Latin American organization. Such a network could serve as a coordinating body for the future.

Population, Human Rights, Youth and the Elderly. Human rights specialists and activists structured their discussions around two main goals: first, to promote human rights for young people, children and the elderly through continual action and the implementation of specific programmes of assistance and development; second, to formulate proposals for better management of the natural environment that reflects the black community's knowledge, experience and needs in relation to nature and natural resources. Participants regarded human rights, care for the elderly and guidance for the young as fundamental to the preservation of their African-American identity.

Conclusions and future prospects

The plethora of proposals, suggestions and resolutions from the five commissions at Montevideo reflected the political, economic and cultural diversity within the Afro-American community. While race was the major factor around which the delegates of these five commissions converged, many Latin American civil rights activists are first and foremost interested in political commitment. However, it is the sense of commitment itself, an awareness of the necessity for collective struggle, that united participants and opposed them to a more individualist and assimilationist outlook. As one delegate put it: 'We are interested in conscious people. It doesn't matter if you're black or white. But we want a commitment.' While race is the indisputable basis of the shared pan-African experience, the history of *mestizaje* and the assimilation of Africans make the issue of levels of commitment an important one among Afro-Latin Americans.

By the end of the four-day encounter, the Montevideo Conference had arrived at a series of resolutions for the short and the long term. Personal contacts and institutional partnerships had been built. Delegates unanimously supported the creation of an intercontinental network that would first be based on regional integration. On the closing day of the conference South American delegates agreed on a second meeting, to be held in April 1995, in the southern Brazilian city of Santa Ana do Livramento, to elaborate on the network, its goals, parameters and methods of working. Delegates from the United States, the Caribbean and Central America were also to be invited to the meeting as observers.[8]

The US delegation also committed itself to establishing future communications among Afro-Latin Americans and African-Americans in the United States. Tentatively planned to be held in late 1995 at Howard University, Washington, DC, the conference on Race, Institutional Development and Human Rights: The Present Status and Condition of Blacks in Latin America would, it was hoped, examine issues of race relations in Latin America on a country-by-country basis, as well as the role of African-Americans in addressing some of those issues.

Whatever the outcome of the international network, Montevideo arguably represented a turning point for pan-Africanism in the Americas. Afro-Latin Americans around the continent are increasingly mobilizing and refusing to allow their national governments to ignore them. They are renewing themselves through forms of political and economic organization, building on international links and partnerships. At the end of the conference, participants shared a more hopeful and purposeful vision of the future, and there was a strong sense of being involved in a process that promises to help release Afro-Latin Americans from the burdens of centuries of oppression.

Notes

1 For purposes of clarity and consistency, the term Afro-Americans will be used to refer to people who identify themselves as of African origin throughout the continent. African-Americans will refer to people of African descent in the United States.

2 The Caribbean islands represent an exception to this generalization in so far as strong Afro-Caribbean middle–classes have emerged in all of the English- and French-speaking islands, but people of African descent make up the majority of these populations.

3 Congreso de Cultura Negra de las Américas, *Proceedings from Primer Congreso de la Cultura Negra de las Américas: conclusiones, recomendaciones y proposiciones*, 24-28 August 1977.

4 Congreso de Cultura Negra de las Américas, 'Segundo Congreso de Cultura Negra de las Américas', *Cuadernos Negros Americanos*, vol. 1, no. 1, 1989, pp. 11-54. This congress saw the participation of Afro-

Americans from Jamaica, Guyana, Trinidad, Puerto Rico, Haiti, the Dominican Republic, Cuba and French Guiana, in addition to North, South and Native American delegates.

5 Congresso de Cultura Negra de las Américas, 'Tercer Congreso de Cultura Negra de las Americas', *Cuadernos Negros Americanos,* vol. 1, no. 1, 1989, pp. 85-9.

6 Ibid.

7 Information on the work of the commissions comes from the official programme of the conference as well as from taped recordings of the plenary sessions of 8-10 December 1994.

8 The Brazilian meeting successfully took place in May 1995, and Afro-Latin Americans welcomed the Paraguayans to their first such international event. Several regional meetings have been held subsequently.

The UN Declaration on the Rights of Minorities

Declaration on the Rights of Persons belonging to National or Ethnic, Religious and Linguistic Minorities
(Adopted by the UN General Assembly; Resolution 47/135 of 18 December 1992)

Article 1
1 States shall protect the existence and the national or ethnic, cultural, religious and linguistic identity of minorities within their respective territories, and shall encourage conditions for the promotion of that identity.
2 States shall adopt appropriate legislative and other measures to achieve those ends.

Article 2
1 Persons belonging to national or ethnic, religious and linguistic minorities (hereinafter referred to as persons belonging to minorities) have the right to enjoy their own culture, to profess and practise their own religion, and to use their own language, in private and in public, freely and without interference or any form of discrimination.
2 Persons belonging to minorities have the right to participate effectively in cultural, religious, social, economic and public life.
3 Persons belonging to minorities have the right to participate effectively in decisions on the national and, where appropriate, regional level concerning the minority to which they belong or the regions in which they live, in a manner not incompatible with national legislation.
4 Persons belonging to minorities have the right to establish and maintain their own associations.
5 Persons belonging to minorities have the right to establish and maintain, without any discrimination, free and peaceful contacts with other members of their group, with persons belonging to other minorities, as well as contacts across frontiers with citizens of other States to whom they are related by national or ethnic, religious or linguistic ties.

Article 3
1 Persons belonging to minorities may exercise their rights including those as set forth in this Declaration individually as well as in community with other members of their group, without any discrimination.
2 No disadvantage shall result for any person belonging to a minority as the consequence of the exercise or non-exercise of the rights as set forth in this Declaration.

Article 4
1 States shall take measures where required to ensure that persons belonging to minorities may exercise fully and effectively all their human rights and fundamental freedoms without any discrimination and in full equality before the law.
2 States shall take measures to create favourable conditions to enable persons belonging to minorities to express their characteristics and to develop their culture, language, religion, traditions and customs, except where specific practices are in violation of national law and contrary to international standards.

3 States should take appropriate measures so that, wherever possible, persons belonging to minorities have adequate opportunities to learn their mother tongue or to have instruction in their mother tongue.

4 States should, where appropriate, take measures in the field of education, in order to encourage knowledge of the history, traditions, language and culture of the minorities existing within their territory. Persons belonging to minorities should have adequate opportunities to gain knowledge of the society as a whole.

5 States should consider appropriate measures so that persons belonging to minorities may participate fully in the economic progress and development in their country.

Article 5

1 National policies and programmes shall be planned and implemented with due regard for the legitimate interests of persons belonging to minorities.

2 Programmes of cooperation and assistance among States should be planned and implemented with due regard for the legitimate interests of persons belonging to minorities.

Article 6

States should cooperate on questions relating to persons belonging to minorities, inter alia exchanging of information and experiences, in order to promote mutual understanding and confidence.

Article 7

States should cooperate in order to promote respect for the rights as set forth in the present Declaration.

Article 8

1 Nothing in this Declaration shall prevent the fulfilment of international obligations of States in relation to persons belonging to minorities. In particular, States shall fulfil in good faith the obligations and commitments they have assumed under international treaties and agreements to which they are parties.

2 The exercise of the rights as set forth in the present Declaration shall not prejudice the enjoyment by all persons of universally recognized human rights and fundamental freedoms.

3 Measures taken by States in order to ensure the effective enjoyment of the rights as set forth in the present Declaration shall not prima facie be considered contrary to the principle of equality contained in the Universal Declaration of Human Rights.

4 Nothing in the present Declaration may be construed as permitting any activity contrary to the purposes and principles of the United Nations, including sovereign equality, territorial integrity and political independence of States.

Article 9

The specialized agencies and other organizations of the United Nations system shall contribute to the full realization of the rights and principles as set forth in the present Declaration, within their respective fields of competence.

CONTRIBUTORS

Jaime Arocha is a Colombian anthropologist with a PhD from Columbia University, New York City. He was a member of the Special Commission for Black Communities which prepared the law legitimating Afro-Colombian ethnicity. He left the direction of the Centre for Social Studies of the National University of Colombia, Bogotá, in order to establish and direct a team to study inter-ethnic conflict resolution among Afro-Colombians and indigenous peoples of the Pacific Basin. Among other publications he is co-author, with Nina S. de Friedemann, of *De sol a sol: genesis, transformación y presencia de los negros en Colombia* (1986). He co-edits the journal *América Negra*.

Eduardo Bermúdez is a Venezuelan anthropologist who graduated from the Central University of Venezuela in 1978 and received his PhD in anthropology from the Venezuelan Institute of Scientific Research, Caracas. He is Director of the Centre for Social Projects and Research and the School of Tourism of the Nueva Esparta University, Caracas, Venezuela.

Osvaldo Cárdenas was active in the Cuban student movement against the Batista dictatorship. From 1961 to 1984 he was a member of the Central Committee of the Cuban Communist Party. In 1982-3 he served as Cuban Ambassador to Suriname. He is a historian and consultant on international relations and has lectured in the Soviet Union, Europe and Latin America. He has also acted as adviser to the Cuban government on Latin American, African and European political affairs. He is vice-chairman of the Cuban Caribbean Studies Association and a visiting professor at the Cuban Institute of International Relations. He currently runs a Jamaican-based consultancy company.

Darién J. Davis teaches Latin American and Caribbean history at Middlebury College, Middlebury, VT. He has worked in Mexico, Peru, Guatemala, Brazil, Colombia, Cuba and Panama and previously taught at Tulane University, New Orleans, LA. He contributed to the *Encyclopedia of Latin American History* (1994), and his most recent book is (as editor) *Slavery and Beyond: The African Impact on Latin America and the Caribbean* (1995).

Anani Dzidzienyo is Professor of Afro-American Studies and Portuguese and Brazilian Studies at Brown University, Providence, RI. He has taught courses on blacks in Latin American history and society, Afro-Brazilians and the Brazilian polity, comparative politics of Africa and Latin America, and the Afro-Luso-Brazilian triangle. His publications include *The Position of Blacks in Brazilian Society* (MRG report, 1971, 1979), 'Activity and inactivity in the politics of Afro-Latin America' (1978), 'Africa–Latin America relations: a reconsideration' (1981), 'The African connection and Afro-Brazilian social mobility' (1985) and 'Brazilian race relations: old problems/new ideas?' (1993). He is a member of the International Advisory Committee of the African Diaspora Research Project (Michigan State University).

Debbie Ewens is a Belizean-Nicaraguan journalist, poet, playwright, educational author, publisher and entrepreneur who writes in both English and Spanish. Her journalism won a UNICEF award in 1992. She is a founder member of the Central American Development Alliance and lives and works in Belize City.

Jane Freeland is Senior Lecturer in Language at the University of Portsmouth, UK, with a special interest in the sociolinguistics of multicultural societies and in particular the question of ethnic and language rights on the Carribean Coast of Nicaragua. She has recently worked among communities of the Coast in connection with the development of a language department for the newly opened University of the Caribbean Coast of Nicaragua. She is the author of *A Special Place in History: The Atlantic Coast in the Nicaraguan Revolution* (1988).

Nina S. de Friedemann, a Colombian anthropologist and writer, is Permanent Research Associate of Research for Social Change, Emory University, Atlanta, GA. She has been a Fulbright professor at various US universities and has taught at the Instituto Venezolano de Investigaciones Cientificas, Caracas. She was nominated in 1987 for the Gabriela Mistral Prize. Currently she is Director of the journal *América Negra*, researches at the Pontificia Universidad Javeriana, Bogotá, Colombia, and is a member of the scientific committee of the UNESCO programme The Route of the Slave. Among her published works she is co-author, with Jaime Arocha, of *De sol a sol: genesis, transformación y presencia de los negros en Colombia* (1986) and author of *La saga del negro: presencia africana en Colombia* (1993).

José Luciano is a Peruvian sociologist and researcher on Afro-Peruvian culture. Formerly a member of the Instituto de Investigaciones Afro-Peruanos, he is an associate of the Instituto de Defensa Legal, Lima, Peru, and the author of various publications and essays about Afro-Peruvians.

Alejandrina da Luz is a Uruguayan scholar and researcher. She currently works with the Proyecto Binacional of the Universidad de la República, Montevideo, Uruguay, and the Universidad de Mar del Plata, Argentina.

Gayle McGarrity is an ethnographic consultant and Research Fellow at the Institute for Social and Economic Research, University of the West Indies, Kingston, Jamaica. She gained her PhD in anthropology at the University of California at Berkeley and conducted graduate studies in public health administration at the Instituto de Desarollo de la Salud in Havana, Cuba. She has conducted research on popular culture and the social, economic, political and medical effects of racism in Peru, Argentina, Nicaragua, Colombia, Cuba and Costa Rica. She is the author of numerous articles and papers on these topics in both Spanish and English.

Jameelah S. Muhammad has studied and researched in Spain, Mexico, Central America and the United States and is currently completing an MA thesis in Hispanic linguistics at the Universidad Nacional Autónoma de Mexico, Mexico City. She is a founding member of the Organization of Africans in the Americas and is the author of numerous articles and papers on the African presence in Mexico.

Pedro Pérez Sarduy is a Cuban writer, journalist and broadcaster currently resident in London. He is the author of *Surrealidad* (1967) and *Cumbite and Other Poems* (1990), and co-editor, with Jean Stubbs, of *AfroCuba: An Anthology of Cuban Writing on Race, Politics and Culture* (1993). He has finished *Journal in Babylon*, a series of chronicles on Britain, and a first novel, *The Maids of Havana* (unpublished). The recipient of several literary awards, he was Writer in Residence at Columbia University, New York (1989), and Rockefeller Scholar at the University of Florida, Gainesille (1993).

Franklin Perry is a Costa Rican of Jamaican descent. He holds a *licenciatura* in English and translation and obtained his BA in English and education from the Universidad de Costa Rica. He has taught English, American and Afro-American literature at the Universidad Panamericana, San José, Costa Rica, and at other universities.

Diego Quiroga took his BA at the University of California, Berkeley, in anthropology and psychology in 1982 and his MA and PhD in anthropology at the University of Illinois, Urbana-Champaign, in 1987 and 1994 respectively. The title of his doctoral thesis is 'Saints, virgins and the Devil: witchcraft, magic and healing in the northern coast of Ecuador'. He is currently Professor of Anthropology and Director of the Social Sciences of the Universidad San Francisco de Quito, Ecuador. His research experience in Colombia and in various regions of Ecuador is published in many works, and he has held several research grants.

Humberto Rodriguez Pastor has a PhD in anthropology and is Professor of Social Sciences at San Marcos University, Lima, and the Catholic University of Peru, Lima. He is a member of the anti-racist Movimiento Negro Francisco Congo and the author of various books and articles about the Chinese influence in Peru.

Kelvin A. Santiago-Valles is Puerto Rican and an Associate Professor of Sociology, of Africana Studies and of Latin American and Caribbean Area Studies at Binghamton University–State University of New York. He is the author of *'Subject People' and Colonial Discourses: Economic Transformation and Social Disorder in Puerto Rico, 1898-1947* (1994). Currently he is researching the development and transformation of US racialization structures positioning Puerto Ricans vis-à-vis racial codes in Puerto Rico, 1898-1950.

Kathleen Sawyers Royal is a tenured professor in the fields of linguistics and comparative literature. She works as a translator and interpreter at the Universidad Nacional, Heredia, Costa Rica, and has been official translator for the Costa Rican Ministry of

Foreign Affairs. She holds an MA in comparative literature from the University of Iowa, Iowa City, and an ABD in linguistics. She has lectured as a visiting professor at the University of Muskingum, OH, and is the author and co-author of several published works and articles.

Rachel Sieder has a PhD in political science and lectures at the Institute of Latin American Studies, London, UK, where she teaches comparative politics of Central America. She chairs the executive committee of the London-based Central American Human Rights Committee. She has lived in Nicaragua and Honduras. Among her publications is the edited volume *Central America: Fragile Transition* (1995).

Alison Spedding has a PhD in social anthropology of the Andes from the London School of Economics, UK. She currently lectures in anthropology at the Universidad Mayor de San Andres, La Paz, Bolivia, where she also organizes popular culture workshops studying Andean oral tradition. She has a special interest in Aymara and Andean culture and is the author of numerous academic articles and of several English-language novels.

Jean Stubbs is a British historian who has combined translation and journalism with teaching and research in Britain, Cuba, the United States and Spain. She is Senior Lecturer in Caribbean Studies and Latin American History at the University of North London, UK. She is the author of *Cuba: The Test of Time* (1989) and *Tobacco on the Periphery: A Case Study in Cuban Labour History, 1860-1958* (1985); is co-editor of *Cuba in Transition* (1992) and, with Pedro Pérez Sarduy, of *AfroCuba: An Anthology of Cuban Writing on Race, Politics and Culture* (1993); and is co-authoring *Cuba: An Annotated Bibliography* (forthcoming).

María Matilde Suárez is a sociologist with a PhD in ethnology from the University of Paris, France. She is Emeritus Researcher in the Department of Anthropology of the Venezuelan Institute of Scientific Research, Caracas, and the author of numerous books and articles concerned with Venezuela's indigenous, rural and artisanal fishing communities and urban popular religious movements.

Silvio Torres-Saillant is a native of the Dominican Republic who holds a BA in mass communication and has studied English, French, Latin, Greek and Portuguese. He received his MA and PhD from the Department of Comparative Literature of New York University's Graduate School of Arts and Science. He belongs to the faculty at the English Department of Hostos Community College and is currently Visiting Professor at the City College of New York, where he is Founding Director of the CUNY Dominican Studies Institute. He is the author of *Caribbean Poetics* (forthcoming), co-author of *The Dominican-Americans* (forthcoming) and a frequent contributor to scholarly journals and collected volumes.

Rosângela Maria Vieira holds a BA degree in human sciences from the Faculdada de Filosofia, Ciencias e Letras de Belo Horizonte, Brazil, and an MA in Romance languages and literatures from the University of Georgia, Athens; and she is completing a PhD in modern foreign languages and literatures at the University of Tennessee, Knoxville. She is currently developing an Afrocentric curriculum of Brazilian Portuguese language, culture and civilization, arts and literatures in the Department of Modern Languages and Literatures at Howard University, Washington, DC. She contributed to the *Encyclopedia of Latin American History* (1994) and is the author of several published works in the field of Afro-Brazilian studies and literatures. She has also published a book of poems, *Chaos, Solitute, Desire* (1993), and a collection of short stories, *Idolo* (1994). She is Founding Editor of the *Journal of Afro-Latin American Studies and Literatures*.

Norman E. Whitten Jr took his BA at Colgate University in 1959 and his MA and PhD in anthropology at the University of Carolina, Chapel Hill, NC, in 1961 and 1964. Past Editor of the *American Ethnologist*, he is currently Professor of Anthropology and Latin American Studies, Affiliate of Afro-American Studies and Senior University Scholar at the University of Illinois, Urbana-Champaign. His grants for research have resulted in such publications as *Class, Kinship and Power in an Ecuadorian Town* (1965), *Afro-American Anthropology* (1970), *Black Frontiersmen* (1974, 1985) and, with Arlene Torres, *To Forge the Future in the Fires of the Past* (1995).

INDEX

Caribbean islands, 8, 14, 92, 77,
99, 109, 164, 190
English-speaking, 49, 103, 116,
181, 204, 215
migrant labour from, 11-12, 86,
90, 116, 183, 203-5, 216-19,
255-56
slavery and, 3, 4, 181, 245, 253,
273
unrest in, 143
Carmen, Juan del, 168
Carnival, 1, 64
in Brazil, 28, 33, 41
in Caribbean, 256
in Mexico, 175, 177
Carpentier, Alejo, 92
Carr, Raymond, 149
Cartaga, Costa Rica, 220
Cartagena de Indias, Colombia,
48, 49, 50, 52, 54, 56, 63
Cartagena Portalatín, Aída, 126
Carter, Jimmy, 206
Castile, Kingdom of, 247, 288
Castillo, Nicolás del, 50
Castro, Fidel, 94, 96, 97, 98
Castro, Rudecindo, 72
Castro, Yeda Pessoa de, 26
Catamoya River, 295
Catholic Church, 65, 123, 168,
236-37, 253
and slavery, 62, 165, 244-45,
246, 293-94
Catholicism, 30, 42, 64, 88, 182,
192, 206, 217, 325
and African religions, 29, 33,
56, 59-60, 127, 195, 257-
59, 304-5
and Garífuna traditions, 237
cattle ranching, 52, 54, 55, 164,
332
and land rights, 239
Cauca district, Colombia, 56, 58,
70
Causa Radical party (Venezuela),
263
Cayo de Cocinos, Honduras, 239
Central Africa, 47, 56, 62, 164
Central America, 181, 182, 198,
225

Caribbean migration to, 11-12,
183, 203-5, 216-19
Garífuna populations, 12, 192-
96, 235
migration from, 230
Centre for Popular Culture
(Nicaragua), 190
Centro de Articulaçao de Popu-
laçoes Marginalizadas
(Brazil), 37, 41
Centro Cultural Afro-Ecuatoriano,
301, 308
Centro de Estudios Afro-
Panameños, 211
Cerro del Congo, Mexico, 170
Chachi people, 292
Chamorro, Violeta, 191
Charla, Sonya Catalina, 300, 306
Charpentier de Castro, Eduardo,
210
Chavelilla, 275
Chicano, Feliciano Antonio, 333
Chico Rei, 30
Chigualeros musical group, 303
Chile, 65, 276
Chirinos, José Leonardo, 250
Chocó region, Colombia, 52-53,
61, 68, 69, 72, 292
resources of, 70-71
Chota-Mira Valley, Ecuador, 292-
94, 296-97, 298, 300, 303-4,
308
Christianity, 32, 56, 110, 128
charismatic, 266
evangelistic, 182, 236-37, 245
Cibola, Mexico, 163
cimarroneras, 249, 253, 275, 297
civil rights, 110, 181, 206, 212,
281, 365
Civil Rights Commission (Puerto
Rico), 144
class, 3, 20, 38
and politics, 38, 91, 186-87,
191, 340
and race, 67, 71, 83, 154-55,
184, 206, 212, 231, 234, 288-
89, 320, 325, 363
cocoa plantations, 216, 244, 245,
247, 249, 250, 251, 255, 262